THE NATIONAL HISTORY OF FRANCE

EDITED BY
FR. FUNCK-BRENTANO

WITH AN INTRODUCTION BY J. E. C. BODLEY

THE SECOND REPUBLIC
AND
NAPOLEON III

THE NATIONAL HISTORY OF FRANCE

EDITED BY FR. FUNCK-BRENTANO

WITH AN INTRODUCTION BY J. E. C. BODLEY

Each Volume Demy 8vo.   Price each **$3.50** *net.*

THE EARLIEST TIMES. BY FR. FUNCK-BRENTANO

THE MIDDLE AGES. By FR. FUNCK-BRENTANO

THE CENTURY OF THE RENAISSANCE. By L. BATIFFOL

THE XVIITH CENTURY. By JACQUES BOULENGER

THE XVIIITH CENTURY. By CASIMER STRYIENSKI

THE FRENCH REVOLUTION. By LOUIS MADELIN

THE CONSULATE AND THE EMPIRE. By LOUIS MADELIN. (To be published)

THE RESTORATION AND THE JULY MONARCHY. By J. LUCAS DUBRETON

THE SECOND REPUBLIC AND NAPOLEON III. By RENÉ ARNAUD

THE THIRD REPUBLIC. By RAYMOND RECOULY

NEW YORK: G. P. PUTNAM'S SONS

THE NATIONAL HISTORY OF FRANCE

THE SECOND REPUBLIC

AND

NAPOLEON III

BY

RENÉ ARNAUD

TRANSLATED FROM THE FRENCH BY

E. F. BUCKLEY

NEW YORK

G. P. PUTNAM'S SONS

MCMXXX

Printed in Great Britain by R. Clay & Sons, Ltd., Bungay, Suffolk.

AUTHOR'S NOTE

HAVING reached the end of my narrative, I feel it incumbent upon me to recall all I owe to an historian whom I have frequently quoted in the body of this book—Pierre de la Gorce, of the Académie Française. His *Histoire de la Seconds République Française* (2 vols. 8vo., Plon) and his *Histoire du Second Empire* (7 vols. 8vo., Plon) have been my guides throughout my study of this period. Although on many points we fail to reach similar conclusions and do not see eye to eye, I should not feel I had discharged my debt to Monsieur de la Gorce unless I acknowledged how invaluable his work has been to me.

I also owe a great deal to Charles Seignobos, who wrote Volumes VI and VII of *l'Histoire de la France Contemporaine*, published by Hachette under the editorship of Ernest Lavisse. If I may borrow an expression frequently used in connection with Napoleon III, he has stood on my Left while Pierre de la Gorce has stood on my Right.

I do not think it is necessary to give a bibliography of the period here. I have, whenever I could, quoted the works of which I have made most use. A good bibliography is printed at the heads of chapters in Charles Seignobos' work.

19300

CONTENTS

CHAPTER I

THE SECOND REPUBLIC

The 24th of February, 1848 : the Provisional Government acclaimed by the mob in the Palais Bourbon. The rival camps : the Socialists *versus* the bourgeoisie. Coalition between the two. The economic crisis : national workshops and the Luxembourg Commission. Lamartine : the red flag and the tricolour (25th of February). A feast of fraternity. The Church rallies to the support of the Government. Financial crisis and expedients. The 45 centimes tax. Ledru-Rollin and Carnot want " to hold the elections." Agitation of the Clubs against the holding of immediate elections. The 16th and 17th of March. Progress of Socialism. The 16th of April. Elections of the 23rd of April for the Constituent Assembly. Triumph of the Republican bourgeoisie over the Socialists and the Legitimists. Session of the 4th of May. The executive commission of the Five. Conflict between the Assembly and Paris on the subject of Poland. Foreign policy of the Provisional Government. The 15th of May : invasion of the Palais Bourbon. Louis Napoleon Bonaparte : his life, his character. The beginnings of Bonapartist propaganda. National workshops. Civil war : 23rd–25th of June. Death of Bréa, and of Monseigneur Affre. Cavaignac's dictatorship : reaction. Foreign policy. The Constitution. Election of Bonaparte to the Presidency (10th of December). The President and the Ministers : incidents. 29th of January, 1849. The Roman question ; the contradiction inherent in French policy : the desire to suppress the " Roman Republic " and at the same time to force certain Liberal measures on the Pope. Oudinot in Rome. Vote of the Constituent Assembly of the 7th of May. Lesseps' mission and the letter to Oudinot. Elections of the 13th of May to the Legislative Body : order *versus* Socialism. The moderates crushed and the triumph of " law and order." The 13th of June. Oudinot enters Rome. Letter to Edgar Ney. The new ministry (31st of October, 1849). The *Loi Falloux*. Reaction. Partial elections of March–April 1850 and the electoral law of the 31st of May. Press Law of the 16th of July. Conflict with the Assembly. Failure of plans for the restoration of the Monarchy. The President's tour (the 1850 Vacation). The Assembly refuses to revise the Constitution (July 1851). Preparations for the *coup d'état*. The 2nd of December, 1851. The rising of the 3rd. The shooting of the 4th. Events in the provinces. The plebiscite of the 21st of December.

B

THE SECOND REPUBLIC

ON the 24th of February, 1848, the riotous mob in Paris, which had driven King Louis Philippe from the Tuileries, invaded the debating chamber of the Palais Bourbon with shouts of "*Vive la République!*" The Royalist deputies fled before the motley crowd of National Guards in blue uniforms with broad white belts and fur caps or *képis*, working-men in overalls or in their shirt-sleeves, and black-coated top-hatted students, who were all armed and gesticulating wildly. Whereupon Lamartine and his Republican colleagues had the names of the men who were to constitute the Provisional Government acclaimed by the howling mob. The list had been drawn up in advance and almost completed in the offices of the *National*, the Republican newspaper, and included Lamartine himself, who, in his recently published *Histoire des Girondins*, had extolled the founders of the Republic; Dupont de l'Eure, the octogenarian, who had been one of the Council of Five Hundred; Arago, the popular old astronomer of the *faubourgs*; Ledru-Rollin, the "ultra-Radical" Director of the advanced journal *La Réforme*; Marie and Crémieux, Republican lawyers under the Monarchy, and Garnier-Pagès, the orator beloved of the populace.

The Provisional Government.

And, in keeping with revolutionary tradition, these seven deputies, raised to power by the mob, made their way to the Hôtel de Ville to obtain the definite consent of Paris to their appointment.

Here they divided the Government offices between them— Dupont was made President, Lamartine Minister of Foreign Affairs, Ledru-Rollin Minister of the Interior, Marie Minister of Public Works, etc. Certain portfolios were entrusted to friends of the *National*, though they were not to form part of the Provisional Government—the Exchequer going to Goudchaux, the banker, the Ministry of Public Instruction to Carnot, whose family had always been Republican, and the Department of Trade to Bethmont. In the evening, however, fresh aspirants to power presented themselves. They had been acclaimed by the *Réforme*, which represented more advanced views than those held by the Republican bourgeoisie of the *National*—the journalists Marrast and Floccon, Louis Blanc the

The Rival Camps.

2

historian and sociologist, and Albert, a working-class mechanic. The two rival camps engaged in an acrimonious discussion—was the Government to be bourgeois or socialist? Eventually they decided to amalgamate; the Provisional Government was to consist of eleven instead of seven members, whereby it was hoped that a reconciliation would be secured between the two rival camps—the Republicans of the *National*, who merely demanded that the vote should no longer be restricted to the possessing classes but granted to every citizen, and the polemists of the *Réforme*, who aimed at the reconstruction of society. In any case, it was understood that the people would immediately be convoked to ratify the Republic. The bourgeoisie, with their customary scruples, refused to proclaim anything before consulting the country. But that very evening the workers, with less regard for legality, placarded the Hôtel de Ville with a phrase reminiscent of '93, written on white canvas with bits of coal picked up in the street : " The Republic, one and indivisible, has been proclaimed in France."

The Coalition.

This enthusiasm for the Republic meant that the people expected something more from it than the realisation of Socialist dreams; first and foremost they wanted bread! For months certain industries and textile factories had been lying idle ; the installation of new machines imported from England meant starvation for the artisan who worked at home. The transport trade was similarly affected, the railways threatening carriers, lock-keepers and lighter-men with ruination. On the 24th of February the mob attacked the factories and stations in several towns and burnt down the mansion of the Rothschilds at Suresnes. The bourgeoisie became uneasy. Was this the upheaval threatened by the Reds? On the 25th of February an armed mob was still blockading the Hôtel de Ville, in which the Government were besieged. A working-man named Marche demanded " the right to work " on behalf of the people. Lamartine tried to speak. " Enough of words ! " retorted Marche. " The people are waiting!" And the Government promised to provide work and founded the National Workshops for the un-employed. On the 28th of February there was another demonstration, under the menace of which it was decided to

Economic Crisis.

National Workshops.

3

appoint Louis Blanc, assisted by Albert, President of a Commission of Works which was to sit at the Luxembourg and devote its energies to ameliorating the lot of the workers.

Clearly the bourgeoisie were going to find it difficult to keep their heads above water. On the 25th of February the red flag **Lamartine.** was within an ace of taking the place of the tricolour of the fallen Monarchy. The two flags floated side by side on the barricades. On the same day the rabble swarming round the Hôtel de Ville picked up the pieces of red velvet which had been torn off the municipal couches and thrown to them out of the windows by a certain doctor, who was either a Socialist or a wag. " The red flag ! " he yelled. Lamartine might possibly have given way, but his colleagues persuaded him to hold his ground. He went out on to the steps, got up on a chair and addressed the mob. He spoke as a poet, and under the charm of his eloquence the tumult was gradually calmed and held in check. He reminded them of the first Revolution and the incident on the Champ de Mars, in '91, when the red flag was used by the military as a signal inviting the insurgents to disperse—before the massacre. But to-day the red flag, by some strange freak, had become the symbol of the insurrection itself. Whereupon with great skill he recalled the glories of the Revolution and the Empire which the tricolour evoked. This Republic of factions, this standard of terror must be suppressed. " The tricolour has borne our liberties and triumphs round the world; the red flag has only been round the Champ de Mars drenched in torrents of the people's blood." He was loudly cheered; and a working-man, his clothes in rags and his face covered with blood, went up and kissed him. The mob roared its approval; the tricolour was to remain the flag of the Republic ! In vain did a fresh demonstration under Louis Blanc return to the attack on the following day. Goudchaux, the bankers' representative, conjured the Government to remain firm; the Reds would drive the Bourse mad. And the Government obeyed.

At first it was no easy matter to set the public mind at rest. To the worthy bourgeois of the day the word "republic" inevitably recalled '93, the Terror and the guillotine. A decree was passed solemnly abolishing capital punishment for political

4

crimes. It was hailed with tears of joy—tears flowed easily in those tender-hearted days. And lo ! the first fright was followed by unanimous rejoicing and a veritable feast of fraternity. The main task of the Provisional Government was to receive the various delegations that presented themselves at the Hôtel de Ville to pay their respects, singing the *Marseillaise* and waving flags and pennants. " Education for the children of the masses ! " was one demand; " Free Trade ! " another. Some pleaded on behalf of downtrodden Poland, others championed the cause of retail trade. The Government promised everything. Clubs and newspapers sprang up like mushrooms, freely calling on the name of Jesus, " the carpenter of Nazareth," to celebrate the triumph of fraternity. The provinces, like Paris, also indulged in demonstrations and illuminations. The Catholic clergy unhesitatingly rallied to the support of the new Government, which was inspired with such deep reverence and love for Christ—had not the revolutionaries carried the crucifix they found in the Tuileries in procession to St. Roche ? The Catholics hoped to enjoy greater freedom under the Republic than they had done under the Gallican kings, who were so mistrustful of the Holy See. Throughout the country bishops and priests blessed the Trees of Liberty, which were planted in the public places to the flourish of trumpets in the presence of the National Guard. It was a unique occasion, when the old ideal of justice and goodness which lies hid in the heart of the mass of mankind seemed at last to have been realised.

A Feast of Fraternity.

Nevertheless it was necessary to keep body and soul together. And the revolution had unloosed, or rather precipitated the economic and financial crisis, signs of which had already been apparent under the fallen Monarchy. A ten days moratorium for the settlement of commercial bills merely aggravated the situation. There was a run on the banks ; more often than not they had invested in State securities, which had steadily gone down since the 23rd of February although the Bourse was closed. In many instances this meant the failure of the bank followed by the bankruptcy of its clients. The President of the *Tribunal de Commerce,* a prominent banker, committed suicide. The Government did all in its power to

Financial Crisis.

5

arrest the panic; the *Comptoir National d'Escompte* was set up in Paris, and similar institutions were opened in the provinces, while interest on the *rente* was paid in advance. All in vain ! Goudchaux sent in his resignation. On the 7th of March the five per cent. stock had fallen from 116 to 89 francs; it was destined to sink to 50 ! Railway shares also collapsed. Garnier-Pagès, who succeeded Goudchaux, launched a scheme for a grand national five per cent. loan at par, relying on " the magnificent wave of patriotism, devotion and self-sacrifice." And, as a matter of fact, delegations of printers, cabinet-makers, bakers and lithographers presented themselves with a flourish of trumpets at the Hôtel de Ville, bringing their small savings and declaring that " the workers still had days of suffering and endurance to place at the service of the Republic." But the bourgeoisie hesitated to pay a hundred francs for a security quoted at seventy on the Bourse, and the loan was not subscribed.

Financial Expedients. The Government was obliged to have recourse to the classic expedients demanded by critical times, which, despite their disastrous effects, will probably be resorted to until the end of time—the savings banks were instructed to limit the payment of cash to 100 francs (£4), the surplus to be made up in five per cent. Treasury Bonds redeemable in four or six months; while holders of Treasury Bonds that had fallen due were forced to renew them or convert them into five per cent. stock at par. Indirectly this was a forced loan at a discount of $33\frac{1}{3}$ per cent. owing to the depreciation of the five per cents on the Bourse. The Bank of France, which held out as long as possible, also stopped payment and the system of the enforced acceptance of bank-notes came into operation.[1] But the crisis did not last long and the bank-note soon recovered its value; for the Government had recourse to heroic measures and imposed a supplementary levy of 45 centimes

The 45 Centimes Tax. in the franc on all direct taxation. This " 45 centimes " tax was extremely unpopular and brought odium on the new Government, though it saved it from immediate bankruptcy.

---

[1] This refers to the law then in existence forcing commercial and financial bodies, as well as private individuals, to accept bank-notes as legal tender, although the Bank of France was under no obligation to give cash in exchange for them.

6

Thus order was restored in Paris and the Government turned its attention to the provinces. What was their attitude towards the new state of affairs? Were not the small towns-people and the peasants still Royalist? It was all very well to give the vote to every Tom, Dick and Harry, as had been done on the 5th of March, but what was going to be the result of universal suffrage? Ledru-Rollin summarily dismissed all the prefects and sub-prefects of the *ancien régime* and sent Government commissioners and sub-commissioners all over the country to mould public opinion—Jacobinism and Bonapartism continued to survive in France under any system. Carnot urged the teachers " to lay the foundations of the Republic and defend it against ignorance and misrepresentation," conjuring them to do all they could to prepare for the elections. Ledru-Rollin was even more outspoken; on the 12th of March, in a circular sent to all his commissioners, he told them to do everything in their power to encourage republican feeling in the country, and to urge and support the candidature of new men drawn from the ranks of the populace. " The country has not been educated; it is for you to guide it ! " These peasants and working-men whose election was to be secured at the expense of the political personnel of the fallen Monarchy would come to the Palais Bourbon and " give the *intelligentzia* the benefit of their practical experience." All this was typical of the simple-minded, generous optimism of '48. How young the world was in those days !

Ledru-Rollin.

Carnot.

This ingenuous command to " arrange for the elections " gave rise to serious qualms in the minds of the bourgeoisie. The Conservative Press attacked the commissioners, " those tyrants, those proconsuls," who had the power to nominate or dismiss the mayors at will. A " Republican " club was formed " to secure freedom for the elections "; in France the Conservative always declared himself " Liberal " when it was a question of opposing a Jacobin dictatorship. Lamartine, who had not been consulted before the circular was sent out, openly disavowed his colleague Ledru-Rollin, and once again the two forces which had come into conflict at the Hôtel de Ville on the night of the 24th of February stood confronting one another.

7

Truth to tell, Paris was giving the bourgeoisie ever fresh cause for alarm; it was full of rabid " incendiary " newspapers, which inflamed unruly passions and preached anarchy, and of Clubs where orators held forth in the evening in the smoke-laden tempestuous atmosphere of electioneering meetings. The names of the Club leaders were whispered in awestruck tones—Raspail, Cabet, Villain, and above all Blanqui, cold, gloved and taciturn, who spread fear wherever he went. And last but not least—what madness !—they had armed all these working-men by allowing them to join the National Guard. Under the fallen Monarchy a man had to pay for his uniform and musket if he wished to join. But now this citizen militia had degenerated into a vulgar rabble. Who could tell whether these muskets, which had been handed out for the defence of the Republic, would not be turned against society ?

The Clubs.

Thereupon the Clubs demanded the postponement of the elections; it was necessary to give Ledru-Rollin's commissioners and Carnot's teachers time " to enlighten the rural population." An immediate election would be " a menace to the Republic," the workers would go to the ballot " led by their masters, the priests and the aristocrats, like blind driven cattle. . . . The people did not know; they must be taught." Ledru-Rollin and Louis Blanc might have been inclined to favour this postponement and for the time being forget Republican principles, if by so doing they could have placed the system upon a surer foundation. But these Jacobins and politicians were confronted by the idealistic Girondists of the Provisional Government, who preferred to sacrifice the *régime* rather than a single principle. Lamartine felt it would be wrong to keep the temporary dictatorship too long in power, and wanted to appeal without delay to the sovereign people. If the purblind populace pronounced in favour of their ancient kings, so much the worse ! It was the everlasting problem of democracy—is the people really sovereign when its will is influenced ?

The conflict broke out in connection with the appointment of officers for the National Guard, which elected all its leaders with the exception of generals and colonels. If these elections took place at once the " unenlightened " working-man would re-elect

8

the old bourgeois officer. The Clubs grew excited, but the Government postponed the election for one week only, though by way of compensation it suppressed the "*bonnets à poil*," picked companies consisting of rich bourgeois. But on the 16th of March, the latter, wearing their famous fur caps, marched to the Hôtel de Ville with shouts of "Down with Ledru-Rollin!" On the 17th, the Reds, put on their guard by Caussidière himself, the Prefect of Police, who was a "whole-hogger," retaliated. A hundred thousand men marched in silence to the Hôtel de Ville to insist upon the postponement of the elections for the National Guard and the Assembly. "This is our 20th of June," exclaimed Lamartine, who sincerely believed he was witnessing a revolution as formidable as that of '89. "When shall we have our 10th of August?" And with a few eloquent words he once more succeeded in soothing the popular lion, who roared notwithstanding and showed his fangs. Finally, the hundred thousand marched past before the Government, who were let off with a fright. Nevertheless, the menace bore fruit—the elections for the National Guard were postponed till the 5th of April, and for the Assembly until the 23rd of April, which was Easter Sunday.

A short enough respite certainly, but the Reds were anxious to turn it to advantage in order to work up the public mind. Some of them went rather too far, more particularly at Lyons, where Emmanuel Arago, the nephew of the Naval Minister, drove out the monks, forbade coin of the realm to leave the town, had all vehicles searched at the gates and at one fell swoop doubled the taxes. The "*Voraces*," the extremists of the Red Cross, feeling that Arago was behind them, rose up in revolt and threatened the town with a species of Communism—a bad advertisement for the new *régime*.

In Paris the Clubs began to grow active. The *Club de la Révolution* was formed, including among its members Proudhon, Pierre Leroux, Pyat and Delescluze, with the object of preparing the way for social reform. Barbès founded the *Club des Clubs*, the central organisation for all the Paris Clubs with delegates in the provinces. At all these assemblies it was declared with the full force of oratory that the staple industries, insurance, transport and banking ought to be State monopolies, and, above

9

all, that, should the elections prove reactionary, insurrection must be the immediate reply. Moreover, Louis Blanc, on the **The Luxem-** Luxembourg Commission, secured the reduction of **bourg Com-** the working day to ten hours for Paris and eleven for **mission.** the provinces—a great social advance for the period —and the settlement by arbitration of all disputes between workers and employers regarding wages. The Commission, which included Socialist theorists like Considérant, Vidal and Pecqueur, launched forth into idealistic dreams—the State was to purchase all private concerns, indemnifying the owners by means of shares. The workers were to perform their labours like brothers of one family, all receiving the same salary, to be fixed according to their needs and not according to their capacity, each man giving of his best for glory's sake, like the soldier under fire. After the salaries had been paid, expenses covered and the interest on the shares met, the residue would be sufficient to redeem the capital, provide relief in case of sickness and help for the old and incapacitated. Nothing is more characteristic of '48 than this belief in the goodness of the working-man, this appeal to social brotherhood, and this oblivion of human egoism, which at bottom is merely the will to live.

Confronted by this torrent of Socialism the Government was split, Albert being enamoured of the new ideas and Lamartine convinced that the elections would be a triumph for law and order. Between the two, Ledru-Rollin made public confession of his faith in democracy, but his hatred of Blanqui alienated him from the Clubs. Lamartine, to preserve the peace, received the Reds, argued with them and tried to persuade them to be patient. This was thrown in his teeth later on, when he confessed that he had conspired with them as the lightning-conductor conspires with the thunderbolt to divert the shock. But would it be possible to ward off the storm for long?

It was already rumbling again. It had been arranged that on the 16th of April, Palm Sunday, the working-men in the National Guard were to go to the Champ de Mars to elect fourteen of their number for staff appointments.

The idea of appointing working-men to the staff is characteristic of the Age. This afforded a good opportunity for returning

10

to the Hôtel de Ville and demanding a further postponement of
the elections, which had been fixed for Easter Sunday, a week
later. On the preceding day, the *Bulletin de la République*,
published by the Ministry of the Interior, allowed a stirring appeal
to be printed in its columns : " If the elections are reactionary,
to the barricades ! " This anonymous exhortation was the work
of a woman, but a woman of letters—George Sand. That same
evening, Lamartine, in the expectation that the following day
would prove his 10th of August, made his last will and testament !

But Ledru-Rollin, after considerable tergiversation, decided
to warn the National Guard to maintain the peace—his hatred
of Blanqui had gained the upper hand. When
16th of April. the demonstrators reached the Hôtel de Ville
on the 16th they found the National Guard already
there, as well as General Changarnier, who had come
by chance—he was just off to Berlin as Ambassador and
wanted to receive his instructions from Lamartine. There
were shouts of " Long live the Provisional Government ! "
and " Down with the Communists ! " A workmen's delegation
entered the Hôtel de Ville demanding " the abolition of the
exploitation of man by man, and the co-operative organisation
of Labour." It received a cold welcome. Meanwhile Lamartine
was congratulating the National Guard. The elections would be
held at Easter, and law and order were secured. Nevertheless,
on the following day, the 17th, the Government could not make
up its mind to arrest Blanqui. On the 20th, however, the Feast
of Fraternity was celebrated at the Arc de Triomphe. The
twelve legions of the National Guard (one for each *arrondissement*, of which there were only twelve at that time), the four
suburban legions, the militia, as well as the regular army, which
now entered Paris for the first time since the 24th of February,
marched past before the Government from early morning until
ten o'clock at night—the Government wanted to show the Reds
that it had might behind it. On the 23rd of April the elections,
which were to put an end to the Provisional Government, at
last took place. This body, at once Conservative and Socialist,
had succeeded in surviving for two troublous months—that was
something !

THE SECOND REPUBLIC

The elections took place on the system of universal suffrage. Before February there had been only 250,000 electors in France —the landed proprietors. There were now to be nine million. It was a sudden and far-reaching revolution, yet no mention of it was made in the Conservative newspapers when it was sanctioned by decree—public opinion had already been won over to the principle. Every Frenchman of twenty-one was to have the vote, even servants, who in 1791 had not been enfranchised, their independence being suspect, and soldiers (the army had not yet become " the voiceless throng "). The elections were conducted departmentally on the multiple-vote system and decided by a relative majority. A man could vote in several departments at once. There were 900 seats allotted according to density of population—34 for the Seine, 3 for the Hautes-Alpes district. A deputy was paid a salary of 25 francs a day (£1).

The Elections.

How could the result of these elections possibly be foretold? Who would these millions of new electors vote for? Many of them were utterly ignorant of politics and some could not even read. The Government had been anxious " to avoid drawing up reports and counting votes," it had aimed at " enlightening France and working openly towards frustrating the intrigues of the counter-revolution," which maintained that the Republic stood for " spoliation, pillage and murder. . . ." And Ledru-Rollin's commissioners prosecuted their campaign on behalf of the Republic energetically, usually appearing in person. . . . The way these prefect candidates behaved and how they used their influence may readily be imagined.

Three categories of candidates stand out conspicuous—the *National* group, including landed proprietors, doctors, lawyers and officers, among whom there were a number of monarchists who had rallied to the support of the Republic after February ; they were all Republicans but not Socialists : secondly, those whose slogan was " Liberty, Equality, Fraternity ! " the workers and the Club men of the *République Sociale*, who wanted to reform society from top to toe; and lastly, in the west, the Legitimists, " the defenders of social order and of religion," who, although they had " accepted the Republic," were nevertheless regarded as reactionaries. In the background were

12

hundreds of other candidates all shouting each other down, one invoking Barbès and another Jesus Christ. Flaubert, who was an eye-witness of these events, has described them better than anyone else in his *L'Éducation Sentimentale*, in the passage relating to the picture by the painter Pellerin : " He represented the Republic, or Progress or Civilisation in the form of Jesus Christ guiding a steam engine through a virgin forest. . . ."

On the 23rd of April, after Mass, the men of every village met together, and, led by the mayor and priest, with flags flying and **Triumph** drums beating, presented themselves at the head-**of the** quarters of their canton to record their votes. Few **Bourgeoisie.** failed to exercise the privilege, eighty-four per cent. of those on the registers going to the ballot. Was such enthusiasm ever to be witnessed again in France? Out of the 900 seats, 700 went to the *National* group, the bourgeoisie of the Provisional Government and anti-socialist Republicans. Lamartine, the hero of the hour, headed the list in Paris and in ten departments. The Club faction and " demagogues " won only a hundred seats, a similar number being secured by the Legitimists. And thus the new Assembly was formed, with a crushing majority in the Centre, and two insignificant opposing groups Left and Right. These results proved a bitter disappointment to the Reds, who immediately began to discuss a *coup de force* against this reactionary Assembly. In the provinces there were disturbances at Nantes, Issoudun and Nîmes, and above all at Limoges, where the unemployed broke into the Hôtel de Ville and occupied it for several days, and at Rouen, where the unemployed, who had been taken on in the communal workshops, rose up against the successful candidate, the attorney Sénard, and put up barricades. Sénard organised the resistance, regulars and the National Guard stormed the barricades with shot and shell, and for the first time since the proclamation of the Republic, blood was shed. It was an evil omen for the Assembly.

It met on the 4th of May at the Palais Bourbon in a temporary structure which it had been found necessary to erect in the **Session** courtyard of the building to accommodate the 900 **of the** deputies. To the salute of the guns in the In-**4th of May.** valides, the Provisional Government marched on foot with a military escort through the boulevards and the Rue

Royale to hand over its powers to the Assembly. The members
of the Government were loudly cheered, above all Lamartine,
their tricoloured gold-fringed belts being particularly admired.
In the Palais Bourbon the deputies shouted again and again,
" *Vive la République !* "—a cry that was to be repeated on seventeen occasions during this one session. In the evening the
deputies descended the steps of the Palais to shake hands with
the workers through the railings. Once again, what confidence,
faith and optimism !

The Assembly elected as President Dr. Buchez, a Christian
Socialist, but as Vice-President the formidable Sénard, the
" mailed-fist " of Rouen. Lamartine paid eloquent tribute to
the work of the Provisional Government and celebrated the
advent of civil peace : " Factions can no longer exist in a Republic in which every man has the right to vote and to carry arms,"
he declared. Alas ! six weeks later this simple-minded
optimism was to be cruelly disillusioned. But let us not smile
at such blindness. If government means foresight, the profession
of statesman needs apprenticeship, and these tyros in the art
had not had time to learn.

The Assembly was essentially a legislative chamber. And
it was considered important that the various spheres of power
The Five. should be kept distinct. In addition to a legislative
body, it was necessary to have an executive, to put
the laws into execution. Would it be best to appoint ministers
and a President of the Council or an Executive Commission of
Five to choose its ministers as the Directory had done ? Everybody was unanimous that Lamartine should be President of the
Council. But he shirked the position, insisting on an Executive
Commission being appointed. This was possibly due to lack
of confidence in himself and dread of the heavy responsibility,
but possibly also, as he himself subsequently confessed, because
he wanted to share the onus with Ledru-Rollin and thus keep
the Reds in check. On the 10th of May the Assembly elected
the Five—Arago, Garnier-Pagès, Marie, Lamartine and Ledru-
Rollin, the latter coming at the tail-end of the list and Lamartine
last but one, because he had dared to defend Ledru-Rollin.
He was beginning to be unpopular in that bourgeois Assembly
which mistrusted " Jacobins," Ledru-Rollin, and the fellow

14

Louis Blanc, who was vainly demanding a Ministry of Progress and Labour. Even for the men of '48 such a Ministry was rather too " forty-eightish."

It was not long before dissensions arose between the Assembly and Paris, between the bourgeois deputies from the provinces and the faubourgs which had voted for Louis Blanc. The pretext for disagreement was Poland. The February revolution had naturally given rise to high hopes among all the oppressed peoples of Europe, the Italian subjects of Austria, the Polish slaves of the Tsar. But Lamartine, who had been in charge of foreign affairs under the Provisional Government, had been extremely cautious; his predilection for the history of '93 did not suffice to make him plunge into adventurous paths; on the contrary, he was anxious to reassure the kings who might take fright at the word Republic, and with laudable good sense protested that the new *régime* would not wage war against anybody. Revolution had broken out in Vienna, Berlin, Budapesth, Milan and Venice; but the revolutionaries would not have welcomed intervention on the part of France—they would have cried Imperialism, remembering that Napoleon's soldiers had paved the way for Prefects who, in the name of the Master, had ruled the French department of the Bouches de l'Elbe and Genoa. So the Provisional Government confined themselves to Platonic assurances of friendship. They sent good wishes to the German Liberals who, with the poet Herwegh, were going to south Germany, sporting the black, red and gold, to found United Germany, but were doomed to failure—it was the black, white and red of Bismarck that was to symbolise German unity. They also sent good wishes and indirect help to the Belgian legion which tried to march out and proclaim a republic in Brussels, but was quickly scattered as soon as it had crossed the frontier; and good wishes to the Republicans of Savoy who had proclaimed a Republic at Chambéry and declared their reunion with France, but were quickly rounded up by the priests and peasants who had remained faithful to the King of Piedmont. In Italy they would have liked to take action against Austria, the hereditary foe. But Charles Albert, King of Piedmont, who had gone out to war against Vienna, was, in his capacity of King, far from enamoured of Republicans, and, as an Italian,

15

extremely suspicious of these Frenchmen. He protested that *l'Italia farà da sè*, that Italy could fend for herself, without the help of anybody. And the French Minister Bixio succeeded in convincing Paris that any attempt at intervention would only lead to war with the King of Piedmont himself. He saw things as they really were : " They will turn to us only when they have been defeated."

And Poland? Poland was a long way off. It is true that Polish legions were formed in Paris and it was loudly proclaimed **Poland.** that " the re-establishment of a Polish nation was a cause as dear to the heart of France as her own.' But there the matter ended, and only extremely half-hearted support was afforded to the King of Prussia when, frightened by a revolt of his Polish subjects in Posen, he tried to act the part of champion of Poland against the Tsar—a paradox which was of short duration, for the Prussians quickly subdued their rebellious subjects in Posen. This aroused great excitement in Paris, where Poland was popular, possibly as popular as Alsace-Lorraine between the two last wars. At the mere mention of the word Poland in public the whole of Paris would rise as one man. The Clubs drew up a petition on behalf of the " heroic and unfortunate " country, and, in keeping with the tradition of '93, arranged to present it at the Palais Bourbon on the 15th of May. No cause could have been more popular nor could a better opportunity have been found for allowing the people of Paris to show their power and prove to that " reactionary " Assembly what their true sentiments were. But the leaders, men like Blanqui, Barbès, and Louis Blanc, were more clear-sighted and tried to stop the proceedings. Other agitators, however, who were less in the public eye and burning to play a part, urged the Clubs to go ahead.

The Assembly took steps to defend itself—General de Courtais, the head of the National Guard, occupying the Palais Bourbon and the Pont de la Concorde with his troops. On the 15th of May a crowd collected at the Bastille, advanced gaily through the boulevards, and gradually growing more and more excited, waxed indignant against the deputies, " those clerks of ours who have voted themselves 25 francs a day and grudge us our 30 sous "—the workers at this time were agitating for

16

THE SECOND REPUBLIC

a minimum wage of 30 sous. This detail throws a light on the real purchasing power of money at this period and proves that it would not be far wide of the mark to put it down at ten times as great as it is to-day. What working-man would be content with 15 francs a day now?—Slowly the crowd made its way to the Rue Royale. Beside himself with excitement, old General de Courtais trotted forward to meet the procession, shouting, " *Vive la Pologne!* " and called upon the leaders to halt. He was cheered, but the march was continued. Would the forces on the bridge fire? Aghast at the thought of civil war, Courtais **Invasion of** ordered his men to stand back and let the people **the Palais** pass. Soon they were climbing the railings, storming **Bourbon.** the steps, breaking into the debating chambers; finally, they reached the rostrum and the amphitheatre. The tumult and confusion was indescribable. Nevertheless, the House continued to sit, and Barbès, Blanqui, Louis Blanc and Raspail harangued the mob and tried to persuade the demonstrators to leave. All in vain! A man named Huber proclaimed the dissolution of the Assembly, and after three hours of torture the deputies at last gave way before the insurgents. Lists were hastily drawn up for the formation of a new Provisional Government consisting entirely of Reds, whereupon the mob marched to the Hôtel de Ville and occupied it. They wanted to call upon Russia and Prussia to reinstate Poland on pain of immediate war. Was this the beginning of fresh adventures, another epic of the year II recently hymned by Hugo:

Contre les rois tirant ensemble leurs epées [1]? . . .

But the good sense of the bourgeoisie and the National Guard, the army that represented them, quickly regained the upper hand. The Palais Bourbon was recaptured without a blow being struck, whereupon Lamartine and Ledru-Rollin rode to the Hôtel de Ville and had Barbès arrested, and shortly afterwards Albert, Raspail and Blanqui were also taken into custody. There were shouts of " Down with the Communists! " and Louis Blanc was hooted in the Palais Bourbon. Once again law and

[1] Drawing their swords as one man against the kings.

order were saved, and people congratulated themselves—perhaps mistakenly—that the leaders were under lock and key. They would not be there in June to moderate the fury of their followers; they might possibly have been able to prevent irreparable disaster.

After the disturbances of the 15th of May everything seemed to be at sixes and sevens—the Executive Commission had already fallen into discredit. To the devil with the Five, the " Pentarchs "! They only knew how to call out the National Guard on the slightest provocation! They were hated by the Left as much as by the Right; by the Left, who met in the Rue des Pyramides, because they had imprisoned the whole-hoggers; by the Right, who met in the Rue de Poitiers, because of their weakness in face of the Reds, who were encouraging strikes, brawls and petty disturbances in the provinces, and because they opposed the Moderates' demand for the prosecution of Louis Blanc. In vain did the Government hold solemn celebrations in honour of the Fraternity of the 21st of May; the ceremony—a civil procession and mid-Lent cavalcade with wagons representing Agriculture and Chastity and patriotic choirs—met with but little success. The people demanded a leader. Would it be General Cavaignac, the son of the member of the National Convention, the brother of a Republican journalist, and himself a Republican and Minister for War? Would this taciturn old African soldier be made Dictator? No! It was another figure that stood out in silhouette—that of Prince Charles Louis Napoleon Bonaparte, who had been elected deputy in four departments.

Louis Napoleon.

He was the son of Queen Hortense and, in the eyes of the law at all events, of Louis, King of Holland, the brother of the Emperor. At the age of forty he had already had a strange career. An old pupil of Le Bas, the son of Robespierre's disciple, he had been brought up on Plutarch. He had joined the Romagna rebels who had taken up arms against the temporal power of the Pope; he had been an artillery captain under the Government of Berne and had written a manual on gunnery and two treatises entitled *Rêveries Politiques* and *Considérations politiques et militaires sur la Suisse*; he was also " a burgess of Sallenstein " and " a citizen of the canton of Thurgau." This

18

philosophic and Liberal gunner further found himself, after the death of l'Aiglon, the heir to the heritage of Napoleon I. In 1836 he had made an attempt at Strassburg to claim his rights. Getting himself up to look as much as possible like the Petit Caporal in his legendary hat, he had endeavoured to induce a handful of gunners (a natural choice) to follow him with shouts of *"Vive l'Empereur!"* Driven into exile, he repeated the attempt at Boulogne, where he landed with a few armed followers and a vulture to play the part of eagle. This escapade cost him six years' imprisonment at Ham and brought him back to the study of philosophy; he wrote *La Question des Sucres*, *Le Recrutement*, *L'Extinction du Paupérisme* and solemnly collaborated in the *Progrès du Pas-de-Calais*. Louis Blanc had a loyal interview with the democrat of Ham. After his escape in 1846 he lived in London, awaiting his hour, with a sentimental belief in his star. This dreamer was typical of his day. Like everybody else, he had his system for reforming society and securing the welfare of the people. He believed in the extinction of pauperism through the triumph of democratic ideas. Uncultivated land was to be given to a huge association of workers, and the necessary credit allowed; between employers and employed an intermediary class of legally recognised " experts " was to be created, elected by the workers, in the proportion of one to every ten of the latter; they were to be paid a double wage and would constitute the non-commissioned officers of the industrial army. What simple-minded faith in human action! Theories with no foundation in reality, a burning desire for social reforms to complete the political reforms and secure true equality! It was all extremely " forty-eightish." But to it must be added that strange combination of militarism and socialism, of " *caporalism* " and humanitarian dreams, which might be expected in a Napoleon.

On hearing of the February revolution he had hastened " to place himself at the disposal of the Republic," but the Provisional Government had politely invited him to take ship again. Nevertheless his friends in Paris, Laity and Fialin surnamed " de Persigny," organised propaganda on his behalf and naturally utilised the legend of the uncle in order to popularise the nephew—portraits, biographies,

Bonapartist Propaganda.

19

journals (*Le Petit Caporal, La Redingote Grise, Le Napoléonien*)
and songs :

> *Napoléon, rentre dans ton palais,*
> *Napoléon, sois bon républicain.*[1]

And in the evening, all along the boulevards, to the stirring
march tune of *Les Lampions,* the workers filed past, crying :
" Poléon, Poléon, we shall have him, we shall have him ! "
The Assembly and the Executive Commission at first saw no
harm in these demonstrations and Crémieux declared from the
rostrum that the glory of Napoleon belonged to the nation.
" We eagerly accept anything in that glory that makes a
popular appeal; the proscription of the Bonapartes would be
a disgrace to France ! " These men of the Left regarded
Napoleon I as the man who had supplanted the fallen Monarchy
and made an end of privilege. His nephew was bound to be
" a good Republican and even a Socialist." In one breath
they shouted " *Vive Napoléon !* " and " *Vive Barbès !* " as well
as " Down with Thiers ! " the Royalist reactionary.

But eventually the Assembly grew alarmed. Apparently
officers had been fired upon to shouts of " *Vive l'Empereur !* "
Once again the deputies cried " *Vive la République !* " and
ordered the arrest of the Prince. But the very next day, on
the recommendation of Jules Favre, this same Assembly confirmed the election of the Prince to the Charente Inférieure
district, although they had proscribed him twenty-four hours
previously. " If Citizen Bonaparte," declared Jules Favre to
the Assembly, " were mad enough to dream of enacting a sort
of parody of what he did in 1840, he would be buried beneath
the contempt of his fellow-citizens and of posterity." What
blissful blindness ! But who could seriously fear the ridiculous
hero of the escapades of Strassburg and Boulogne ? Moreover,
on hearing of the political unrest, the Prince, who was no hero,
remained in London and sent in his resignation—the ground
had not yet been prepared. But he wrote from London : " If
the people set me a task I shall not fail to carry it out." It was
only later that the full significance of this phrase was understood.

For the time being a very different problem was agitating
the public mind—the question of National Workshops. On

---

[1] Napoleon, return to your palace; Napoleon, be a good Republican.

the 25th of February, in order to relieve the crisis of unemployment, the Provisional Government had proclaimed the right **National Workshops.** to work and had passed measures for the establishment of National Workshops, whereby Louis Blanc and the Reds hoped to organise Labour on co-operative lines, and place all skilled artisans in one common category—it was an admirable opportunity for putting the Socialist theory into practice. But Marie, the Minister concerned, regarded these National Workshops merely as an extension of the charity workshops which had already been inaugurated under Louis Philippe in times of unemployment—out-of-work blacksmiths and jewellers were to be paid a dole for working on the land. The State was not rich enough to launch out into Socialistic experiments. And thus in March, under the supervision of Émile Thomas, an engineer from *l'École Centrale,* a regular army of navvies was organised with flags and banners, squads and companies, a daily roll-call and a salary—for two pins it would have been called pay—of two francs a day. Little by little the army grew, its ranks swelled by unemployed from the provinces, strikers who threw up their jobs to come and loaf in the national yards; by May they numbered 100,000. The Government was at a loss to find them employment. It first set them to replant the trees along the boulevards, rebuild the Gare de l'Ouest (now the Gare Montparnasse), and lay out the Champ de Mars, or else paid them an " inactivity " dole of one franc which enabled them to while away their time playing *loto* or *bouchon* and talking politics.

At first the Government was not perturbed. Possibly it was not altogether sorry !—what a fine refutation of Socialist **Disturbances of May 15th.** theories ! And these battalions of workers might on occasion form an army of " Yellows " to fight Louis Blanc's Reds. At the elections they were induced to vote against Louis Blanc. But gradually the gangrene of Communism crept over these idlers, and on the 15th of May they formed the van of the insurgents who broke into the Assembly.

At last the latter took fright. Moreover, the unemployed constituted an expensive luxury. On the 23rd of May the Executive Commission was in favour of abolishing the Work-

21

shops. But Émile Thomas, the Director, protested. Whereupon, by virtue of a Republican *lettre de cachet*, he was carried off from the Public Works Office and, with many a friendly handshake, driven away in a post-chaise accompanied by two police officers who, on the pretext of some mission, conveyed him to the wilds of les Landes. In the Assembly Falloux demanded the termination of " this permanent organised strike which was costing 170,000 francs a day " (£6,800), though he proposed less heroic measures than dissolution pure and simple. The Assembly and the Executive Commission hesitated. Eventually, on the 21st of June, with the desperate energy of the weak, the Commission brutally offered the 110,000 unemployed the choice between joining the army or clearing the land in the provinces, which being interpreted meant—between being shot by the Arabs in Algeria or dying of fever in the swamps of Sologne. On the evening of the 21st and on the 22nd bands were formed under the leadership of a certain Pujol, an ex-seminarist and sometime African hunter, a mystic and fanatic, who had recently published *La Prophétie des Jours Sanglantes*, in which he declared that " the Governments were trying to reserve the days of suffering for the people and to keep the festivals and gold-grabbing for themselves." Marie received a deputation, but his attitude was threatening. In the Place St. Sulpice, Pujol climbed on to the fountain and harangued his followers. There were shouts of " Bread or bullets ! Bullets or work ! " and " We're going to stop ! " was set to the tune of *Les Lampions*. In the evening there was more speechifying at the Bastille and the Panthéon, and to the light of torches the crowd sang the *Marseillaise* and shouted " *Vive la République sociale !* " The authorities were powerless, although they had foreseen the drama and had even called out **Civil War.** the troops. But the Executive Commission could not bring itself to arrest the leaders and stifle the insurrection at birth. On the morning of the 23rd civil war broke out.

On that day, which was a Friday, Pujol's followers assembled at the Panthéon and made their way towards the Bastille, with drums beating and the Workshop banners flying, led by their Workshop brigadiers in blue caps trimmed with gold braid.

22

They sang the *Ça ira*—" Lamartine to the nearest lamp-post !
. . . Lamartine to the gallows ! " At the Bastille they took
off their caps and knelt down round the July column, whilst
Pujol recalled the memory of the heroes of '89 who on this very
spot had stormed the Bastille; and he pinned a bouquet to one
of the flags. There were shouts of " Liberty or death ! "

This mysticism boded no good—drunkards would have been
less dangerous than these fanatics ready to lay down their lives.
The mob then made for the boulevards and overturned an
omnibus at the Porte St. Denis—the first barricade. Immediately barricades sprang up here and there in all directions,
flying the red flag or even the tricolour, and soon half Paris was
covered with them. Paving-stones and scaffold-poles were
torn up and placed across the streets; in the Faubourg St. Denis
a half-finished locomotive was used, and in other places mail-
coaches. Thus solid walls were constructed, thick enough to
protect the men firing behind them and to break the onslaught
of the troops. The task was all the easier because the streets
were narrow. We must remember that the boulevards of St.
Michel, Sebastopol and Strasbourg, the Rue de Rivoli beyond
l'Oratoire, the streets and squares surrounding the Hôtel de
Ville were not then in existence. Instead of these wide thoroughfares there was a labyrinth of dark and noisome alleys—the
ancient quarters of the people where they could easily entrench
and defend themselves. To-day the district is roughly covered
by the 10th, 11th, 3rd, 4th, 5th and part of the 12th and 13th
arrondissements, and between the Gare du Nord and the Observatoire, faced the west end of Paris, where the bourgeoisie and
the partisans of law and order lived. Its rear rested on the
octroi wall skirting the boulevards, which are still sometimes
called the outer boulevards, and separating them from the
present peripheral *arrondissements* (the 18th, 19th, 20th, etc.),
where la Chapelle, la Villette, Belleville, Ménilmontant and
Gentilly were at that time communes independent of Paris,
although they were inside the recently constructed fortifications.
This town in revolt set to work to organise itself, and though it
had no pre-arranged plan it possessed discipline. There was no
lack of arms, for the men, who had all been members of the
National Guard since February, had their muskets. They

had no great leaders; the latter were in prison or had fled, and Pujol was unable to replace them. But on every side there were energetic men to take command of the barricades, most of them members of the Clubs. But no shops were looted and the *octroi* dues continued to be paid. Placards were posted on the barricades proclaiming: " Hands off private property, death to robbers ! " " Organisation and Work ! " They believed that the new age had dawned. A " slave " revolt, observed Lamartine. Yes, a social war, the uprising of the oppressed !

The Government took no notice. Was this deliberately done in order to pave the way for a greater victory? We must beware of interpreting mere inertia as Machiavelism. Arago cursed when he was informed that the National Guard was coming to the Palais Bourbon : " Good God ! " he cried, " who can have given such orders? Run quickly and stop them ! " Nevertheless, the civilian population began to get alarmed. They turned to Cavaignac; but the old African was not a Prefect of Police; he wanted to keep his troops in hand—30,000 regulars, 12,000 militiamen and the National Guards from the bourgeois quarters—and to avoid dividing them up into small patrols who would get disarmed, as had happened in February 1830. He insisted on arranging his forces with a centre and two wings, as he had been accustomed to do against the Arabs, and advancing in force. But that meant bloodshed ! Well, it was war; and Cavaignac was a soldier to whom Paris for the moment was merely a battle-field; possibly too he forgot that the enemy facing him were really Frenchmen.

On Friday, at midday, the National Guard—companies " in yellow gloves and patent-leather boots "—hurled themselves at the Porte St. Denis and broke down a barricade, killing two women one after the other—two street women, says Hugo—who, their shoulders bare, were brandishing the red flag. Meanwhile, at the Panthéon, Arago, the aged scientist, was courageously haranguing the insurgents. " Monsieur Arago," they replied, " you have never been hungry, you do not know the meaning of poverty ! " Among them were old working-men who in days gone by had fired by the side of Arago against the soldiers of Louis Philippe. But to-day there was a great gulf fixed between

24

the Republican bourgeoisie and the Socialist masses. In despair Arago went back to fetch the National Guard and led the assault. " For heaven's sake, fire at the base of the barricade ! " he shouted. For the time being the Panthéon was cleared. The National Guard, which was apt to bring a smile to men's lips, had not done so badly. These members of the bourgeoisie may have hesitated to plunder, but they could show as much devotion to the cause of law and order as did their adversaries to liberty. And to maintain, as some do, that they only carried a position under the lash of fear, in a heroic " flight forwards," is to display complete ignorance of the truth regarding the fight.

At last, in the afternoon, the army went out to battle—Lamoricière on the left, Bedeau in the centre, to protect and clear the Hôtel de Ville, Damesme on the right (the left bank of the river). Lamoricière's troops were engaged at St. Vincent de Paul, the Rue de Bellefond, the church of St. Laurent, the Faubourg du Temple and the Rue St. Maur. From there Cavaignac, who came in person, wanted to fall back on the Bastille and take the Faubourg St. Antoine in the rear. But he had difficulty in carrying the position, which had to be attacked with heavy artillery and surrendered only at nightfall. In the centre Bedeau endeavoured to parley—because, says Tocqueville, " he is as human as if he had never waged war in Africa." Such a testimony, in the mouth of a Tocqueville, is sufficiently eloquent and throws considerable light on the nature of " Africans." But the negotiations ended in smoke, and Bedeau attacked the barricades on the Petit Pont and the Pont St. Michel, in order to give Damesme a helping hand. But he was held up at the Rue St. Jacques, where he was obliged to bombard the barricade from the wards of the Hôtel Dieu, where the guns were mounted between the beds of the patients. The troops stormed the position. Intoxicated with rage and the fumes of battle, the militia massacred or shot down the insurgents, hurled the fugitives from the roofs, and laughed to see them crash on to the pavement. But elsewhere the barricades held firm. Not far off one of the commandants of the National Guard, a solicitor named Masson, tried to parley with the insurgents : " Don't shoot ! " he shouted. " Don't start a

25

civil war!" And he fell like a hero. Bedeau was wounded, and his troops were obliged to fall back. Damesme also was making but little headway round the Panthéon. In short, on the evening of the first day the insurgents were still holding their own.

As the hours dragged by the Assembly continued to sit without adjourning. They imagined they were in duty bound to prolong the session, though they had no very clear idea of what to do, and debated the question as to whether the State should not resume control of the railways, which at the moment were almost bankrupt. After which certain deputies made speeches on the situation, some proposing to go to the barricades, others suggesting that a proclamation should be issued. In the end the Assembly were unable to reach any decision. What could these deputies, nearly all of whom came from the country, do in this Parisian revolt? Towards the Executive Commission Cavaignac adopted the tone of a master. To secure unity of command he begged Ledru-Rollin to refrain from giving any orders. On trying to reach Lamoricière he was held up in the Rue St. Maur, some distance away from the place where he should have been, and the Executive were at their wits' end to know how to meet the demands for reinforcements received from Bedeau and Damesme. Ledru-Rollin, feeling himself bound to Cavaignac, refused to give any orders, and instinctively took refuge behind the military, as civilians usually do in such cases, and was naturally accused of treachery by the various staffs which were demanding reinforcements. When Cavaignac came **Cavaignac.** back, Ledru-Rollin had a violent scene with him. This meant a rupture between Cavaignac and the Executive. On the following morning, when the fighting had already started again, the Assembly proclaimed a state of siege and put Cavaignac in supreme command.

On that Saturday morning the insurgents had received reinforcements. During the night they had cast bullets out of zinc taken from the wine-shop counters, and printers' type, and lead and copper from the railway workshops; they had manufactured powder at Ruggieri's, the firework-maker, founded a cannon in a factory, where they cooled it immediately by suspending it with ropes and getting women and children to throw

26

moist sand on the metal while it was still hot. Thus they easily equipped themselves. And at dawn the battle was renewed with redoubled fury. The insurgents recaptured the Panthéon and threatened the Hôtel de Ville. Cavaignac issued proclamations at once resolute and moderate in tone to the National Guards, " volunteers representing the intelligent sections of the nation," to the regulars who were to remain " faithful to the laws of honour and of humanity," and finally to the insurgents : " If in your ranks there are criminal instigators, there are also your own brethren who have merely gone astray. . . ." This was not exactly African in tone. By means of visual signalling he summoned the National Guards from the provinces. From near and far they came, from Versailles or Finistère, and these warriors in their shakos filed past before the Palais Bourbon. Pray do not laugh at these village firemen who rushed to put out the Paris conflagration !

Throughout the day the battle raged without reaching a decision. There was mutual slaughter. The tragedy had its humorous side—a street urchin in his death agony asked for a drink : " Madeira ! I have never tasted it ! " A general entered a café in search of members of the National Guard : " Come, gentlemen, you will have plenty of time to quench your thirst this evening; go and rejoin your comrades under fire. . . ." Maxime du Camp, who relates all these incidents, also describes his return from the barricades. When he was being carried back wounded, all the sentinels in turn saluted him, exclaiming, " All honour to courage in misfortune ! " And he had to end by laughing. Meanwhile the efforts of Lamoricière and Lebreton in the Faubourg du Temple were all in vain. Duvivier, who had taken Bedeau's place, could make no headway. In the south Damesme failed in his attack on the Panthéon. But eventually he succeeded in capturing it, though soon afterwards he fell mortally wounded.

It was only on the third day that the situation cleared, as had been the case in 1830 and also in February. The Assembly was terror-stricken, and Thiers proposed that it should retire to Bourges. Cavaignac was furious at the suggestion and threatened to have Thiers shot. A Republican dictator, he wanted to have the representatives of the country at his back.

27

Paris was in despair. The dismemberment, burning and castration of militiamen by female insurgents, and the violation of convent girls by the Socialists formed the sole topics of conversation. On one insurgent was found an order entitling " the bearer to three ladies of the Faubourg St. Germain." One red flag bore the inscription : " Two hours of plunder and of silk petticoats ! " On the barricades, on the other hand, tales were told of the murderous fury of the militia, who savagely killed anybody in a blouse, while their hands seemed to reek of powder. Everybody saw that the end was near, and on both sides the watchword was the same—No quarter ! At last Lamoricière and Lebreton succeeded in advancing step by step as far as the yard of the Hôpital Lariboisière, which was being built at the time, the Chapelle and the Faubourg du Temple. Hugo, who was watching the struggle, tried to intervene, but declares that he was met by musket-fire. In the Rue St. Antoine, Duvivier attacked the houses which had been fortified and the crenelated barricades. He advanced, but was mortally wounded, whilst his brigadier, Regnault, was treacherously killed by a prisoner, and Négrier, who took Duvivier's place, also fell at the Bastille. Meanwhile Bréa, who had replaced Damesme and had reached the Barrière d'Enfer (now the Place Denfert-Rochereau), tried to hold a parley and put a stop to the fighting by announcing that the Assembly had voted relief for the unemployed. He advanced alone to the barricade across the Barrière d'Italie (the present Place d'Italie), where he was lured over by the insurgents, captured, dragged into a house in the Avenue d'Italie, insulted and beaten. Whereupon his staff-captain, Mangin, tore open his tunic in exasperation and shouted : " For God's sake shoot, and have done with it ! " A few kind souls were trying to help them to escape, when a woman cried : " The militia ! " and they were shot down like mad dogs. Bréa had

Death of Bréa. his own sword buried in his belly—a sword " presented to the brave Bréa in memory of Waterloo. . . ."

This terrible incident became famous in France and inspired the bourgeoisie with an almost morbid terror of the Reds.

That evening, Monseigneur Affre, Archbishop of Paris, whom certain young Catholics—among them Ozanam—had begged to intervene to put a stop to the bloodshed, at last decided to take action, and making his confession, he set out for the Bas-

Death of Affre. tille. On his arrival the firing ceased. Did this mean a truce? But owing to some misunderstanding the insurgents, thinking they had been betrayed, reopened fire. The bombardment started once more and a bullet, fired doubtless by one of the regulars, hit the Archbishop in the back. He was taken to his palace, at that time situated in the Rue St. Louis, amid the respectful homage of insurgents and soldiers alike. Two days later he was dead. . . . But the sacrifice hastened the end. During the night negotiations were opened, though they proved fruitless. On the Monday morning a further final assault swept away the last show of resistance, and at twenty minutes past eleven, Sénard, in the Assembly, was able to return thanks to Almighty God, whilst the deputies shouted: *" Vive la République! "*

Thus ended the terrible civil war, which had cost the lives of 1,500 of the defenders of law and order, and possibly of 3,000 insurgents, most of whom were shot in the heat of battle where they stood. Others were arrested and thousands deported. From that day forward a river of blood separated the Socialist workers from the Republican bourgeoisie. Henceforward France was to be haunted by the memory of those terrible days of " anarchy " and " barbarism," that first Commune which another Commune was destined to make her forget. When the saviour of law and order appeared he would be welcomed with open arms. And thus it came about that Louis Napoleon Bonaparte owed his success chiefly to the massacres of the 23rd, 24th and 25th of June and to the blood of men like Affre and Bréa.

As soon as the massacre was over there was a longing on all sides for order with bivouacs

la République des honnêtes gens ! "   On the same day the Assembly cheered Cavaignac, who " had deserved well of his country,"

Cavaignac Dictator. and placed the executive in his hands with the title and powers of President of the Council and the right to choose his own Ministers, the latter to be responsible to the Assembly.   Thus, says Monsieur Seignobos, the parliamentary system was put into practice for the first time. Cavaignac surrounded himself with strong men—Lamoricière, Sénard and Goudchaux, and dismissed Carnot, the head of the Ministry of Public Instruction.   The Assembly held him suspect on account of his *Manuel Républicain de l'Homme et du Citoyen*, an infamous publication edited for the use of schools and electors by the philosopher Renouvier.

A reaction, natural enough after civil war, now set in.   Some of the Clubs were closed, others put under supervision.   They

Reaction. were forbidden to discuss motions hostile to public order and decency—an expression sufficiently vague to warrant any measures the police might choose to take— private meetings were forbidden, as well as addresses and delegations from the Clubs.   Newspapers were suspended, and Émile de Girardin was arrested, because he had complained of " having once again fallen beneath the despotism of the sword." Every newspaper was obliged to lay down a large sum by way of deposit for the payment of fines that might be incurred later on. Lamennais, who was poor, was obliged to suspend the publication of his journal.   Offences against the Republic, attacks " on the principle of private property and the rights of the family " —once more an expression sufficiently vague to justify any repressive measure—were punishable as misdemeanours.   Lastly, a commission of inquiry was appointed to hunt down those responsible for the recent disturbances; it frightened Ledru-Rollin   who took flight.
                                                                                                           ssed for

and the voice of authority. Paris, filled
and patrols, was like a captured city. The siege fever
that had convulsed the town did not immediately abate. The
whistle of an engine or dressmakers burning the midnight oil in
an attic gave rise to cries of "Conspiracy!" On the 28th of
June the National Guards, who had come from the country,
marched past in review order to shouts of "Down with the
Montagnards!"—an expression aimed at the Reds—and "*Vive*

...r and decided to prosecute Louis Blanc, w...
At the same time, however, Cavaignac had measures passe...
the relief of unemployment—loans for cabinet-makers and the
bronze-workers of the Faubourg St. Antoine, and exemption
from taxation for houses to be built in 1849. And at every turn
he proclaimed himself a Republican, even suspending the royalist
Gazette de France. Meanwhile Goudchaux was endeavouring
to replace the finances on a firm basis. He refused to allow the

THE SECOND REPUBLIC

State to buy back the railways, which at that time showed a
deficit, and insisted on levying the unpopular taxes on salt and
liquor, as well as the 45 centimes tax, which provoked a rebellion
in Guéret, where the people, with delightful irony, wanted to
hang on the nearest tree of liberty anybody who consented to
pay it. Goudchaux also wanted to tap legacies, property
enjoyed " through the accident of birth or the caprice of private
affection." But the Assembly, which, as is ever the case in
France, consisted of Conservative country-folk, did not support
him. It also condemned a Socialistic scheme advanced by
Proudhon by which one-third of all agricultural rents and debts
was to be cancelled, the State to benefit equally with farmers
and debtors. And Ledru-Rollin incurred considerable odium
for taking upon himself the task of unearthing money for the
Treasury " from places where it was hidden or turned to selfish
purposes. . . ." In fact, it was a system of reaction, at once
sincerely Republican and whole-heartedly Conservative.

In his dealings with foreign countries Cavaignac continued
the temporising and pacific policy of the Provisional Govern-

Foreign Policy. ment. The Piedmontese, defeated by the Austrians,
were invoking the aid of France; but Cavaignac,
born soldier though he was, proved himself a statesman, by refusing to intervene. His Minister, Bastide, declared
that the Government did not believe in " the enthusiasm and
love of Italians for France," and would intervene only if Austria

Ticino. invaded Piedmont. " We shall defend the Ticino
frontier as we would the Var." This was an axiom
of the day equivalent to the determination of England to protect
Antwerp from annexation of any description. Cavaignac even
refused to send reinforcements to the Pope, whose temporal
power was menaced in Rome. The country had been too
severely shaken by civil war for him to wish to launch out into
adventures.

Meanwhile the Assembly confirmed the Constitution, for the
passing of which it had been convened. It also ratified the

The Con- stitution. establishment of the Republic, since France " wished
to maintain her position as the pioneer of progress
and civilisation in the world." Happy youth !—
but in this respect all revolutionaries are young. Their slogan

31

was " Liberty, Equality, Fraternity ! " The two first words dated from '93, the third was the creation of the period. The Assembly was to consist of 750 deputies elected for three years by universal suffrage; by the same method a President of the Republic was to be elected, who could not seek re-election immediately after the expiration of his term of office. He was forbidden, on pain of being arraigned for high treason, to dissolve or suspend the Assembly, and was to appoint his own Ministers, who were to be responsible to him and not to the Assembly.

During the debate on the Constitution certain points were acrimoniously discussed—first and foremost the right to work, which the Montagnards were anxious to see proclaimed. " Vain promises ! " declared Thiers, who could not bring himself to admit that it was the duty of the State to provide bread for all. The Assembly, however, agreed to the obligation " within the limits and resources of the Republic." The question of creating a second Chamber, to balance the first, was also brought up. But there were outcries of " Reaction ! " and " The House of Peers again ! " and a Council of State, elected by the Assembly to frame the laws, had to suffice. Finally, there was the debate on the President. It was maintained that he should be elected by the people and not by the Assembly. But Grévy, disquieted by the success of Louis Bonaparte, who had been elected in five departments in September, pointed out the danger presented by ambitious men who, if they were elected by the nation, would try to overthrow the Republic and remain on the Presidential throne. " Hitherto," he declared, " every Republic has been swallowed up in despotism." Parieu, a future Minister of Napoleon III, predicted that unending conflict between the Assembly and the President would be inevitable. But Lamartine, probably with the object of annoying Cavaignac, whom the Assembly, if they could have had their way, would certainly have elected, and hoping to secure the favour of the country himself, harangued them with his usual poetic fervour, pointing the moral from history : " To risk an 18th Brumaire, two things are necessary—long years of terror behind, and Marengos and victories ahead." He forgot that although historically there is nothing new under the sun, in form, at least, everything

32

is new, and that while two periods may have many points in common, they are never wholly alike. He ended with a challenge : " Let God and the people decide ! If the people wish to resign their freedom and place themselves in the hands of a dim shadow of the Empire, so much the worse for them ! " Such challenges are always dangerous. But, as a matter of fact, who could believe in the possibility of such a menace ? Louis Napoleon, shy and awkward, when called upon to make his maiden speech from the rostrum, had not been able to utter a word ; at his second attempt he had spoken in hollow tones with a foreign accent. Surely this ridiculous hero of Boulogne and Strassburg could not be taken seriously by anybody !

But as the election drew near it was suddenly discovered what power the name of Napoleon still had in France. The other candidates were Raspail, the Socialist, Ledru-Rollin, the social-democrat—to-day he would be called a Radical-Socialist—and Cavaignac, representing the moderates. The latter was the only one who held a chance. He was already in power and had officialdom and the *National* behind him. But for some he was too reactionary, for others too much of a Jacobin. Moreover, he " had deserved well of his country "—a bad qualification for a politician in France. Girardin, furious at having been sent to prison, led the campaign in his journal *La Presse* against the man who " had purposely allowed the insurrection to grow in order to be hailed as saviour." And after all, what could be done against a Napoleon ?

Louis Napoleon had no party that he could really call his own. He borrowed from everybody. But on his side he had Thiers, who regarded him " as a booby whom it would be easy to lead by the nose " and hoped that in his efforts to restore the Monarchy this puppet would be as clay in his hands. Never for a moment did he imagine that one day this booby would lead him—to the Mazas prison. Thus the party of law and order, and Girardin out of hatred for Cavaignac, embarked upon a campaign in favour of the Prince. His chief asset was his name—it inspired confidence, and the country as a whole was in favour of Napoleon. The imperial legend still lived. Béranger, in one of his songs, makes the " grandmother " conjure up the memory of the *Petit Caporal :*

Candidature of Louis Napoleon.

D

THE SECOND REPUBLIC

Il avait petit chapeau [1]
Avec redingote grise.
Près de lui je me troublais. . . .
Il vous à parlé, grand'mère,
Il vous à parlé !

The legend had effaced the horrors of massacre and bloodshed,
and allowed only visions of triumphal processions through
captured cities, flying flags and glory to remain ! It was eight
years ago that the hero had returned to his beloved Paris, and
had descended the Champs Élysées on his way to the tomb of
his apotheosis under the dome of the Invalides. The country
would vote for the new Napoleon. Medals stamped with his
effigy were hawked about and papers singing his praises. He
declared that he was neither a Socialist nor a lover of war, that
he would be a Liberal, pacific Napoleon. But did anybody
trouble to read his manifesto? It was his name that was
acclaimed. At the ballot of the 10th of December
His Election. he received five and a half million votes out of a
total roll of seven million voters, leaving Cavaignac,
Ledru-Rollin and Raspail far behind. On the 20th of December
he took an oath to remain true to the democratic Republic, one
and indivisible; and of his own accord he added : " I shall
regard as enemies of my country any who shall attempt by
illegal means to change what France herself has established."
A politician's promise is even more brittle than a lover's oaths !
Nevertheless, in this instance, it was not a case of making
promises in the hope of being able to break them with impunity
later on. On the 20th of December, 1848, Prince Napoleon
was undoubtedly sincere. But human nature can be sincere in
different and contradictory ways at different times.

It was not long before the President fell out with the Ministers
whom Thiers had forced him to choose from among Guizot's old
The President and his Ministers. adversaries, that is to say, from the ranks of the
monarchists; for in this Cabinet of the Second
Republic, of which Odilon Barrot was the head,
there was but one Republican, Bixio, and he soon sent in his
resignation. But lately returned from exile, and dreaming of

---

[1] He wore a little hat and a grey frock-coat. In his presence I was
stirred. . . . He spoke to you, grandmamma, he spoke to you !

34

social reform and of personal rule by the head of the State, what could this Prince possibly have in common with these Conservative members of the bourgeoisie, hidebound by parliamentary tradition? At Cabinet meetings this shy, irresolute man held his tongue, with a far-away look in his lack-lustre eyes. Yet he was capable of sudden disconcerting bluntness and obstinacy. It seemed as though this gentle dreamer occasionally remembered the name he bore and in his desire to be a Bonaparte did violence to his true nature. When his Ministers refused to allow him to examine the *dossiers* of Boulogne and Strassburg, as he wished to do—he was devoured by all the curiosity of a criminal suddenly allowed to look through the judge's papers—and when he asked in vain to be given the reports sent by the Prefect of Police to the Minister of the Interior, he grew angry. " I insist upon having those *dossiers*," he wrote, adopting the tone of his uncle. " I shall not allow Ministers of my own creation to treat me as though the famous constitution of Sieyès were still in force." To use his uncle's expression, he had no intention of being a pig battening on a few millions. But when the Ministers sent in their resignation he immediately gave way and apologised. He was a man of caprice rather than of determination. At all events, with all the eagerness of the upstart, he surrounded himself with a certain pomp and ceremony. At the Élysée he had a full military establishment, with liveried flunkeys, Swiss halberdiers, a coach emblazoned with the imperial arms, and two horses that had once been the property of the Duc d'Aumale. He liked to appear on horseback—being short in the legs, he looked puny and insignificant on foot—dressed in the uniform of a General of the National Guard with a white plumed hat. He was already masquerading—innocently?—as Emperor.

Meanwhile the Constituent Assembly, having completed its work on the Constitution, decided, somewhat reluctantly, to give way to the Legislative Assembly which was to be elected. Faucher, the Minister of the Interior, made preparations for the elections betimes, keeping a sharp eye on *La Solidarité Républicaine*, the party which included Ledru-Rollin and the Reds as well as Delescluze and Félix Pyat in its ranks. He would also have liked to suppress the Clubs, and did actually disband

35

unruly units of the militia. On the 29th of January, 1849, Changarnier, the Governor-General of Paris, dispersed a band of demonstrators. The troops cheered the President, already shouting "*Vive l'Empereur!*" and Changarnier suggested to Louis Napoleon an immediate *coup de force* against the Assembly. He refused. Did he do so because it would place him under too deep an obligation to Changarnier? The more likely reason is that he could not make up his mind, because he had not got at his elbow the man who was to prove the embodiment of his will on the 2nd of December—Morny. This earned him the contempt of Changarnier. " Did you see the face the President made? " the latter inquired of Thiers. " After all, he is only a . . ." The word he used is too reminiscent of the barrack-room to be set down in print.

But it was not long before the Executive and the Legislative Assembly came to serious loggerheads over the Roman question. **The Roman Question.** The Pope, put to flight by the revolutionaries, had taken refuge at Gaeta. Austria meditated intervention, in order to crush the Roman Republic and restore the temporal throne of the Holy Father she thought fit, that is to say, in accordance with absolutist principles. But French diplomacy in Italy, by supporting the Liberals, had always aimed at being a thorn in the flesh of Vienna. Yet France too wished to see the temporal power of the Pope restored. Hence the thousand and one contradictions in French policy, which was constantly endeavouring to reconcile irreconcilables, endeavouring to reinstate the Pope in Rome without crushing the Roman Liberals, and to restore his subjects to the Holy Father while at the same time protecting them from a reaction which was nevertheless inevitable. The President himself was the living embodiment of these contradictions. In 1831, at the age of twenty-three, he had fought in Romagna for the cause of Italian independence side by side with those who had now proclaimed the Republic in Rome. It was at this time that he had lost his elder brother, though, as a matter of fact, his actual death was due to measles. Like a good Bonaparte, he had kept alive his hatred of Austria and his love of Italy, while the latter, for her part, still did homage to his uncle, fondly imagining that Napoleon I would have liked to see her united and independent. But the sometime conspirator, now that he had come into power, was anxious to preserve law and order, and instinctively leant on the Catholics, who were demanding the restoration of the Pope, and on the military party, the dream of whose ambition was to go to fight in Rome.

Towards the end of March the news was received that the Piedmontese army had been defeated by the Austrians on the 23rd at Novara. The President was in favour of declaring immediate war on his ancient foes of Vienna. But Thiers intervened, pointing out to him that France was not ready, and at the same time persuading Austria to show moderation and refrain from violating the integrity of the Ticino frontier, which it was the policy of France to protect as she would protect the Var frontier. Nevertheless, it was imperative to forestall victorious Austria in Rome. Accordingly, supplies were obtained from the Assembly for an expeditionary force which " was to secure for the Roman people a Government based upon Liberal institutions." In short, the French Government imagined it could effect a reconciliation between the Pope and the Roman people, and secure the restoration of the Holy Father as well as Liberal reforms. Vain delusion ! When General Oudinot and his men disembarked at Civita Vecchia, the Pope categorically refused to make any promises about Liberal institutions; and on the 30th of April a presumptuous attack on Rome by French troops resulted in a signal defeat.

Oudinot in Rome.

A repulse such as this cried aloud for vengeance, and the situation became proportionately complicated. The Government sent immediate reinforcements to Oudinot. But the Assembly insisted on having a finger in the pie. They had been taken in, and told that it was the aim of France to support the cause of Liberalism in Rome. But she was doing so with shot and shell ! On the 7th of May, Jules Favre lodged a protest : " French blood has been spilled in the cause of absolutism ! " he exclaimed. The Assembly, which could not countenance the crushing of the Roman Republic by soldiers of the French Republic, insisted that " the Italian expedition should no longer be diverted from the object for which it had been sent out." But the Government was not perturbed. They were on the eve of the elections and relied upon the Legislative Assembly, which was to supplant the Constituent, openly declaring in favour of energetic intervention on behalf of the Pope. Accordingly, in order to gain time, Ferdinand de Lesseps was sent on a special mission to Rome, to endeavour to arrange matters and reconcile irreconcilables. The President gave him a personal letter to Oudinot, which was published in Paris on the 9th of May and caused great excitement, for it was frankly hostile to the vote of the 7th of May : " I cannot allow our military honour to be assailed. . . . Your soldiers can always count on my support and gratitude." The Prince, being a Bonaparte, instinctively ranged himself on the side of the army, entirely oblivious of what was at stake. Carried away by his love of the soldier, the old Carbonaro forgot that the adversaries of the French troops had once been his companions in arms in the Romagna—they were the enemy, and that was enough. Changarnier, when he communicated contents of the letter to the garrison in Paris, declared it ought to " strengthen the devotion of the army to the head of the State," and that " it presented a happy contrast to the language used by those "—meaning the Assembly—" who wanted to disown French soldiers facing enemy fire." Thus from May 1849 the future Emperor, trying his hand at personal rule, relied on the support of the army against the Assembly. At a review on the 21st of May there were shouts of " *Vive l'Empereur !* " as he passed by. In the light of subsequent events all this becomes perfectly clear.

Lesseps' Mission.

Meanwhile Lesseps was parleying and negotiating, and at last after infinite trouble he obtained, on the 31st of May, the signature by the Romans to the draft of a treaty arranging for a truce of at least a fortnight. But on the 1st of June Lesseps was peremptorily recalled and Oudinot was given orders to attack in spite of the promised truce, that is to say, in violation of the right of nations, the reason being that the Constituent had been replaced by the Legislative Assembly, which openly sided with the Pope against the Roman Republic.

Indeed the elections of the 13th of May, 1849, had marked the definite triumph of the party of law and order. The horrors of June had not yet been forgotten, and were the less likely

38

to be forgotten seeing that the courts-martial and the assizes had just passed sentence on the murderers of General Bréa and the other insurgents. Furthermore, an opportune parliamentary report had exposed the financial anarchy of the Provisional Government, the mad extravagance of its commissioners costing 6,000 francs a month (£240)—they insisted upon travelling between their departments and Paris by special train. The party of law and order turned these memories and fears to their own purpose in order to discredit the February Republicans. The Committee of the Rue de Poitiers founded a powerful organisation, the *Union Electorale*, to defend social order against anarchy and rally all right-minded citizens round the man who had been elected head of the State on the 10th of December. Two hundred thousand francs (£8000) was raised for the Union by public subscription, a huge sum for the period, which enabled the organisation to inundate the country with pamphlets against Socialism, signed by Bugeaud, Wallon, the future " father " of the Third Republic, and many others. Bugeaud dubbed the schemes for social reform " nefarious absurdities emanating from our big schools and polytechnics . . ," while Wallon roundly abused the " Red " : " The Red is not a man," he declared, " he is a Red; he does not reason, and he has ceased to think. He has lost all sense of truth and justice, of the beautiful and the good. . . . He sacrifices his liberty, his instincts and his ideas on the altar of the most brutal and uncivilised passions; he is a fallen and degenerate creature." A portrait of him follows : "A brutal face, with dull, shifty eyes, furtive as those of a pig . . . a low forehead, a mouth dumb and insignificant as a donkey's . . . thick, bulging lips, indicative of low passions; a great big nose, insensitive and wooden, glued in the middle of his face. . . ."

Elections of May 13.

Against this " reactionary " current, Socialism struggled valiantly, using pedlars to circulate pamphlets and almanacs throughout the country. These " partitioners " won adherents in the country districts where there were still hopes of another partition of land such as had taken place after '89. Moreover, an idyllic picture was drawn of Socialism, with its mutual benefit society to which everybody contributed 20 sous a month to pay for remedies for

Socialistic Activities.

any comrade who should fall ill. And better still : " We shall not allow his work to suffer—those who are well will meet together, lots will be drawn, and those on whom the choice falls will turn out on Sunday morning to work on his field. . . . By getting up betimes they will have finished before Mass and go home content. . . ." A simplicity of mind which, although it was 1849, still savoured strongly of '48. Democrats and Socialists alike, Ledru-Rollin and Pyat, united against the parties of the Right and claimed the right to work, to the use of capital and the means of production, a graduated income tax, the nationalisation of the railways, mines, insurance, etc. And the strides made by Socialism were all the greater seeing that there was now practically nothing separating it from the party of law and order. There were no moderates; a man had either to be Red or White. On the very eve of the elections the Minister of the Interior, emboldened by a vote in favour of his Ministry, declared in a despatch to the Prefects that the agitators were only awaiting a hostile vote in order to rush to arms and renew the disturbances of June. " Paris is quiet." The manœuvre was hardly honourable, since there was no threat of trouble, but it was shrewd.

And indeed the ballot of the 13th of May resulted in a signal success for the party of law and order. It is true that the poll **Triumph of** was not nearly so heavy as it had been in '48—only **Law and** 60 per cent. of those on the registers voting. The **Order.** enthusiasm of Easter of the preceding year was very far from being repeated. It is also true that the Social-Democrats had secured 180 seats, a figure that gave rise to a sort of panic and made the five per cents drop by almost five francs—a huge depreciation ; for law-abiding people feared that the Ledru-Rollins and the Pyats, who had been elected in several departments, would renew civil war as they had done in June '48. But the Right was none the less triumphant, since it was certain of almost 500 seats, including 200 Legitimists and a few Bonapartists. The February party, the moderate Republicans, were crushed between the Reds and the Whites—Lamartine and his old colleagues of the Provisional Government had not been re-elected, and their party had retained only 75 seats. Falloux pointed the moral from the result of the ballot which

40

condemned the weakness of these moderates as well as the
excesses of the Reds : " France has no further use for the
timorous, nor those who make others timorous. She wants
neither men who are capable of nothing nor those who are
capable of anything."

But to return to Rome—an explanation was given of Lesseps'
sudden recall and of the order to attack, and by the middle of
May the wind had changed. On the 3rd of June, Oudinot
captured a Roman outpost, the Villa Pamphili, though at a
price. On the 9th the news reached Paris. The Social-Democrats became excited, declaring that there had been a violation
of the Constitution, Article V of which stipulated that " France
. . . should never turn her arms against the liberty of any
nation." On the 11th, in the Palais Bourbon, in the very
chamber where the 750 deputies were huddled together—the
quarters of the Constituent Assembly being under repair—
Ledru-Rollin spoke in an atmosphere of civil war, amid much
abuse and heckling. He recalled the vote of the Constituent
on the 7th of May : " It is no use telling us that because the
French have suffered a reverse, it is necessary to have a victory
to-day—there can be no victory if the law of nations is violated."
He tried to inculpate the President and his Cabinet. " The
Constitution has been violated ! " he exclaimed; " but we shall
defend it by every means, even by force of arms ! " The Right
retaliated with cries of " Order ! Order ! " but the Montagne,
raising their fists, echoed : " Yes, by force of arms ! " Did
this mean civil war again ?—the war prophesied and apparently
almost desired by the Conservatives in order to have done with the
Reds. But as soon as the fatal word had escaped his lips, Ledru-
Rollin began to have qualms. Would the people support him ?
At that time everybody was far more concerned about the
epidemic of cholera which was killing 200 people a day in Paris,
and to which Bugeaud fell a victim on the 11th of June. But
once again the leaders were obliged to follow the movement
they had let loose in order not to be outdistanced by their
subordinates.

On the 13th of June, a procession of National Guards under
Etienne Arago marched along the boulevards shouting, " *Vive
la République Romaine !* " But the onlookers were indifferent,

41

almost hostile. In the Rue de la Paix, Changarnier debouched
with his dragoons and light infantry, charging and dispersing
the demonstrators without difficulty. Whereupon the
June the 13th. troops made their way to the *Conservatoire des Arts
et Métiers*, where Ledru-Rollin and the Montagnards,
wearing their sashes, had gathered together, doubtless awaiting
the result of the demonstration before risking their persons.
There was a shout of " The soldiers ! " and a general rush for
safety. Ledru-Rollin fled and took refuge in England. Pyat
went into exile. It was the end of the Montagne. In the
evening the mob greeted the President with cheers. The mad
escapade of the 13th of June had also served to increase the
popularity of the representative of law and order. At Lyons,
General Magnan bombarded and destroyed the barricades
erected at the Croix Rousse by the Club known as the *Voraces*.
Reactionary measures naturally followed—newspapers were
suspended, Clubs closed, and a Press law was passed against
" the spirit of revolt and disorder." The *Revue des Deux Mondes*
was very severe on the political " disturbers of the peace."
" Who would have anything to do with them as lawyers,
doctors, clients or patrons? They are no good except as
masters ! " And the President gave utterance to a phrase
which was to become famous and represent ten years of reaction
and peace : " It is high time for the good to take heart and for
the wicked to tremble in their shoes."

The party of law and order was also triumphant in Rome—
Oudinot sapped his way towards the city, and after a bombard-
Oudinot enters Rome. ment lasting several days, took two bastions on the
21st of June and a third on the 30th. Garibaldi,
who had come to the rescue of the Roman Republic,
abandoned the struggle. On the 3rd of July Oudinot entered
Rome. The Pope immediately embarked upon a reactionary
and repressive policy which even the French Government
found disconcerting; reactionary in Paris, it would have liked
to be Liberal in Rome if only for the sake of annoying Austria.
And at this juncture the President again intervened and seized
the opportunity to take personal action. Now that the military
honour of France had been avenged, the old Carbonaro remembered the promises of his young days and his enthusiasm for the

42

cause of Italian freedom. On the 18th of August he wrote to one of his aides-de-camp, chosen doubtless on account of his **Letter to** name—Edgar Ney—a letter which raised an even **Edgar** greater commotion than his letter to Oudinot : **Ney.** " The Republic did not send an army to Rome to stamp out Italian liberty in that city," he wrote, and added that a general amnesty must be demanded of the Pope, together with the secularisation of the administration, the adoption of the *Code Napoléon* and the appointment of a Liberal Government, reminding him that the armies of Napoleon I had everywhere " done away with the abuses of feudalism and sown the seeds of liberty." Thus he identified himself with the tradition of Napoleon as a democrat, an egalitarian and the adversary of the *ancien régime*, the man who had put a stop to the excesses of the French Revolution whilst safeguarding its achievements.

The excitement such a letter provoked on its publication in Italy and France may well be imagined. It precipitated the rupture between the President and his Ministers. There had never been much love lost between them. These members of the bourgeoisie despised the adventurer who was riddled with debt and had great difficulty in preventing the furniture belonging to his " fair Englishwoman," Miss Howard, from being seized. Before a Cabinet meeting they used generally to foregather at Barrot's house and arrived at the Élysée unanimous on all points, so as to be able to forestall any discussion upon which the President might embark. They were suspicious of the caprices of this visionary, and his personal intervention in affairs— especially his letter to Ney—more often than not seemed dangerous folly in their eyes. In this respect the majority of the Assembly was on their side; Thiers, during a debate on the Roman question, systematically omitted all reference to the Ney letter, a fact which the Left were quick to turn to account. The President silently raged against his Ministers, against that fellow Thiers, against the whole bourgeois class which **The New** had nothing in common with him except the love **Ministry.** of order, but whose conception of what order was differed so widely from his own. And on the 31st of October, 1849, he insisted upon the resignation of the Cabinet, and summoned new men chosen outside the parliamentary majority

43

—Rouher and Parieu, two deputies who were lawyers from Auvergne, a banker named Fould and two generals. He refrained from appointing any President of the Council. His aim was to put into practice the system which had triumphed on the 10th of December. "For the name of Napoleon is in itself a whole programme. It means at home, order, authority, religion and the welfare of the people; abroad, the dignity of France." It was necessary to have a firm Government in the hands of one man, and for the personal will of the chosen leader of December the 10th to be made manifest. It was the duty of his Ministers to understand him and, both in deed and word, to concern themselves with his responsibilities as well as their own.

Already there was an outcry that the *coup d'état* was taking place. But at the same time the President remembered the oath of allegiance he had sworn to the Constitution and protested that he was aiming at restoring authority without prejudice to real freedom, and establishing religious principles without abandoning anything the revolution had won—a fantastic conciliation of opposites entirely in keeping with his nature, which was a bundle of contradictory whims and fancies. But he was undoubtedly sincere. It was at this time that Morny was deploring the Prince's hesitation to proclaim the Empire, and his "honest scruples." Two years were to pass, bringing about the deadlock created by the end of his term of office, before the President at length lent an ear to Morny the tempter, and carried out the *coup d'état*, or rather allowed others to carry it out for him.

The new Ministry had an Education Bill passed which was really the work of their predecessors in power and was known by the name of a member of the previous Cabinet— **The *Loi Falloux*.** the *loi Falloux*. For several years the Catholics, led by Montalembert, had been conducting a campaign against the "Voltairian" University and against the teaching monopoly conferred upon it by Napoleon, maintaining that the Church should have the right to mould the rising generation according to her own lights. And by a curious irony of fate, what they had been unable to obtain under the Monarchy and the rule of the Jesuits they were to win under the Republic, thanks to the revolutionary disturbances which had terrified

44

the bourgeoisie. For the latter had "returned to the only moral authority that remained—the Church" (P. de la Gorce). Moreover, the heroes of February, in the name of "the great principles" they upheld, were in favour of liberty of instruction. Thus the ground had been prepared when, on the 20th of December, 1848, Monsieur de Falloux, a member of the Barrot Cabinet, was given the portfolio of Public Instruction and Religion. Falloux, a Catholic and Legitimist, a confidant of the Abbé Dupanloup, and the author of works defending Louis XVI and the Inquisition, happened to be the friend of Persigny, the President's faithful satellite, and received his appointment through the latter at the command of the master. A statesman in the eyes of historians of the Right, according to historians of the Left a knave, he was in any case a man of ability. The President had promised the Catholics that they should be given the right to teach, and Falloux accepted office for the express purpose of carrying out the reform. He was helped in his task by a Commission over whose debates Thiers presided, and which counted Montalembert and Dupanloup among its members.

On the main principle they were all agreed—that in order to strengthen society against the Socialists and revolutionaries, the rising generation should be taught by the Church "ideas concerning religion and morality that were true for all time" as Falloux put it. Montalembert added that there was "only one recipe for making those who possessed nothing believe in the principle of private property, and that was to make them believe in God, the God who had dictated the Ten Commandments and sent robbers to eternal perdition." It is somewhat astonishing to find in a sincere believer this utilitarian conception of a God who was to act the policeman against the people. It is less astonishing in Thiers, who had no religious beliefs, but maintained that the Church "represented the last remnant of social order," and in his work *De la Propriété*, which appeared in September 1848, declared that the basis of society was religion. This law was to prove a Roman campaign at home, as Montalembert put it—to fight Communism and support the clergy.

As regards elementary education, Thiers declared himself opposed to free education for all, "a Communistic principle." Society was no more bound to provide education than work.

45

Moreover, what was the point of giving everybody an education which meant " the beginning of a life of ease " ?   The only result would be to make the son of the peasant discon-

Thiers on Education. tented with the plough, " and to light a fire under a cauldron that contained no water "—or, as we should put it, to rear a disgruntled and botched generation.   Thiers was above all suspicious of teachers, " those lay parsons, with no religion to act as a brake and no spirit of resignation . . . 37,000 Socialists and Communists, anti-clericals."   He wanted to see the elementary schools placed entirely in the hands of the monks or their pupils, who would inculcate the sound philosophy which taught men that they were born on this earth not for a life of pleasure but for a life of pain.   The Commission did not go as far as this.   The Law in its final form made it legal for anybody to open a private school provided he had a certificate, or had been a probationer in a school for five years, or was the minister of a religious body recognised by the State, or—in the case of a woman—if she had a *lettre d'obédience* from some teaching religious community.   The teacher in a State school might be chosen by the municipal council from the members of a religious order—the departments even having the right to do away with their ordinary elementary schools—but was in any case to be under the supervision of the mayor and the *curé* as well as of the Prefect, who could suspend him.   The right of deciding which children were to be given free education was vested in the mayor and the *curé*.   Finally, the Bishop was to have a seat on the departmental Council.   He was to exercise supreme power in conjunction with the Rector, the latter no longer having authority over a whole academy, but only in a single department; men who were products of free education were eligible for the office.   Thus, on the one hand, clerics were given the right to teach, and, on the other, the teachers were placed under the supervision of the Church; in fact it was a law establishing a system of moral and intellectual supervision, as Henry Michel has pointed out in his book on Falloux' Law.

In the realm of secondary education Thiers was far less rigid; he wanted the middle classes " to be allowed free philosophic discussion " and not to be limited to the " scheduled truths

46

necessary " for the masses of the elementary schools. And, like a good bourgeois, he was suspicious of the Jesuits, who at Freibourg and other places abroad learnt to hate the Government of their own country; religious orders which eluded public control were ever suspect in his eyes. He was only too ready to repeat the famous dictum : " I fear that sword the handle of which is in Rome and the point everywhere." It was the duty of the State to mould the youth of the country in its own image. Thus Thiers was in favour of the monopoly of secondary education granted by Napoleon. In the end, however, he gave in to the arguments of the Catholics. Lastly, the law did away with the necessity for the certificate of study hitherto required of candidates for the *baccalauréat*, proving that they had gone through a course of " rhetoric and philosophy " in a *lycée*. They were now allowed to go in for their *baccalauréat* on leaving a seminary or a private school. But most important of all, anyone who had passed the *baccalauréat* or held the *brevet spécial* could open a free secondary school in which anybody could teach, experience making up for any deficiencies in the way of diplomas. This too meant the end of the monopoly. The free school might be subsidised by the Municipal Council, the General Council or the State. It is true that the State reserved the right of supervising the morality and hygiene in all educational establishments and seeing that the laws and regulations were observed; but on the supreme Council the eight University representatives appointed by the President of the Republic were in a minority to the Bishops, the Protestant ministers, the Members of the Institute, and the members of the free scholastic establishments, who were also appointed by the President—and thus a check was put on the University.

These were the main clauses of the *loi Falloux*, which on the 15th of March, 1850, established a sort of concordat between the University and the Church, the latter being put in a position to compete with the former and given the right to control it, though powers of supervision over the educational activities of the Church were reserved by the State. The Universities protested that they were " being shoved right back into the Middle Ages " ! whilst Hugo in the Assembly lashed the " clerical party " with the scourge of his rhetoric : " France

47

will never accept the rule of the sacristy," he declared, "the darkness cast over the minds of men by the shadow of cassocks, and the curbing of genius by beadles." On the other hand, certain Catholics, above all Louis Veuillot, were of opinion that Falloux had not gone far enough; he felt for Falloux all the hatred and contempt of the controversialist for the shrewd diplomat, of the Catholic democrat for the Conservative bourgeois. He thought that far too many privileges had been left to the University, that "hearth of atheism, unbelief and the spirit of anarchy," as one of the Bishops called it. And indeed the law did not result in the destruction of the University or even in subjecting it to the absolute control of the Church, but side by side with the University a rival educational body came into being—the monks' schools for the masses, and colleges for the middle classes.

Henceforward public education supported the aims of the party of law and order. And indeed the years that followed **Reaction.** were years of reaction, in which every effort was made to combat the subversive doctrines of Socialism, "which is nothing but barbarism." It was the duty of the Prefect, "the first soldier of order," to go down into the arena and influence public opinion. The Colonels of the gendarmerie and the Attorney-Generals had to send in periodic reports on the state of feeling in the country and the "attitude" of the officials. A spy system was organised to give information against the Reds. Meanwhile, Carlier, the Prefect of Police, had the Trees of Liberty cut down—an ominous symbol—on the pretext that they impeded traffic. Important military commands were created in the departments for the purpose of keeping seditionmongers under stricter supervision, the country being still haunted by recollections of June '48 and the Commune. And people nearly went mad when in March and April 1850 the electors, in spite of official pressure, returned twenty-one deputies of the Left instead of the thirty-one Montagnards who had compromised themselves on the 13th of June in the preceding year, among them Carnot, Vidal the Socialist, Eugène Sue the popular novelist who had "unmasked the Jesuits," and Flotte, one of the June insurgents. Securities fell, foreigners left Paris, and the savings banks were depleted.

48

A month later a debate was held and an electoral Bill was passed—the law of the 31st of May, 1850—to modify the system **Electoral** of universal suffrage by eliminating almost three **Law of** million dangerous electors from the 9,600,000 on the **May 31st.** registers. This was secured by the proviso that in order to have a vote a man must have resided three years continuously in the same canton, and shut out from the ballot the casual labourers who wandered from one workshop to another and from farm to farm. In vain did the Left protest that this was a violation of the Constitution, which declared that all Frenchmen of twenty-one in enjoyment of civil and political rights were entitled to the vote. "We want to wage legal war against Socialism in order to avoid civil war," retorted Montalembert, and Thiers hurled his invective against "the odious masses."

Shortly afterwards a Press law—the law of the 16th of July, 1850—completed the measures taken by Cavaignac in '49 by **The Press** imposing a stamp duty on minor publications, **Law.** periodic or otherwise, and on serial stories, and forcing journalists to publish replies made to their articles by private individuals. The Attorneys rained down fines on Socialist newspapers—any working-man who took an interest in politics must necessarily be a malefactor—prosecuted Republican societies whether secret or not, forbade the wearing of sashes, ties, red caps, Phrygian bonnets and portraits of Barbès or Ledru-Rollin. The cry of "*Vive la République!*" was already held to be seditious. . . . And thus the way was prepared for imperial despotism.

The common menace of demagogy brought the President and the Assembly together for a while; but dissensions soon broke **Conflict** out. The President had his own newspapers, *Le* **with the** *Napoléon* and *Le Pouvoir*, which openly made fun **Assembly.** of the Assembly and its anxiety about legal representation, and of the conflicts in the Palais Bourbon, and openly advocated "taking the high hand." The President nursed his popularity by staking, so to speak, on both sides—he wanted to raise the pay of non-commissioned officers and at the same time he pardoned the insurgents who had been deported after the June disturbances. The Assembly was far from pleased

E

and went one better by raising the pay of corporals and re-engaged men, and also insisting that the Presidential favours were to be submitted to it for ratification. The President wanted to appoint all the mayors, even in communes of less than 6,000 souls, where they had hitherto been elected by the municipality. The Assembly refused to grant him this right. Lastly, disputes arose over money matters. Extravagant and up to his ears in debt, the President, whose allowance was only 1,200,000 francs a year (£48,000), of which 600,000 was for entertainment expenses, demanded that the latter should be raised to three millions. The Assembly hesitated, and but for Changarnier the President would have gained nothing. He never forgave the Assembly for this, nor Changarnier.

The Assembly, the majority in which was monarchist, was dreaming of a restoration. But at this juncture it was impossible **Plans for** to secure any agreement between the Comte de **restoring** Chambord, the grandson of Charles X, to whom the **the** Legitimists gave the title of Henry V, and the **Monarchy.** partisans of the young Comte de Paris, the grandson of Louis Philippe, who died just about this time in exile (26th of August, 1850). Chambord, who had no children, might have adopted this boy as his heir, but he would not admit the principle of appealing to the people, and took his stand upon the doctrine of divine right. Consequently the restoration was postponed.

Meanwhile the President spent his holidays in trying to increase his popularity by means of banquets given at the **The** Élysée to officers and non-commissioned officers, **President's** and by touring the provinces, as he had already done **Tour.** in 1849. He boldly went to places where he was not popular—travelling through Burgundy and visiting Lyons, Besançon and Strassburg, and was met with varying cries of "*Vive la République!*" and "*Vive l'Empereur!*" He repudiated any idea of a *coup d'état*: "The man who has been elected by six million voters," he declared, "carries out the will of the people and does not betray them." He also visited Normandy, where he was given an ovation. Here he spoke more ambiguously about "strengthening authority and warding off the dangers of the future," in order to give the country canals and

50

railways, redress the grievances of agriculture, and infuse fresh life into industry and commerce. . . . Here a glimpse of the future Emperor appeared.

Was he already contemplating a *coup d'état?* It is certain that he was not, and his denials were sincere. But he dreamed of a revision of the Constitution whereby he could stand for re-election in May 1852, which under the existing regulations he was not allowed to do. The Prefects submitted the proposition to the vote of the General Councils, many of which expressed themselves in favour of it. On his return to Paris, his adherents of the *Société du Dix Décembre* (the anniversary of his election) hailed him with enthusiasm. In October, at reviews held at St. Maur and Satory, the troops shouted " *Vive Napoléon! Vive l'Empereur!* " Changarnier, who was Governor of Paris with quarters in the Tuileries, vaingloriously contemptuous of the ruler in the Élysée, came forward with a reminder that troops under arms were forbidden to make any vociferous demonstration. Whereupon a rumour was circulated to the effect that a Bonapartist Society, called the *Société du Quinze Août,* was contemplating the assassination of Changarnier and Dupin, the President of the Assembly. Did this mean war between the Legislative Assembly and the Executive?

Nevertheless, the winter of 1850–51 at first witnessed a truce. The President was constantly referring to " his duty " and " the religion of law." Meanwhile the Assembly prosecuted social reforms of some importance—a campaign against slums, the establishment of savings banks and mutual benefit societies, the granting of pensions and legal assistance. The *loi Grammont* was also passed for the prevention of cruelty to animals. Lastly, the telegraph system was thrown open to the public and a charge of 25 centimes ($2\frac{1}{2}d$.) fixed for the delivery of letters to any distance. But the political struggle broke out again in January 1851. The President dismissed Changarnier in spite of the Assembly. The latter became excited, Berryer predicting that one day the Palais Bourbon would be occupied by " dumb legislators "; whilst Thiers openly declared that if the Assembly gave way . . . the Empire would be established. But what could that hybrid Assembly, the hearth of political feuds, avail against a Napoleon who had millions of votes behind

51

him? It is true that in February it refused to raise his grant, but, in order to curry favour with the public, he ostentatiously reduced his establishment and borrowed—from the Spanish Ambassador. And thus it became more than ever necessary to him to be re-elected in 1852.

A revision of the Constitution, which all enlightened people regarded as indispensable, was again discussed, and the month **Suggested** of May 1852, when a new President would have to **Revision of** be elected and a new Assembly installed, was **the Con-** anxiously awaited. The Legislative Assembly and **stitution.** the Executive would both have to be renewed simultaneously. What could be more dangerous? At the critical moment when power was changing hands, and there was no strong controlling body in existence, the path would lie open to all the hosts of demagogy. And who would prevent those who had been deprived of the vote from still exercising the right? In the end " the crisis of 1852 " became a current topic of conversation, and at the Élysée this was naturally referred to more than anywhere else in order to frighten the lovers of law and order. What an argument in favour of a revision of the Constitution! A movement in this direction was duly encouraged, and all the officials were mobilised to collect signatures to the petitions that were circulated. But the Assembly, which alone had the power to authorise such a revision, could not make up its mind to the step. The President became impatient and roundly took them to task in a speech of the 1st of June, in which he declared that he would carry out the will of the country—thus hinting at the *coup d'état*. Changarnier reassured the Assembly : " Nobody can force the army to march out against the Assembly," he declared. " . . . You have the mandate of France, so proceed with your deliberations in peace ! " The general was but a sorry psychologist. And Hugo opposed the Prince with a violence that the latter never forgot : " Because we have had a Napoleon the Great, are we bound to have a Napoleon the Little? " he exclaimed. In the end, the Bill for a revision, which before it could be passed had to be voted by a majority of three-quarters, was thrown out (July). This meant that if the Prince wished to remain in power he must have recourse to violence.

He accordingly made his plans and summoned his young "Africans" to his side—St. Arnaud, Canrobert and Espinasse,

Preparations for the *Coup d'Etat*. men whose strength had not yet been sapped by politics and who were ready to treat the people of Paris as they had been accustomed to treating the Arabs—with the whip. General de St. Arnaud was the first to be chosen. An ambitious man, riddled with debt, he hated the masses and the Republic. His title to glory had just been secured by supplying him with a nice little expedition in Kabylie. He would make an excellent Minister for War. The Paris army was under the command of Magnan, who had always been a Bonapartist and was also riddled with debt. Other military men also frequented the palace of the Prince—Fleury and Vaudrey, two of his intimates, the latter of whom had compromised himself on his behalf on the occasion of the Strassburg venture, and both of whom had won facile popularity in the army by supplying the officers with information about forthcoming promotions.

The Prince also appointed a civil staff, which included Mocquard, his private secretary, and Persigny, the companion of the Boulogne and Strassburg escapades. He had already singled out Maupas, the iron-fisted Prefect, who sent reports about his department direct to him and would make a perfect Prefect of Police. Last but not least he had his half-brother Morny. It was Morny who was to be the master mind behind the *coup d'état*, to inspire the Prince with the determination in which he might be lacking and to watch over the smallest detail.

Morny had a distinguished ancestry; he was the son of Queen Hortense and the magnificent General Comte de Flahaut,

Morny. and was thus the illegitimate grandson of Talleyrand, since Flahaut was the latter's illegitimate son. He had fought in Algeria, manufactured beet-sugar in Puy-de-Dôme, was deputy for Clermont-Ferrand and set the fashions for men in Paris. An ex-officer and business man, this dandy and sceptic had a knowledge of men and a strength of will that were to serve him in good stead in a crisis, all the more so since he was also endowed with the cold daring of the poker-player. It is not difficult to imagine the tone of authority he adopted towards his half-brother, that " dreamer awaked out of sleep,"

53

who knew nothing of life except what he had learnt from the pages of the books he had read or seen through the bars of the prisons in which he had indulged in meditation.

From that moment, whilst the Montagne loudly declared that it expected to be signally avenged by the elections of '52, the *coup d'état* was no less loudly discussed by the Élysée party. Romieu saluted the sword which had become the weapon of civilisation and declared that the day of the bourgeoisie was done : " Social order is supported, not by your ridiculous tangle of laws and regulations, but by the stronghold bristling with bayonets and artillery which is called the army." And the nearer the fatal month of May 1852 approached the more vivid became the terrible memories of June '48, which froze the bourgeoisie to the marrow. The saviour of law and order would be hailed with enthusiasm. Taking the bull by the horns, the President, with a view to conciliating the humbler folk and possibly also moved by sincere sympathy for the poor, proposed the rescinding of the law of the 31st of May, 1850, whereby three million voters had been deprived of the right to go to the ballot. The idea was worthy of a Napoleon, at once despot and democrat, aiming at absolute power but maintaining that he held it by the will of the people. Whereupon the struggle with the Assembly, which threw out the President's electoral Bill, broke out again with renewed violence. Bedeau, who was a vice-President, and General Leflô, a quæstor, moved that the President of the Assembly should be granted the right to call out the troops for the protection of the deputies. St. Arnaud and Magnan retorted by reminding them that it was the duty of a soldier passively to obey the orders of his superiors without question. And Magnan promised that they should all have their orders in writing duly signed, which would relieve those who carried them out of all responsibility. He knew the military mind better than Changarnier did. Whereupon the Assembly, utterly in the dark and possibly afraid that the troops would one day be called out against them, threw out Leflô's Bill on the 17th of November. " There is an invisible sentinel protecting us," Michel de Bourges eloquently declared, " the people ! " Wonderful optimism ! Had Leflô's Bill been passed, that 17th of November would have been the date of the *coup d'état!* As it was, it was merely postponed. Everything was in readiness. After successive postponements to the 20th and 26th of November, the 2nd of December was finally decided upon. Morny had triumphed over the last traces of vacillation and weakness.

During the night of the 1st–2nd of December,[1] police commissioners were sent by Maupas to arrest the leaders of the Assembly and other dangerous persons at dawn—they numbered 78 in all. It was Morny who was responsible for the idea. "There is no longer any need for people to suffer hardship in prison, and intelligent arrests may prevent civil war," he observed, ironically adding: "To arrest a man in such circumstances is to do him the greatest service." And it did indeed prevent him from risking his life on a barricade should he have felt any inclination to do so. Cavaignac and Changarnier were also arrested, as well as Bedeau, who vainly endeavoured to alarm the garrison, together with Thiers, who shed tears of rage, Lamoricière, Charras, etc. Colonel Espinasse slipped at early dawn through the gate of the Palais Bourbon, which was opened for the cleaners and sweepers, and occupying the building with his men, arrested his friend Leflô. Magnan had the city occupied by troops. Finally, Morny had had a proclamation printed during the night announcing the dissolution of the Assembly, the rescinding of the law of the 31st of May, the restoration of universal suffrage and the convocation of the French people "in their comitia." The President represented himself as the saviour of the Republic and proposed a new Constitution to be framed on the pattern of the Consulate—a chief to be elected for ten years, and two Assemblies instead of one, with a Council of State to frame laws. In appealing to the army he said: "I rely upon you not to violate the laws, but to see that respect is shown to the first law of the land—the sovereignty of the people." And he conjured up "the memories which his name revived" by proclaiming the dogma of "passive obedience to the head of the Government." At an early hour Morny installed himself as Minister of the Interior and communicated with the Prefects.

Dec. 2nd.

[1] Details of the events of these days will be found in *Le Coup d'État du 2 Décembre* by the present author (Hachette: Series "Récits d'Autrefois").

During the morning of the 2nd of December some of the deputies tried to meet at Barrot's, and then at the Palais Bourbon; but they were dispersed, although they reminded the gendarmes and the soldiers of Article 68 of the Constitution, which made it high treason for the President to dissolve the Assembly. Dupin, the President of the Assembly, did not cut a very heroic figure on this occasion. Nevertheless, at eleven o'clock 300 deputies, most of them Royalists, met at the *mairie* of the tenth *arrondissement* (the present Carrefour de la Croix Rouge). Berryer was the soul of the gathering and had a vote passed for the compulsory resignation of the President and the requisitioning of the National Guard and the regulars, and had Oudinot appointed Commander-in-Chief, in spite of the protests of certain Republicans who had not forgotten Rome. But bodies of troops arrived upon the scene, and all that remained of the Assembly set out in procession for prison under the protection of General Forey—220 more prisoners whom Morny quickly set at liberty, as he would want them later on to reinforce his political personnel. Everything seemed to be settled. On the morning of the 3rd the President appointed his new Ministry, consisting of St. Arnaud, Morny, Rouher, Fould and Magne. Apparently the *coup d'état* had been carried out without a drop of blood being shed—as Morny had intended.

But on the 3rd of December Paris rose in revolt. The Montagnard deputies tried to gain the support of the masses, but the latter, disarmed and embittered by the repressive measures of June '48, were at first quite uninterested in this quarrel between the President and a reactionary Assembly. Nevertheless, a barricade was erected in the Faubourg St. Antoine. The troops attacked, and a deputy named Baudin, whom a working-man had taunted about his pay of 25 francs a day, allowed himself to be killed " for twenty-five francs "—an episode of which few knew at the time. By the afternoon the barricades had spread to the Quartier du Temple, and street fighting began under the leadership of General Herbillon. Maupas was at his wits' end and demanded guns. There was a slump on the Bourse. Morny held his hand, proclaimed a state of siege, ordered the immediate execution of all rebels, and told Magnan to imitate the tactics

Revolt of Dec. 3rd.

of Cavaignac—to allow the insurrection to grow in order to stamp it out the more effectually in the end. In the evening the troops retired. There were shouts of " *Vive la République!* " on the boulevards. Paris was under the impression that the *coup* had miscarried.

Accordingly, on the following day, December the 4th, barricades were put up in the Rue St. Denis and the Rue Rambuteau, **The Shoot-** and in the Faubourg St. Martin and the Faubourg **ing of** St. Antoine. On the boulevards there were cries of **the 4th.** " Down with the Prætorians ! " Maupas became frantic. " You wanted barricades," sneered Morny, " and when you get them you are not satisfied." Early in the afternoon Magnan mobilised his 30,000 men, each armed with sixty rounds of shot. They made an attack from the four points of the compass on the hotbed of the insurrection, centred in the present 1st, 2nd, 3rd and 4th *arrondissements*, where a labyrinth of narrow streets made the barricades easy to defend. But owing to lack of arms and a concerted plan of action, the resistance was short-lived and the rebels were shot down on the spot. The western column under Canrobert set out from the Madeleine in the direction of the Porte St. Denis, through the boulevards. The mob blocked the way and insulted the soldiers, who grew angry. One soldier fired, whereupon for ten minutes shops and spectators were fired upon and bombarded. A hundred— possibly two hundred—were killed. After this massacre the success of the *coup d'état* was assured, although a few barricades still remained to be cleared away that night and on the following day. Paris was terror-stricken and subdued for the next nineteen years. Thanks to the shooting, which had taken place, as it were, accidentally, the venture had succeeded.

The provinces, informed of events by Morny himself, with the usual precautions, accepted the situation without any serious disturbances, except in Clamecy and in the Var district, where two uprisings were quickly suppressed. Those in power did not hesitate to exploit these revolts, to exaggerate their importance and misrepresent their true significance, declaring that they constituted the crisis that had been expected in 1852, and which the *coup d'état* had merely precipitated. Paris regarded them as uprisings of peasants and " cannibals." " You have been through some trying days," wrote Morny to the Prefects, " having experienced in 1851 the social war which was to have broken out in 1852." Republicans who had rebelled were regarded as vulgar insurrectionaries and communistic robbers, hot on rape, murder and pillage, which justified the severest repressive measures. There were 27,000 arrests in Paris and the provinces. The informers had the time of their lives, and parties to village feuds were able to gratify their animosities. It was decided, on the plea of " public safety," to deport all these suspects without trial to Algeria or Cayenne. But there were too many of them, and a mixed commission was appointed in each department, consisting of the Prefect, the Attorney and the General, to examine each case without giving the accused a hearing, and to decide what was to be done. In the end 6,000 persons were released, 5,000 placed under supervision in their own town, 3,000 interned in some town other than their own, 1,500 sent into exile, and almost 10,000 deported to Algeria, half to be confined in a fortress or camp (*Algeria +*), half to reside in a place of their own choosing (*Algeria —*); some hundreds of old offenders were sent to Cayenne. But in March 1852 the Prince, who was too weak to be capable of hatred, and possibly also a prey to remorse, sent commissaries to the provinces —Quentin-Bauchart, Canrobert and Espinasse—to revise the sentences passed by the Commissions. They pardoned between 3,000 and 4,000, though this did very little towards palliating the brutality of the repressive measures. Espinasse was the least indulgent of the three; he granted only 300 pardons, and that unwillingly, being of opinion that too little severity had been shown. It was during this period that there came into being the implacable hatred for the Prince and his *régime* which was destined to be " the weight he dragged on his foot all his life," as the Empress observed when she was in exile.

The time had now come to consult the country. Still haunted by recollections of June '48, it voted solidly for the saviour of law and order who had once and for all put an end to peasant risings and " social war," and had checkmated the Reds and the Communists. The Church was won over by restoring the Panthéon as a place of Catholic worship and making the observ- ance of Sunday obligatory in Government workshops. More-

58

over, was it not the President who had reinstated the Pope in Rome? Montalembert recommended the people to vote for Louis Napoleon. "If you do so," he said, "you will arm authority with the power necessary to overcome the forces of crime, to defend your churches, your homes and your women from those whose covetousness holds nothing in respect." Thus the very disturbances in Paris and the Provinces contributed to the triumph of the Prince by making him appear in the light of the victor over anarchy. On the 21st of December

Plebiscite of Dec. 21st. every citizen—for universal suffrage had been restored—voted *Yea* or *Nay* to the following motion, when his name was called : "The French people desire the maintenance of the authority of Louis Napoleon Bonaparte and delegates to him the powers necessary for the establishment of the Constitution on the foundation proposed by the proclamation." At one time Morny had contemplated insisting upon open voting, but he returned to the secret ballot, because he doubtless mistrusted the factious spirit of the Frenchman. He also wanted to force officials to give their support in writing, but was obliged to think better of it, as the magistrates and the University men proved recalcitrant.

Voting accordingly took place on the 21st and was very heavy; the calling by name, which was the system enforced throughout the existence of the Empire, made it easy to discover abstainers, and the justices of the peace and the mayors warned the electors that if they failed to record their votes a black mark would be set against their names. There were over eight million voters, more than there had been in April '48. The Prince, who had won five and a half million votes in December '48, now won seven and a half millions with only 600,000 *Nays*. Six hundred thousand was very little, but it was also a great deal, for it meant that 600,000 reasonable beings had escaped from the bleating herd. An even graver omen was that in Paris, out of 300,000 on the registers, the Prince secured only 133,000 *Yeas*— 80,000 Parisians voting *Nay*, and 80,000 abstaining. Thus Paris, the brain of France, in spite of the absolute silence to which the Opposition Press had been reduced, returned a hostile majority. But these details were disregarded in the triumph of the moment. On the 31st of December, 1851, Baroche reported the official result of the ballot to the Prince. " France has faith in you," he said. " Restore the principle of authority in the country. . . . Wage unceasing war against those forces of anarchy which are attacking the very basis of society. . . . May France at last be delivered from those who are ever on the alert for murder and pillage. . . . Give back to the country . . . order, stability and confidence." And the Prince, faithful to the Napoleonic tradition, replied that his aim was to reconcile authority with equality, and to lay the foundation of " institutions which should meet both the democratic interests of the nation and the universally expressed desire henceforward to possess a strong Government commanding the respect of the people." And he added : " France has understood that I broke the law only in order to do what was right. The suffrages of over seven millions have just granted me absolution." Absolution—the word is eloquent of his doubts, his remorse. This man, who was being hailed as the saviour of society, and whose supporters had made him a despot, was at heart too weak to be a villain.

CHAPTER II

THE ORGANISATION OF THE IMPERIAL *RÉGIME*

The Constitution of the 14th of January, 1852. Powers of the President. The Legislative Body. The Senate. The plebiscite. First measures of the legal dictatorship. The property of the House of Orleans. Quarrel with Morny. Press regulations : the warnings. Officials, mayors and prefects. Economic and financial measures. Official candidature. Precautionary measures for the elections. Elections of the 29th of February. Session of the 29th of March. First activities of the Legislative Body : Montalembert. Speculation. The Festival of Empire begins. Towards the Empire. The President's tour of the provinces. Speeches at Lyons and Bordeaux : " The Empire means peace." The *Senatus Consultum* of the 7th of November. The triumphant plebiscite of the 20th–21st of November. The attitude of foreign countries. Marriage with Eugénie. The Court.

ACCORDING to the terms of the plebiscite, Louis Napoleon had been granted the powers necessary for the establishment of a Constitution. He had been invested with what was known as the " legal dictatorship." Within a fortnight his legal advisers, chief among them Rouher and Troplong, had drawn up the plan of a Constitution " on the basis proposed in the Proclamation " of the 2nd of December, that is to say, on the pattern of the Constitution of the year VIII. On proclaiming the establishment of the Constitution of the 14th of January, the President declared that " he had no pretension—a pretension so common in our days —of substituting any personal theory for the experience of centuries." He had preferred " the doctrines of genius to the specious doctrines of the professors of abstract ideas." And he added : " Since France has been able to carry on her government for the last fifty years only by virtue of the administrative, military, judicial, religious and financial organisation of the Consulate, why should we not also adopt the political institutions of the Consulate ? For the scaffolding of our social edifice is undoubtedly the work of the Emperor and has sur-

The New Constitution.

61

THE SECOND EMPIRE

vived his fall and three revolutions.   So why should not political institutions deriving from the same source be equally durable? " It was a specious argument and double-edged into the bargain; for it might well be asked why these political institutions had not also survived the fall of the Emperor?   But there was no question at that moment of embarking on any such discussion of principle.

Louis Napoleon was made President of the Republic for a period of ten years.   And he proceeded to arrogate to himself **The President.** the most extensive powers, the powers of a quasi-absolute monarch.   He had the right to command the armies, to declare war, to conclude treaties, to make all appointments, to receive the oath of allegiance from all the officials, to choose his Ministers, who would be answerable to him only, to be alone competent for the initiation of legislation and the framing of regulations for putting it into practice.   He was to be responsible " to the French people."   But to be responsible to millions means in practice to be responsible to none.

Nevertheless, the Dictatorship was anxious to show some deference to public opinion, and, to satisfy it, allowed some **The Legis- lative Body.** semblance of representative institutions to survive. It professed to support the doctrine of the division of power—in addition to the Executive there was the Legislative Body, to whom the power of legislation was entrusted.   It consisted of members elected (unless a dissolution had intervened) for six years by universal suffrage—for under this democratic system everybody possessed the right to vote, the single-vote method being substituted for the multiple-vote method.   As a guarantee of peace, the Chamber was to be strictly limited in numbers and to consist only of 261 members. After the proclamation of the Empire they were granted a salary of 2,500 francs (£100) a month during session.   There was to be one representative for every division of 35,000 electors, the Government cutting up and modifying these divisions as it pleased—a convenient way of splitting up and reducing to scattered minorities any group that might have constituted a dangerous majority.   " You must understand," ran the circular addressed to the Prefects, " how great an influence

62

the more or less intelligent arrangement of the divisions will have on the results of the elections."

Parliamentary procedure was a masterpiece of minute mechanism. As we have said, the President alone had the right of introducing a Bill, the Chamber no longer enjoying the parliamentary initiative " that allowed any deputy to take the place of the Government." Thus the Bill had to go from the competent Ministry to the Council of State charged with the duty of drawing it up, whereupon it was presented to the Legislative Body, or rather to the Commission of seven members to be appointed by that body. Here it was defended by Councillors of State. It was now, and now only, that amendments might be proposed; if the Commission accepted these amendments, the Bill had to be returned to the Council of State, who accepted or rejected the new text without appeal. Thus the Council of State, a body of officials, " a gathering of practical men," exercised, *in camera*, " a sort of control over the representatives of the nation " (P. de la Gorce). Finally, the Bill was again presented to the Legislative Body in plenary session, but a deputy who had moved an amendment that had been thrown out was not allowed to repeat his amendment or on the spur of the moment introduce a new one " and disturb the whole working of the system "; he had but one alternative—to propose the rejection pure and simple of the entire clause in dispute. Here he once more recovered his sovereign power as against the Council of State—the sovereign power residing in the right of veto. It was obviously expected that he would refrain from taking so grave a step, and by laying down the rule of all or nothing it was hoped that he would choose nothing. Moreover, no reasons were allowed to be given for the order of the day. But as though all these precautions were not sufficient to keep the unfortunate Legislative Body in leading-strings, more especially as it sat for only three months in the year, it did not even choose its own Presidents and Vice-Presidents, who were appointed by the Government. Naturally there were no more interpolations in Parliament, no more ministerial crises, since Ministers were not allowed to be deputies or enter the Palais Bourbon. The Cabinet too was at an end, for the Ministers had no corporate existence, but were merely

63

the servants of the Executive. As the Bill ingenuously put it : " Since the Chamber is no longer faced by the Ministers, no time will be lost in foolish interpolations and frivolous objections . . . the sole object of which is to overthrow a Ministry in order to put another in its place. . . . The representatives of the nation will give their serious attention to weighty matters." Care was to be taken to avoid giving the slightest publicity to important questions; eloquence and " oratorical display " were to be regarded with suspicion; the sittings were to be public, but the reports of proceedings given in the newspapers were to be confined to the publication of the summary drawn up by the President of the Legislative Body. And thus, declared the Bill in a tone of delightful complacency, " the reports are not exposed to the Party spirit of the various newspapers."

In addition to the Legislative Body there was the Senate, which was to consist of at most 150 life members, some of whom sat *ex officio*—Cardinals, Marshals and Admirals—whilst the rest were chosen by the President " from the ranks of men whose fame, wealth, talent or conspicuous public services qualified them for the position." They might be paid a salary of 30,000 francs (£1,200) a year. Apparently Montalembert, who was " extremely forty-eightish," told the President to his face that nobody would accept a salary. " Do you really believe that ? " replied the President, who was more sceptical and was doubtless surrounded by more impecunious friends. When the Empire was proclaimed, this salary was regularly paid. This Senate had a peculiar part to play; it was not to be called upon to debate or pass Bills already passed by the Legislative Body; all it had to do was to examine them *in camera* to make sure that " they were not prejudicial to the Constitution, religion, morality, freedom of worship, individual liberty, the equal rights of all citizens, the sanctity of property and the permanence of the magistracy." In addition to this it was to promulgate *senatus consulta* to interpret or complete the Constitution, subject always to the consent of the President. It might even lay down the principles of Bills of great national importance. And if the Legislative Body were dissolved it could, on the motion of the President,

The Senate.

64

undertake the settlement of urgent business. It was a strange creation! Appointed by the Executive, it was officially called upon to give the country certain guarantees in regard to this same Executive, whilst the Legislative Body elected by the people enjoyed practically no power.

Lastly, the people, who in theory were the sovereign people, exercised their power in two ways only—they elected the mem-

The Plebiscite. bers of the Legislative Body and they might be called upon to vote by plebiscite, that is to say, to answer *Aye* or *Nay* to any question put to them by the President of the country. Nevertheless, this amounted to recognising the importance of public opinion and giving it, though in an extremely rudimentary form, the opportunity of expression. This appeal to the people was a characteristic of the new *régime*, which, maintaining that it derived its powers from the will of the people themselves, set itself up against the Legitimist doctrine of divine right, and further, by only allowing a Parliament without real power and without authority over the Ministers to survive, also differentiated itself from the constitutional monarchy established by Louis Philippe. The President was to be a tyrant in the old interpretation of the word, who, deriving his powers from the people themselves, was free to act as he pleased, though from time to time he might make a direct appeal to the people over the heads of their pseudo-representatives. " I do not mind being baptised with the water of universal suffrage," declared the Prince, " but I refuse to live with my feet in it." He considered it quite sufficient to repeat the inaugural ceremony on important occasions.

One or two decrees completed the work of the Constitution. Two new Ministers were created—the Minister of State, who acted as a link between the Government and the Assemblies, since individual Ministers were never allowed to be present at the sessions, and the Minister of Police, who, as had been the case under the First Empire, was entrusted with the task of carrying out " the laws relating to the police in general and peace and order at home," and above all of controlling the Press and the theatre. Apparently the Government was not afraid that such an official might be regarded as symbolic of the new *régime*, which relied upon a system of espionage and

F

summary arrest. Maupas was appointed to the office as a reward for the services he had rendered on the 2nd of December. His chief inspectors were to be sent out into the provinces " to make the victory of order over anarchy bear fruit."

This Constitution could not become operative until the Government bodies had been formed. Until this had been done, the President continued to act as Dictator, and his proclamations, issued, in the absence of a representative Assembly, without any legislative sanction, were legal decrees. The new *régime* lost no opportunity of profiting from the delay and the absence of all control even of the mildest description, to issue decree after decree and establish " social order " by means of a series of more or less anomalous measures. The device " Liberty, Equality, Fraternity " was obliterated from the cornices of public monuments, for it recalled " times of disorder and civil war," it was " a vulgar inscription . . . that saddened and disquieted passers-by." And the last remaining Trees of Liberty were also cut down. Any celebration of the anniversary of the 14th of February was forbidden, since " it recalled the memory of civil disturbances "; but, on the other hand, the 15th of August, the birthday of Napoleon I, was made a national holiday. The word Republic was not suppressed, but the eagle was introduced into the standards, and on the 1st of January, 1852, at Mass in Notre Dame, after the *Salvum fac Rempublicam* the priests intoned *Salvum fac Ludovicum Napoleonem.*

But an even more important measure was the disbanding of the National Guard. " Arming everybody indiscriminately " merely amounted to preparation for civil war—the lesson of June 1848 had borne fruit. Moreover, how could such an institution, which was essentially the champion of public liberty, if necessary against the Government, survive under the new *régime?* The principle of it was preserved, but it was to be reorganised only " when its help was regarded as necessary for the defence of public order "—as a matter of fact the National Guard was not destined to be revived during this reign. The co-operative societies, which had always been suspected of being republican centres and in reality secret societies, were

66

also broken up, and all associations and meetings were forbidden unless they had been sanctioned by the Government. Morny was even anxious to prevent meetings of supporters of the Government. And a Prefect's licence, which was liable to be cancelled at any moment, was required for the sale of intoxicating liquor, for there was always the possibility of a café developing into " a centre of political propaganda."

On the 23rd of January further decrees were issued which gave rise to considerable public astonishment. When Louis Philippe came into power in 1830, he had, with the characteristic caution of the good bourgeois, or rather of the good father, taken steps to insure himself against the results of a fall which was always a possibility in those troublous times, and had secured his own private property and estates; instead of adhering to the ancient law of France, by which they would have reverted to the State, he had transferred them by deed of gift to his children, with usufruct for himself, with the result that in '48 the House of Orleans did not lose everything—very far from it—although it lost the Crown. It was this state of affairs that Louis Napoleon was determined to end, and he not only forbade the Princes of the House of Orleans to possess any property in France and compelled them to sell all they had, but also rescinded the gift made by Louis Philippe in 1830, " whereby he had defrauded the country," and decreed that the property thus given away should be returned to the State. It was to be sold and the allocation of the proceeds of the sale was arranged in advance—10 millions to the Mutual Benefit Societies, 10 millions to Workmen's Dwellings, 10 millions to the *Crédit Foncier*, 5 millions for Homes for Sick Clergy, and the surplus to the Legion of Honour. It is possible that this step was dictated by old feelings of bitterness against those who had kept him for six years a prisoner at Ham. But any such spirit of rancour seems alien to Louis Napoleon. It seems more likely that, following the advice of Persigny, he imagined he would add to his popularity by levelling a blow at the Royal Family whom Paris had overthrown in '48, and by using the opportunity to give the country a gift of happy augury.

But he was very much mistaken. Public opinion at this

The Property of the House of Orleans.

juncture found its only outlet in the salons. And the salons were animated by a feeling of sympathy for the Orleans family and of fellowship with anybody who had possessions. They regarded the measure as ill-bred, and considered that any such confiscation undermined the principle of private property. " It is the first flight [1] of the Eagle," declared Dupin, making some small atonement for his weakness of the 2nd of December. The phrase became all the rage ! Montalembert, who until that moment had been in favour of the new *régime*, ostentatiously withdrew his support. Berryer pleaded on behalf of the Orleans family before the Seine Tribunal, who, in defiance of the administration, had declared itself competent to judge of the validity of Louis Philippe's gift. And the Government was obliged to stop the case and bring it before the Council of State; and even there it had great difficulty in winning it. Furthermore, four Ministers who did not approve of the " flight of the Eagle " sent in their resignations—Rouher, Magne, Fould and lastly Morny.

It is true that in the case of Morny the decrees provided a pretext rather than a real reason for resignation. There had been an unpleasant incident between him and his half-brother. An illegitimate son of Queen Hortense, Morny had no doubt already assumed what Monsieur Marcel Boulenger called the speaking, not to say shrieking, coat-of-arms with the hortensia flower and the motto : *Tace sed memento* (Keep silent but remember). He had remembered only too well, and on the occasion of a certain banquet had not been able to keep silence regarding the ties that bound him to the Prince. The President was somewhat incensed at having his mother's weaknesses recalled to the public mind in this way. Might it not lead to his own legitimacy being questioned? Moreover, Persigny, who had no liking for Morny, did all he could to blacken his character with the Prince. Morny, who had been the friend of the Orleanist Princes, seized the honourable pretext provided by the Royal Property case to resign from the post of Minister of the Interior; and his place was taken by Persigny. It was not long before he made

Quarrel with Morny.

[1] " *C'est le premier vol de l'aigle*." It is impossible to render the pun on the word *vol* in English.

68

his reappearance, however, though his eyes had been opened with regard to the Prince. " The Prince feels no real friendship for anyone," he wrote shortly afterwards, " and he finds my peculiar relationship to him a nuisance. . . . He accepted my presence unwillingly and my services were burdensome. He is suspicious and ungrateful and likes only those who slavishly obey and flatter him." It is true that allowance should be made for the bitterness of a man whose resignation, after all the services he had rendered on the 2nd of December, had been accepted with such alacrity. At the same time it would certainly seem that the Prince was incapable of true friendship; like so many humanitarians, he was animated by too deep an affection for mankind at large to be able to feel particularly drawn to individuals.

Meanwhile the Government continued to be carried on by means of legal decrees. A decree of the 17th of February, 1852, regulated the control of the Press, which was **Press Regulations.** put on the same footing as under the Restoration. The permission of the Government was required before a political or economic journal could be started, as well as for any change of proprietorship, management or editorship, and the publication of the most insignificant drawing or picture. The deposit to be paid by a newspaper was raised to 50,000 francs (£2,000) in Paris and Lyons, two cities that were suspect, and to 25,000 (£1,000) and 15,000 (£600) in the case of other towns. Every copy of a newspaper had to pay stamp duty (which was raised from 5 to 6 centimes), and also a postal duty of 4 centimes, making a total of 10 centimes (a penny) a copy. The following additions were made to the list of press misdemeanours liable to prosecution—the publication of details in connection with the Legislative Body and the Senate other than those contained in the official summary or in the *Moniteur*, " false " news, even though it might have been published in good faith and with every reservation, failure to publish material sent for insertion by the Government and reports of Press trials. But apparently even these judicial precautions were inadequate. For newspapers, which in their general editorial outlook were regarded as constituting a danger to order, religion and morality, were subjected by Rouher and

Persigny to further Government supervision, which, without officially restoring the censorship, had virtually the same result—the Minister of the Interior or the Prefect issuing a *warning* to any newspaper which had published an objectionable article, and requiring the insertion of the warning in the said journal. After two warnings, and a repetition of the offence, the Minister could suspend the newspaper for two months. Moreover, a newspaper was always liable to summary suspension without warning by presidential decree. Such was the new *régime*, which seemed to draw its inspiration " from the system of punishment in barracks or the graduated pains and penalties inflicted in boarding-schools " (P. de la Gorce). The aged Bertin, of the *Débats*, whose smooth chin and the wart in the corner of his eye have been immortalised by Ingres, used to say : " The decree has made me the supervisor of my own newspaper, an unpaid official charged with the task . . . of maintaining order for the benefit of the Government." The printer and the bookseller were also licensed by the Minister of Police.

The Warnings.

To be appreciated the system must be studied in operation. The warnings issued were less numerous than might have been supposed; the maximum was reached during the first six months and never exceeded sixty. Some of them are delightful. One newspaper was warned because " it had displayed a serious lack of prudence and moderation which are the prime requisites of a periodical publication "; another because " in printing in italics and emphasising the words *people* and *legitimate*, it clearly intended to pour ridicule upon these two words "; another for having called Napoleon the missionary of the Revolution, " an article which was an insult to truth as well as to the hero and legislator to whom France owed her salvation "—Louis Napoleon alone had the right to point to his uncle as the militant defender of the principles of '89; another for having criticised certain steps taken by the Government " in such a way as to assail regard for authority "; and others for having " gone beyond the limits of good taste "; so that under this *régime* it became extremely difficult to be a journalist. Only five or six newspapers were able to continue publication, and willy nilly their editors acquired an

70

admirable gift for insinuation, innuendo and equivocality, sufficiently clear for the reader to understand at the merest hint, and yet sufficiently veiled to make it impossible for the Government to take action. And this game of hide-and-seek eventually had the effect of developing the talent for saying everything without seeming to do so.

Other decrees secured discipline among the officials, all of whom, including the deputies, were called upon to swear " obedi-

The Officials. ence to the Constitution and fidelity to the President." Many University men, rather than take this oath, sent in their resignation. Fortoul, the Minister of Public Instruction, and a Professor of Law, was anxious to set the University in order. And thenceforward he had the power to dismiss at his own will and pleasure the Professors of Higher Education, who hitherto had been called upon to resign only by decree of the Supreme Council of the University; and the members of this Council, who had hitherto been elected, were now to be appointed by the President. Professors were reminded that they should be dignified in their bearing and were forbidden to wear beards, " it having been agreed that the last traces of anarchy should be done away with." Since the *École Normale Supérieure* had given preference to historical and philosophic studies at the expense of advanced literary courses, the Philosophy and History Fellowships were abolished, to the great chagrin of the young Taine. University Professors were required to give a written synopsis of their lectures in advance, while the teachers in the *lycées* had to outline their class lessons in a " journal."

An attempt was also made to bring influence to bear on the Mayors and their deputies, the Government arrogating to itself

The Mayors. the right of nominating them all, even in the small communes where they had hitherto been elected, and if need be choosing them from outside the ranks of the Municipal Council. The system of nomination was everywhere substituted for that of election. Mayors and deputy-mayors had to wear uniform at all ceremonies—the cocked hat with black feathers, a blue coat embroidered with gold or silver, a white waistcoat, white or blue trousers, and a sword. They were turned into soldiers—soldiers of the new *régime*.

71

The Prefects were also called upon to play an important part. In order to effect " decentralisation," they were endowed with authority to decide minor matters and appoint subordinate officials without referring to Paris.

The Prefects.

Thus the Prefect became the absolute master of his department, on condition, of course, that he rendered implicit obedience to instructions from the central power. There was no fear of resistance on the part of the elective bodies. The Prefect was paid a salary in keeping with his position—20,000 to 40,000 francs (£800 to £1,600). Naturally, care was taken to secure complete subservience on the part of the Prefects left in office—some were recalled, some dismissed and others placed under supervision. Before his fall, Morny had time to arrange the policy for the choice of Prefects; the position was a good one, but the work to be done was far from easy; one man was suspected of Royalist leanings, another " was common and vulgar, abrupt, violent and lacking in tact "; this man was engaged " in dubious money transactions," another was mean and a third was " over-zealous "—doubtless the worst of all shortcomings in Morny's eyes.

At the same time economic improvements of all kinds, which the slow working of the legislative Commissions had failed to realise, were hastened on by decree and made practical realities in the twinkling of an eye under the dicta-torship—new railways to Lyons, to the north, to Strassburg, Wissenburg and Bâle; telegraph lines,

Economic and Financial Measures.

a *Crédit foncier* for advancing money to farmers; pawn-shops, Mutual Benefit Societies. It is characteristic of every autocracy to maintain that it gives the people an increase of material prosperity and wealth in exchange for their lost liberty. The President also tried to introduce financial legislation. So confident was the tone of the Bourse that the five per cents had reached and gone above par, with the result that the Government felt in a position to force the fundholders to accept redemption at par or a four and a half per cent. standard. Naturally the Treasury had done all in its power to stimulate a rise in railway and other similar shares, so that the fundholders, rather than have recourse to these investments, would be forced to accept the four-and-a-halfs. But finance is less amenable than other concerns to dictatorship; and in a few days the five per cents, which had risen to 103, fell below par and it became necessary to call in the help of the Banks to stop the depreciation. Lastly, in the absence of a Parliament, the President issued a decree passing the Budget of 1852, which had been drawn up by the Legislative. But he did not publish the real sum-total of expenditure amounting to over fifteen thousand millions (£600,000,000), and exceeding the estimate of the Legislative by almost 67 millions (£2,680,000). Although the new *régime* might be doing all in its power to increase the national wealth, it would undoubtedly also lay a heavy hand on the country's income.

It was impossible, however, to carry on government for any length of time solely by the promulgation of decrees, and **Official** eventually it became necessary to create the pseudo-**Candida-** representative bodies provided for by the Constitu-**ture.** tion. But naturally all the necessary precautions were taken for preventing a surprise at the ballot. Under Louis Philippe official candidature had been a tradition, and while a certain amount of discretion was used, steps were taken *sub rosa* to secure the support of the influential electors, the most important people of the district, the "ruling classes," and to make them vote for the Government candidate. But with universal suffrage the situation was very different. As Morny observed to the Prefects, "It is impossible to suspect the Government of bribing such a huge number of voters. . . . To-day there is only one motive force, a colossal one which no power on earth can divert or suppress, and that is public opinion." Nevertheless, the Government set to work to influence it. In January 1852 Morny gave the Prefects their instructions—instead of a politician he would prefer a man who "had made his fortune by work, industry or agriculture, who had ameliorated the lot of the workers, and made a good use of his wealth," and who would bring "a practical mind to bear on the making of laws and support the Government in its work of pacification and reconstruction." The Government were to put forward their own candidates, but before doing so Morny expected them to have secured the sympathies of the electors "by showing the greatest deference and attention

73

to the humblest." And he warned the bureaucracy against imagining that they existed for the purpose of raising objections, creating delays or being obstructive. "Subordinates are apt to fancy that they are increasing their own importance by creating difficulties and troubles," he declared. This showed a profound knowledge of the administration, but Morny was unduly optimistic in thinking it could be reformed by sending out a circular note. Persigny, who succeeded Morny, expressed the wishes of the Government with an ingenuous frankness which was not lacking in cynicism : "The French people would be hopelessly embarrassed unless the Government intervened," he maintained. "How could eight million electors possibly agree in picking out from among so many candidates with various qualifications . . . 261 deputies animated by the same spirit, devoted to the same interests and all equally anxious to complete the popular victory of the 20th of December? It was the duty of the Government to enlighten the electors on the subject. . . . The people must be placed in a position to distinguish between the friends and foes of the Government they had just set up." The Prefects were therefore instructed to make the official candidates known by every means in their power, if necessary by placarding proclamations in the communes. And they did not hesitate to do so, making full use, legitimate and illegitimate, of the poster to recommend the Government candidate. They also mobilised all the officials and mayors, instructing them to do likewise and bring pressure to bear upon public opinion.

Further precautions were also taken. Soldiers and sailors, young men of whom the Government could not be certain, **Precau-** though still allowed the right to vote, could be **tionary** enrolled only in the commune in which they were **Measures.** domiciled, which meant that the army was indirectly debarred from voting. All political offenders, of whatever category, were also deprived of the vote; this was a blow aimed at the Republicans. Voting took place in the commune and lasted for two days, and the Mayor, who was a Government official, kept the ballot box in his possession during the night— he thus had ample leisure to make sure that his commune voted " rightly."

74

A candidate could not be elected in the first round unless he had polled a quarter of the number of votes on the register and obtained an absolute majority. In the second round that candidate was elected, whoever he might be, who had secured a relative majority. Monsieur Seignobos points out that the term balloting was incorrectly applied to this second round, whereas it ought to have been reserved for the fight between the two rival candidates who headed the poll in the first round.

The electoral campaign accomplished all that was required of it. The Government Press alone could make its voice heard, and re-echoed Morny's contention that " by voting for the friends of Louis Napoleon the people would have a second opportunity for voting for the Prince himself." This amounted to making the forthcoming elections merely a supplementary plebiscite (P. de la Gorce). The official candidates were nearly all new men, either landowners or industrialists. And what possibility was there of opposing them in a country which had been in a state of siege ever since December? Print notices? The printer would have run the risk of losing his licence. Distribute circulars? But the distributer had to have a permit, in default of which he would be guilty of infringing the regulations against itinerant trading. The unofficial Press merely had the right of publishing the name of the independent candidate without comment. Candidates' manifestos were to be strictly censored by the Prefects " in accordance with what they regarded as necessary for the public peace." Election meetings were, of course, forbidden. Moreover, the candidates who were returned had to swear the oath of allegiance, which neither Republicans nor Royalists could do. Nearly everywhere the official candidates presented themselves for election unopposed.

The Elections. The elections were held on the 29th of February. Out of 261 deputies elected there were only 3 Legitimists, 2 Independents and 3 Republicans—Cavaignac, Carnot and Hénon. Cavaignac and Carnot, who stood for Paris, did not even show themselves at the election, while the victory of Dr. Hénon, who was extremely popular in Lyons, came as a surprise. In order to prevent sharp practices at the election, it was arranged that the workers should vote only on the second day, the Monday; but during the night of Sunday

THE SECOND EMPIRE

to Monday they went round slipping voting-papers for Hénon under all the doors. And thus the Government was tricked. But the proceeding was destined to be practically fruitless, since Carnot, Cavaignac and Hénon preferred to resign rather than swear allegiance to the President.

A list of 72 Senators had been published as early as January. It included ex-Ministers of the President, ex-members of the Legislative Body, former peers of the realm, Generals, and magistrates, among them Troplong. In addition there were the *ex officio* members—four Cardinals, and eight Marshals and Admirals. The most important members of the Council of State, presided over by Baroche, were Rouher and Magne, who were Presidents of Sections.

As all the organs of the new Constitution had been created, the new *régime* was now in a position to come into force. On Session of the 29th of March the President summoned the March Senators and deputies to meet not in the Palais 29th. Bourbon but in the Tuileries. The President, who on his entry was met by a salute of 101 guns, took his seat on a raised chair, which was already almost a throne, surrounded by diplomatists in Court dress, Generals, magistrates in their robes and fashionable ladies. Opposite him the parliamentarians were humbly seated on benches. " It was more like a royal levee than a political assembly " (P. de la Gorce). In the course of his speech the President made use of a bold metaphor : " Society has all too long resembled a pyramid turned upside down and balancing itself on its apex; I have set it once more on its base." This solid base was composed of the landed gentry, the industrialists and moneyed classes; the apex upon which the pyramid had been swaying was doubtless what Thiers called the vile multitude. The President was expected to proclaim the restoration of the Empire on this occasion, and he did actually allude to it : " I should accept changes in the present condition of affairs only if I were constrained to do so by obvious necessity . . . if the Parties tried to undermine the foundations of my Government . . . it might be reasonable to ask the people, in the interests of the country's peace, to confer upon me a new title which would irrevocably place upon my head the symbol of that power with which they have

76

already endowed me." But he added : " Let us keep the Republic."

On the following day the Legislative Body met in the ancient hall of the Palais Bourbon, which was quite large enough for it—the temporary building of '48 had been demolished. The rostrum had been done away with—a symbolic action; the representatives were to speak from their seats. At the feet of the President, instead of the rostrum and in the space it had occupied, was the bench for the Councillors of State— another symbol; the deputies were to be seated like school- boys facing these officials and the President chosen for them. The President in this case was Billault, a former Orleanist deputy, who opened with a diatribe against parliamentary Government—a good beginning !

The first measure with which the representatives were called upon to deal was a Bill for a fresh issue of copper coins. They then passed on to the Budget of 1853. This Assembly, from which the stars of previous Governments had been carefully excluded, was, but for a few exceptions, a gathering of medio- crities. " The present *régime*," declared Tocqueville, " is the paradise of the envious." And, indeed, all who were endowed with any talent, and might therefore have been dangerous, had been reduced to silence. But the Legislative Body was none the less called upon, by virtue of its functions, to amend, or rather to endeavour to amend, the Budget proposals of the Government and thus came into conflict with the administra- tion. The Commission appointed to consider the Budget did not dare to reject *en bloc* the clauses of the Budget which were in dispute—the only power still left them; but in its report it felt it had the right to express its doubts and difficulties, to point out that expenditure was increasing, that the deficit amounted to 40 millions (£1,600,000) and the floating debt to 750 millions (£30,000,000), an enormous sum for that period. At this sitting the Catholic Montalembert, who was the only orator in the Assembly, and had broken with the President

Montalem- bert. although he had previously been on his side, waxed eloquent in his criticism of the Constitution and the decrees issued by those in authority with regard to the Legislative Body : " Our rules and regulations have

77

been imposed upon us," he declared; "we are not allowed either to discuss them or to vote them; we have been deprived of the right of electing not only the President and Secretaries of the Chamber, but also the Presidents and Secretaries of the Government Departments. The Press has been forbidden . . . even to mention what takes place in the Legislative Body; indeed one might almost think that a gathering of 250 honourable gentlemen like ourselves was something in the nature of a dissentious body. . . . I had hoped that the Legislative Body would have had a modest but useful part to play, similar to that of a General Departmental Council on a large scale, with no oratorical or political pretensions. . . . But is this the case? Certainly not! We are indeed a kind of General Council, but a General Council at the mercy of the Prefectoral Council we see before us." And he pointed to the Councillors of State. "I refuse to vote for the Budget," he added. "I am not free to vote for a Budget which I cannot amend. . . . I regard the destruction of all control and the humiliation of the only elective body left in the French Government as a serious evil." Finally, he placed his finger on the sore by drawing a comparison between the Legislative Body and the Council of State: "The one," he said, "is an elective, unpaid assembly which is demanding economies, the other a permanent paid assembly which refuses to consider them." And thus he emphasised the contradictory principles inseparable from the new *régime* which was making a vain endeavour to reconcile the absolute authority of those in power with the sovereignty of the nation, the settlement of the Budget by the Government with the financial control of the representatives of the people; and he proceeded to pour scorn upon the sham presented by this democratic façade to an autocracy, and the illogicality of a pseudo-popular Cæsarism.

The President happened to be in the Chamber when Montalembert made his furious "sortie," and he was all the more incensed. A message from the Minister of State dryly reminded the deputies of the limits laid down for them by the Constitution. Nevertheless, Monsieur de Kerdrel, a Legitimist, ventured to criticise the extraordinarily rapid promotion of Espinasse, who had been made a General after the *coup d'état*. "I was not

78

aware," he retorted when the Government commissioner referred to the exceptional services rendered by the General on the 2nd of December, " I was not aware that General Espinasse had done anything great or glorious on the 2nd of December ! " But, worse still, the Legislative Body had the audacity to vote in favour of Montalembert having his speech printed ! But this quasi-revolt had no sequel. It was but an echo of the liberties of yore, and years of autocratic Government would be required before that Liberal Empire could be established of which certain minds were already vaguely dreaming.

Nevertheless, a certain revival of political life took place at the elections for the municipal councils, especially in the east, where hostile votes were recorded against the Mayors and deputy-Mayors, who, though nominated by the Government, were not members of the Council. This was a means of showing disapproval of the Government, though it had no practical result, for in spite of not being on the Council, the Mayors and deputy-Mayors retained their powers. Except for this, the whole country was calm; only very rarely came the report that red ties had been worn, Socialist songs sung, or a poplar planted by a body of young men. The *régime* inaugurated on the 2nd of December had undoubtedly cowed the country.

Everybody acquiesced. A certain African General gave up politics and declared that " he would build himself a hut and curl himself up in it in peace." And thus everybody retired into their shells. The bourgeoisie applauded the restoration of law and order and the working classes resigned themselves, though the Socialist theorists hoped for great things in the future as the outcome of this period of subjection and authority. " It is under the sway of the sword," wrote Proudhon at this time, " that the work of the revolution will begin in good earnest." But the peasants blessed the name of Napoleon.

Paris now began to speculate in the new railways, shipping companies and industrial concerns, and there were rumours **Speculation.** of gold-digging in Australia. Building on a large scale in Paris was also beginning to be discussed. There were meetings at the *Institut*, and in January 1852 Guizot received Montalembert at the *Académie Française*, when the two orators seized the opportunity to refer to the new *régime*,

with all the more zest seeing that the censor had made some
pretence of recasting their speeches. The Spanish pictures
belonging to Marshal Soult, who had recently died, also formed
a popular topic of conversation, and it became the fashion to
go to the Champs Élysées to see the President drive at a smart
pace down the avenue in his phæton. People read Mrs. Beecher
Stowe's *Uncle Tom's Cabin;* and *La Dame aux Camélias*, which
had just been produced at the Vaudeville and was enjoying
a *succès de scandale*, was applauded to the echo. " This play
of the younger Dumas is a disgrace," wrote Viel-Castel. " Every
evening the Vaudeville is packed and fashionable carriages
crowd the Place de la Bourse. Even ladies of the best society
do not hesitate to show their faces in the boxes." For Paris
in those days was a small community, even smaller than the
fashionable Paris of to-day. Everybody was known by sight
and by name, and at certain entertainments only women of
the *demi-monde* dared to appear openly; respectable women
hid in the shadow of the *baignoires*. " For five acts," continued
Viel-Castel in his diatribe, " *La Dame aux Camélias*, or the
kept woman, regales a cultured public with the details of her
life as a prostitute. Nothing is omitted from the picture; the
procuress, the nights at the baccarat table, the cynical conversation, and scenes borrowed from the lowest haunts of vice are
all there. The whole play reeks of vice and debauchery."
This gives an idea of the moral tone of the period. In the
salons and between the acts at the theatre there was plenty
of opportunity for carping tongues to riddle the Government
with epigrams. But meanwhile there were celebrations and
rejoicings—banquets to the Mayors, a distribution of eagles
to the regiments who shouted " *Vive l'Empereur !* ", a ball to
which 5,000 guests were invited at the Tuileries, and another
for 12,000 at the *École Militaire*, dinners at St. Cloud, reviews,
a solemn *Te Deum* on the 15th of August, a salvo of guns and
fireworks representing the crossing of Mont St. Bernard by the
Emperor, and free performances in the theatres. The Festival
of Empire had opened !

Empire—the word slipped from my pen. For as yet there
was no Empire; on the coins the word *République* was still
engraved round the head of the new master. Louis Napoleon

presided over ceremonies and festivities at the Tuileries, he had his military establishment and his civil establishment, as well **The** as his private secretariat, his packs of hounds and **Festival** his horses, but he still lived at the Élysée. On **of Empire.** the 5th of May a solemn memorial service was held in Notre Dame on the anniversary of the death of the Emperor; but on the previous day, the 4th of May, which was the anniversary of the meeting of the Constituent Assembly in '48, the priest, by virtue of an old decree which had not been rescinded, had held a thanksgiving Mass in the selfsame nave of the church. The building, it is true, was empty. Nevertheless, everything was pointing towards the restoration of the Empire; the President had succeeded in obtaining from the Senate a Civil List of 12 millions (£480,000); Émile de Girardin had been cautioned for daring, in the columns of the *Presse*, to express his disapproval of the proclamation of the Empire; while the menace of strikes, secret societies and seditious propaganda was again discussed, with the result that petitions were circulated, particularly in the Charente districts, demanding the restoration of the Empire. At the elections for the General and District Councils the absolute success of the official candidates was a foregone conclusion, and several General Councils—though not all—demanded, either directly or indirectly, that the imperial system should again be put into force.

Nevertheless, Louis Napoleon still hesitated. " He was seized with qualms which made his head swim," declared Persigny. Ambitious though he was, he suffered from scruples and doubts which are not compatible with ambition. In fact he was frankly convinced that his dictatorship should be rooted in the sovereignty of the people and that he ought to seize the crown only in obedience to the formal demand of the country. He accordingly made up his mind to ascertain the popular will by making a grand tour of France in September. " I don't want the answer to be dictated," he said. But Persigny hastened to send instructions to the Prefects whom the President was going to visit, bidding them incite the crowd to shout " *Vive l'Empereur! Vive Napoléon III !* "

With the same spirit of bravado as he had shown in 1850, the President chose for his tour the central departments and

G

the valley of the Rhone, where disturbances had broken out after the *coup d'état*, returning *viâ* Toulouse, Bordeaux and **The** the Charente districts. He listened to the cheers **President's** which had been arranged at Bourges, where the **Tour.** General, who was a friend of Maupas, ordered his troops to shout as they were bidden, as well as at Nevers, Moulins, La Palisse and Roanne, where the display of enthusiasm was obviously not spontaneous, since a fortnight later the town elected a democratic Municipal Council which had to be dissolved. At St. Etienne, and lastly at Lyons, there were similar displays. Apparently Louis Napoleon was not deceived by these acclamations, since at Lyons he had a speech printed in which he refused the Empire. And it required all the persistence of his supporters, Persigny, Mocquard and St. Arnaud, to persuade him not to use it. And even then he actually declared before a statue of Napoleon I which he was unveiling : " The cry of *Vive l'Empereur!* is an echo that touches my heart rather than a hope that flatters my vanity. . . . If the modest title of President can help me to carry out the mission that has been confided to me . . . far be it from me to wish for personal interests to change it to that of Emperor." And he continued his journey towards Marseilles *viâ* Grenoble. Here precautionary measures had been redoubled. Certain democrats, who might have been dangerous, were put under lock and key, and out of diplomatic courtesy the representative of the King of Piedmont and Sardinia even had the French exiles, who had sought refuge in the province of Nice, interned in case they came out and held hostile demonstrations. The Mayor of Valence gave orders for decorations and illuminations; any disobedience to instructions was to be reported. The President was acclaimed at Avignon and Arles. At Marseilles a plot against him was opportunely discovered—a plot which had probably been arranged in the same way as the popular enthusiasm. Louis Napoleon laid the foundation stone of the new cathedral with the assurance that his Government supported religion for its own sake, " not as a political instrument or to please any Party "—doubtless he had in mind the Monarchists, who regarded the Altar as a mainstay of the Throne. At Montpellier the Prefect had carried out his task inadequately, for the crowd shouted : "*Vive l'amnistie!*" But after that enthusiasm increased. The President was welcomed with triumphal arches bearing such inscriptions as : "*Ave, Cæsar Imperator!*" "*Fiat imperium! Vox populi, vox Dei!* To Napoleon, the saviour of property! To Napoleon, the Emperor!" The acme of servility was reached in the inscription which read : "*Quel bonheur que le 2 Décembre!*", while one Prefect in his address said, "Welcome to the land over which Charlemagne and St. Louis once reigned."

At Bordeaux the Prefect Haussmann had an opportunity of displaying his talent for organisation. At last the President **The Empire** was convinced. "France," he declared, "apparently **means** wishes to return to the Empire." But he im- **Peace.** mediately forestalled the serious objection that might be raised. "Certain persons maintain that the Empire means war. But I say—*the Empire means peace*." And he outlined his programme, a programme consisting of peaceful victories : "My conquest will consist in the reconciliation of dissentient parties and in turning hostile tributaries back to the main stream of the popular will. . . . I shall win over to religion, morality and comfort those large sections of the people who . . . still hardly know the precepts of Christ, and . . . are barely capable of enjoying the meanest necessities of life "— a curious mixture of idealistic aspirations and material concerns. " We have enormous uncultivated districts to clear," he added, " roads to lay, harbours to dig, rivers to render navigable, canals to finish, and our railway system to complete. Opposite Marseilles we have a great kingdom to unite to France, while in the west we must join all our great ports to the continent of America by swift means of communication which are at present lacking. . . . That is what I mean by the Empire, if the Empire is to be restored. Those are the conquests I have in mind, and all of you who are standing round me now, eager, as I am, for the welfare of your country—you are my soldiers." And thus with further formal modifications and cautious provisos the momentous word was spoken.

The President returned *viâ* Angoulême, Rochefort, La Rochelle, Tours and Amboise, where he informed Abd-el-Kader, at that time a prisoner in the castle, of his forthcoming release.

THE SECOND EMPIRE

On the 16th of October he entered Paris, where he was received by the President of the Municipal Council, and, to the ringing of bells, the salute of guns, and shouts of " *Vive l'Empereur !* " drove through the decorated boulevards beneath triumphal arches. Nevertheless, Hübner, the Austrian Ambassador, made a note on the same day : " The public more or less indifferent." Possibly among the crowd were some who had not forgotten the shooting of the 4th of December which had stained with blood the very boulevards that were now so gay with flags.

On the 7th of November the Senate, convoked to " give its opinion in regard to certain changes in the form of the Govern-ment," on the motion of Troplong passed a *senatus consultum* proposing the restoration of the imperial power in the person of Louis Napoleon Bonaparte, and his heirs after him. The motion was carried unanimously except for one dissentient—Narcisse Viellard, the Prince's old master in the art of war. Troplong recapitulated the details of the triumphal tour that had just ended, " the colossal petition presented by a whole people pressing on the heels of their saviour . . . that premature plebiscite welling from the hearts of millions of agriculturists and workers, industrialists and merchants." And he added : " After great political upheavals, the peoples invariably throw themselves joyfully into the arms of the strong man sent them by Providence. It was the weariness following upon the civil wars that founded the monarchy of the victor of Actium. It was horror at the excesses of the Revolution, quite as much as the glory of Marengo, that raised the imperial throne in France. In the midst of the dangers threatening the country, this strong man presented himself on the 10th of December, 1848, and the 2nd of December, 1851, and France has placed her drooping standard in his hands."

Senatus Consultum of November 7th.

The argument was misleading only on one point—what had been true just after June '48, when Cavaignac had been appointed dictator for the maintenance of social order, was already less true in December, when the Prince was elected, and quite untrue three years later in December '51, when absolute order reigned in France, secured by three and a half years of reaction.

84

Not a finger was raised, all the democratic leaders being in exile. And the success of the *coup d'état* had been due far less to the presence of any real danger to society than to the still vivid recollections of the disturbances of June '48 and the fears that had cleverly been fanned into existence regarding " the crisis of 1852." The President had known how to turn these recollections and fears to his own advantage. Finally, Troplong emphasised the " democratic " nature of the new *régime*: " The Republic is virtually contained in the Empire, since the institution partakes of the nature of a contract and the power has been expressly delegated by the people."

On the 20th and 21st of November the electors were convoked to a plebiscite—they were to say whether or not the French **The** people desired " the restoration of the imperial **Triumphant** dignity in the person " of the President. The Pre-**Plebiscite.** fects did everything in their power to influence public opinion in their departments so that there might be the maximum of *Ayes*, the minimum of *Nays* and above all the minimum of abstentions, which they feared as much as the *Nays*. The Bishops brought similar pressure to bear, one of them hailing the Prince as " the man from the right hand of God, the weapon of divine Providence." The result was all the Prince could wish—there were 7,800,000 *Ayes* to 250,000 *Nays*. The only blot on the picture consisted in the number of abstentions— 2,000,000, most of them occurring in the Legitimist departments of the west, and in the great Republican towns such as Marseilles, Lyons and Bordeaux. Nevertheless, the magnificent total was a further advance on the plebiscite of December 1851.

On the 1st of December the Senate, the Legislative Body and the Council of State drove to St. Cloud in gala coaches heralded by mounted torch-bearers, to convey the result of the vote to the Prince. " France delivers herself up entirely into your hands," observed Billault as he saluted the Emperor. The latter adopted the title of Napoleon III, the Duc de Reichstadt having been proclaimed Emperor in 1814 with the title of Napoleon II. He also announced that he would recognise the Governments that had preceded him and would not regard his reign as dating from 1815, declaring that his power was not founded upon violence or strategy. Probably for the moment

85

he was sincere; the acclamations, the triumphal arches and the millions of votes in his favour had made him forget the violence and bloodshed of the *coup d'état*. He was also sincere in saying that he wished the foundations of his Government to be laid upon " religion, probity, justice, and love for the suffering classes." On the 2nd the new Emperor of the French made his entry into Paris. To celebrate his accession he granted a wide amnesty, which included certain political prisoners of 1848 and 1849 and most of the exiles of December 1851, on condition that they recognised the new *régime*. He cancelled all the warnings issued to the Press up to date. St. Arnaud, Magnan and Castellane, Governor-General of Lyons, were made Marshals, and Morny was promoted Grand Cross of the Legion of Honour.

The Civil List, thanks to Persigny and Troplong, was raised to 25 millions (£1,000,000) and a *senatus consultum* laid down that the Emperor alone, and not the Legislative Body, should have power to modify the customs dues, although they belonged to the realm of finance, and to order the undertaking of great public works, provided the Legislative Body subsequently sanctioned the expenditure involved. The Government could also issue a decree authorising the application of sums voted for one item in the budget to another, which gave it an extraordinarily free hand in financial matters, and the Budget was to be passed not item by item, but by Departmental votes. This meant a still further curtailment of the rights of the Legislative Body. As for the rest, the Constitution had already conferred upon the President powers which were all that the Emperor could require.

How was the rest of the world going to receive the restoration of the Empire? The Congress of Vienna had excluded the **Attitude of** Bonaparte family for ever from the throne of France. **Foreign** Though the Emperor had doubtless derived his power **Countries.** from the popular vote and the plebiscite, the fact that he had adopted the title of Napoleon III seemed to indicate that he wished to attach himself to Napoleon I by the tie of heredity and restore the principle of imperial legitimacy. And was it not to be feared that his traditions would lead him to dream of war and prove a menace to Europe? In this connection the historical expression he had used at Bordeaux : " *The Empire means peace*," was addressed quite as much to the foreigner as to French public opinion. The election of the Prince and the *coup d'état* had been fairly well received by the rulers of Europe, who naturally favoured order and authority. But would they prove equally enthusiastic about the proclamation of the Empire ?

The King of Piedmont and Sardinia was one of the first to recognise the Emperor. He foresaw what a valuable ally he would find in Napoleon III against Austria, and he kept in close touch with him through his personal friend Arese. The King of the Belgians recognised the new *régime* " not from sympathy but from fear " (P. de la Gorce). And as a matter of fact constant causes of friction arose between him and the Prince in connection with French refugees in Brussels and articles in the Belgian Press hostile to the new *régime*. Moreover, the King had heard rumours of vague ambitions which had been floating in the Prince's brain ever since 1850; at that time Louis Napoleon had sent Persigny to Berlin to offer the King of Prussia the help of France against Austria and to encourage him to establish German unity by means of a Union of all the German Princes, in return for which he had hinted that he expected annexations on the left bank of the Rhine. This might prove a menace to Belgium, who regarded her redoubtable neighbour with suspicious eyes.

Furthermore, Persigny, who was no diplomat, had talked too much and threatened war, with the result that he had to be recalled. Since then there had been an attempt to come to an understanding with Austria and the German Princes. And as a matter of fact the latter made no delay about recognising Napoleon III; Austria too was not hostile. Prussia showed greater hesitation. Frederick William saw in the Prince " the revolutionary incarnate," adding : " Belgium is the next objective of the recently crowned bird of prey "; and he talked of making an alliance with Austria, England and Russia and offering 100,000 men to guarantee the territorial *status quo*. But he did nothing ! His imaginative, mystical mind could wish without willing. Moreover, Great Britain did not regard the Belgian menace as serious. London was friendly to the

Prince, who had lived in England and liked the English. The Press, it is true, had waxed indignant over the shooting on the boulevards, and Queen Victoria had forbidden her Ambassador to be present at the *Te Deum* in honour of the *coup d'état*. But the Foreign Office did not share these prejudices. Had not this nephew of Napoleon I sent a representative of the French Government to the funeral of the Duke of Wellington? Thus it was in London that the representatives of the four signatory Powers of 1815 signed a secret protocol recognising the Emperor in consideration of his promise to preserve the peace, and they further agreed to keep watch over the maintenance of the *status quo*.

Russia had signed this protocol together with England, Prussia and Austria. Nevertheless, the Tsar Nicholas regarded the restoration of the Empire with a far from friendly eye; he was anything but pleased that there should be a new Emperor in Europe, and he despised the upstart. In writing to Napoleon III he did not use the expression *Mon bon frère*, by which sovereigns usually addressed one another, but merely *Mon bon ami*— a diplomatic offensive on a small scale which was destined to have important results. The Russian Ambassador explained that the title of *brother* could be used by the Tsar only in the case of sovereigns whose power had an origin similar to his own. Whereupon Drouyn de Lhuys, the Minister for Foreign Affairs, ironically expressed surprise that it should fall to the youngest Court in Europe thus to uphold the cause of tradition. The Emperor made a show of thanking the Tsar for the title. " One has to put up with one's brothers," he said, " but one chooses one's friends." Nevertheless, he did not forget the little insult.

He was exposed to further rebuffs when he began to look about him for a foreign princess to marry. As Emperor it was imperative for him to secure direct heirs. But what European Princess would consent to marry an upstart whose future seemed far from secure? Morny and Fleury had urged the Prince in 1852 to take steps towards a settlement, more especially as the beautiful Englishwoman, Miss Howard, was at that time in residence at St. Cloud and playing the part of official favourite. The Prince had no hesitation in allowing her to appear at balls
88

and even at reviews, and Morny and Fleury were afraid that the influence of this adventuress might prove dangerous. Offers of marriage were made to certain Princesses—a Swedish Princess, the daughter of the Prince of Vasa, and an English Princess, a niece of Queen Victoria. They were refused.

But Napoleon already had his eye on a Spanish lady of twenty-six—Eugénie de Montijo, Countess of Teba. She was extremely beautiful, seductive and lively, with " a cameo-like profile, a high arched forehead, almond eyes, golden hair," and a slim and elegant figure. She was in the habit of travelling with her mother, who had been a widow for years, from capital to capital. In 1849 she had visited Paris and had returned in 1852. During the winter of 1852–53 she was invited to Compiègne, and it soon became evident that the Prince, despite his forty-four years, loved her with all the ardour of a schoolboy. They went for walks in the park surrounding the palace and for rides in the forest. On one of these walks she noticed a curious-shaped clover leaf heavy with dew; on the following morning he presented her with a jewel of the same design with the dew represented by brilliants. It was impossible for her to ignore his passion and devotion, but she made him understand that she would not be content with the position of favourite, but would insist upon a wedding ring. As early as the beginning of January 1853 the Emperor had made up his mind and the news was bruited abroad. His associates, and more particularly Persigny, were hostile rather than the reverse; the young lady was of good family, no doubt, but she was not a Princess. At a ball held at the Tuileries on the 12th of January, Rothschild, the banker, led her and her mother to the seats intended for the most important guests. But the wife of one of the Ministers was ill-advised enough to remark sarcastically that the seats were reserved. The Emperor intervened and found places for the two ladies with his own family.

On the following day he announced his engagement to his Ministers. " I do not ask your advice," he said. " I merely

Marriage with Eugénie. state the fact." Like all weak men, he showed determination only in his whims. On the 22nd of January, in the Throne Room, he made the official announcement of his marriage to the representatives of the

89

Senate, the Legislative Body and the Council of State. Regardless of the fact that they might think the grapes were sour, he pretended to despise a royal alliance. " When before the eyes of the old Europe," he declared emphatically, once more recalling the Cæsarian nature of his office, " one has been raised by the power of a new principle to the level of the ancient dynasties, one wins recognition not by pretending one's coat of arms is older than it really is or by trying at all costs to insinuate oneself into the family of kings, but rather by being ever mindful of one's origin, by preserving one's own character, and by frankly adopting before all Europe the position of an upstart, a glorious title when it has been won by the free suffrage of a great people." And he proceeded to sing the praises of Eugénie : " She is French by choice and upbringing, and by the memory of the blood her father shed in the cause of the Empire." (The Count of Montijo had been an officer in the service of France.) He used the argument to forestall any objections that might be raised against her as a " foreigner." And he added a further trivial argument which raises a smile : " As a Spaniard, she possesses the advantage of having no family in France on whom honours and dignities would have to be conferred." " A devout Catholic . . ." he continued, " good and gracious, she will revive the virtues of the Empress Josephine in the position the latter once occupied." Clearly, since a Bonaparte had once been content with a Beauharnais, a Spanish Countess could very well be Empress of France. Nevertheless, in view of the sorry termination of Josephine's marriage, the comparison was not altogether felicitous. The Emperor ended with a sentence which ought to have won him the heart of every woman : " I have preferred to take a woman I love and respect rather than an unknown wife, marriage with whom would have entailed sacrifices as well as advantages. Before long I will go to Notre Dame and present the Empress to the people and the army; the confidence they have in me makes me certain of their sympathy for the woman I have chosen. And as for you, gentlemen, when you have learnt to know her, you will be convinced that on this occasion I have once again been inspired by Providence."

Possibly he was sincere in saying that he saw the finger of

God in a chance caprice. On the 29th of January the civil marriage was celebrated in the Tuileries; on the 30th the couple went to Notre Dame in the coach used by Napoleon I at his coronation. In order to win the hearts of the people of Paris, the young Empress had refused a set of diamonds worth 600,000 francs (£24,800), the purchase of which had been voted by the Municipal Council, asking that the sum should be distributed among the poor. Nevertheless, the reception accorded to the royal couple as they drove through the streets was cold. Crowds of Spaniards filled the balconies of the hotels to see their country-woman drive past. One of them, says P. de la Gorce, had noticed the pearl necklace worn by Eugénie at the civil marriage, which reminded her of a Spanish proverb : " The pearls women wear on their wedding-day are symbols of the tears they are destined to shed."

During the first few months of 1853 the organisation of the imperial Government was completed, and the body of officials **The Ministry.** appointed remained unchanged for some years. Troplong was President of the Senate, Billault of the Legislative Body (he was succeeded by Morny in July 1854), while Baroche was President of the Council of State, supported by Magne, Parieu and Rouher, who was to play a more important part later on. Persigny was Minister of the Interior (Billault took his place in 1854), Drouyn de Lhuys Minister for Foreign Affairs, Fould Minister of State (later on he was given the Treasury), Walewski, a natural son of Napoleon I, was sent as Ambassador to London, Delangle was the First President of the Court of Appeal, St. Arnaud was Minister of War and Maupas of Police. All were already well known and all remained in office, with the exception of Maupas (who fell out with St. Arnaud on the question of the gendarmerie, which he wanted to control, although it really came under the War Office, a dispute which brought about his downfall) and Persigny, whose clumsy and exaggerated zeal ended by getting on the nerves of his master. But as a matter of fact Napoleon did not like to see fresh faces about him. Moreover, where could he find new helpers? Press and Parliament had been silenced and the best men either held their tongues or lived in exile. The general mediocrity of the high officials under the Empire was a direct result of the *coup d'état*, and so to speak the price paid for it.

The Court was framed on the model of " the Other's " Court. High offices, carrying large salaries, were revived. Marshal **The Court.** Vaillant was Lord High Steward of the Palace, Marshal St. Arnaud Master of the Horse with a salary of 300,000 francs (£12,000), Marshal Magnan Master of the Hounds with 200,000 (£8,000), and Colonel Fleury First Equerry. There were hosts of equerries, chamberlains, aides-de-camp, secretaries, and maids-of-honour. There were festivals and banquets galore. Knee breeches were worn again at a ball in the Tuileries on the 12th of January, 1853. There were dances at the Luxembourg and dances at the Palais Bourbon. " The chief item of news," wrote Tocqueville sarcastically to a friend in England, " is that the new Court ladies have already returned to trains and little page-boys, and the new courtiers go stag-hunting with their master in the Forest of Fontainebleau, clad once more in the hunting costume of Louis XV with the plumed cocked hat." The Cent-Gardes were created for ceremonial occasions—they were men chosen for their looks, like the grenadiers of Frederick William. On the 15th of August, 1853, the Emperor, in gold-embroidered Court dress, had the *Corps Diplomatique* presented to him. " Etiquette is all the stricter because it is of recent date," observed Hübner, the Austrian Ambassador, with the contempt of a member of an old Court for all upstarts. The fact was that the old French nobility were sulking and this new world of fashion was somewhat mixed.

But at the same time interest was shown in " the suffering classes " and the economic progress of the country. It was a weapon of power—if the poor were given comfort and the bourgeoisie wealth, nobody would think of talking politics. But the Emperor was also sincerely interested in such matters. The Empress was President of Maternal Welfare Societies, the Emperor dreamed of easing the burden of taxation, of colonising the Sologne and les Landes, and founding Transatlantic steamship companies. In 1852 he ordered the building of the *Palais de l'Industrie* in the Champs Élysées, and meditated arranging an International Exhibition. Lastly, with coloured chalks he designed the Paris of the future, tracing wide avenues

92

and squares planted with trees. Already water and gas had been installed and the Bois de Boulogne was being laid out. Moreover, a drastic curtailment of the army was announced— the Empire meant peace! Nevertheless, in 1853 war was already looming on the horizon.

CHAPTER III

THE CRIMEAN WAR

The dispute over the Holy Places : Catholics and Greeks, France
and Russia. Incidents of 1850. Nicholas, Menschikoff and the
" Sick Man " (1853). The war : the Anglo-French Alliance
(1854). Gallipoli. Expedition into the Dobruja. Outbreak of
cholera. Diversion in the Baltic. In the Crimea. Battle of the
Alma (20th of September). Death of St. Arnaud. Canrobert.
Sebastopol. Unsuccessful bombardment of the 17th of October.
Balaklava (25th of October). Inkerman (5th of November).
The winter campaign. The Emperor wishes to direct the siege.
The Austrian alliance. The Emperor's visit to London.
Suggested visit to the Crimea. Pianori's crime. Unsuccessful
bombardment of April 1855. Pélissier. The Mamelon (7th of
June). Reverse of the 18th of June. Traktir (16th of August).
Queen Victoria in France. Assault of the 8th of September :
the Malakoff. Fall of Sebastopol (10th of September). The
Peace Congress (25th of February, 1856).

FOR many years two Powers and two races had been at
loggerheads in the Holy Land under the eyes of the Turkish
rulers, disputing the custody of the Holy Places at Jerusa-
lem and Bethlehem—the Roman Catholics, of whom, by virtue
of agreements made with Turkey in 1740, France was the tra-
Dispute ditional protector, and the Orthodox Greeks, who
over the relied upon Russia. In 1850, Louis Napoleon,
Holy Places. anxious to conciliate the Catholics, had tried to
put a stop to the continual encroachments of the Greeks, who
had gradually obtained possession of all the keys, altars and
tombs. He had reminded the Turks of the Treaty of 1740.
Caught between France and Russia, the Sultan temporised,
and finally reached a compromise, allowing the Greeks to keep
certain privileges but otherwise upholding the claims of the
Catholics. Tsar Nicholas, however, a " barbarous " mystic
Tsar and autocrat, took up the cudgels on behalf of the
Nicholas. Greek subjects of the Sultan and lodged a protest.
The latter imagined he had settled the matter by
granting the Greeks a firman rescinding the former compromise.
94

THE CRIMEAN WAR

The incident of the "Holy Places" might have had serious developments had it not been merely "a dispute between monks." Nevertheless, it had served to rouse some ill-feeling on the part of the Tsar against France and Louis Napoleon, who in the meantime had assumed the imperial purple and become his equal. Moreover, he despised this "*bon ami*."

He thereupon conceived the grand plan of turning the Eastern Question to his own advantage—Turkey was a "sick man," and plans must be made for the succession and the partition of the Empire—to the exclusion of France. Like all the Tsars, he dreamt of entering Constantinople in triumph. He tried to bribe England by offering her Egypt; but she did not rise to the bait. And he forthwith decided to act single-handed. In March 1853 he sent Prince Menschikoff on an extraordinary mission to Constantinople, where he was received by the Greeks with open arms and immediately adopted a threatening tone towards Turkey. In Paris there was a slump on the Bourse; movements of troops were reported in southern Russia and military preparations at Sebastopol, and fears were immediately entertained that France might be dragged into a war between Russia and Turkey. The Mediterranean squadron was despatched to Greece. England, at first convinced that the affair was merely a quarrel over the Holy Places, was not so quick to move. But at last Menschikoff unmasked his batteries, and demanded nothing less than the right of protection over the ten million Greek subjects of the Sultan. As the English Ambassador at Constantinople declared, this did not mean amputating a limb from Turkey, but infusing the poison into her whole system. Menschikoff presented his ultimatum, and when the Turks refused to give way, he took ship for Odessa. The whole of Europe, and above all France, lodged an emphatic protest. In July the Russian army crossed the Pruth and entered Moldavia, a province which was at that time a vassal of Turkey. The Anglo-French fleet approached the Dardanelles.

At this juncture Austria intervened and offered her services as mediator. Napoleon III had drawn up with his own hand and sent to Vienna a plan for effecting a compromise between Russia and Turkey which he trusted would settle the matter.

In August 1853 there was still hope that war might be averted. But Turkey refused to accept the compromise, which she regarded as too favourable to Russia; moreover, the latter was at heart irrevocably wedded to Menschikoff's ultimatum. Turkey declared war against Russia. Negotiations were still in progress in Vienna, when, on the 30th of November, the **War between Russia and Turkey.** Russian Black Sea Fleet surprised and destroyed the Turkish Fleet at Sinope. Tense excitement reigned in Europe. In London the influence of Palmerston, a friend of Napoleon III, which had for a time been under an eclipse, suddenly burst forth once more in full splendour, and he urged on his country to declare war. France and England agreed to make common cause and to send their squadrons to the Black Sea to protect the Turks.

The entry of the Anglo-French fleet into the Black Sea, that " Russian Lake," was virtually a declaration of war. It meant **Anglo-French Alliance.** at all events a rupture of diplomatic relations. But after forty years of peace there was a general desire to avoid war if possible. Napoleon III at least already had reason to congratulate himself—ever since 1814, France, suspect in the eyes of Europe, had been hedged in by a Holy Alliance of Sovereigns which to all intents and purposes was still in existence. But in the game of diplomacy this " concert of Europe " had just been broken up and France and England had joined hands against a common foe—Russia. At a certain banquet, Palmerston had proposed a toast, " a toast that had not been drunk since the time of the Crusades "— he had raised his glass " to the united fleets of France and England." The change was all the more remarkable since it meant the reconciliation of two ancient foes, at a moment, moreover, when the throne of France was occupied by a Napoleon.

In intervening on the side of Turkey, France was only carrying on the traditional policy she had adopted from time immemorial. It was war, no doubt, but a short, far-distant war, which would win more in glory than it would cost in blood— a colonial expedition, that was all. And fancy-dress balls were still given in Paris. On the 29th of January, 1854, in a final effort to secure peace, Napoleon III wrote a personal letter to Nicholas I, suggesting an armistice; the Russian army was to evacuate Moldavia and Wallachia and the Anglo-French squadron to leave the Black Sea, after which negotiations would be opened. Doubtless this letter, which was meant for publication, was primarily intended as a sop to public opinion. But, at the same time, it is probable that Napoleon III, anxious though he might have been to provide his army with opportunities for glory, sincerely hesitated to break the peace and run any adventurous risks. His vacillation drew down the attacks of his enemies on his head—Hugo, in exile, dubbed it a "retreat." But the waverer was confronted by a will of iron. "Russia will prove that in 1854 she is still what she was in 1812," replied Nicholas. In March 1854 the Legislative Body voted the raising of a loan of 250 million francs (£10,000,000). On the 10th of April France and England concluded an alliance and undertook " not to pursue any private aim."

Since the die had been cast, Napoleon allowed himself to indulge his dreams. Officially France was intervening only in defence of the Sultan, to maintain her influence in the Mediterranean, and to protect Germany and the rest of Europe against possible encroachments on the part of the " northern colossus." But under cover of this war the Emperor hoped to recast the map of Europe by increasing the power of Prussia in Germany, delivering Poland, and giving Austria Moldavia and Wallachia in exchange for Lombardy, which was to be returned to the King of Piedmont and Sardinia. With the name of Napoleon it became second nature to play the part of master of the world. But there was to be a rude awakening which would not allow of the realisation of such vast ambitions.

A year had passed without war having been declared and yet nothing was ready. At first it was thought that a diversion, a demonstration involving the disembarkation of a few troops in Turkey, would suffice. Public opinion also had to be considered. The *Moniteur*, announcing that the contingent forming the 1853 class had been raised from 80,000 to 140,000 men, observed : " There is every prospect that the majority of these forces will remain at home." At last, after considerable hesitation, it was decided to send three, then four and finally five divisions. St. Arnaud, who had handed over the Ministry

H

of War to Vaillant, and had set out for the campaign, already
a victim to attacks of *angina pectoris*, was to be the Commander-
in-Chief of the Eastern Army, consisting of 30,000 men. Trochu
was his aide-de-camp. The 25,000 men of the English army
were to be under the command of Lord Raglan, who had fought
under Wellington against France at the beginning of the century.

Gallipoli. Gallipoli on the Dardanelles was chosen as the
base of operations; it was easy to supply and easy
to defend and afforded protection to Constantinople, " one of
the finest cities in Turkey," said the *Moniteur* in tones of official
optimism. As a matter of fact it consisted of wooden houses
and narrow streets filled with refuse and garbage. The work
of transport was extremely difficult. The railway between
Lyons and Valence had not been finished, and the quays at
Marseilles were inadequate. The harvest had been so bad
in Europe in 1853 that the merchant service was fully occupied
in carrying grain, and there was a lack of ships. It took a
week to reach Gallipoli from Marseilles by steam, and twenty-
five to thirty days by sail. Men and material were despatched
in the greatest confusion, and it was only at the end of May
1854 that the expeditionary force was assembled in Gallipoli.
In spite of ancient feuds, the French and English got on very
well together. Meanwhile the Piræus had been occupied with
a view to putting a stop to the machinations of King Otho of
Greece, who naturally took sides with Russia; and the Anglo-
French fleet had bombarded Odessa.

At one moment St. Arnaud meditated opening an immediate
offensive on the Danube. But as yet he had no cavalry, no
artillery and inadequate transports, and he was dissuaded from
taking a step that would have been sheer madness. He then
thought of conducting operations in the Balkans north of
Adrianople. Finally, it was decided to move a little further
north to Varna, to support the Turkish army under Omer
Pasha, who was defending Silistria against the Russians. At
this juncture the Tsar, on the urgent solicitation of Austria,
who was growing more and more perturbed by the occupation
of Moldavia and Wallachia, raised the siege of Silistria, and
his troops retired across the Danube and the Pruth. " The
Russians have run away and robbed me of my chance ! "

98

exclaimed St. Arnaud. The situation was indeed peculiar; in this war there was only one thing lacking—the enemy. What was to be done? But it was imperative to fight somewhere and win a victory. The idea of taking action in the Crimea and attacking the great military port of Sebastopol had already been entertained. " It is a jewel, and I dream of nothing else," declared St. Arnaud. " I have an idea that there is something to be done in that direction." Obviously such strategy had been as little weighed and considered as a surprise attack or raid in Algeria. Moreover, the adventure terrified him. It was Palmerston who decided the matter in London— everything would be over before the winter and everybody would have " a merry Christmas and a happy New Year." And English merchants waxed enthusiastic over this attack on a port which commanded the Black Sea. About the middle of July, while St. Arnaud was dreaming of a more distant attack, at Anapa, beyond the Crimea, the decision was taken.

Meanwhile cholera had broken out at Marseilles, and was naturally carried to Varna. While awaiting the departure for the Crimea, St. Arnaud took the absurd step of sending his troops north of Varna, into the Dobruja, a region of pestilential swamps, where some Russian cavalry had been sighted. **Expedition into the Dobruja.** Possibly he was aiming at throwing dust in the eyes of the Russians by this diversion, or at fighting the cholera by marching out into the open. It was to be a lightning raid in true Algerian fashion before embarking for the Crimea. The army advanced for some days through jungle and stagnant pools. On the 30th of July cholera swooped down upon the already exhausted forces. They had to return, **Cholera.** and the retreat was terrible. There were no medicines or conveyances, and stretchers had to be improvised. Often the stretcher-bearers themselves staggered and fell by the side of the invalid they were carrying. The dead were hurriedly buried : " heads were bared and one of the officers recited a short prayer, a handful of earth was thrown over the poor bodies which were hardly cold," and the procession set forth once more. Sometimes the grave-diggers collapsed and were buried in the trench they had themselves begun (P. de la Gorce). At Mangalia they embarked again

99

for Varna amid heartrending scenes—the sick tore off their clothes and threw themselves into the sea to extinguish the flames that devoured them; many of them died on the barges which were conveying them from the beach to the ships. A division of 10,000 men lost nearly 2,000 and there were 5,000 deaths during this period.

To crown all, Varna was burnt down on the 10th of August and large quantities of stores were destroyed. A powder magazine was surrounded by flames; St. Arnaud, who was suffering from one of his attacks, hurried up, panic ensued, and some of the soldiers took flight. By a miracle the sappers succeeded in putting out the fire and preventing an explosion. "That would have been the last straw!" exclaimed St. Arnaud. "I shall pull through, but it will be the death of me." After all these trials there was some hesitation about embarking for the Crimea. But St. Arnaud overcame all his scruples, and in September the English, French and Turkish armies weighed anchor—a force of 50,000 men all told. It was in the Crimea that the war was to be decided. It is true that in August an Anglo-French squadron had entered the Baltic and landed troops in the Åland Islands and Bomarsund had **Diversion in the Baltic.** been taken. But this success, on the eve of winter, was bound to lead to nothing, as it would have been too risky to attempt an assault on Cronstadt. It was destined to be a futile diversion and provided further proof of the extraordinary lack of resolution displayed in the conduct of this war.

After considerable hesitation it was decided to disembark at Old Fort, near Eupatoria, about twenty-five miles north of Sebastopol. The landing was accomplished with- **In the Crimea.** out a blow being struck on the 14th of September. St. Arnaud, worn out by his illness, managed by a great effort of will to pull himself together. Menschikoff, who had been taken by surprise, resolved to face his assailants; in great haste he collected together a body of 40,000 men—one regiment did a forced march of over 170 miles in five days— and occupied the rugged heights between Old Fort and Sebastopol, south of the little river of the Alma. His main object was to defend his centre, a ravine between hills through which

100

the road from Eupatoria to Sebastopol ran. On the 19th of September, 1854, the Anglo-French forces were facing him, and that night the two armies could count each other's camp fires and try to estimate the strength of the enemy.

On the 20th the attack was opened. Bosquet on the right wing, supported by the fleet, was to follow the coast, scale the hill and drive back the Russian left. Canrobert and Prince Napoleon (the son of Jerome) were to attack in the centre, and the English on the left. It was a misty morning when réveillé was sounded. Bosquet set out, but was obliged to call a halt—the English were not ready. The whole morning was lost in waiting for them. At last, in full view of the Russians, Bosquet approached the Alma. The Russians thought he was merely creating a diversion in this direction and imagined they were protected by the precipitous heights. But the Zouaves, the Algerian sharp-shooters and the infantry forded the river and scaled the heights which the Russians believed to be insurmountable. Even the artillery followed. They were now on the further slope and exposed to view. Suddenly the Zouaves appeared on the crest and opened fire. The Russians fell back. St. Arnaud, who was still in the valley, was scouring the plain with his field-glasses. " I see the red trousers," he exclaimed; " ah ! and I recognise my good old African Bosquet over there ! " And he gave orders for the frontal attack to be made. " Gentlemen," he said, " this battle will be called the Battle of the Alma." Canrobert and Prince Napoleon advanced, but were stopped by the fire of the Russians, who were awaiting them; whereupon, under the protection of their own artillery, they crossed the river. Menschikoff sent reinforcements after reinforcements to his left, but they were only small bodies of men sent in relays. Bosquet held his ground with 12 guns to 40. " Remember," he had observed on the previous day, " I cannot face heavy fire for more than two hours." At last Canrobert debouched on to the plain, and St. Arnaud brought reserves into play under Forey. The Russians stood their ground for a time and then fell back. Eventually the First Zouaves planted their standard on the summit of the Telegraph Hill.

The English, who had been late in starting, reached their

Battle of the Alma.

objective towards evening. They had advanced under gun fire and over barricades of felled trees, and had suffered enormous losses (2,000 men put out of action). The French had 300 dead and 1,000 wounded, the Russians nearly 2,000 killed and 3,000 wounded. These figures, which to-day seem very small, were extremely high for that period. Were they going to pursue the enemy? But owing to a lack of ships the cavalry was still at Varna. The troops were exhausted, they had had nothing to eat since dawn, and some of the units were in disorder, as the men had come down to the Alma again to look for their bags. It was decided to encamp and not exploit the victory further.

Sebastopol, lying north and south of a long tongue of water running inland for over three miles in an easterly direction, was strongly defended on the side facing the sea by the arsenal of Catherine II, " the holy city," but on the land side it was practically unprotected, as an attack from that direction had never been contemplated as a possibility. The Allies were about twelve miles from the town and were expected to make an attempt to take it by storm, while the Sebastopol fleet could not cope with the Anglo-French fleet, which would no doubt force the roadstead. Menschikoff thereupon heroically decided to block the entrance to the port by sinking one of the finest Russian ships in it. On the 22nd Admiral Korniloff carried out Menschikoff's orders, and the latter immediately resumed fighting with the forces at his disposal. About 20,000 men were left to defend the town. The attack was expected to come from the north. But the blocking of the port had deprived the Allies of the support of their fleet, which had to remain outside the roadstead and was consequently out of range. In these circumstances an attack would have been too hazardous, and the Allies accordingly skirted the town on the 25th with the object of crossing the Tchernaya, which flows into the roadstead, and approaching the town from the south. With any other enemy this flanking movement might have been dangerous, not to say fatal. It is true that Menschikoff himself was veering in an easterly direction at this moment, and the two armies just missed meeting face to face. On that very day St. Arnaud was struck down by

102

THE CRIMEAN WAR

cholera and handed over the command to Canrobert. On the
26th he drove through the camp and shook hands with his
Death of St. Arnaud. Zouaves. On the 29th he was put on board ship
a dying man, lying on a litter with the flag at his
feet. He was put on the poop of the vessel and a
priest kept watch beside him. He died eight hours after the
ship set sail. The Emperor had this soldier and adventurer,
whose death had been surrounded with a halo of glory, buried in
the Invalides.

To the south of Sebastopol the troops were encamped on
the plain of the Chersonesus, an almost desert table-land, with
no trees or running water, swept by the wind and cut up by
deep ravines leading to the roadstead. A few bastions, most
of them unfinished, covered the town. But the whole population of Sebastopol had been mobilised, and under the energetic
leadership of Todleben, a lieutenant-colonel of the Engineers,
were feverishly working at completing these defences. Admiral
Korniloff and the priests kindled enthusiasm in the breasts of
their fellows and encouraged them to hold out to the death.
Canrobert, a good executant but a poor strategist, and the
Canrobert. aged Raglan did not dare to risk their troops in a
surprise attack. Possibly also it was already too
late to make such an attempt. They decided to wait, encamp-
ing some of their troops at about two miles from the bastions
to keep watch on the town, and making the rest face inland,
where Menschikoff was still manœuvring freely and keeping
in constant communication with Sebastopol, which the Allies
had not sufficient forces to invest. Thus it was not so much
a siege as a war of positions.

General Bizot, in command of the Engineers, decided to
attack in the direction of the South Bay, a deep inlet running
Sebastopol. from north to south and debouching in the roadstead, thus separating the town from the suburb
of Karabelnaya. During the night of the 9th to the 10th of
October trenches were dug at about half a mile from the ramparts, and batteries were built. On the 17th of October the
town was bombarded, and it retaliated with heavy fire. In the
clouds of smoke the Allies were shooting by guesswork, guided
only by the flashes of the enemy's guns. A French powder

103

magazine blew up, and the explosion was loudly cheered by the Russians. It was necessary to cease fire without being able to launch an infantry attack. The English, who had demolished the Russian defences by their bombardment, did not dare to advance unsupported—the opportunity was lost! During the night the Russians, profiting by the silence of the guns, which it was impossible to lay again in the dark, repaired their defence works, and the bombardment, which was resumed during the two following days, proved ineffectual. Korniloff, it is true, was killed, but the place was by no means ready to surrender. Before the 17th of October it was hoped that a prompt settlement would be reached on the French side, but the English said at the time, "We are here for the whole winter!" And after the 17th it had to be admitted that they were right.

Moreover, the recent success gained by the Russians made them decide to take the offensive. The English had made **Balaklava.** Balaklava their base of operations; it was a small roadstead on the south-east of the plain of Chersonesus, and was covered by redoubts occupied by our Turkish allies. On the 25th of October Menschikoff attacked these redoubts and finally took them. In attempting to push on further the Cossacks were met by the fire of the Highlanders. As the enemy were making preparations to remove the guns from the redoubts, Lord Raglan ordered the English cavalry to come into play. When the order reached them, the situation had already changed, the Russians having evacuated the redoubts and re-formed further off. Lord Cardigan, who was in command of the Light Brigade, expostulated, but nevertheless obeyed the order, shouting, "Forward the last of the **Charge of** Cardigans!" The brigade advanced to the gallop, **the Light** broke through the first enemy lines beneath a mur- **Brigade.** derous fire, and was forced to retreat to the accompaniment of heavy losses. Out of 700 men, 250 were killed or wounded. The heroic but mad charge of the Light Brigade was to win undying glory in England.

A few days later, Menschikoff, who had received fresh reinforcements and now had 100,000 men at his disposal, decided to attack the Allies, who did not number more than 70,000.

104

THE CRIMEAN WAR

He hoped by this means to free the town, whose situation was becoming more and more precarious, the French trenches at one point having reached within five hundred feet of the salient of one of the Russian bastions. During the night of the 4th to the 5th of November, his troops massed round the plain of Inkerman, on the east of the town, near the suburb of Karabelnaya. This constituted the British sector. It was raining and the men on guard were exhausted. The English could hear the church bells ringing in the middle of the night, but they often rang in this way; they could also hear the rumbling of wheels, but they thought they belonged to peasant carts conveying supplies to the town. Nevertheless, General Codrington, who on the west of the plain was inspecting his sector on horseback before dawn, felt uneasy. The men on outpost duty were making tea. Codrington went on. Suddenly there was a burst of musket fire. The Russians in grey coats, without a bugle-call or allowing a single camp-fire to be seen, and regardless of all the rules of the game at that period, debouched on to the plain on the left of the English. The English officers rallied their troops, who were all at sixes and sevens in the morning fog. The Russians penetrated right into their camp. But the English pulled themselves together and with their quick-firing carbines inflicted heavy losses on the Russians, who fell back. At this moment the English right was attacked by another body of Russians, who, had they arrived earlier on the scene, might have put their adversaries to flight. But the latter, though they were outnumbered, held their ground and pushed back the Russians into the Careening ravine.

At last the main body of the Russian troops in the centre reached the plain, singing the Tsar's hymn which the regiments had sung during the night in the churches to the sound of the bells. At the " Sandbag Battery " hand-to-hand fighting took place between the Russians and the English—they shot each other at close quarters, used their bayonets and the butt-end of their muskets and pelted each other with stones. They fought in dead silence, not a cry was heard. The Coldstreams lost a third of their strength, an enormous figure for that period. The English gave way. Raglan despatched reinforcements,

Inkerman.

105

who failed in their effort; the Coldstreams lost and retook and again lost the Battery. Whereupon, at nine o'clock in the morning, Raglan summoned the French to his help.

Bosquet was already holding two battalions in readiness under the command of Bourbaki. To the blare of trumpets and the ringing cheers of the English, the red trousers advanced and captured the Battery, and then fell back under the weight of numbers. Colonel de Camas was killed, and the flag was in danger—for in this war the flag was always in the forefront. " To the flag, boys ! " shouted the lieutenant-colonel, rallying his men. This counter-attack made the Russians hesitate, and Bosquet had time to bring up some light infantry, Zouaves and Algerian sharp-shooters, who, " bounding out like panthers," once more captured the Sandbag Battery and again drove the enemy back into the Careening ravine. The Russians counter-attacked, but were forced down the steep ravines under the fire of the French guns. Two Russian diversions, one under Gortchakoff in the direction of Balaklava, and the other on the far west of the town against General Lourmel, who was killed, also failed.

It had been a terrible battle. " What a shambles ! " exclaimed Bosquet when he reached the Sandbag Battery. The bodies were heaped up on the top of one another. The English had lost 2,800 in dead and wounded, the French 800, or 10 per cent. of the forces engaged, the Russians 3,000 dead, 6,000 wounded and 1,600 missing. After the battles of the last war —the French troops at Verdun were relieved only after they had lost 75 per cent. of their strength—these figures appear to us surprisingly small, but at the time they seemed terrible. And France, who was always dreaming of the glories of the first Empire, compared Inkerman with Eylau.

After such a blow all idea of attacking the town had to be abandoned and the Allies were obliged to resign themselves to wintering on the spot. On the 14th of November **The Winter Campaign.** a terrific storm broke over the camps, blowing away the tents and huts, flooding the trenches and sinking the boats, and a period of terrible hardship began. " The Chersonesus," said an eye-witness, " is like the bottom of a half-empty pond; our encampment has been turned into a

106

THE CRIMEAN WAR

swamp, and dead horses are littering the ground." No
arrangements had been made for a winter campaign; moreover, the African forces despised heavy baggage, "*impedi-
menta*." Warm clothing was ordered from France, but woollen
vests and flannel body-belts were a long time arriving. There
was also a shortage of wood for fuel, scarcely enough being
procurable for supplying the kitchens. The cartage of munitions and supplies was extremely difficult. They had to be
brought up from the harbour of Kamiesch, which was packed
with Levantine merchants, by a road full of deep ruts to the
camp. Sometimes it took several days to cover these six miles,
and the horses died by scores. The camp consisted of tents,
huts and even hollows dug in the ground. Finally, in the
trenches the soldiers on guard, in spite of their sheepskins,
their hoods and their Russian boots, suffered terribly from the
cold and rain, while the navvies were worn out constantly
repairing the earthworks and digging the frozen ground. There
was a great deal of illness and as many as 6,000 men a month
had to be taken away sick. After a most uncomfortable crossing they were taken to Constantinople, where huge hospitals
had been organised. The French were nursed by the Sisters
of Saint Vincent de Paul and the English by the volunteer
nurses under Florence Nightingale. During the winter operations at the front slowed down—the guns were almost inactive,
the work of entrenchment progressed extremely slowly, and
there were occasional surprise attacks on the part of the Russians. But the classic formula in the *communiqués* was : " There
is nothing further to report." Meanwhile the Russians succeeded in strengthening their defences. The hours dragged
by on leaden feet. The men read newspapers that were a
month old which the ships brought in, and were irritated
by the wonderful plans mapped out in France by theorists
sitting in their warm bedroom slippers. " Do they imagine
that Sebastopol is going to fall like Jericho to a blast of trumpets ? " they exclaimed. " It is the siege of Troy." On the
31st of December a parade was held and Canrobert distributed
crosses and thanked his men.

At the end of September Paris had been under the impression
that Sebastopol had fallen or was on the point of falling. It

was bitterly disappointed. Moreover, cholera was levying its toll in France, the harvest of 1854 had been almost as bad as that of 1853, and amid the silence of the Press, " defeatist " rumours spread through the country. It became necessary to keep under the colours soldiers whose discharge was due; a levy of 140,000 men from the 1854 class was voted, and a fresh loan of 500 million francs (£20,000,000), which incidentally was subscribed four times over, was floated. In February 1855 the frigate *la Sémillante*, carrying about half a battalion of infantry to the Crimea, was totally wrecked off the coast of Sardinia with the loss of all on board. Nevertheless, official optimism persisted, and in January the *Moniteur* wrote with reference to the Crimea : " It might almost be Italy, the weather is so mild."

The Emperor, provoked by these delays, was anxious to intervene. Having written an Artillery Manual and being an old **The** artillery captain of the Swiss army, he considered **Emperor's** himself thoroughly qualified. Moreover, with the **Anxiety.** name of Napoleon, it was only natural that he should imagine himself a born military genius. So he set to work at his maps and plans, and came to the conclusion, like the good theorist he was, that " no common sense " had been applied to the construction of the siege works. And he forthwith despatched several *missi dominici*, chief among them General Niel of the Engineers, who had won distinction at Rome and at Bomarsund. The Emperor and Niel were both anxious that the town should be invested and cut off from all communication with the outside world. But for this heavy reinforcements would have been required. Conferences were held, the days slipped by and the siege seemed endless.

Meanwhile the diplomatists were not idle. Since it had been impossible to avoid war, the least that could be done was to define its aims. In August 1854 a Note had been drawn up in Vienna, in conjunction with the French and English Ambassadors, laying down four points : (1) the Russian protectorate over the Danubian principalities (Moldavia and Wallachia— the Roumania of to-day) was to be replaced by a joint protectorate of the Powers ; Austria was opposed to the Tsar sharing the privilege; (2) the free navigation of the Danube;

(3) the independence of Turkey, to be secured by prohibiting or limiting the entry of fleets into the Black Sea; (4) the protection of the Christians in Turkey in a manner compatible with the sovereignty of the Sultan, that is to say, in such a way as to prevent the Tsar from exploiting it to establish his suzerainty over Constantinople. In December 1854 Austria signed a treaty on these lines and formed an alliance with France and England; indeed at one time it seemed as though **The** Austria would join in the conflict. Drouyn de **Austrian** Lhuys naturally brought pressure to bear on Vienna **Alliance.** to induce her to act, threatening to make peace with the Tsar on generous terms as soon as victory had been secured. For neither Moldavia and Wallachia nor the free navigation of the Danube were of any particular interest to France : " We might make the present conflict a mere matter of military honour between Russia and ourselves, and after forcing the Tsar Nicholas to recognise the superiority of our arms and resources, hand him back his sword unconditionally." Nothing was better calculated to prove the vanity and futility of this bloody war which was being prolonged merely for the sake of honour. Russia succeeded in gaining time and preventing the intervention of Austria. But at this juncture Piedmont joined the Anglo-French alliance and despatched 15,000 men to the Crimea. This step on the part of her worst enemy was ill calculated to conciliate Austria or induce her to throw in her lot with the Allies.

On the 2nd of March, 1855, Nicholas I died. This led to the immediate belief that peace would soon be signed, and on the Bourse Government securities rose five francs. But Alexander II carried on his father's policy. Negotiations were still being conducted in Vienna; Russia accepted the four points in principle, but disagreed as to detail, more especially on the question of the neutralisation of the Black Sea, in which the English and French were chiefly interested. Drouyn de Lhuys went in person to Vienna to suggest this neutralisation, or at least the limitation of Russian forces in the Black Sea, and to persuade Austria to force acceptance of these proposals on Russia on pain of launching an ultimatum against her. He did not succeed. It was clear that Austria was not prepared to intervene.

THE SECOND EMPIRE

Napoleon III was so firmly convinced that he alone could end the war that he conceived the idea of going to the Crimea himself. He confided his plan to the English, who endeavoured to dissuade him. Doubtless they had no confidence in his military genius; moreover, his presence at the seat of war would completely have overshadowed the small British army. They raised objections, pointing out that it would take months to convey to the spot the reinforcements necessary for complicated and extensive operations. As yet no anxiety was felt in the Emperor's immediate circle. Persigny was frantic. " If he goes," he declared, " the army is lost and there will be a revolution."

It was just at this time, April 1855, that the Emperor and Empress paid the visit to Queen Victoria which was destined **The Emperor's Visit to London.** to cement the alliance and which had been discussed for the past year. Napoleon III was given an ovation. He stayed at Windsor Castle. The two sovereigns held a review in which the Crimean wounded took part, chief among them Lord Cardigan, the hero of Balaklava. They visited the Crystal Palace, were present at a gala performance, and attended balls. The Emperor received the Order of the Garter from Queen Victoria and was invited to a banquet at the Guildhall given in his honour by the City of London. He returned thanks in English and immediately sprang into popularity. Queen Victoria was charmed by his calmness and candour and his belief in his star, and his " invincible determination." " Is it not strange," she naïvely wrote, " that I, the granddaughter of George III, should be dancing in the Waterloo room with the Emperor Napoleon, the nephew of England's greatest enemy, who is to-day my closest ally, though eight years ago he was living in this country an obscure exile? " They naturally discussed the Crimea, and the Queen tried to dissuade the Emperor from carrying out his plans by emphasising the distance and the dangers. " Danger is everywhere," replied Napoleon III, with the fatalism of the man long since resigned to attempts on his life. But still he could not make up his mind. It was about this time that Bismarck wrote : " They say that the Emperor Napoleon is going to the Crimea to teach the generals their job, and then,

110

if Sebastopol refuses to surrender, he will lead his army to Constantinople to secure the succession to the throne of the Sultan and found a Roman Empire. It is a fantastic enterprise, but for that very reason all the more probable." Bismarck already knew his future victim.

Chance decided the matter. On the 28th of April, at five o'clock in the afternoon, the Emperor was riding from the Tuileries to the Bois through the Champs Élysées, when an Italian named Pianori, a native of the Papal States, fired two shots at him. He remained calm and collected and continued his ride. The defence put forward by Pianori for his crime was that the Emperor had fought in the Roman campaign and ruined his country. The incident proved the dangers that might attend his absence, and nothing more was said about going to the Crimea. At this juncture the Conference of Vienna definitely ended in failure. Drouyn de Lhuys, in conjunction with the Austrian Cabinet, had tried to draw up a complicated system for securing the balance of power in the Black Sea. The Allied Fleets were to have the right of keeping a certain number of ships permanently beyond the Bosphorus to counterbalance the Russian fleet. But Napoleon III, under the influence of England, refused to countenance the plan, and Drouyn de Lhuys was replaced by Walewski. The war alone—that is to say, the capture of Sebastopol, and that without the intervention of Austria—could provide a solution. The alliance with Austria had vanished in smoke.

Pianori's Crime.

With the advent of spring preparations were made to have done with Sebastopol. The French army now consisted of 80,000 men, the total Allied forces numbering 130,000. All idea of attacking the town itself had been abandoned; at one point the trenches were still 600 yards away from the Russian bastion, and it was impossible for a storming column to advance that distance under fire. At another point they were nearer—about 130 yards— but the Russian defences were formidable and protected by mines. It was therefore decided that it would be better to attack in the direction of the suburb of Karabelnaya on the east of the town, concentrating more particularly on Fort

Renewed Activity at Sebastopol.

Malakoff, which commanded the suburb, the roadstead and the town, and the Mamelon, an advanced redoubt which covered the fort at a distance of about 600 yards. But Todleben was too quick for them, and during the night had redoubts constructed at the points from which the Allies might have been able to destroy Fort Mamelon by the fire of their guns. They were hollowed out in the chalk and nicknamed the White Works—a term familiar to those who fought in the Great War. Thereupon Todleben turned his attention to the fortification of the Mamelon itself. The Allies wanted to end the whole business by a *coup de force* and avoid wasting time over siege works, and during the night of the 8th to the 9th of April their troops unmasked the embrasures of 500 guns in the rain. At five o'clock in the morning fire was opened all along the line. The Russians retaliated with their 1,000 guns; for, as Sebastopol was not invested, they were able to receive constant reinforcements of men and material. During the night the Russians repaired the damage done to their trenches. The bombardment was continued on the 10th, many of the Russian embrasures were destroyed, the salients of the bastions were demolished, and it is possible that an assault might have been successful. But the Allies did not dare to make it. The bombardment continued until the 19th of April with no result except the infliction of losses in both camps, and above all the death of General Bizot.

This fresh rebuff, for it could not be regarded in any other light, was ill calculated to appease Napoleon III. He insisted that the place should be invested, but for this a long inland campaign in the Crimea was a pre-requisite. He sent note after note and aides-de-camp after aides-de-camp. Better still, the Black Sea cable joining the Crimea to the west became operative on the 25th of April, and the Emperor made an almost unjustifiable use of it. Canrobert, courteous, modest and weak, and anxious to spare the lives of his men, spent his time in interpreting the notes he received from Paris, which were sometimes contradictory. Moreover, unity of command had not been established, and incidents arose between the French and English Staffs. It had been decided to send an expedition to destroy Kertch, one of the ports from which

112

the Russians obtained supplies. The ships had already set sail when an order arrived from Paris commanding them to be recalled and an immediate offensive against Sebastopol to be arranged. The attack on Kertch, however, was merely postponed for a while. Niel continued to insist that the place should be invested; the English raised a thousand and one objections, and, sick of the war, Canrobert resigned his command in favour of General Pélissier, of the African army, who had taken Forey's place at the New Year and was also the man appointed by the Commander-in-Chief to take over the command. Canrobert was allowed to return to the command of his own division under the orders of Pélissier.

Pélissier had but one idea—" the vigorous prosecution of the siege," cost what it might. And he adhered to it in spite

Pélissier. of the protestations of Niel, the Emperor's confidant, and regardless of the Emperor's own plans for investment on a grand scale or for operations at a distance. Abrupt, biting and sarcastic, he instilled fear even in the breasts of the *missi dominici* from Paris. His subordinates wrote direct to Napoleon III to inform him of their feelings with regard to the conduct of the campaign, and Pélissier had his work cut out to deal with the Emperor : " It is not a matter of discussion between us," the latter telegraphed, " but of giving and receiving orders." To which Pélissier, without beating about the bush, replied, " It is easy to draw up a magnificent plan of campaign on the map." In order to appease the Emperor and postpone the grand " external attack," he pleaded the opposition of the English, the cholera, etc. At the same time he did all in his power to speed up operations against Sebastopol.

He now had 120,000 men at his disposal. At the end of May he captured some of the enemy's outposts and the army at last felt it was being guided by a strong will. And they set eagerly to work, extending the trenches, widening the parallels for the forming-up of attacks, and providing them with steps, and collecting gabions, fascines and sandbags. Frossard pushed forward his approaches, whilst Bosquet, with his eye on the Mamelon, made plans for its capture. On the 6th of June a bombardment was opened against all the

Russian defences before Karabelnaya. During the night of the 6th to the 7th, which was a short one, the Russians did not have time to repair all the damage before dawn. On the 7th the bombardment was renewed on a wider front. At half-past six in the evening rockets were fired giving the signal for attack. The French troops, under General de Failly, captured the White Works, and at the same time Wimpffen covered the 500 yards separating him from the Mamelon, the undulating nature of the ground fortunately affording him occasional cover. His men jumped into the ditch, scaled the crumbling parapet, and captured the position. Colonel de Brancion was killed just as he was planting his colours on the parapet. An attempt was even made to pursue the Russians and to take the Malakoff tower by storm; it lay about six or seven hundred yards further on. But the Russians counter-attacked; they succeeded in driving back the units that had advanced too far, and in the confusion that ensued, recaptured the Mamelon. Whereupon Bosquet brought his reserves into action and again took the position, and during the night, in full view of the Russians, the sappers hastily fortified the defences of the works that had been captured during the day. The action had cost the army over 5,000 killed and wounded.

The Mamelon.

It was now hoped that all would soon be over. Pélissier was determined to win, and to win quickly in order to disarm Niel and the Emperor. On the 17th of June the Malakoff and its surroundings were bombarded, as well as the town, where numerous fires broke out. The Russians, thus warned, made preparations to repulse the attack, which they expected would take place on the following day, the anniversary of Waterloo. In the morning the French opened the attack, but some of them started too soon, others too late. Mowed down by the Russian fire, they were obliged to take cover behind any shelter the ground afforded and to open fire themselves. An isolated battalion of Chasseurs reached the Malakoff and barricaded themselves in, but were eventually forced to beat a retreat. On the 19th an armistice to allow for the burial of the dead was concluded.

Reverse of June 18th.

On the 22nd of June the *Moniteur* published the news word

114

for word as Pélissier had telegraphed it : " The attack of the 18th of June has failed, although our troops, who showed great spirit, for a time found a footing in the Malakoff. I was obliged to order a retreat to the parallel. It was carried out in orderly fashion without panic of any sort. It is impossible for me to compute our losses to-day." Such a *communiqué* produced great excitement in France. The Press, it is true, was dumb. But this only served to make " defeatist " news circulate all the more readily, and the huge reinforcements that were continually being sent out to the Crimea, the heavy losses suffered, more especially by the sappers, the constant stream of sick and wounded returning home and the temporary hospitals organised in the south formed universal topics of conversation. And in spite of the regulations, public opinion occasionally found an outlet. One day Grassot, the actor, complained that the waiter in the café was very slow in serving him : " What," he cried, " is it the same here as at Sebastopol? Can't one get anything? " There was always some spy lurking about public places, and Grassot was immediately arrested and imprisoned. But such incidents gave the authorities cause for anxiety. In July the Legislative Body voted a levy of 140,000 from the 1855 class for 1856 and a fresh loan of 750 million francs (£30,000,000). And Napoleon III declared in public that he " had every hope of concluding an honourable peace." He was no longer asking for much, and was becoming more and more nervous. " All the African generals are the same," he observed to a certain Englishman, " I cannot see much difference between Changarnier, Lamoricière, St. Arnaud, Pélissier and Canrobert. The kind of fighting they were accustomed to in Algeria has not fitted them for military operations on a grand scale." On the 3rd of July the Emperor decided to replace Pélissier by Niel. Marshal Vaillant, who knew his master, took it upon his own shoulders not to telegraph the order but to send it by post. On the following day the Emperor's immediate circle, and chief among them Fleury, succeeded in making him change his mind, and there was time to have the order intercepted at Marseilles.

There was also discontent in the army. Bosquet, Niel and even Canrobert began to grumble. " We are getting tired of this idiotic war they are making us wage," wrote one of the generals. " God alone knows how it will end." Cholera had broken out again, complicated by scurvy due to lack of vegetable food. On the 28th of June Lord Raglan died of cholera, as St. Arnaud had done before him. Nevertheless, the command succeeded in surviving this moral crisis. The Russians too were becoming exhausted. Todleben had been seriously wounded and Nakimoff had been shot in the head on the 10th of July when he was inspecting the French works. St. Petersburg, like Paris, was growing impatient, regarding a defensive war costing 250 men a day as utterly futile, and insisting that the army should take the offensive against the Allies in the open country. Gortschakoff replied that it would be madness to attack the enemy's trenches. Nevertheless, he was obliged to consent to take the offensive on the Tchernaya, between Inkerman and Balaklava, on the Traktir bridge. On the 16th of August he made a series of furious attacks,

Traktir. each of which was in turn repulsed by the French and the Sardinians. The latter had 28 killed and 160 wounded and all Europe was informed of the fact. Cavour, the Minister of Piedmont and Sardinia, was not slow to turn this sacrifice to account at the psychological moment. In France this news had the most salutary effect on public opinion.

It was just about this time that Queen Victoria and Prince Albert were paying their return visit to the Emperor and

Queen Victoria in France. Empress at St. Cloud, and for the first time since 1422 an English sovereign set foot in Paris. They visited the International Exhibition held in the *Palais de l'Industrie*, and the Queen went to the Invalides and paid her respects to the tomb of Napoleon I, her country's erstwhile foe, while the organ in the chapel played *God save the Queen*. She was enchanted with the gaiety and beauty of Paris and became the devoted friend of the Emperor, in whose company she spent the ten days of her visit. She was with him for " twelve or fourteen hours a day, often *tête-à-tête*." The festivities were so brilliant that they aroused considerable ill-feeling in Sebastopol. " They are having a fine time in Paris," wrote an officer, " a very fine time. Surely they might have postponed all this merrymaking until peace had been made."

116

THE CRIMEAN WAR

The Russians continued to work at their defences, laying mines in all directions. But their losses reached 1,000 men a day. Certain positions which were constantly bombarded were untenable, and were dubbed Hell Bastion, Butchery Bastion and Pestle Mill. Meanwhile the French sappers had advanced to within twenty-five yards of the Malakoff; the Russian spades and pickaxes could be distinctly heard. " All is well," said Pélissier in a telegram of the 3rd of September, " we are getting on and making headway." The only thing that still inspired terror were the mines which the Russians were said to be preparing for blowing up positions that had only just been won—nothing was more demoralising for a body of men than this sinister and invisible danger against which the infantry had no protection.

At last on the 5th of September the 800 French guns opened a terrific bombardment. There was firing on all sides, but more particularly on the Malakoff, which was blown to bits by the mortars. At first it retaliated, but was soon silenced. During the night the Russians repaired the damage, but the French continued to shoot by the light of the fires that had burst out. On the 6th the bombardment was continued; at intervals it suddenly ceased in order to give the Russians the impression that the moment for the assault had come. They would then bring out their reserves from cover, whereupon the firing would start again more savagely than ever, and inflict heavy losses upon them. On the 7th, the anniversary of Moskowa, the bombardment was continued with redoubled fury. The Russians were unable to repair the damage or remove their wounded, who lay groaning surrounded by the troops defending the works. Whole quarters of the town were on fire, a boat with a cargo of spirit caught alight, and boats carrying powder were blown up—powder destined for charging the mines of the Malakoff.

At dawn on the 9th of September preparations were made for the assault. Bosquet was determined to succeed, and his officers assured him that they would win him the Marshal's baton. At eight o'clock the troops entered the trenches. A violent north-east wind was blowing, and the sea was so rough that it was impossible for the fleet to fire, but the dust and

117

smoke hid the movements of the Allied troops from the Russians. Moreover, the latter were expecting the attack to take place either at dawn or in the evening, but it was at midday precisely—the whole command having synchronised their watches with headquarters—that the men leapt up the steps of the parallels and rushed forward. Bosquet planted his headquarters flag on the parapet. To the beating of drums and the blowing of trumpets the officers with swords drawn led on their men. MacMahon's Zouaves swarmed up the Malakoff, where the exhausted defenders had just had their midday meal in their armoured shelters, cleared the ditch, scaled the escarpment without waiting for the sappers' ladders, and forced their way into the embrasures. A hand-to-hand fight ensued, and at the end of half an hour the colours of the First Zouaves were floating over the Malakoff.

The English redcoats attacked on the left, at the Great Redan, but as they had to advance 200 yards under fire, they suffered heavy losses, and were unable to keep the position they had won. Another French attack in the direction of the town failed and Trochu was wounded. On the right of the Malakoff, at the Little Redan, desperate fighting took place, but no decision was reached and Bosquet was wounded. A powder magazine blew up. Did this mean defeat? No! MacMahon was still holding the Malakoff, after having cleared the fortifications with the help of Vinoy, and repulsed one furious counter-attack after the other in conjunction with Wimpffen. As the Malakoff was the key to the whole defensive system of the town, Gortschakoff had the place evacuated that evening; in the dusk the French saw the Russian soldiers, wagons and guns crossing the great bridge which had been constructed during the siege to join the south bank of the roadstead to the north. All through the night the Russians were busy blowing up powder magazines, throwing all the material they could not take away with them into the water, and sinking the ships. After which they dismantled the bridge. Before day dawned the last defenders were conveyed to the north bank by boat. Among them was Osten-Sacken, the Governor, who was the last to leave the town. But the Russians remained on the north bank of the roadstead only 800

THE CRIMEAN WAR

yards away. On the 10th of September, 1855, after a siege
lasting 332 days, and nearly a year after the Battle of the Alma,
Pélissier, who had been made a Marshal, entered Sebastopol.

Fall of Sebastopol. On the same evening the great news was announced
in Paris with a salute of guns. But several days
passed by, and the news had been confirmed from
all quarters, before France could make up her mind to believe
it. The last onslaught had cost the French 3,000 dead and
4,500 wounded, while the English casualties amounted to
2,500 and the Russian to 12,000.

On the fall of Sebastopol the Emperor returned to his grand
schemes—an offensive was to be opened in the Crimea, Russia
was to be attacked in the Baltic with the help of the Swedes,
the ancestral foes of the Tsar, and the Poles were to be roused
to rebellion. But the combatants were exhausted. Pélissier
gave no thought to future victories and the war dragged wearily
on. A Council of War was held in Paris, but it accomplished
nothing. In France there was a general demand for peace,
especially in the rural districts and centres of trade. But
England did not want to end the matter with her defeat at
the Great Redan, and talked of attacking Cronstadt, criticising
" the passion for peace which was paralysing the French
market," as the Prince Consort declared with reference to the
Bourse. Semi-officially, and more particularly through the
mouth of Herr von Beust, the Saxon Minister, Napoleon III
conveyed to Russia that all he demanded was the neutralisation of the Black Sea. Beust did all in his power to persuade
the Tsar to accept. " I am certain," he added, with a scepticism
which the issue was to justify in 1870, " that in ten or twelve
years' time some diplomatist or other will propose a return
to the *status quo ante bellum*." Moreover, Alexander II was
tired of the war. The defence of Sebastopol had been sufficiently
glorious for the demands of honour to be satisfied, and some
Russian troops had just captured the Turkish fortress of Kars
in Asia Minor. Thus there was a basis for negotiations.

Whereupon Austria intervened, and in conjunction with
the Allies proposed to the Tsar the four points which some
months previously had been decided upon in Vienna, adding
the neutralisation of the Black Sea, a rectification of the frontier

119

in favour of Moldavia and the right to insert supplementary clauses. The Tsar wanted to abide by the four points, and in Paris there was a slump on the Bourse. But Prussia brought pressure to bear on Alexander II and he gave way. French Government securities immediately rose five francs.

The Peace Congress opened in Paris on the 25th of February, 1856, under the Presidency of Walewski, who was assisted by **The Peace Congress.** Benedetti, the Minister for Foreign Affairs. Only the belligerents and Austria were represented. It was the revenge for the Congress of Vienna— France, hitherto suspect, " had been allowed to return to the great European family," observed Hübner. The neutralisation of the Black Sea was proclaimed, confirming the situation which had existed in practice ever since the disappearance of the Russian fleet and the fall of Sebastopol. The Sultan, on his own initiative, issued a firman promising " to ameliorate the lot " of all his subjects, whether Christian or not, and communicated the said firman to the Powers, who undertook not to meddle in Turkish affairs. Navigation on the Danube was to be free, and an international commission was to see that the regulations were carried out. Moldavia and Wallachia were to be independent States under the suzerainty of Turkey. Napoleon III was anxious to establish an independent Roumania forthwith; but Austria and Turkey were opposed to it, and a commission was appointed to organise the two principalities in accordance with the wishes of their inhabitants. Russia ceded a slice of Bessarabia to Moldavia and thus ceased to be a Danubian State—a sacrifice which she found extremely painful and for which she bore Austria a grudge for having wrested from her.

In the course of the negotiations it became clear that France was anxious for a *rapprochement* with Russia. The French **Franco-Russian Rap-proche-ment.** delegates did everything in their power to spare their erstwhile enemies all humiliation, and during the festivities that followed Napoleon III was particularly friendly in his attentions to the Tsar's emissary, Count Orloff. The Emperor and Walewski felt they had made sufficient advance with Russia to put forward a plea on behalf of Poland, but Orloff replied vaguely that it was a matter of domestic policy and that the Tsar alone was competent to decide the fate of the Poles. Although Napoleon III was just as friendly to them, the English felt a little bit jealous of this Franco-Russian *rapprochement*. The Congress was closed by the announcement of a great event—the Empress was expecting a child. On the 16th of March the guns of the Invalides boomed out. It was known that twenty-one shots meant a daughter, and a hundred and one a son. At the twenty-second shot the populace went mad with joy—the Emperor had an heir. The future of the Empire seemed assured !

Meanwhile Napoleon III had himself insisted that Prussia, although she had played no part in the drawing up of the Treaty of Vienna, should be admitted to the Congress to guarantee the integrity of Turkey in conjunction with the other Powers, and he gave Herr von Manteuffel an extremely courteous reception when, like the other plenipotentiaries, he came to sign the Treaty on the 30th of March with a symbolic pen—an eagle's feather plucked from a bird in the *Jardin des Plantes*. But the fair fabric raised for the safeguarding of Turkey was destined to be shortlived—thirty years later not a sign of it was left. Certain far-sighted minds in Europe felt sure this would be so, but the Tuileries were none the less convinced that the Eastern Question had at last been settled. At all events French influence, or at least French prestige, had been restored, and this was the most important advantage gained from the war that had cost France so dear. During the winter of 1855 to 1856 men were still dying of cold in the Crimea, as well as of typhus and other diseases, which accounted for 9,000 deaths. It was only in July 1856 that the final evacuation of troops was carried out. The French had lost in all nearly 100,000 dead, of whom 75,000 had been carried off by sickness—at that time there were more deaths in hospital than on the battle-field; the English losses reached a total of 20,000, of whom 16,000 died of sickness; the Sardinians 2,000, nearly all of whom were victims of disease; the Turks 30,000 and the Russians 110,000. It was a sorry bill to pay for a Quixotic war in which nobody knew what they were fighting for and which, in the absence of all ill-feeling on the part of the combatants, was carried on as though it were a polite but dangerous sport. And when it was all over what remained? A silver medal with the effigy of Queen Victoria, held by a light blue riband with a yellow border and clasps—*Alma, Balaklava, Inkerman, Sebastopol!*

The Congress afforded an opportunity of settling certain matters of common interest—Napoleon III loved to pose as the arbiter of Europe. In April the Congress introduced certain alterations in international maritime law—the abolition of privateering, the neutral flag to cover enemy's goods, with the exception of contraband of war, neutral goods not to be liable to seizure under the enemy's flag, blockades to be binding must be effective. Furthermore, the Emperor thought the moment opportune to give free expression to his grand dreams about Italy. On the 9th of April, Walewski called upon his colleagues to exchange views " on various subjects." It was the first foreshadowing of a meeting of the League of Nations, without, however, any prearranged programme. Walewski discussed every subject under the sun—the attacks of the Belgian Press on the Empire, the rule of tyranny in Naples, the evacuation of the Piræus, and finally, through association of ideas, the evacuation of Rome by the French and of the Romagna by the Austrians, who were still there. Cavour, the Piedmontese delegate, who was eager to have the Italian question raised, was responsible for this. Naturally Austria protested—the Congress had been called to discuss the Eastern Question and nothing else! The delegates were therefore confined to expressing themselves in favour of the evacuation of the Papal States. No matter! The question had been raised, and thenceforward Napoleon III was convinced that " something must be done for Italy." And thus the seed for future wars was sown.

CHAPTER IV

THE IMPERIAL AUTOCRACY

The Emperor—his "mission." His character—a man of '48. The Empress, the imperial family, the Court. Balls, charades. Compiègne, Paris. The Government. Laws relating to the army. Great public works. Speculation, the rush for money. The theatre. The St. Simonians. The *Crédit Foncier*. The *Crédit Mobilier*. The railways. The telegraph system. Ocean transport. Paris—Haussmann. Politics and æsthetics. Speculation. Disasters and catastrophes. The Exhibition of 1855. The Council of State, the Legislative Body—Morny. The Senate. The clergy. Incidents connected with the *Articles Organiques*. Coronation plans. The Press. The spy system. The Legitimists, the Orleanists; opposition of the *Institut*; the Republicans. Elections of 1857. Conspiracies. Orsini (1858). Protests. The Law of Public Safety. Espinasse. Incidents with Belgium, Switzerland, the Piedmont, England. Favre's defence of Orsini. Orsini's letter—heading towards the Italian War.

UNTIL the end of the year 1860 no change was made in the organisation of the imperial *régime* established in 1852 and 1853; this constituted the period known as the imperial autocracy. " The elective bodies have no real power. . . . Political life is at an end " (Ch. Seignobos). It was **The Emperor.** the Emperor who governed. During the first years of his Presidency he had bided his time, knowing that his hour would come. " I am convinced," he wrote to a lady friend in 1847, " that from time to time men are created, whom I shall call men of destiny, to whose hands the fate of their country is entrusted. And I believe that I myself am such a man. . . . If I am right, Providence will put me in a position to carry out my mission." Like his uncle, " The Other," he had faith in his star, a simple and superstitious faith. And strange to say, in a few years' time Destiny munificently granted his request and placed a crown upon the head of the poor exile riddled with debt. During these first years of his reign he was justified in thinking that the future lay in the hollow of his hand.

Even when he had ascended the throne he still remained simple and kindly. " He can be very charming when he wishes," wrote the Ambassador Hübner, " and extremely talkative when he takes it into his head to cast aside his usual solemnity." He gave everybody the impression of being a good fellow, being open-handed and liberal in the cause of charity as he was towards the members of his own immediate circle, and finding it impossible to be severe except in writing. " In conversation he has the gentleness and patience of a saint," wrote Marshal Valliant, " but in his letters all this vanishes. I have received some extremely disagreeable communications from him, but he always apologised for them afterwards." He inspired affection though possibly he himself never really loved anybody. But friendship, which is in any case rare in life, is in all probability a closed book for crowned heads. At all events he had fits of benevolence towards the people and the country, and was inspired by a sincere desire to ameliorate the lot of the " working classes." He tried to get into touch with those of humble rank and " was for ever shaking hands with people when he went out for a drive," said Piétri, his Prefect of Police, adding, however, that he himself knew his duties and saw to it that the Emperor shook hands only with people employed by the police. As Seignobos observes, he was the exact opposite of Thiers, who felt only contempt and indifference for " the vile multitude." Thus, if Thiers was a true representative of the period of Louis Philippe, Napoleon III may be said to have been typical of '48, sympathising with the humanitarian impulses and socialistic dreams of his period, and even when he came into power retaining traces of the political and social romanticism that characterised it.

Unfortunately he was endowed with more heart than head, and was anything but clear-sighted. He had some sort of vague idea of the goal he was aiming at, but did not possess the lucidity calmly to consider ways and means of reaching it, nor was he able to foresee the consequences of his decisions. His was not the enlightened strength of will of the statesman, but the obstinacy of the weak man. He had no capacity for keeping himself well informed. " He never examines the arguments put before him," said Hübner, " and has neither wish nor aptitude for discussion." The fact was that in the middle of a

124

conversation he was still obstinately pursuing his airy visions. And he was too much of a fatalist really to be animated by a strong desire, being too sincere a believer, if not in the guidance of a divine providence, at least in the force of circumstances, to be able to bend them to his own will. The influence his immediate circle was able to exercise over such a man may well be imagined.

His education had been neglected. He knew Italian, English and German, which was a good deal, and meant more in his day, when people did not learn foreign languages. He prided himself on his knowledge of artillery and political economy, the art of war and social philosophy. With but little of the artist in him, he took no interest in either literature or art.

He was supported by a wife, the beautiful Empress, who also had more heart than head. She liked books, but only for their bindings. She was talkative, " but flitted from one **The Empress.** subject to another," said Hübner, " like most Spanish women do; they are more vivacious than witty and more witty than profound." She was religious, but in a superstitious way, and did not care to have priests about her. She worshipped Marie Antoinette and collected souvenirs of the Queen who fell a victim to the Revolution, imagining that she too was destined to die on the scaffold. During the first few years of their married life the Emperor was in love with her, but he soon had fresh favourites.

The imperial family also included the old King Jerome, the brother of Napoleon I, and, more important still, his two **The Imperial Family.** children, the cousins of Napoleon III. Prince Jerome, who resembled Napoleon I in profile and cultivated the likeness, lived in the Palais Royal. One of the Montagnards of the Legislative Assembly, intelligent and brutal, he was fundamentally anti-clerical and democratic in tendency, and " kept to the Left of his cousin "; while Princess Mathilde, who was separated from her husband Demidof, was interested in art and literature and thus played a part in the intellectual history of the day.

Etiquette at Court was extremely strict. At the official receptions the Emperor and Empress were seated on a dais under a canopy. On their left stood the Ministers and cour-

125

tiers, on their right the ladies. On the 1st of January, 1854, four hundred ladies in Court dresses with long trains were pre-

The Court. sented and made their curtsey to the two sovereigns. "Very few of them bore aristocratic names," observed Hübner with his usual malice, " but they got on fairly well all the same." This ceremony was repeated on the 1st of January, 1855, but Napoleon III was suffering from his first attack of gout and leant on a stick—he was already ageing.

The Court would have died of boredom had not every nerve been strained to provide entertainment. The Empress had a

Festivities. reception every afternoon from four to six, while in the evening there was always a ball, a concert or some sort of show. At first the Emperor was afraid of public opinion; after a dinner to a hundred guests at Fontainebleau there was a dance, but the music was provided by a barrel-organ which a General and the Grand Master of the Ceremonies took turns to grind. Napoleon was afraid that if musicians were employed they might describe " what they had seen and what they had not seen." Little by little he overcame these fears. Every Thursday there was a Court function to which eight hundred guests were invited. On the other days of the week officials and Ministers gave parties. The objections that carping tongues were ready to raise against " this whirl of festivities and pleasures " were forestalled in the columns of the *Moniteur*, where it was pointed out that " the money spent on a grand ball fell back in a rain of gold on the various industries." Dancing was a necessity—it " was good for trade." And so dances were given. Before long fancy-dress balls with masks became the fashion—there were pierrots and pierrettes, Turks, Greeks, Neapolitan peasants, grand ladies, shepherdesses and follies ; the most dignified Ministers and the highest ladies in the land dressed up and made caricatures of themselves. The Emperor and Empress wore dominoes, " fondly imagining they would not be recognised." To prevent any possibility of foul play, the guests were requested not to wear their masks when they first arrived. At the Carnival of 1857 the Empress made two " appearances," first as Diana the Huntress, and afterwards as the wife of a Doge. The Emperor was a knight in black and red. On another occasion, Madame de Castiglione, of whom

126

the Emperor was very fond, appeared as a gipsy fortune-teller, with her hair hanging loose over her bare shoulders, and her short skirts revealing an extremely fine pair of legs.

They tried to amuse themselves in other ways as well—with table-turning and experiments in hypnotism. In 1857 a Scottish medium named Hume made the table talk in the name of Queen Hortense and predicted a two-years war. An accordion was seen to rise in the air and play all by itself. Amusement **Charades.** was also provided by very simple diversions such as charades, which were extremely fashionable. A certain well-known dancing hall at that time was known as the *Bal Musard ;* the name provided the word for a charade in which the word *muse* was first represented, and then the word *arrhes* (deposit), the " whole " being a dance *à la musarde* performed by the Emperor and Empress. At an open-air festival held at Villeneuve-l'Etang in 1857, the storming of the Malakoff was acted, the Empress and her ladies defending a mound representing the tower, while the Emperor and his courtiers stormed the position. It was whispered in horrified Orleanist salons that " the Emperor had made the attack on all-fours " and that " he had caught hold of the ladies by their feet." They also played Blind Man's Buff, Eugénie's favourite game. Charming puerilities, but not devoid of danger ! Malignant tongues talked about the " orgies " held at Court. At all events, on occasion the strictest etiquette was changed almost in the twinkling of an eye into carnival pranks and the familiarity of children at play. The sedate bourgeois life of Louis Philippe's Court was at an end.

In 1856 the house parties at Compiègne began—the guests were invited in relays to stay for a week. Everything was **Compiègne.** arranged down to the minutest detail. The guests were received between rows of lackeys, with a pair of *Cent Guardes* at each door, and were welcomed by the Prefect of the Palace, who placed a valet at the disposal of every member of the party. A hundred sat down to dinner, a military band played throughout the meal and a footman stood behind every chair. After which, " to while away the evening," there was dancing. At midnight everybody retired to bed. Nothing was arranged for the morning, but at two o'clock the whole party went hunting or drove out in char-à-

THE SECOND EMPIRE

bancs to visit the ruins at Pierrefonds. And this occupied the interval until dinner-time.

Town life naturally vied with that of Court circles in brilliance. Marcel Boulenger in his *Morny* describes the stream of carriages **Paris.** driving up and down the Champs Élysées in the afternoon : " Gently swaying on their luxurious springs these open carriages, drawn by four horses, these cradles, rocked Lilliputian sunshades and billowing crinolines from side to side. Or else light broughams like lacquer chests glided through the mist. A constant jingling of soft harness and steel curbs fell on the ear. The high-stepping horses hammered the ground as they trotted along or else hardly seemed to touch the ground with their hoofs, the postilions of the four-horsed carriages rose rhythmically in their stirrups, stiff as ramrods in their leather breeches, the coachmen held their whips, their reins and their heads high in air. . . . O gorgeous luxury ! O the joy of being alive ! " Morny drove by in his phæton, " perched up on huge wheels," driving his two black-and-white trotters. On the pavement the men and women about town, of whom Constantin Guys has given us a picture, watched the carriages drive past, whispering some scandal about one or other of their occupants. And already strangers were flocking to Paris to witness the glories of the Empire !

While the public mind was occupied in the contemplation of this pomp and splendour, the Emperor " governed through his **The Govern- ment.** Ministers." The latter used to meet twice a week, but the order of the day was decided by the Emperor himself, who put on the agenda only those subjects he thought it worth while to discuss. This ministerial council, which did not vote any measures or sign any documents, was an advisory committee and nothing more. The Emperor would listen, and after the meeting would come to a decision alone in his cabinet with the Minister concerned. He insisted on knowing everything and held himself alone responsible, the Minister having no power to act without his authority. But he soon saw that the mere desire to imitate Napoleon I was not sufficient to ensure success, and he sent his officials to glean information on the spot. But they were met by the sullen opposition of the bureaucrats and the apathy of the administra-

128

tion, while the weakness of the master was frequently unable to overcome these obstacles, which might possibly have defied the efforts of the First Consul himself.

Nevertheless, the achievements of the new *régime*, more particularly in connection with the army, must in all fairness be **Army Laws.** recognised. Thus, by a law of 1853 a separate fund was formed for Government pensions, of which the army reaped the advantage, as the military received their pensions sooner than civilians, and they were also higher in proportion to their contributions. Another law, passed in 1855, introduced changes into the recruiting system. Ever since 1818 a conscript had been allowed to find a substitute if he was rich enough to pay for one obtained through a private agent, the " purveyor of men " as he was called. Naturally these substitutes, who formed over a third of the strength, were nothing but riffraff. The law of 1855 put an end to the traffic of these dubious agencies by allowing the conscript to procure his discharge by paying a fixed sum to the State, the proceeds of which were to be applied to providing a bounty, increased pay (10 and later on 20 centimes a day) and a pension for those who re-enlisted. Finally, in 1857 the codification of military law was completed. Ever since 1797 justice had been dispensed by court-martial, the regulations of which were extremely severe, offences against discipline in time of peace being punishable with death, with right of appeal only to a military Appeal Court. The Code of 1857 was less strict and afforded greater safeguards for the prisoner without, however, admitting the plea of extenuating circumstances.

Furthermore, the Government turned its particular attention to economic reforms and enterprises which would provide work for the masses and money for the bourgeoisie, the aim of the dictatorship being to spread prosperity and thus breed oblivion of lost liberties. As Albert Thomas points out in his " Second Empire " in *l'Histoire Socialiste*, this policy was a direct development of Guizot's policy : " During a similar absence of parliamentary life, the Government of that day had proclaimed that its programme was 'to conduct the affairs of the nation efficiently' and to do its best to satisfy the demands of a 'healthy and peaceful nation.' " These, as we know, were

K

Guizot's words, "but they might have been Monsieur de Morny's." A good many of the men forming the Emperor's immediate circle had made their entry into public life under Guizot : men like Fould, the deputy for Tarbes; Magne, the deputy and Government official who was a protégé of Bugeaud; Billault, the lawyer and deputy; Morny, the beet-grower and sugar refiner, whom, under Guizot, Marrast had denounced as "the youngest and baldest of the smug and satisfied." As early as January 1847 Morny, writing in the *Revue des Deux Mondes*, called the attention of the ruling classes to the " practical solutions " and the material reforms which would do far more for the happiness of the people than any Socialist dreams. And thus the Second Empire merely carried on the policy of Guizot.

In this domain everything was in the hands of the Government; by merely issuing a decree it had the power of ordering the construction of great public works and arranging the contracts for them; it granted concessions for exploiting the land and authorised the floating of joint stock companies. Those who had inside information and were in a position to get wind of the schemes that were being hatched, and to receive favourable **Speculation.** or adverse news, could seize the opportunity of speculating advantageously in land that was to be expropriated, or on the Bourse. Morny was undoubtedly one of those who profited most by his official position. In Paris it was quite enough to tell capitalists that " Morny was in it " to make them part with their money. For Morny to have an interest in any concern was regarded as the best security. And everybody speculated in railways, War Loan, gas and mines. Women stole from their husbands in order to gamble, and the market fluctuations tallied with good or bad news from the Crimea. The telegraphic system made gambling possible even in the provinces, and there was a mad rush for money. In the end the Government became perturbed and made an unsuccessful attempt to put a stop to it. The worthy François **The Theatre.** Ponsard wrote a scathing denunciation of gambling in classic verse in his comedy *La Bourse* (1856); a few years previously (1853) he had depicted the conflict between honour and money in *l'Honneur et l'Argent*, and had made honour win the day—as it always does in the theatre. And good Émile Augier described the power of money in *Le Gendre de Monsieur Poirier* (1854, written in collaboration with Jules Sandeau), in which the " Old Liberal " Poirier, after working fourteen hours a day for thirty years and amassing a fortune, dreams of being made Baron Poirier. The scene, it is true, is laid in 1846, in the time of Louis Philippe, but the state of society in 1854 was a repetition of what it had been under Guizot, and the voice of authority could once more say : " Get rich ! " Again, in *Ceinture Dorée* (1855) Augier makes old Roussel, who is too clever and too rich for any gentleman to be ready to marry his daughter, exclaim : " There now, so I am no gentleman, I who have three millions ! " Last but not least, the younger Dumas dealt with the financial question in his play *La Question d'Argent* (1857), in which gambles on the Bourse provide one of the mainsprings of the plot.

This mania, in many respects so disastrous, did at least lead to one or two lasting institutions. There was a whole school of economists, disciples of St. Simon, who expected universal happiness to result from material progress, the development of public works, the establishment of the credit system and of co-operation in work and industry. They took little interest in politics and had held themselves aloof throughout the turmoil of 1848. But now their day had dawned. Père Enfantin dedicated books to the Emperor. " The rostrum and the Press must be silenced for a time," he wrote, " so that the hammer alone may ring out where shot and shell once boomed, so that man may inscribe his iron hieroglyphics on the ground instead of putting political conundrums on paper." But this did not make him renounce his profound idealism : " The spirit slumbers, the flesh keeps watch and works. . . . The hands of the workers are full of power, their heads swim in frenzy, and in their wild bacchanalian dance they curse the spirit, the mind, so that it would seem to have vanished and returned to the bosom of its Maker. But it is still there, the rogue, rubbing its hands and whispering : ' Go on, sing, dance the *cancan* and pull the puppet strings.' Meanwhile earth and labour are in travail ; they are creating a new world ; and if this new world should be born in the midst of all this filth and squalor, what matter ?

The St. Simonians.

We shall make it clean." His was the curious attitude of the intellectual surrounded by hedonists and money-grubbers, puppets whose strings he could see and who in their blind dance were making towards a distant goal of which he alone was aware. Barrault sang the praises of the railways : " Europe will soon have her network of railways from the Ural Mountains to the Sierra Nevada; she will be fed by a single financial system and will breathe the same moral atmosphere everywhere." There were several St. Simonians in the immediate circle of the Emperor—the Pereire brothers, who studied problems connected with credit, Michel Chevalier, a Councillor of State, and an advocate of Free Trade, and last but not least, Géroult, a journalist and friend of Prince Napoleon. They were not mere theorists, but practical men and they played a direct personal part in the great enterprises of the day.

By a decree of February 1852 Land banks (*banques foncières*) were organised for the purpose of granting landed proprietors long loans on first mortgages, redeemable by annuities (interest 5 per cent. with a further 1 or 2 per cent. for redemption), and authorised to raise capital by the issue of debentures on the security of the mortgages, the object being to put at the disposal of the landowner the funds necessary for improving his estate and for building. The innovation in the scheme, which was borrowed from Germany, consisted in redemption by annuities over a long period, which was not such a crushing burden on the landowner as an ordinary mortgage. The idea had been studied under Louis Philippe and an attempt had been made to put it into practice under the Second Republic. It was left to Napoleon III to make it a reality after the *coup d'état*. Land banks were opened in Paris, Marseilles and Nevers, that is to say, in the very towns and districts where the *coup d'état* had met with the worst reception—clearly those in power were confident that these institutions would do much towards securing the welfare of the people and calming men's minds. Before long, in order to attain greater unity and facilitate payment, it was decided to merge these banks into a single institution under Government control, and on the 10th of December, 1852, the *Crédit Foncier de France* was founded, the activities of which were to extend over the whole country. It received a subsidy of 10 million francs (£400,000) from the sale of the property belonging to the House of Orleans, but was allowed to charge only 5 per cent., to include redemption, its loans not **The *Crédit*** to exceed half the value of the property mortgaged. **Foncier.** In practice it advanced loans chiefly to owners of urban property—rural landowners were more suspicious and less enterprising—and it was by its help that many of the buildings constructed during this period came into being.

In November 1852 the Pereire brothers founded the *Société Générale de Crédit Mobilier*, the object of which was to finance commercial undertakings, to issue loans on securities **The *Crédit*** held, to facilitate the prosecution of great public **Mobilier.** enterprises by providing them with capital, and to develop the powers of credit. Isaac Pereire extolled the genius of Law, who had " revealed to the world the power of co-opera-tion." His *Crédit Mobilier* was destined to fail just as Law's Bank had done, but in the meantime it provided a powerful impetus to the growth of railways in France, Spain and Italy, it secured the monopoly for fifty years of the six gas companies in Paris, which it amalgamated into one concern, and created the Transatlantic Company. In 1855 the *Crédit Mobilier* paid its shareholders a dividend of 178 francs 50. The Bank of France was also authorised to make advances on securities deposited with it, being granted the privilege for fifty years, and it soon had at least one branch in every department.

The most important undertaking of the period, however, consisted in the development of the railway system. The lines had been begun by Louis Philippe, by virtue of a law **The** of 1842, but they were very far from complete in **Railways.** 1848, and under the Second Republic very little was done to them. The lines from Valenciennes, Boulogne, Calais and Le Havre were finished, but in other directions the railways from Paris went no further than Chartres, Poitiers, Nevers, Chalon-sur-Saône and Nancy, making a total of 2,250 miles as compared with 6,875 in England, 5,000 in Germany and about 530 in little Belgium. The system was in the hands of about twenty separate companies, each of whom had its own tariff, and the expenses of running were ruinous for some of them, while travellers were obliged to be constantly changing.

133

The companies did not dare to build new lines, especially over cross-country routes, which would certainly not pay expenses. Furthermore, there was an inclination to think that a railway would in some cases merely be competing with water transport— between Paris and Marseilles the railways ran from Paris to Chalon and from Avignon to Marseilles. What need was there to complete the line between Chalon and Avignon, since the Saône and the Rhone, those " moving roadways," were available for transport ? In short, things were at a standstill and at a discount, and there was a slump in railway securities on the Bourse.

Whereupon the Emperor and Morny decided to take action. A week after the *coup d'état* a decree was issued arranging for the opening of a line round Paris on the right bank, inside the fortifications. In order to facilitate the redemption of capital the concessions granted to the companies were extended for a term of 99 years, and a minimum rate of interest of 4 per cent. was guaranteed for half the duration of the concession. And, more important still, in order to reduce expenses, large companies were formed, so that deficits on the small lines could be met by the surplus from the large ones. The *Nord*, the *Orléans*, the *Paris–Lyon* and *Lyon–Méditerranée* companies were already in existence. In 1853 the *Midi* and the *Grand Central* companies were formed (the latter was abolished in 1857, being divided between the *Orléans* and *Lyon* companies); in 1854 the *Compagnie de l'Est* and in 1855 the *Compagnie de l'Ouest* came into being. In 1858 the *Paris–Lyon* and *Lyon–Méditerranée* systems were amalgamated. At the end of 1858 there were over 10,000 miles of railway. Between 1854 and 1857 the important line from Paris to Marseilles and the Saint-Quentin–Erquelines line to Liége and Germany were finished. The railway ran to Nantes, Bordeaux, Limoges, Clermont, Issoire, Grenoble, Bâle, Mulhausen and Metz. A series of accidents at one time alarmed the public mind, but the regulations for the running of the trains were improved and confidence was restored. The opening of a railway in distant towns always afforded the occasion for a ceremony at which the authorities blessed the Government which had been responsible for bringing the metals and the heavy engines to such a vast distance. And the admiration felt by

134

the populace made no distinction between the new invention and the power which had brought it to their door (P. de la Gorce).

At this time the telegraphic system was also developed; it had been in use since 1850 for private messages only. In 1855 **The Telegraph System.** the electric telegraph reached Mende, the only prefecture which had not been placed in communication with Paris. Telegrams were extremely expensive; there was a fixed charge of 2 francs for twenty words and an additional charge of 10 centimes for every six miles. The scale of charges was reduced in 1858, telegrams were nevertheless rarely used—on occasions of great rejoicing or great sorrow.

The Government also took an interest in maritime transport to supplement the railways. Here too previous Governments **Ocean Transport.** had limited their activities to arranging for subsidies, although in England steamship companies had long been in existence. The Emperor had the Chambers of Commerce, naval engineers, and makers of machinery and ships consulted, and in 1857 a law was passed to subsidise three transatlantic lines—from Le Havre to New York, from Saint Nazaire to the Antilles, Mexico, Colon and Cayenne, and from Bordeaux to Senegal, Brazil and Buenos-Ayres.

In addition to all this there was the rebuilding of Paris. Immediately after the *coup d'état* it was decided to build the **Rebuilding of Paris.** *Palais de l'Industrie,* to enlarge the Halles which Baltard was engaged in building, to complete the Palais du Louvre and lay out the Bois de Boulogne. The Gare de l'Est was joined to the boulevards by the Boulevard de Strasbourg, the Rue de Rivoli was continued eastward beyond the Louvre and the Rue des Écoles was begun. But the Prefect of the Seine was not the right man for the job, he was an "ædile of the old days." On the 1st of July, 1853, his place at **Haussmann.** the Hôtel de Ville was taken by Haussmann, who remained there for sixteen years, that is to say, almost throughout the reign. On the occasion of his grand tour before the proclamation of the Empire the Prince President had noticed this Prefect—a brawny Alsatian, a talker and an epicure, an ogre for work, despotic, insolent, self-confident, full of initiative and daring and caring not a straw for legality. "Everything in him is great," observed Rouher, "both his

135

virtues and his vices." Haussmann was given a far from cordial welcome in Paris by Delangle, the President of the Municipal Council, although the latter owed his office to the Emperor. " We promise you our support in advance for all such measures as are not beyond the resources of the city," he observed. But Haussmann paid no attention to him. He set to work cutting and hewing into the flesh of the ancient city with all the devil-may-care freedom of a sapper captain digging trenches and parallels on a battle-field. His aim was to have open spaces round the palaces, churches and barracks so that they might be more easily defended in case of disturbance and be accessible at ordinary times, to pull down the tortuous alleys of old Paris, the refuge of insurgents where recruits to defend the barricades were raised, and to cut broad boulevards allowing for the circulation of troops and civilians both in the heart of the city and in the neighbourhood of the railway stations. He wanted to make Paris a city where, in case of disturbances, the police and the military could intervene swiftly and easily. Thenceforward the erection of barricades, which had been far too much in evidence under Louis Philippe and in 1848, became practically impossible. This " haussmannisation " was animated by political rather than æsthetic considerations. The expense? Rubbish ! " Extraordinary expenditure is not detrimental to the budget; if it is intelligently applied it enriches rather than impoverishes a community and leads to a general increase of revenue." Foreigners and provincials were expected to contribute to this end; they would be attracted to the fine new city and would flock there to spend their money and " would pay the expenses of the new buildings." The shops would reap a harvest, the bourgeoisie would invest their money in the ground rents of the new streets, and the working classes would be provided with full-time employment. Thus everything would be for the best under the best of all possible Prefects !

The first task to be carried out was the cutting of the " great cross roads " through Paris, an artery running north and south from the Boulevard de Strasbourg, called the Boulevard du Centre (after the Crimea it was renamed Sebastopol), and extending to the Observatoire, and an artery running east and west formed by the extension of the Rue de Rivoli as far as the

136

Rue St. Antoine. The Boulevard du Centre and the new Rue de Rivoli " disembowelled " the old quarters of St. Denis, St. Martin and St. Antoine, the haunts of insurgents. The Hôtel de Ville was also cleared and the avenue leading to it was named after Queen Victoria on the occasion of her visit to Paris. And everywhere bourgeois houses of uniform height and style were built, and are still the most common type of building in Paris, at all events in the central quarters.

These vast alterations were by no means universally welcome, and an outcry was raised against the various loans the city had to raise to pay for them, the expenditure naturally being far in excess of the estimates; and the public complained of the rise in rents. A cartoon by Daumier depicts Monsieur Vautour, the Paris landlord, in his dressing-gown, with his hands on his belly, watching the demolitions from his window : " Good," he exclaims, " there is another house being broken up. . . . I shall raise the rents of my tenants two hundred francs." The *Moniteur* did its best to reassure the public, declaring that the crisis was only temporary, that wages would also rise and that a large number of workmen's dwellings would be built to replace the old hovels. Moreover, there were a great many people who did very well for themselves; expropriated tenants and landlords demanded huge compensation, and the jury appointed to decide their case nearly always gave it. In order that heavier damages might be claimed, leases were ingeniously renewed just before the work of demolition was started, people even deliberately settling down along the route of the projected new thoroughfares, and some of them managing to secure compensation several times over. False inventories and account books were produced and borrowed goods were displayed (P. de la Gorce). " How did you make your fortune? " Maxime du Camp inquired of one man who had suddenly grown rich. " I was turned out of my house," was the reply. Those in the immediate circle of the Prefect were extremely advantageously placed for specula-

Speculation. tion and they took full advantage of their opportunities. These abuses, however, did not prevent the work that was carried out from being a remarkable achievement. On Sundays crowds of working-men and shopkeepers went to see how the building was progressing and were filled with

THE SECOND EMPIRE

admiration of the half-finished streets with their water and gas
mains under the macadam which had replaced the old paving-
stones, the rows of lamps which would light them at night,
and the young saplings which in due course would provide shade
and green foliage in the avenues and boulevards. The provincial towns, and first among them Marseilles, Le Havre,
Lyons and Lille, naturally followed the example set by Paris.

Nevertheless, the years during which these great building
operations were being carried on were not as prosperous as had
been hoped. This was due to the fact that in 1853 the harvest
was extremely bad, and in 1854 it was not much better—the
price of wheat rose to 26 francs the hectolitre, and then to 30
Disasters. and 33, although the importation of foreign corn
was allowed, help and subsidies were given, and an
attempt was made to control the price of bread by means of a
Bakers' Fund, which provided compensation by putting on a
duty when the harvests were good and thus preventing a rise of
prices in bad years. The agricultural depression was universal
throughout the country, potatoes, vines and silkworms all being
attacked by disease. In 1854 and 1855 there was a plague of
cholera which carried off 150,000 victims. To crown all, in
1855 and 1856 the Garonne and then the Rhone and the Loire
overflowed their banks, and the authorities undertook to deal
with the floods. " I regard it as a point of honour," the Emperor
declared in 1857, " that under my rule the rivers, like the forces
of revolution, should keep to their beds and be unable to leave
them."

The new *régime* was anxious to provide Paris with an ocular
demonstration of its activities, and in spite of all these catas-
The trophes and the tedious prolongation of the war
Exhibition in the Crimea, it organised the International Exhibi-
of 1855. tion of 1855. It was an old idea which had first been
mooted in 1830, and which some attempt at realising had been
made in 1849. But England had taken the lead and had held
an International Exhibition at the Crystal Palace in 1851. The
Empire wished to do likewise and to go one better. On the
8th of March, 1853, it was decided that an International Exhibition should be opened in Paris on the 1st of May, 1855, and
Prince Jerome was made President of the *Commission Centrale*
138

de l'Exposition. Although the space provided by the *Palais de l'Industrie* was somewhat cramped, the building of annexes enabled it to serve the purpose of the exhibitors. Of course everything was behindhand, and on the 15th of May, when the Exhibition was opened, nothing was ready. It was only at the end of June that it was really in full swing. There were 20,000 exhibitors, half of whom were foreigners. It included an Art section in which the works of living French and foreign artists were on show. The crowd naturally flocked to the sections where clothes and jewellery were exhibited. But a certain number also visited the galleries where gas radiators, agricultural machinery and railway engines were displayed—the latter were so new that they were regarded as fit exhibits. Here the masses were shown the commercial uses of rubber, food-preserving and photography. The Exhibition, which was visited by 5,000,000 people, was a great success (at the Exhibition of 1867 there were 15 millions, and at the Exhibition of 1889, 82 millions). In addition to Queen Victoria and Prince Albert several crowned heads came to Paris for the Exhibition, among them the King of Portugal and the King of Sardinia. While this first Exhibition was not the glorious function of 1867, it nevertheless already reflected the dawn of the prosperity that was to characterise the Second Empire.

Throughout the period just described political life was almost at a standstill in France. The Emperor himself expounded the theory of the imperial autocracy : "Liberty has never helped to found a lasting political edifice," he declared; "she crowns it after time has consolidated it." But these early years were still years of construction and the time for liberty had not yet come. The most important body in the State was clearly the one that initiated schemes of legislation in accordance with the wishes of the authorities, that is to say, the Council

The Council of State. of State. Of this body Baroche was President; he was an ex-President of the order of French advocates, and erstwhile Attorney-General of the Court of Appeal, an opponent of Guizot, a Republican in '48, a supporter of law and order in '49, and of the *coup d'état*; under his dignified exterior he was a clever man, an accomplished orator and a good official. He had as his colleague Parieu, a native of Auvergne, who came into prominence in '48 when he opposed the election of the President by universal suffrage, although subsequently, when the latter had been returned to power by these suffrages, he got on very well with him; he was instrumental in having the *loi Falloux* passed. He was a learned jurist with a philosophical turn of mind.

The Legislative Body, which sat for three months in the year, in the spring, was mainly composed of rural landowners, **The Legislative Body.** moderate Conservatives, though they were not as docile as might have been supposed. They could not, of course, be expected to oppose a Government of which they had been the official candidates, but, on the other hand, they occasionally rebelled against the servile part they were called upon to play. They complained, for instance, that the Council of State too frequently sent them Bills at the end of the session, when they had not sufficient time to study them at leisure, and that the reports of their debates were sent to the newspapers three days late and were moreover quite colourless. And their opposition to the proposed pension for the widow of Marshal Ney was so pronounced that in the end the Government withdrew the Bill. (The imperial Government, however, put up a statue to Ney at Port Royal, on the spot where he had been shot, which afforded an opportunity for Rude to produce a masterpiece.) They declared themselves protectionist with such firmness and determination that for the time being all idea of lowering the customs dues was dropped. They were always endeavouring to reduce expenditure, discussing ways and means *in camera* with the Councillors of State or the heads of Government departments. They protested against the increase of loans and local dues. But in the end they were nearly always persuaded to give way; if necessary the Emperor summoned the recalcitrant members one by one to the Tuileries and overcame their scruples.

In 1854, when Billault was made Minister of the Interior, the Legislative Body was provided with a suitable President in the **Morny.** person of Morny, who had returned to favour after his half-brother had for some years turned the cold shoulder on him. "The cleverness of Monsieur de Morny

140

consisted in the fact that although he had been appointed by Napoleon III, he immediately came forward not as the servant of the Emperor but as the mouthpiece of the Assembly. "With consummate art he applied himself to espousing its cause, to safeguarding its dignity, and defending its privileges against all and sundry, from mere councillors of State to the sovereign himself" (P. de la Gorce). And it was small wonder that he could get all he wanted from "his" Legislative Body, seeing that an assembly naturally respects a leader who succeeds in making it respected. He knew exactly how to talk to every one of the deputies, discussing agriculture with one, industry with another, and behaving as a man of the world towards them all. A conversationalist rather than an orator and affecting a certain contempt for rhetoric, he would preside over debates " lying back in his armchair, looking as though he were asleep and tired out," just as Alphonse Daudet depicts him in his *Souvenirs d'un homme de lettres*. Again, in *Le Nabab*, of whom Morny is the original, Daudet writes : " Nobody knew better than he did how to ascend the rostrum with a smile. . . . A paradoxical air of distinction ! . . . He was easy in his smallest gestures, which were in any case extremely rare, allowing half-finished sentences to fall carelessly from his lips, the shadow of a smile illumining the gravity of his face, and hiding beneath an impenetrable mask of courtesy the bottomless contempt he felt for men and women alike." No one was better gifted than this grand gentleman at ending a dangerous debate with a word, or stopping a speech with the ghost of a smile. He allowed Montalembert " to make remarks put forward with tact, loyalty and good-will." It was to this that interpellations were reduced ! In short, Morny was the ideal President for transforming the Assembly into a polite gathering. When the Legislative Body was dissolved on the 29th of May, 1857, a year before its mandate ended, the *Moniteur* sang its praises : " Deprived of the dangerous privilege of making and unmaking Ministers . . . it was able to discuss Bills in peace undisturbed by political passions " and to pass 979 laws in five years.

The Senate, an assembly of venerable greybeards, who were supposed to confine their activities to making sure that the laws did not infringe the Constitution, naturally went beyond their

141

powers and discussed the laws themselves, as had been the case with the old Chamber of Peers, of which some of the senators **The Senate.** had been members. Although these debates were held *in camera* and were not reported in the Press, they disquieted the authorities, who on more than one occasion sharply reminded the senators of their real duties : " The Senate, in discussing measures which it has no right to modify, is performing a futile and consequently unauthorised duty, unless the measures under discussion infringe the Constitution. The senators would be better advised to scour the country, to discover its needs and suggest reforms." In order to drive the lesson home, the Government had it reported in the *Moniteur*—and thus the Senate was never heard of except when it had been reprimanded. This admonition wounded the senators to the quick—the Vice-President resigned, and to have its revenge the Senate rejected as unconstitutional a proposed tax on luxury carriages and horses in Paris on the plea that a sumptuary tax of this description was illegal. Another incident arose between the Senate and the authorities after the birth of the Prince Imperial on the question of the regency of the Empress in the event of the death of the Emperor ; one of the senators, suspicious of the religious intolerance of the Spanish woman, insisted that the oath she would be called upon to swear should include the following words : " I swear . . . to respect the laws of the Concordat and freedom of worship." And this amendment was rejected only by a very narrow majority. This was all petty warfare, but, even had it wished, the Senate was not armed for anything else.

One of the most solid buttresses of the new *régime* was provided by the clergy. It was in keeping with imperial traditions to **The Clergy.** support the Church and be supported by her, and she was accordingly granted all manner of favours. The laws affecting the recognition of convents of nuns were simplified, new Catholic secondary schools were founded, especially in the north, Lacordaire was allowed to reopen the College at Sorèze in Tarn, and the *Congrégation de l'Oratoire* was also re-established ; the conferences at Notre Dame as well as the charitable works of the Order of Saint Vincent de Paul and the

142

Little Sisters of the Poor were encouraged; the Bishops' stipends were raised; part of the proceeds of the sale of the property belonging to the House of Orleans was applied to a pension fund for superannuated clergy; the hawking of anti-religious works was forbidden; cabarets were ordered to be closed on Sundays during the hours of divine service; priests were paid to recite the last prayers for the dead in the case of poor persons and met the funeral processions at the entrance to the cemeteries; and whereas all other gatherings were forbidden, the Church was left perfectly free to hold her little councils, a privilege she had not enjoyed under the Monarchy, but which the Republic had granted her; gifts and subsidies were made to religious buildings—Ste. Clotilde was finished at this time, and the restoration of Notre Dame, while Hippolyte Flandrin decorated the ancient church of St. Germain des Prés with frescoes; the Government and the army were officially represented at the Corpus Christi processions, and some of the Prefects attended Mass, "without quite knowing what they were doing," says Schoelcher, as they were not sure at what point in the service they were expected to stand up, to kneel down or to take their seats.

Nevertheless, those in the immediate circle of the Emperor took care to see that the Church did not acquire too much power over him, chief among them Jerome Napoleon, Persigny, Piétri, the Prefect of Police, Delangle and the " legists," that is to say, certain jurists inclined towards Jansenism and Gallicanism. And they put a stop to several schemes advanced by the religious party. The Church was anxious to secure the suppression or **The Articles Organiques.** revision of the *Articles organiques*, measures adopted for regulating the administration of divine worship, which had been added to the Concordat on the sole responsibility of the State without the consent of the Church. The Government allowed them to fall into disuse, but would not consent to revise them. The Church refused to admit that the religious solemnisation of marriage should be regarded as subordinate to the previous civil ceremony, but the authorities curtly refused to make any alteration in the law. The Church wished Sunday to be made a day of rest by law, but here again she met with a blank refusal in the *Moniteur*: " This is a ques-

143

tion which the conscience of every man is free to decide for itself and allows of neither constraint nor intimidation." Finally, in 1854 the Church was forced, willy nilly, to sanction a modification of the *loi Falloux*; in order to infuse fresh life and vitality into higher education, the departmental council, on which the Bishop and the Prefect each had a seat, was put under a Rector whose jurisdiction extended over five or six departments (there were sixteen Rectors for the whole of France), assisted by an academic council consisting entirely of University men. This reform had the inevitable result of increasing the autonomy of the University and decreasing the power of the departmental councils, which played a very minor part under these all-powerful Rectors, and at the same time it deprived the Bishop of a large part of his influence.

Last but not least, negotiations were carried on for months between the Vatican and the Tuileries. Napoleon III, with the memory of his uncle ever before him, wanted to be **Coronation** crowned in Paris by Pius IX as Napoleon I had **Plans.** been by Pius VII. And he brought pressure to bear on the Pope, not through the medium of his regular Ambassador but by means of secret envoys—a General and later some of the Bishops. The Vatican tried to turn the occasion to account to secure a revision of the *Articles organiques*. In the end the years rolled by and nothing was done.

About 1857 a certain coolness supervened in the tacit alliance between the Empire and the Church. " Obviously Napoleon is merely Louis Philippe to the *n*th," Veuillot wrote in one of his letters at this time; warnings were also issued to *l'Univers* and the *Correspondant*, an old Catholic review that had recently been revived. Nevertheless, in August 1858 the Emperor and Empress made a triumphal tour of Brittany, a Catholic and Royalist district, and Bishops and priests supported the Prefects in organising an enthusiastic reception. But the outbreak of the Italian War was destined to put an end to the alliance between the imperial Throne and the Altar.

The Press was dumb. The Government itself appointed the editor of every newspaper, even the Opposition journals, and those organs alone survived that the authorities allowed to do so. The Paris newspapers could be counted on the fingers

144

—the *Constitutionnel*, the *Pays*, the *Patrie*, which were Government organs, and *l'Univers*, a Catholic publication which supported the Empire and to which Louis Veuillot contributed. **The Press.** An ardent and intolerant Ultramontane, a vigorous not to say vulgar controversialist, though a finished stylist, Veuillot was extremely popular with the country clergy and openly at loggerheads with the more Liberal Catholics like Montalembert, Lacordaire, Dupanloup and Falloux. He had violent altercations with Monseigneur Sibour, Archbishop of Paris, who forbade his priests to read *l'Univers*. The conflict was ended only by the death of the Archbishop, who fell under the knife of an assassin early in 1857 at St. Etienne du Mont. The murderer was an unfrocked half-mad priest named Verger, who refused to accept the new dogma of the Immaculate Conception. " Down with all goddesses ! " he cried, as he plunged his knife into the Archbishop's body. The *Gazette de France*, *l'Union*, and *l'Assemblée Nationale* were Legitimist ; the *Journal des Débats*, Orleanist ; the *Siècle*, moderate Republican under the patronage of Prince Jerome ; and lastly the *Presse*, under Émile de Girardin, had a purely personal and somewhat capricious policy. In the absence of competition and with the help of advertisement, each of these journals was an extremely paying concern, " and all the more dependent on the Government, which could ruin it at one fell swoop " (Ch. Seignobos). " Warnings " were rare. The *Phare de la Loire*, published in Nantes, one of the two Republican newspapers tolerated in the provinces, received a warning for having said that a speech by Napoleon III had, " according to the Havas Agency, been several times interrupted by cries of *Vive l'Empereur !* " " . . . in view of the fact," ran the warning, "that this equivocal expression ill describes the outburst of enthusiasm which the Emperor's speech provoked." From the point of view of the Government the warning was justified, and the case brought against the *Phare de la Loire* was a typical example of the campaign of innuendo and ironic allusions which some of the independent organs waged against the Empire.

Even private conversations were subjected to official eavesdropping and people were prosecuted for having given utterance to " defeatist " sentiments, as we should say nowadays,

L

THE SECOND EMPIRE

regarding the price of corn, the plague of cholera and the vine mildew. The police called Jules Simon to order for imagining he could talk politics in his own house. At the beginning of the Crimean War, Persigny summoned the Presidents of the three aristocratic Clubs in Paris, and told them to hold their tongues on all political matters.

The Spy System.

Under such a rigorous system of supervision signs of opposition became more and more rare—silence reigned supreme. " Terrible corruption in Paris, terrible oppression in the provinces, and dark and painful silence everywhere," observed Duchâtel, who had been a Minister under the Monarchy. " All resistance is dead," said Cousin. " Nobody dares to raise his voice in the provinces or to write to Paris. The bourgeoisie . . . think only of money-making." When the economist Lavergne was asked for information about the state of the country, he replied, " How could I possibly get news? Nobody tells us anything, except the Government, and we do not believe what it says."

Nevertheless, in spite of all the activities of the police, signs of Royalist and Republican opposition were not lacking.

Owing to the fact that the clergy had rallied to the support of the Empire, the Legitimists had very little influence. " They sulk rather than act," remarked a certain Attorney-General with reference to their Party in the Limousin district. " They criticise everything the Government does, refuse to attend the salons of those in authority, and welcome bad news." Information reached Paris from the provinces that banquets in honour of the Pretender were being organised for St. Henry's Day, at which the halls were to be decorated with white flags and portraits of Henry V, and the names of the noble families mentioned who had the Holy Bread distributed in church stamped with the fleur-de-lis—nothing very dreadful. At the time of the Crimean War some of the Legitimists openly espoused the cause of the Tsar, the champion of authority and the enemy of the Revolution, and contrived to forget that one of the main objects of this war had been to safeguard the privileges of the Catholic clergy at the Sacred Places against the demands of the Greek Church. Their opposition was most in evidence in the west of France, and was characterised chiefly by abstention from voting and

The Legitimists.

146

refusal to perform any public office, the Comte de Chambord having forbidden his followers to take the oath of allegiance to the Empire.

The Orleanists, who were advocates of the parliamentary system, were more dangerous, and therefore more suspect. It is true that the majority of the bourgeoisie, who **The Orleanists.** were naturally Conservative and supporters of law and order, had rallied to the Empire. But the Party leaders, suddenly cut off from all political life, did not lay down their arms. Changarnier and Lamoricière, who were in Belgium, refused to take the oath, conveying their refusal in letters which Napoleon III regarded as offensive, while Thiers, Guizot, Broglie, Rémusat, Duchâtel, Molé and Barante gathered together in the salons, and hurled their epigrams at the new *régime*, and the upstarts who put on airs and graces at the Court of the Tuileries, and whispered a thousand and one anecdotes in one another's ears, which were eventually published abroad in *The Times*, the *Journal de Genève* and the *Indépendance Belge*. Meanwhile they made good use of the leisure afforded them by the absence of all political life; Thiers continued his *Histoire de l'Empire*, Tocqueville wrote his *Ancien Régime et la Révolution*, Prince Albert de Broglie went on with his *Histoire de l'Église au XVᵉ Siècle*, and Duvergier de Hauranne with his *Histoire du Gouvernement parlementaire en France de* 1814 *à* 1848, while Guizot finished his *Histoire de la Révolution d'Angleterre* and began his *Mémoires*. In none of these historical works was it easy to indulge in criticism of the imperial institutions, which found a more suitable outlet in the *Journal des Débats*, in the shape of innuendoes, allusions and veiled insults, the full savour of which only the initiated could enjoy. The editors of the journal were more or less celebrities—Samuel de Sacy, St. Marc Girardin, Laboulaye, John Lemoinne, Jules Janin, Cuvilier-Fleury and Hippolyte Rigault, ephemeral journalistic lights. One fine day the *Débats* reminded its readers that man doth not live by bread alone and that all was not for the best in the best of all possible worlds because the market price of cattle and the three per cents were rising. On another occasion the journal declared that the dictatorship was only a temporary expedient and that a normal and healthy system of Government ought to follow upon the period of convalescence. Detailed reports were printed of the debates in the English, Belgian and Piedmontese Parliaments. And these full accounts appearing cheek by jowl with the curt official communications on the Legislative Body provided further pinpricks for the Government. In due course a new editor was appointed in the person of Prévost-Paradol, who had been educated at the *École Normale*, " the school which leads to every profession, including that of teaching," and he made opposition by means of innuendo his speciality.

Another centre of Royalist opposition was to be found in the *Institut*. The *Académie Française* was the only independent elective body, and it turned the circumstance to **The Institut.** account. In 1854 the Academicians elected Monseigneur Dupanloup to their body. He enjoyed considerable moral prestige in the Church and had been one of the few Bishops to refrain from expressing his opinion or singing the praises of those in power. In 1855, Berryer, the great Legitimist orator, was elected; he referred to the Parliament as " the ruined theatre of his labours," and managed to avoid the usual presentation at Court after his election. In 1855 Samuel de Sacy, of the *Débats*, was added to the number; he deplored the fact that in the case of the Press " use had been suppressed at the same time as abuse, and that liberty had been subjected to regulations drawn up to deal with licence "; and in 1856 the Duc de Broglie became a member.

The Duke referred to the time " when France prided herself on having at great cost won a whole class of institutions of which the spoken word was in a sense the life and soul . . . in which there was a close alliance between literature and politics." Referring to the 18th Brumaire, he exclaimed : " Happy the man who succeeded in that world, happy not only because of his success, but because his faults were forgotten or redounded to his credit ! " And turning to the subject of his predecessor, Monsieur de St. Aulaire, the noble Duke added : " He was not allowed to die in time. . . . He saw the leaders of the State persecuted, proscribed and driven into exile." As P. de la Gorce says, the words rang out like a clarion call in the universal silence. And Broglie went on to pour anathema on " the

148

THE IMPERIAL AUTOCRACY

ungrateful oblivion of the past, the indifference to matters of principle, the eagerness to burn what yesterday had been adored, the thirst for change, for fresh possessions, the greed for gold, luxury and ease. . . . The glory of letters consists in refusing to suffer or endure the debasement of the human mind. . . . It is for us," he continued, addressing his colleagues, " to revive the cult of the eternal verities in the hearts of our contemporaries, to speak in its voice to the generation to come, to that generation which is reeling from its fall, which is swallowed up in doubt, and intoxicated with the interests of the day and the hour." Last but not least, the Legitimist Falloux was elected to fill the place vacated by Molé. There was a regular scramble for tickets to be present at the inaugural ceremony when these new members were received, and they became the topic of conversation in the salons for long afterwards. The Government pretended to be indifferent. It is true that it created in 1855 a new section of the *Académie*, the Moral Science Branch (administration, politics and finance), the ten members of which it appointed itself. But this new " batch " of Academicians, not unlike the " batches " of peers under the Monarchy, was not sufficient to change the character of the *Institut*. Apparently the Tuileries at one time thought of creating a rival *Académie*, which was to be more democratic and entirely dependent on the Emperor. But the idea was abandoned, and quite rightly. Such a creation would have been wrecked on the rock of ridicule. And Napoleon III confined himself to making fun of this opposition on the part of the Academy. " I hope, Monsieur le duc," he said, when Broglie was presented to him after his speech, " that your grandson will speak of the 2nd of December as you have spoken of the 18th Brumaire." This petty warfare was at bottom perfectly innocuous and gave the Government no cause for anxiety.

The Republican opposition was more formidable and a stricter watch was kept on this Party. The Attorneys-General carefully reported all its activities—the contraband importation of prohibited books, such as *Les Châtiments* by Victor Hugo, then in exile, which was smuggled through hidden in game baskets, in plaster busts of the Emperor,

The Re-publicans.

149

and the linings of clothes; parcels of red ties, of silk handkerchiefs with portraits of outlaws, seditious songs and cries printed on them, " seditious labels " on bottles of liquor, the circulation of penny-pieces on which the Emperor with his eye out and his throat cut was represented wearing a beard like Christ. But most of the leaders were abroad, chiefly in Belgium, where they foregathered at the *Galeries St. Hubert* in Brussels and published violent articles against the Empire in the Belgian Press, which on more than one occasion gave rise to diplomatic incidents between Napoleon III and Belgium. Chief among them were Deschanel, the father of the future President of the Republic, Challemel-Lacour, Edgar Quinet and Charras. The last two were engaged in historical studies and before long were obliged to make their way to Switzerland. Hugo, who wrote his account of the *coup d'état* in Brussels, under the title of *Histoire d'un Crime*, which was not published until 1877, as well as his *Napoléon le Petit*, was expelled from Belgium after the issue of the latter work in 1852 and settled down in Jersey, where he published his *Châtiments* in 1853, completed *Les Contemplations* (published in 1856) and began *La Légende des Siècles* (published in 1859). In 1855, on the conclusion of the Anglo-French Alliance, he was expelled from Jersey and took refuge in Guernsey. In London the exiles found Louis Blanc and Ledru-Rollin. They were living in great poverty in spite of the funds collected for them by Goudchaux in France. Barbès, the old prisoner of Belle-Ile, wrote a letter in 1854 sending his best wishes to the soldiers in the Crimea who were fighting against the reactionary Tsar. Napoleon III ordered him to be set free. He refused, and had to be driven out by force, whereupon he decided to go and live in Holland. The activities of all these leaders separated from their flock were necessarily of but little avail. The smuggling of cheap editions of the *Châtiments* and *Napoléon le Petit* into France was not enough to bring about the downfall of the detested *régime*.

The Opposition had its own organ in France, the *Siècle*, but it could say only what the Tuileries allowed it to say, while the authorities found it a useful medium for " sending out feelers " outside the inspired Press and for launching at will an anticlerical offensive whenever there were strained relations between the Church and the Empire. " The *Siècle* is under the protection of the police," observed Veuillot of *l'Univers*, " and *l'Univers* is under their supervision."

The Republican students found opportunities for holding demonstrations against their masters who had rallied to the Empire, organising a " rag " against Sainte Beuve at the *Collège de France* and against Nisard at the Sorbonne. They read Hugo with avidity, as well as Proudhon and *l'Histoire de la Révolution* by Michelet. The latter had retired to Nantes on being deprived by the imperial Government of his Chair at the *Collège de France*, and forced to resign his post at the *Archives Nationales* because he refused to take the oath of allegiance to the Emperor. Republican members of the working classes flocked to the funerals of the democrats—Marrast, Madame Raspail and Arago in 1853, Lamennais in 1854, David d'Angers in 1856, and Béranger and Cavaignac in 1857. But in order to avoid disturbances the authorities nearly always " confiscated the body to which honour was to be done," official delegates, troops and bodies of police were sent to the funeral and the obsequies were hurried through as quickly as possible in order to prevent demonstrations.

In spite of all the efforts of the authorities there were still Republicans in France, and above all in Paris, and great care was taken at the elections of 1857 to prevent them **Elections of 1857.** from raising their heads. The Government naturally had its own official candidates " and openly made public the names of those who carried its confidence and seemed deserving of that of the electorate "; they were nearly all deputies from the Legislative Body. Over-zealous busybodies at Court made an attempt to exclude anybody who showed any signs of independence, but Morny took up the cudgels on their behalf. In the departments there were many leading lights who dreamt of a seat in the Legislative Body, and the Prefects had their work cut out to ward off these people, who maintained they were " the Emperor's candidates," and to secure the privileged position of the genuine official candidate. The Prefects conducted the electoral campaign with a high hand, forbidding the non-official candidate to post up his programme, prohibiting the formation of electoral committees of

151

any kind, and all " special meetings," but above all doing everything in their power to prevent abstentions which would have provided proof positive of the Laodicean attitude of the country towards the Empire. " The name of the Emperor," cried the Prefect of the Dordogne district, waxing lyrical, " shines out like a beacon whose light the mists born of intrigue cannot hide; its rays illumine this urn and reveal to every eye the right road along which for the last six years we have found safety and honour. . . . The Government desires the triumph of its candidates as God desires the triumph of good, though He leaves to every man the free choice of evil."

In Paris the authorities did not have such an easy task. The *Siècle*, it is true, was sent a warning for having dared to say that official candidature constituted an attack on the principles of '89 : " The Imperial Government, founded upon the sovereignty of the people and the principles of '89, cannot allow any calumniation of the ideas of order and progress which it represents and of which the mass of the electorate approves." But the Government found it impossible to prevent the Republicans from forming a Committee to prepare the ground for the elections in the Seine district. The latter, however, had some difficulty in coming to an agreement. A preliminary list was drawn up consisting chiefly of men of '48—Cavaignac (who died a few months later), Carnot, Goudchaux, Bethmont, Garnier-Pagès and Bastide, with the addition of two young men, Jules Simon and Émile Ollivier, the latter the son of one of the exiles of 1851.

But this list was far from pleasing to the younger generation of Republicans, who wanted to have done with a personnel that had had its day, " old greybeards," and were anxious to take the reins into their own hands, to swear the oath of allegiance to the imperial Government if necessary, and to fight it with the weapons provided for them by the Constitution. Some young lawyers led the dance. One of them, Ernest Picard, in conjunction with Nefftzer, the future founder of the *Temps*, who at that time was contributing to the *Presse*, secured from the *Siècle* permission to draw up a modified list on which the chief changes introduced were the substitution of Ollivier for Garnier-Pagès, of Darimon, a democratic journalist, for Bastide,

152

and the addition of Laboulaye, of the *Débats*, as a sop to the Orleanist bourgeoisie. In spite of being thus divided against itself the Opposition won five out of the ten Seine seats; the successful candidates were Carnot, Goudchaux, Cavaignac, Ollivier and Darimon. Like Lyons, where Hénon was again elected, and other provincial towns, Paris was still a Republican city which had never laid down her arms and would never do so. Out of the total number of votes registered, there were, even according to Government figures, 665,000 against the official candidates and 5,471,000 for. The Empire had against it all who were not included in the ranks of the indifferent, the great Conservative mass who voted as they were told to. And however overwhelming its majority, this minority provided sufficient cause for anxiety—and the Emperor was indeed anxious.

But he allowed nothing of all this to be seen in the official festivities of the moment. 1855 had been the year of the Exhibition and the visit of Queen Victoria, 1856 had witnessed the Congress of Paris and the birth of his son. In 1857 the Emperor presided in person over the manœuvres held at the camp of Châlons. On the 15th of August he opened the new Louvre and had a new medal struck called the *médaille de Sainte Hélène*, bearing the image of Napoleon I and held by a red and green ribbon like the recent *Croix de guerre*. It was to be presented to all the veterans who had " served between 1792 and 1815 "; on the reverse of the medal was the inscription : " To my companions in glory my last thoughts. Saint Helena, 5th of May, 1821." Shortly afterwards a home of refuge at Vincennes for *industrial patients*, members of the working-classes who had been injured at work and convalescents, was opened with great pomp and ceremony. It was about this time too that news was received that Marshal Randon had completed the subjugation of Kabylie, and the Emperor paid another visit to Queen Victoria in England, and shortly afterwards had an interview with the Tsar at Stuttgart. As he was not enamoured of the things of the spirit, the intellectual activities of the Court were limited to the charades at the Tuileries and Compiègne. It was left to the magistrates to see to the censorship of morals. During this year two masterpieces were published whose names appeared in the judicial reports—Flaubert's *Madame Bovary* and Baudelaire's *Fleurs du Mal*—which led to the prosecution of their respective authors. Thus the only common bond between these two works, which will defy the hand of time and have outlived the ephemeral system of their day, consists in the judicial proceedings taken against them!

But in this atmosphere of authority and triumph there was an element which caused the Emperor even more anxiety than the opposition at the elections—and that was the existence of conspiracies. The imperial police were constantly frustrating or forestalling them; occasionally they took action too late. Ever since the beginning of the reign proceedings had been taken in one case after another. In 1852 and 1853 emissaries of the *Commune révolutionnaire*, a group of exiles in London who were accused of fomenting civil war, were arrested; in Lyons the *Voraces*, and in the west and central provinces a Republican Society known as *Marianne* were prosecuted. In June 1853 some working-men were arrested; apparently they had planned to kill the Emperor at the Hippodrome or the Opéra Comique. In 1854 an infernal machine was discovered on the railway over which the Emperor was to travel on the following day. This was followed in 1855 by Pianori's crime, which has already been described in connection with the Crimea, and shortly afterwards a lunatic named Bellemare made another attempt on the Emperor's life. In August of the same year a regular insurrection broke out among the slate-workers of Trélazé, who were said to belong to the *Marianne* and complained of the dearness of living. Six hundred men occupied the gendarmerie barracks, seized some arms and marched to Angers, where they came up against the military and were dispersed. In 1857 some Italians were arrested, among them a certain Tibaldi, who had plotted to kill the Emperor. Mazzini was found to have been implicated in the plot and also a certain *Drou-Rolline* of London, as one of the Italian prisoners pronounced the name. Naturally the police at once recognised Ledru-Rollin. Shortly afterwards, on news having been received that the Republic had been proclaimed in Paris, an insurrection broke out at Chalon-sur-Saône. Last but not least on the 14th of January, 1858 . . .

154

THE IMPERIAL AUTOCRACY

On the 14th of January, 1858, at half-past eight in the evening, Napoleon III and the Empress Eugénie were going to the Opera, at that time situated in the Rue Le Peletier almost at the corner of the great boulevards, to see a performance for the benefit of a famous singer of the day, the baritone Massol. In the carriage, which was preceded and surrounded by blue-and-white lancers, was the Emperor in black and the Empress in evening dress under a white cashmere cloak, accompanied by General Roguet, the son of a Waterloo hero. As they drove past the crowd shouted " *Vive l'Empereur !* " The carriage was just about to drive under the awning in front of the theatre when in a blinding flash there was a loud detonation like a cannon-shot, followed by two others at intervals of a few seconds. The windows were shivered to bits, the gas lamps on the front of the building all went out, and in the pitch darkness the horses belonging to the carriage and to the nearest lancers reared and pranced; people were knocked down and others who were wounded fled screaming like mad or dragged themselves groaning along the ground—lancers, gendarmes, police, footmen and pedestrians all pell-mell.

Meanwhile the Emperor and Empress, very pale but unwounded, descended from the carriage, the front of which was blown to pieces. The Emperor had a slight graze on the face, while Roguet, who had been seated facing him, was wounded in the neck. The Empress said something about " the risks of their trade," and the Emperor, who quickly regained his composure, turned his attention to Princess Mathilde's carriage, which had just driven up and asked somebody to help his cousin to get out, remarking that the step had not been lowered. He wanted to go and cheer the wounded, but he was begged to go into the opera-house in order to prevent a panic. The first act of *William Tell* had just ended when the sound of the explosions was heard. The Emperor and Empress appeared in their box, the news of the crime ran like wild-fire through the theatre, the audience rose as one man and cheered the Emperor, while the orchestra played *Partant pour la Syrie*, a song attributed to Queen Hortense and which had become the official anthem of the Empire.[1] Morny, Persigny, Billault and

[1] The words of the song are remarkable for their platitudinous insipid-

THE SECOND EMPIRE

Walewski, who were in the theatre, hastened to the vestibule of the imperial box to tender their congratulations. "The police are covering themselves with glory!" the Emperor observed with biting brevity to Billault, the Minister of the Interior, and Piétri, the Prefect of Police. Shortly afterwards the Emperor and Empress retired and once more drove through the boulevards amid ringing cheers and under windows which were already illuminated and hung with flags.

Apparently the police might have prevented the crime. They had been warned of the affair, having been informed from Brussels of the arrival in France of a dangerous Italian named Pieri, who had been arrested that same evening just as it was striking eight o'clock in the Rue Le Peletier, by an official of the municipal police, who had recognised him. A revolver had been found on him, as well as a dagger and a bomb. There was time to warn the Emperor, but nothing was done. The police were sure of themselves. In the Opera, a few minutes before the crime, Fleury remarked, "The policing of the streets is perfect."

---

ity: "Setting out for Syria the young and handsome Dunois" begged the Virgin Mary that he might "love the fairest and be the bravest." "He inscribed upon the stone the oath of honour," and covered himself with glory, so that his lord gave him the hand of his daughter Isabella: "At Mary's shrine they both plighted that sweet troth which alone brings happiness." The music is a melody and not like the *Marseillaise*—a march.

156

THE IMPERIAL AUTOCRACY

But thanks to fortuitous circumstances and the stupidity of Pieri the police were able to arrest all the conspirators that same night—Count Rudio, Gomez, and the leader of the band, Felice Orsini, who had been wounded during the explosion. All four were Italians and came from London, and all, except Pieri, who had been arrested in time, had hurled a bomb. Orsini, who had escaped from an Austrian prison in Italy, had met at the Swiss café in London a certain Frenchman known as Bernard " the Clubist," who had at one time been a naval surgeon, but had been obliged to go into exile after June '48. The two together had hatched a plot to kill the Emperor in order to provoke revolution simultaneously in France and Italy. It also afforded an opportunity of executing the Carbonaro who had broken his oath, the man who, after having solemnly sworn to his secret society to deliver Italy and seen his elder brother die in his own arms at Forli in the middle of a war against Austria, had so far forgotten his promises as to send French troops to crush the Roman Republic.

This crime exasperated the Government. The weapon used by the conspirators was a new one. Hitherto sovereigns had been called upon to guard against the dagger and the revolver only. Henceforward there was the added terror of bombs. The number of innocent victims also served to increase the horror felt for such a crime—there were eight killed and a hundred and fifty wounded—a regular massacre. Napoleon III was naturally courageous, being endowed with the bravery of the dreamer and the somewhat melancholy resignation of the fatalist. These risks were part of his trade and provided one more point of similarity between the career of the nephew and the uncle—apparently, after the crime Napoleon III asked to see the documents relating to the infernal machine that had exploded in 1800 in the Rue Saint Nicaise. But however brave a man may be, and however proud of running risks similar to those run by Napoleon I, he cannot undergo such an experience entirely unmoved. Those about him were even more upset, Ministers and courtiers suddenly perceiving the abyss into which they ran the risk of being hurled if the Emperor were to die. Everything depended on this man. If he were to go, what would remain? An ignorant woman and a baby in its cradle!

(marginal note) **Orsini.**

Even the tradition, which in similar circumstances had saved many a monarchy, was lacking.

It is true that on February 1st the conditions of the possible regency of the Empress were to be settled, and a Privy Council appointed which, in addition to King Jerome and his son Prince Napoleon, would include high officials of the State, the Army and the Church. But even these safeguards were fragile and uncertain. Insecurity of tenure is the inevitable price paid for a dictatorship. Founded upon violence, the imperial Government tried to strengthen its position by blindly increasing the violence of its methods.

On the 16th of January representatives of the great State institutions presented themselves at the Tuileries in solemn procession to congratulate the Emperor on his escape. Troplong, in the name of the Senate, waxed eloquent on the subject of the revolutionary lairs abroad and on the risks run by the man who, since the Congress of Paris, all his associates regarded as the arbiter of the nations : " It is from these external strongholds, **Protests.** raised against Europe in the very heart of Europe itself, that fanatical hirelings and cut-throats are sent forth with fire and sword against the Prince whose mighty arm bears aloft the shield of European law and order." Morny, as the mouthpiece of the Legislative Body, spoke out more openly, and this almost brutal frankness was all the more remarkable seeing that it fell from the lips of the most courteous and reserved of men : " The masses are disquieted by the results of your clemency, in which your good-nature plays too great a part, and they are asking themselves why it is that the Governments of neighbouring States friendly to us have been unable to destroy what are regular laboratories of murder." This amounted to demanding repressive measures at home and publicly indicting England and the other haunts of the revolutionaries. Morny was the hero of the *coup d'état*; but he was also the hero of the Russian Alliance which he had advocated ever since France had been openly coquetting with Russia after they had gallantly cut each other's throats at Sebastopol.

The voice of Morny was not the only one to be raised. Between the 22nd and 31st of January the *Moniteur* published a whole series of congratulatory addresses sent to the Emperor
158

by the Colonels of various regiments. As Monsieur Marcel Boulenger points out in his *Attentat d'Orsini*, they constituted a sort of military plebiscite organised by Morny himself : "Reaching him as they did from all the garrisons in turn . . . these addresses were calculated to give the Emperor the impression that they really expressed the voice of the country itself." As a matter of fact they merely repeated what Morny had already said, though with greater vehemence—one Colonel laying the blame upon England, " that haunt of assassins whom they would one day go and hunt out of their island retreat." Morny, in these hours of uncertainty, had instinctively secured the intervention of the real mainstay of the Government, the force that had brought it into being and which alone had the power to maintain it—the army, the regular army, a body existing within the State itself, which had its own opinions and did not hesitate to express them whether by cheering the Emperor at reviews or by sending addresses for the *Moniteur* to publish. One of these addresses openly declared that the army would in future be called upon to play a political part in times of crisis.

The result of all these demonstrations was quite unexpected. On the 18th of January, at the opening of the session of the Legislative Body, the Emperor announced that repressive measures would have to be taken. Because four Italians had met together in London and plotted to kill the Emperor of the French, the Government was going to keep a stricter watch than ever on all suspects in France, that is to say, on all who were opposed to it. " Unfettered freedom is impossible," he declared, " as long as there exists in the country a handful of people who persist in disregarding the fundamental bases of the Government, for in these circumstances freedom is merely a Party weapon to be used against it. . . . The danger . . . consists . . . in the absence of repressive measures. . . . The last elections . . . afforded in certain districts an extremely sorry spectacle, and the hostile parties seized the opportunity to raise disturbances in the country. . . . Since the nation's peace of mind must be our constant concern, you must help me to seek means for reducing these extremist factions to silence." The Paris elections and the 665,000 Opposition votes were still lying heavy on the Emperor's chest, and once again the criminal attempt of

159

a lunatic was to be used as a pretext for the police and the authorities to adopt brutal measures against opponents who had no intention of using any but legal methods in their struggle. To all intents and purposes it meant a return to the state of siege of 1852.

The control of passports, which were demanded even for travelling inside the country itself, was made stricter. On the 27th of January a decree was issued dividing France into five military commands, each under a Marshal—Paris, Nancy, Lyons, Toulouse and Tours. The threat, however, proved more or less ineffectual, though it did at least provide a moral sop for the army, which was now able to consider itself one of the active organs and not merely the instrument of the Govern-

The Law of Public Safety. ment. A much more serious measure was the *Law of Public Safety*, the Bill for which reached the Legislative Body on the 1st of February. Morny constituted himself its sponsor. It was necessary to have recourse to exceptional defensive measures, and " to adjourn the day of liberty." By this law fresh offences were created punishable by imprisonment—public incentive to murder, the fabrication or distribution of explosives, any word or deed whether at home or abroad tending " to disturb the public peace or inspire hatred or contempt of the imperial Government "—this last offence was sufficiently vague to allow of any form of opposition, however trivial, being prosecuted. But more important still, the Minister of the Interior was empowered to intern in France or in Algeria or to expel from the realm not only all those who had been condemned for these offences or for conspiracy, rebellion, riotous assemblage, harbouring weapons of war and affronts against the person of the Emperor, but also anybody " who, having been condemned, expelled or deported in connection with the disturbances of June 1848, June 1849 and December 1851, was once more convicted by grave occurrences of being a menace to the public peace." Thus the main object of the law was to authorise the police to put once more into safe custody all those who had already been rendered suspect by sentences passed long ago, which had been "unearthed from dusty documents," or, as P. de la Gorce puts it, " debts to society which had long since been liquidated."

160

THE IMPERIAL AUTOCRACY

Public opinion immediately gave this law its proper name; it was a new " law against suspects," which would allow the Government, the executive, to imprison or to expel from the realm without trial or the intervention of the judicial authorities all the old adversaries of days long since gone by whom they regarded as dangerous. Baroche, speaking in the name of the Council of State, openly declared that the Empire despised " the exaggerated respect for the scruples of the legists which had brought about the revolutions of 1830 and 1848." The *régime*, founded on force, did not hide its contempt for law. The Legislative Body, docile though it was, at first showed some reluctance to pass such a Bill. After all, would not a decree have sufficed? Why compromise the deputies in the venture? It was necessary for the *Moniteur* to assure it that the proposed law had no connection with Orsini's plot—an exceedingly audacious statement—and above all it required the full weight of Morny's authority and his shrewd powers of persuasion to overcome the objections. And even then two guarantees were insisted upon : the Minister of the Interior was granted discretionary powers only for seven years, until 1865, and nobody was to be interned or expelled without the advice of the Prefect, the General and the Attorney-General having first been asked. This return to the mixed commissions of 1852 was but a sorry safeguard, but still it was a safeguard.

Émile Ollivier was almost the only member of the Legislative Body to oppose the measure; he condemned this confusion of executive and judicial powers, anathematised these prosecutions without trial or defence of unfortunate people who had already been hounded down for other offences, all those " whose attitude and tone were displeasing." The official orators retorted that the law was directed " not against the salons, the reviews, the books, the malicious historical allusions and pinpricks, but actually against daggers," and scoffed at " the scruples of the Faculty of Law and the traditions of the *Palais*." In the end the Bill was passed by 227 votes to 24, among those who voted against being Curé, Darimon, Hénon, Ollivier and various Legitimists. In the Senate also some objections were raised. Haussmann, who was too much of the " high-handed Prefect " to trouble about legality, remarked with some show of sense

M
161

that " in time of peace such a weapon was useless, whereas in time of extreme peril every man had to act as best he could, at his own risk and peril, in which case laws were of little importance." But only one senator made a public protest—General MacMahon. " Never had he been more brave," Marcel Boulenger very justly remarks.

The point of the law became plain as soon as it was known who was to be charged with the task of administering it. **Espinasse.** Billault, who was in ill odour at Court after the crime, sent in his resignation, and his place at the Ministry of the Interior was taken by General Espinasse—Espinasse who on the morning of the 2nd of December had quietly crept into the Palais Bourbon and occupied it. He had afterwards been sent to the provinces to revise the decisions of the mixed commissions and make them less severe, but had granted only a few pardons, and that very unwillingly, being of opinion that the sentences had erred on the side of leniency rather than the reverse. He was made *Minister of the Interior and of Public Safety*. He proclaimed his intentions in a circular addressed to the Prefects : " An execrable crime has just opened our eyes and revealed the savage resentment and the guilty hopes which are still lurking in the revolutionary Party ! " And he repeated the menacing formula which had already been used even before the *coup d'état* : " It is time for the good to be reassured and for the wicked to tremble." The wicked were all those in France who had shown any opposition to the imperial Government and who were arbitrarily classed with Orsini, the Italian who had come from London. Espinasse gave the Prefects their instructions and sent each one of them a list of arrests to be made, " which were apportioned to the general temper of the department." The weapon of fear was to be used. In the provinces it was the leading lights of the district who were singled out—solicitors, notaries, lawyers and doctors. The required number was made up somehow or other—an unfrocked priest was placed on the list, or a foreman who had been denounced by one of his men dismissed for theft. And Duvergier, the Orleanist Duvergier, maintained that public opinion listened with indifference to such tales, which, had they been told a little while back about Russia, would have made

162

France set out on a crusade against the Tsar : " How low have we sunk after six years of slavery ! " It must in all fairness, however, be added that after " making some examples " the Government soon returned to a more normal attitude, and in June Delangle took the place of Espinasse at the Interior.

But the blow had been struck, and the Empire insisted upon acting more autocratically than ever and, far from advancing towards the more Liberal institutions it had vaguely promised, took the opposite course and revived the exceptional measures it had adopted at first. Nevertheless these violent expedients did not subdue Paris; in April 1858, when the reaction was in full swing, the city elected Ernest Picard and Jules Favre, the lawyer who defended Orsini at the assizes, to fill the places of Carnot and Goudchaux, who had refused to take the oath of allegiance. Favre and Picard, together with Ollivier, Darimon and Hénon, were to constitute the " Five," the nucleus of the Republican Opposition in the Legislative Body until 1863. It is true that in February, before these bye-elections took place, it had been decided to insist upon the candidates swearing " obedience to the Constitution and loyalty to the Emperor " in advance. But the young members of the Republican Party, convinced that the policy of abstention was sterile, had resolved to take the oath and to fight the Empire on constitutional grounds.

Orsini's crime had other results, more particularly in connection with the relations between France and foreign countries. **Belgium.** Like every dictatorship, the Empire held neighbouring States, in which its enemies had sought refuge, responsible for political crimes committed by the latter. Belgium, the refuge of many Republicans, whence conspirators had entered France, was naturally the object of diplomatic pressure on the part of the imperial Government. One Belgian newspaper had even gone so far as to express approval of the crime. " We are awaiting the decision of the Belgian Government," declared the *Moniteur*, and its tone was eloquent of the opinion that the France of Napoleon III had of little Belgium. As a matter of fact several newspapers were prosecuted in Brussels, including the one that had defended the crime, some Frenchmen were expelled from the country, and a law was passed making it a punishable offence to insult the head of a State. Remon-

Piedmont. strances were also forwarded to Switzerland as well as to Piedmont, where Cavour refused to suppress certain violent journals which were displeasing to the Paris Cabinet, though he had a law passed to put a stop to plots against ruling sovereigns. Victor Emmanuel, King of Piedmont and Sardinia, cleverly succeeded in maintaining his dignity without quarrelling with Napoleon III. He sent him an aide-de-camp and wrote the latter a letter the most interesting contents of which dealt with the remonstrances addressed by France to Piedmont : " Tell the Emperor," ran the missive, " that this is not the right treatment of a faithful ally; that I have never suffered violence from anybody; . . . that for 850 years we have held our heads high and that no one will make me bow mine; lastly, that in spite of all this I desire nothing else but to be his friend." It required some courage to remind Napoleon, the upstart, that the House of Savoy was the oldest dynasty in Europe. But it was this very fact that secured the success of the move—Napoleon III was conquered by the tone of the letter and the incident was closed.

Lastly, a regular crisis supervened at this time in the Anglo-French alliance. It will be remembered that Morny, who was

England. in favour of an alliance with Russia against England, had rudely informed the Government of this friend and neighbour what he thought of it for failing to prevent the conspirators from hatching their plot in London. He regarded it as a unique opportunity for breaking with London and drawing closer to St. Petersburg. He had been sent as Ambassador Extraordinary by France to Russia on the occasion of the coronation of Alexander II in the summer of 1856, and had done all in his power to reconcile the two erstwhile foes, astonishing the Russian Court by the splendour of his retinue, his carriage with its six windows, its gilt wheels and its embroidered upholstery, drawn by three pairs of English horses. And out there he had married a pretty fair girl with brown eyes, Princess Sophie Troubetzkoy, a lady of exalted rank; indeed, if any credence can be placed in the tales of those who remembered the interest the late Tsar Nicholas had taken in her mother, her rank was even more exalted than was generally supposed.

164

THE IMPERIAL AUTOCRACY

Morny had returned a confirmed advocate of the Russian alliance and more than ever suspicious with regard to England. The crisis of 1858 was calculated to forward his designs. On the 20th of January Walewski telegraphed to Persigny, the French Ambassador in London, reminding him that Pianori and Tibaldi as well as eight other abettors of crime had come from London during the past six years : " Is hospitality to be given to assassins? " he demanded. Palmerston, who was Prime Minister at the time, and Clarendon were at first conciliatory, though they could not contemplate the idea of abolishing the right of refuge or of driving the stranger from their shores, declaring that this would amount to suggesting to Parliament the annexation of England to France. However, a Bill was introduced to treat as felonies, and not as misdemeanours, any plots hatched in England against foreign princes. But the virulent addresses of the Colonels, inspired by Morny and published in the *Moniteur*, and the sentence " that haunt of assassins whom they would go and hunt out of their island retreat," incensed public opinion in England. After the courteous though not really friendly relations which had connected the armies of the two countries in the trenches at Sebastopol, did not this incident afford a preliminary excuse for returning to the ancestral hatred of England for France and for Napoleon? When Palmerston presented his Bill in the House of Commons he was put in a minority and resigned. Disraeli, who then came into office under Lord Derby, subsequently maintained that when they took over the reins of government, " peace was a question not of months or of days, but of hours." That was saying a good deal. Paris climbed down and Napoleon III, wavering between two lines of policy, could not bring himself deliberately to forget his friendship with Queen Victoria, however tempted he might feel to seek an ally elsewhere.

At the very moment when Bernard " the Clubist," the Frenchman domiciled in London who had been an accomplice of Orsini, was acquitted by an English jury—which might have wrecked everything—Persigny, ever a clumsy Ambassador, sent in his resignation, and in his place the Emperor sent the " Duke of Malakoff," that is to say, the old veteran Marshal Pélissier. As a certain Englishman remarked, he was not exactly cultured and knew as little about diplomacy as he did about astronomy

165

or music. But recollections of the Crimea were still too vivid for his name to be anything but a symbol. He was welcomed, acclaimed and made much of, and the sky of the *entente cordiale* was once again cloudless. In August Napoleon invited Queen Victoria to come to Cherbourg to be present at the festivities in connection with the completion of the port and at the unveiling of the statue of Napoleon I, her ancient foe. The Queen must have been somewhat perturbed at seeing so many battleships at Cherbourg, so close to England. But once again the Emperor paraphrased the famous words : " The Empire means peace ! " which he had first uttered at Bordeaux. " The more powerful a nation, the greater the respect she commands," he declared. " And the stronger a Government, the greater the moderation of its councils. . . . In such case the peace of a country is not risked for the satisfaction of empty vanity or the winning of an ephemeral popularity. A Government which rests upon the will of the masses . . . makes war only when it is forced to do so in defence of the national honour or in the highest interests of the peoples."

This pacific declaration was a somewhat bold assertion to make only three years after the Crimean War, though, it is true, in this case the national honour was supposed to have been involved; and it contained one word which might have given rise to anxiety—the Emperor mentioned the highest interest of the *peoples,* and not the highest interests of the country. The full significance of the expression becomes evident when one remembers that at this very moment Napoleon III had just met Cavour at Plombières in order to arrange for the war against Austria. Thus, throughout his career, the Emperor continued to intoxicate himself with his own verbosity and to protest his pacific intentions when he was all the while preparing for war after war and adventure after adventure, just as he exercised the most crushing police tyranny while calling upon God to witness his democratic spirit and loyalty to the principles of '89. Machiavellism? Alas, no !—this would perhaps have been better ; a Machiavelli would coldly and dispassionately have seen the goal he wished to reach. Nay, it was illusion, sincere belief in a chimera, a mystic groping after the phantom of peace and also after the ghosts of glory.

166

THE IMPERIAL AUTOCRACY

And it was now that the Italian policy of the Emperor became manifest. Did this mean that he wanted to liberate Italy in order to forestall further attacks on his person and prevent another Italian from springing out upon him with dagger, revolver or bomb in hand? No, this was not his motive; he possessed the courage of all those who believe in their star and are resigned to the risks of their trade. It is probable that Orsini's crime had the unexpected result of suddenly reviving all the old memories which were slumbering in his breast—his oath as a Carbonaro, when as a young man of twenty he had sworn to liberate Italy, the mysteries of the secret meetings and the plots against the detested Austria, the death of his elder brother in his arms at the back of an inn in Forli in 1831, when they were both fleeing from Metternich's soldiers, his friendship in New York (after the mad escapade at Strassburg in 1836) with Count Arese, exiled by Austria from Italy . . . all these visions of the past floated once more through his dreamy brain and were to play their part in determining his action, and with it moulding the destiny of the country.

When, on the 26th of February, Jules Favre, Orsini's counsel, made his speech for the defence in reply to the speech for the

Jules Favre. Crown by Chaix d'Est Ange, the public prosecutor, he maintained that he was making no attempt to save his client's head—an impossible task. Orsini would lay down his life to redeem the murders he had committed. But, added Favre, " I am anxious to shed upon this immortal soul which is about to return to the bosom of its Maker a ray of that eternal truth which will protect his memory against unmerited accusations . . . the motive for such a crime is to be found in the aberrations of an ardent patriotism, the feverish desire for the independence of his native land which is the dream of all noble minds." And he recapitulated the career of the prisoner, the son of a soldier of the Empire who had fought for France in Russia : " He has spent his life in a ceaseless and energetic struggle against the foreigners who are trampling his country underfoot." And he reminded the Court that in 1831 Orsini had attacked the Papal Government " in conjunction with illustrious accomplices "—the allusion was transparent and there was not a person present who did not understand it.   After

167

THE SECOND EMPIRE

all, the criminal and his proposed victim were old comrades in arms who had fought in the same cause. And he adroitly conjured up " the bloody memories of 1815," France's day of humiliation after the fall of Napoleon, pointing out that this oppression of Italy beneath the yoke of Austria was the work of the disastrous treaties of Vienna, which had also sanctioned the humiliation of France. To wipe out all trace of these treaties and to place his country once more in her proper place in Europe, the Emperor of the French had one certain means at his disposal—he must deliver Italy and substitute the principle of the national will for the antiquated machinations of diplomatists and kings.

A most dramatic scene followed—Jules Favre, declaring that he had received the express permission of the Emperor himself,

Trial of Orsini. read aloud a letter addressed by Orsini to the sovereign; as a matter of fact Jules Favre had dictated it to him. " Upon your will hangs the fate of my country for good or for ill," it ran, ". . . I adjure Your Majesty to return to Italy the independence her children lost in 1849 through the fault of France. . . . As long as Italy is not independent the peace of Europe and of Your Majesty will be but a will-o'-the-wisp. Let not Your Majesty deny the last prayer of a patriot on the steps of the scaffold, but deliver my country, and the blessings of five-and-twenty millions of citizens will follow you down the ages." The Emperor had given Favre permission to publish this letter, which was at once threatening and suppliant, thus already announcing a fundamental change in his policy. To tolerate this reminder of the Roman expedition was to admit that a mistake had been made in 1849 and to promise that it should be rectified. Such a declaration coming from so exalted a source through the lips of so eloquent a speaker made a profound impression, which was only increased by the publication of the letter in the *Moniteur*. Orsini became the " hero of the day." People admired his dignity, his resignation and his grandeur of soul—it was a case of " Orsinomania." Even the Emperor and Empress were inclined to pardon the martyr, and it was necessary for the Archbishop of Paris at the Privy Council to call to mind the blood that had been spilt, and the eight innocent victims, who are always forgotten in such

168

cases, for it to be finally decided to execute Orsini and Pieri. Orsini went to the scaffold on the 13th of March, dressed in a long white shirt, his head covered by the black veil of the parricide and regicide. At the foot of the guillotine his sentence was read out to him. He listened, and when it was finished he cried, " *Evviva l'Italia! Evviva la Francia!*" and delivered himself up to the executioner. He died like a man. Four months later Napoleon secretly summoned Cavour, the Piedmontese Minister, to Plombières, and arranged for war against Austria.

CHAPTER V

THE ITALIAN WAR

Austria in Italy. Piedmont and France. Cavour and Napoleon III;
Plombières (21st of July, 1858). Diplomatic precautions.
On the verge of war. Opposition. War. Transport of the
army. Disorder. Montebello (20th of May, 1859). Palestro
(31st of May). Magenta (4th of June). Entry into Milan.
Solferino (24th of June). Sudden armistice (7th of July).
Reasons for the cessation of hostilities. Interview of Villa-
franca (11th of July). Preliminaries. Italian disappointment.
Return of the Emperor to Paris. The march past of the 14th
of August. Italy's difficulties. Central Italy desires union with
Piedmont. The Roman question. Struggle between the
Emperor and the Church. The bribe—Savoy and Nice.

ITALY of this period, the creation of the Treaties of 1815,
was still a coat of many colours. In the north, following
the course of the Po, from the Alps to the Adriatic, was a
chain of states consisting of Piedmont—the Kingdom of the
House of Savoy, whose authority extended from Turin to
Austria in Chambéry, Nice, Genoa and the island of Sardinia—
Italy. and Lombardy and Venetia, which were dependent
upon Austria. To the south of the Po, further
down the peninsula, were the Duchies of Parma, Modena and
Tuscany, which were theoretically independent, though the
Austrian white-coats were still garrisoned in Florence, as
they were in Milan and Venice. Next came the Papal
States, from Bologna to Ancona and Ancona to Rome, the
temporal domain of the Holy See, occupied by the Austrians
in the north, and by the French, who had remained in Rome
ever since 1849; and finally the Kingdom of the Two Sicilies,
distant and isolated, almost outside Italy.

Thus throughout the basin of the Po, from the Ticino to
beyond the Apennines, Austrian armies kept watch and ward
and held in check the Liberal and National movement which
they had arrested in '48. The dreamers and poets who were
aiming at the deliverance of Italy might well be filled with
170

despair. But at the foot of the Alps, facing the Austrian garrisons of Milan and Parma, there was the independent kingdom of Piedmont ruled by an ambitious monarch, King Victor Emmanuel, and a Minister of genius—Cavour. Both King and Minister wanted to make their country the nucleus of a great and free Kingdom of Italy. The policy of Piedmont was already prepared; if the Austrians had been in occupa-

Piedmont. tion of Milan ever since 1815 it was only to forestall another French adventure in Italy, an attack *à la Bonaparte*, a second Rivoli. Thus Piedmont, the ancestral foe of Austria, was the natural ally of France, and this alliance was one of the dogmas of French diplomacy. " We shall defend the frontier of the Ticino like that of the Var," had been Bastide's famous dictum in '48. Piedmont was the advanced guard of France against Austria. And Napoleon III, by virtue of his birth, had been from the very beginning a supporter of the plans of Cavour. " The day will come," he observed in 1852 to the Piedmontese Ambassador, " when our two countries will be companions in arms in the noble cause of Italy." They had already fought side by side in the Crimea, at Traktir, and little Piedmont had taken her place among the great Powers of Europe. At the Congress of Paris the Sardinian Ministers had been treated exactly like the other plenipotentiaries. Cavour had done all in his power to win

Cavour. over Napoleon III. " I warn you," he wrote to a friend on the 20th of February, 1856, " that I have added a recruit to the ranks of diplomacy in the person of the lovely Countess of Castiglione, and have invited her to flirt with the Emperor, and if necessary seduce him. . . . I am trying to stimulate the patriotism of our fair Countess." A charming device to present Italy to the impassioned gaze of the Emperor in the guise of a beautiful woman—a beautiful woman whom unfortunately he was called upon to love and deliver from bondage !

The Congress of Paris, it is true, had not brought Cavour all he had hoped for; the Italian question had been raised, but no attempt had been made to solve it. Napoleon III had not yet made up his mind to break with Austria. " I cannot enter into conflict with her just now," he had, however, remarked to Cavour, " but do not worry; I have a presentiment that the present peace will not last for long." But would these fancies develop into a real desire? There were those in the immediate circle of the Emperor who did not regard Piedmont with over-much sympathy; the little State was a frog trying to puff itself up to the size of the Austrian ox, and Cavour, its whippersnapper of a Minister, was giving a great deal too much trouble. Clearly the Emperor was undecided.

It required the bombs of Orsini to convince him by reviving all the dreams of his youth, and to determine him to take action. This was the opportunity for which he had been waiting to recast the map of Europe and to wipe out the treaties of 1815 which had confirmed the defeat of his uncle. Queen Victoria declared that he wanted to avenge himself on Europe, and treacherously added that' he was afraid of being assassinated. Orsini's famous letter appeared in the official Gazette of Turin, as well as in the Paris *Moniteur*, also at the express desire of the Emperor. At the end of May 1858, Doctor Conneau, the Emperor's physician, went to Turin to announce that Napoleon III was going to drink the waters at Plombières that summer. The Emperor did not trust his Ministers, and, as the Piedmontese Ambassador observed, did not share with them " the great ideas he was harbouring in his mind," but preferred to have his own secret agents. In July he sent his aide-de-camp to Cavour, and on the 21st of that month the two men met at Plombières and had a conversation lasting for four hours.

Plombières. They must have smiled when the Emperor was handed a telegram from Walewski, the Minister for Foreign Affairs, in which he gravely informed his master that Monsieur de Cavour had been seen in France. The Emperor promised Cavour the help of France against Austria, but, to avoid upsetting Europe, arrangements must be made for the war to have a diplomatic origin and not to arise out of revolutionary disturbances; an incident would be engineered between Piedmont and Modena, whose Duke was under the protection of Austria. As soon as victory had been won— and naturally no doubts were entertained on this score—Italy would be free as far as the Adriatic; Victor Emmanuel would extend his power over Lombardy, Venetia and the northern

172

THE ITALIAN WAR

portion of the Papal States; another kingdom would be formed in central Italy consisting of Tuscany and the Duchies, together with Umbria, at that time the property of the Holy See. By way of compensation for this loss of territory, the Pope would be President of the Italian Confederation, which would also include Naples. The Emperor hoped that this would forestall any objections on the part of the French Catholics, who would certainly wish to defend the temporal power of the Pope. Moreover, he had no intention of fighting for nothing, but demanded the return to France of Savoy and Nice—the old departments of Léman, Mont-Blanc and the Alpes-Maritimes under Napoleon I. These were to be France's only conquests, and the Emperor, by giving up all idea of making annexations on a large scale as his uncle had done, imagined he would conciliate Europe and also secure for himself "powerful allies" beyond the Alps, who would come to his rescue in case of danger. Cavour soon agreed to ceding Savoy, but protested in the case of Nice, which was "Italian territory." And the matter was left in abeyance. In the evening the Emperor took Cavour out in his phæton, which he drove himself, for a trip in the Vosges, and, to ratify the agreement, proposed that his cousin, Prince Napoleon, should marry the young Princess Clotilda, daughter of Victor Emmanuel. The Prince, he explained, was better than his reputation, and he added quite seriously that as he was touchingly faithful to his mistresses, he would make a good husband! In principle this family matter was also agreed upon.

Later in the summer of 1858 shrewd observers might have guessed that "something was in the air"; the *Siècle* and the *Presse* made furious onslaughts on the unduly despotic attitude adopted by Austria in Lombardy, and no warning was issued against them by the Ministry of the Interior. Worse still, the *Moniteur*, the official Government organ, published some articles by a young journalist named Edmond About, an old student of the *École Normale* who had turned his back on the University; in limpid, vivacious and easy prose, resembling Voltaire in style, he denounced the abuses of the Government of the Pope in his temporal domain. When the articles were published in book form in Brussels it was said that the Emperor

173

himself had read the proofs. Such rumours were not calculated to win him the support of the Catholics, but the Emperor sincerely imagined he could reconcile irreconcilables, and establish Italian unity without really undermining the prestige of the Pope.

Just at this juncture a fresh incident arose to put a spoke in the wheel. A little Bolognese Jew, named Mortara, had been secretly baptised by a Christian maidservant when he was ill. Three years later the girl informed a priest of the fact, and Rome, unwilling to allow a Christian soul to grow up an infidel, had the child kidnapped and placed in a convent. This raised a tremendous outcry. It was an unexpected opportunity, observes P. de la Gorce, of pointing out the danger of uniting spiritual and temporal power in the hands of one person and of introducing the rigours of religion into civil law. That section of the Press which was hostile to the Pope even went so far as to suggest that a League of Fathers of Families should be formed to fight the abuses of the theocracy. The only newspaper to support the Pope was *l'Univers*, under Veuillot; and it sneered at those who wanted to make the little Mortara " the Uncle Tom of the Church." In the end the *Moniteur* insisted upon peace and silence, but the incident served to alienate the Emperor even more from the supporters of the temporal power of the Pope.

Meanwhile the Emperor was endeavouring to conciliate public opinion in Europe. From Biarritz, whither he re-

Diplomatic Precautions. paired when he left Plombières, he sent his cousin, the happy bridegroom to be, to Warsaw, to beg an alliance with the Tsar, in return for which the clause in the treaty of 1856 forcing the neutralisation of the Black Sea upon Russia was to be rescinded. And in this direction Napoleon III did at least succeed in obtaining a promise of neutrality and of diplomatic support. To curry favour with the Tsar, he postponed all thought of realising his dreams regarding Poland; for this visionary, who wanted to recast the map of Europe by arousing the dormant spirit of nationalism, had at one time thought of liberating Poland as well as Italy. And in order to secure the co-operation or at all events the good-will of Prussia, he suggested that, under

174

cover of the Austrian war, she should annex Holstein and Hanover. King William, however, had but little love for him, and, suspicious of the adventurer, refused his tempting offer. Finally, in the autumn, the Emperor invited the English Ministers, Palmerston and Clarendon, to Compiègne, where he unfolded his plans to them, but succeeded only in terrifying them. By embarking on the Italian venture he would run the risk of losing the friendship of England for ever. What matter! He would do without it. In vain did Queen Victoria write him a personal letter begging him to renounce his bellicose plans. He was already poring over the map of the Po valley, dreaming of battles and of new frontiers.

The *Presse* was anxious for war against Austria and was allowed to say so. The *Patrie*, an inspired journal, joined the chorus. In vain did the *Moniteur* protest that the intentions of the Government were pacific. At that very moment a secret treaty with Piedmont confirmed the agreements reached at Plombières (the 10th of December); in the event of any act of aggression on the part of Austria, France would send 200,000 men to Italy. Finally, when he received the *corps diplomatique* on the 1st of January, 1859, Napoleon III observed to Hüber, the Austrian Ambassador, " I regret that our relations with your Government are not so good as they have been in the past; but I beg you to inform the Emperor that my personal sentiments have not changed." A deliberate threat? No, probably merely a mistake, a sudden access of candour to which all reserved natures are prone, possibly also a desire to imitate his uncle, Napoleon I, who, before violating the Peace of Amiens, had said some hard things to the English Ambassador. But at all events it was a blunder. An attempt was made on the following day to recall the words, and the Empress was particularly amiable to Hübner. But meanwhile there was a slump on the Bourse; the commercial world was afraid of war, and a reassuring statement in the *Moniteur* of the 7th of January, made in the hope of calming the fears of the public, only served to confirm them—the inevitable result of *communiqués* at critical moments.

Three days later, in the Parliament at Turin, King Victor Emmanuel, in the Speech from the Throne, said that he was

175

not deaf to the " cry of pain " which had reached his ears from so many parts of Italy. But Napoleon III had seen and personally corrected the text of the speech. And Prince Napoleon, when he presented himself in Turin for his marriage, was accompanied by General Niel, who was entrusted with the task of making a sort of military inspection of Piedmont. Last but not least, a pamphlet appeared at the beginning of February, *L'Empereur Napoléon III et l'Italie.* The author remained anonymous, but it was immediately attributed to the Emperor himself. And, as a matter of fact, he had furnished the draft to a paid publicist, and had revised the text and even corrected the proofs. It was an extraordinary way of bringing pressure to bear on public opinion. But this man, who never ceased to be a conspirator, retained, even when he was on the throne, a love of intrigue, of anonymity and of secrecy; and this particular secret was soon to be no secret at all. But he was not endowed with sufficient strength of will to dare to speak out openly. The pamphlet poured anathema upon the heads of those Italian States which owed allegiance to Austria, extolled Piedmont to the skies, and openly proclaimed the new theory of nationalities, tracing it to an august source—to Napoleon I himself. Had the latter not declared that he wished to create a free and independent Italy, had he not expressed a wish from St. Helena " for the centralisation of all those geographical entities whom revolution or politics h___nen___ up or disintegrated " ? But while professing to follow___ably___ple of his uncle, the nephew endeavoured to go one be___. The Emperor Napoleon I thought it his duty to conquer the peoples in order to set them free; it is the aim of Napoleon III to set them free without conquering them." The pamphlet ended by sketching the foundation of a federative Italian State under the Presidency of the Pope.

It was about this time, on the 7th of February, that the Emperor opened the session of the Legislative Body and made **On the Verge of War.** a speech which was extremely characteristic of him—announcing peace and war alternately in the same breath. He repeated, " *The Empire means peace,*" and then reminded his hearers of the points at issue with Austria. He protested that his attitude was

176

one of moderation and conciliation, declaring that he would never indulge in a provocative policy, and then proceeded to talk about the power of France and swore that he would not be pusillanimous, but would know how to take a firm stand. It would have been difficult to make head or tail of all this rigmarole. Clearly he wanted war but hoped that Austria would take the initiative, for he had bound himself to Piedmont only in the event of an act of aggression against her, and he was not the man to take upon his own shoulders the responsibility for opening hostilities. Ever a dreamer, action terrified him.

He hesitated all the more because those around him were hostile to his idea. Nobody approved except the worst enemies **Opposition.** of the *régime*—the Republicans. The Empress, who insisted upon playing her part, and was jealous of her rival, the lovely Italian Countess, did not approve of the policy of the liberation of the peoples, and regarded it as a " fool's job." Persigny, who had again returned to London as Ambassador, was too anxious to maintain the alliance with England to support an adventure which was disquieting the Foreign Office. Fould was by no means pleased at the slump on the Bourse, and even the Generals declared that they were not ready. Walewski, the Minister for Foreign Affairs, who hated Cavour, was frankly against war. Last but not least, Morny cleverly constituted himself the mouthpiece of the deputies in the Legislative Body who did not dare to say openly that these plans for war were not at all popular in the country. " Religion, philosophy, civilisation, finance and labour," he declared, calling to mind eternal verities, " have made peace the greatest blessing of modern society." And he added a new and interesting rider : " The rapid means of communication with foreign countries and publicity have created a new European power with which all Governments are bound to reckon—and that is the power of public opinion. It may at times be undecided or erratic, but in the end it always ranges itself on the side of justice, right and humanity." It was a strange definition of that new international life, which owed its inception to the creation of railways and the telegraph system, of that moral League of Nations which was already faintly looming on the horizon. And this reminder of the

N

power of public opinion in Europe was also a shrewd move on the part of Morny, who doubtless hoped it would make the Emperor stay his hand.

For Europe did not support him. The South German States, prompted by Vienna, threatened to intervene on the Rhine in favour of Austria, and to conquer Alsace. And most important of all, England deliberately set to work to prevent war, securing the support of Prussia, conjuring Napoleon III not to endanger the peace of Europe, and imploring Vienna to show a conciliatory spirit and grant Liberal reforms to the Italians in Milan and Venice, and thus deprive Cavour of all excuse for setting match to the powder. The Ballplatz was still ready to hear the voice of reason. Austria was not yet ready for war; there were only 50,000 men in Italy, the railway from Semmering, which was to connect Vienna with Venice, was not finished, and the heavy guns destined for the Venetian fortresses were still held up at the end of the completed section. In Paris no decision had yet been reached. At one moment it seemed as though the opposing forces both at home and abroad would put a stop to the Emperor's plans. The *Moniteur* of the 5th of March denied the rumours of war and securities went up on the Bourse. Then Prince Napoleon, the pawn in the Piedmontese alliance, resigned from the Ministry of Algeria. And finally there was a suggestion that an international Congress should be convened to regulate the " abnormal situation " in Italy—the proposal emanating from France and Russia. Austria replied by insisting on Piedmont disarming before anything else was done. Whereupon Cavour rushed to Paris and did his utmost to persuade the Emperor to take up arms instead of parleying. Queen Victoria's husband wrote that the Emperor had sold his soul to the devil, and that Cavour could do as he pleased with his honour. And indeed Cavour was in a position to create a fine scandal by publishing the results of their secret negotiations. Nevertheless, Napoleon III, somewhat flattered by the idea of a Congress at which he would once again act the part of the arbiter of Europe, asked Cavour to disarm. England, to clinch the matter, suggested a general disarmament. In the end, Cavour, sick and tired of the thought of war, gave his consent and renounced

178

his grandiose schemes, when suddenly Austria herself, at the end of her patience and at last ready for war, rejected the English proposal of disarmament, though, in a brutal ultimatum of the 23rd of April, she called upon Piedmont to disarm.

Such a demand was the greatest possible blunder imaginable. It provided Cavour with the opportunity for which he had been longing and Napoleon with a pretext for intervening to defend Piedmont against the invader. Ill-fated Austria thus flung herself into the jaws of the wolf and roused even public opinion in England against her. Prussia, although she was already prepared to fight France, maintained her expectant attitude, waiting to intervene in her own good time, and refusing the alliance offered by Vienna.

On the 24th of April, which was Easter Sunday, the troops from Paris marched to entrain at the *Gare de Lyon* amid the cheers of the crowd, above all in the Faubourg

War.

St. Antoine, the old-time quarter for revolutions and barricades, where the idea of this war of liberation was extremely popular. On the 26th the Legislative Body voted a loan of 500 million francs (£20,000,000) and passed a Bill allowing a levy of 140,000 men instead of 100,000 for the next contingent. On the 3rd of May a proclamation was issued to the country to induce it to acquiesce in the war. "Austria has brought things to such a pass that either she must extend her sway as far as the Alps or Italy must be free as far as the Adriatic. . . . I have no desire for conquest. . . . The object of this war is to return Italy to herself." And, as a sop to Catholic susceptibilities, the Emperor added : "We are not going to Italy to foment disorder, nor to shake the power of the Holy See, but to deliver her from the heel of the foreigner." Henceforward the honour of the flag was involved, and everybody, even Morny, silenced their objections. It was announced that the war would be localised and limited in its sphere. On the 10th of May the Emperor crossed Paris, which was decorated with the colours of France and Sardinia, to shouts of " *Vive l'Empereur !* " and " *Vive l'Italie !* " and in his turn took his departure from the *Gare de Lyon* for Marseilles and Genoa. Like his uncle, he too was to have his Italian campaign.

179

Ever since January preparations for war had been carried on in France with the utmost secrecy. Vaillant and Castellane were collecting troops round Lyons, and some of the regiments had been recalled from Algeria. Marvellous tales were told about the new rifled cannon which fired armour-piercing shot or fused shells at the rate of two a minute; the eight-pounders shot an eight-pound shell with a range of from twelve hundred to eighteen hundred yards; the twenty-four pounders a twenty-four pound shell with a range of from 1,000 to 1,900 yards with a maximum of 3,000 yards. It was an extremely up-to-date weapon at the time, although it was still muzzle-loaded. It was said that the Emperor himself, calling to mind his knowledge of artillery and his term of service with the Berne gunners, had worked on its design. But Austria too had hastened on her preparations and had a force of 107,000 men ready who could very quickly be conveyed by rail to the Ticino. France, on the other hand, was obliged to send her troops either by sea to Genoa, or overland *viâ* Mont Genèvre or **Transport** Mont Cenis, the railway (the Lyons–Geneva Com-**of the** pany) breaking off at Saint Jean de Maurienne and **Army.** beginning again at Susa. Thus they had to cross the mountains, covering four stages on foot, one or two of them being through snow. And Piedmont had only 50,000 men. Was Austria going to steal a march on France, scatter the Sardinian army, enter Turin and dictate the terms of peace before a single Frenchman had crossed the Alps?

Everything was done to move more quickly than Austria. On the 24th of April Canrobert was urged to reach Susa with the utmost possible speed with his own and Niel's forces. And he arranged for the railway to convey 5,000 men a day, which for the period was a very large number. They set off anyhow, without tents, camp-kettles and water-bottles, blankets, forage or mules, provided only with a few rounds of shot. Bourbaki, in command of a division, grumbled and growled, but advanced quickly notwithstanding. At the same time Baraguay d'Hilliers and MacMahon landed at Genoa with the troops under their command. Canrobert did not trouble to cover Turin, but preferred to concentrate his forces at Alessandria and on the Po, below Turin. The Austrians, advancing from Milan, would never dare to march direct on Turin with such a menace on their left flank. And as a matter of fact, Gyulai, the Austrian Commander-in-Chief, lost time, apparently awaiting the result of a last unsuccessful effort at mediation on the part of England. He crossed the Ticino only on the 29th of April, menaced Turin on the 9th of May, and then, fearing he would be surrounded, beat a retreat as far as Mortara. These Austrians of 1859 had made too profound a study of the campaigns of 1796 and 1797, and the new Bonaparte terrified them. Would he not swoop down upon them and rout them as his uncle had routed Wurmser and Alvinzi?

If only they had been aware of the disorder that reigned in the ranks of the enemy! Suddenly Randon, who was **Disorder.** about to be promoted Major-General, was made Minister of War instead of Vaillant, who was made Major-General, it having been discovered, somewhat late in the day, that Vaillant had failed to make preparations and that Randon was a better administrator. And indeed, when the Emperor reached Alessandria on the 14th, nothing was ready; there were no artillery, cavalry, doctors, nurses, biscuits or boots. "We have assembled an army of 100,000 men," wrote the Emperor to Randon, "without providing them with anything to live upon. . . . We always behave like children who have never made war before." Randon subsequently confirmed this statement. "Everything was lacking," he declared, "except courage." There were only 68 guns of the new rifled pattern, while for the old smooth-bored guns there were no longer any projectiles to be had. The troops were also provided with a new rifle with a conical bullet; all it lacked was the backsight, and the rifleman had to use his thumb to help him to aim. Fortunately the days slipped by without the Austrians making an attack! On the 18th of May the Franco-Sardinian army, 150,000 strong with 432 guns, was at last concentrated and almost fully equipped. They were full of confidence, for memories of Arcole and Rivoli were as vivid as they were in the ranks of the enemy: "The Austrians are fine soldiers," they said, "but they always get beaten." Taking the offensive and victory was all that was thought of.

THE SECOND EMPIRE

Gyulai was afraid that the Franco-Piedmontese army would descend the right bank of the Po, cross the river at Placenza and suddenly appear on his flank and rear. Event-**Montebello.** ually, in order to see his way clearly, he decided to send out two divisions to reconnoitre in the face of the enemy to the south of Pavia on the right bank of the Po. On the 20th of May these 20,000 men advanced in three separate columns—one of which came up against Forey, who, with only one division of 6,000 men, courageously opened the attack, supported by the Piedmontese cavalry, and drove back the Austrians. The latter rallied the other columns, collected in the village of Montebello, which was situated on a height, and put the houses and walls in a state of defence. Forey again made a furious onslaught, captured the houses and the cemetery and in the end forced the enemy to retreat. Whereupon he returned to his quarters. He had lost 700 men killed or wounded in the fray, while the Austrians had 1,200 put out of action. The delight in the French camp may be imagined! It was at Montebello that Lannes, on the 11th of June, 1800, three days before Marengo, had defeated 20,000 Austrians with his 8,000. . . . What a presage of brilliant victories to come!

Gyulai became more and more convinced that the Allies were trying to turn his left flank. They made a feint of slipping towards Placenza and attempting to cross the Po. But meanwhile, behind a screen of outposts, the army was suddenly conveyed a distance of over thirty miles to the north-east by road and rail, hoping to surprise Gyulai on his right in the direction of Novara, and to cross the Ticino and capture Milan. This grand strategic idea was due to the Emperor, and according to P. de la Gorce was " the only one in the whole campaign." It was a flanking movement which might involve considerable risk. On crossing the river the troops fell in with the extreme Austrian right; on the 30th of May Victor Emmanuel took Palestro, near Vercelli, and was **Palestro.** violently attacked there on the 31st. He held his ground, but was just on the point of being overcome when a regiment of Zouaves glided through the corn and, under the poplars, leapt the acacia hedges, forded a canal in which the
182

men were up to their waists in water, debouched on the left flank of the Austrians, to the south of the village, charged the enemy with their bayonets, and captured five guns, which they presented that evening to Victor Emmanuel, whom they acclaimed as " Corporal of the Zouaves."

It was only on the day following the capture of Palestro that Gyulai understood the Emperor's manœuvre; and he immediately fell back in all haste behind the Ticino, the frontier of Lombardy, to bar the passage and defend Milan. The manœuvre had fired the French army with enthusiasm; " it was a move worthy of the great Emperor," observed Ducrot. It was even hoped that on leaving Novara it would be an easy matter to cross the Ticino under cover of the surprise and disorder in the Austrian ranks. And on the 3rd of June MacMahon did succeed in crossing the river at Turbigo, and after a successful battle at Robecchetto, in which the " Turcos," or Algerian sharpshooters—a recently formed body—played a part, took up his position in Lombardy north of Magenta.

Magenta. On the same day Espinasse's division without striking a blow occupied the San Martino bridge over the Ticino, where the road and the railway ran east and west from Novara to Magenta and Milan. But about two miles from the river, half-way between San Martino and Magenta, there was a formidable obstacle in the shape of the Naviglio Grande, running north-west and south-east, a canal about twenty yards broad and extremely deep, protected by a perpendicular embankment lined with a prickly acacia hedge. The road crossed the canal by the Ponte Nuovo at Magenta; it was round this bridge and the hamlet close by that a desperate battle was fought on the 4th of June.

The country formed a regular death-trap—a level plain intersected by ditches, canals and swamps, covered with mulberry bushes, poplars and willows where it was impossible to see two hundred yards ahead. The only observation posts were the square red-brick campaniles in the villages, from which the eye wandered over the medley of green fields and lines of trees, bounded on the north by the blue-and-white crests of the Alps, while to the east the silvery turrets of Milan Cathedral were visible. The French wanted to press on to Milan, and

183

Gyulai tried to attack them on their left flank. But on both sides the forces were scattered over a wide area, and the battle was fought in detail. In the morning the Emperor waited for MacMahon to reach Magenta from the north. And Mac-Mahon did indeed succeed in putting the enemy to flight and advancing to within a mile and a half north of the Ponte Nuovo. Whereupon at midday Napoleon III, thinking that MacMahon, whose guns he could hear, would push on, ordered the Guards to advance and force the Naviglio Grande. The Zouaves and the Grenadiers engaged in a furious battle at the Ponte Nuovo, which the Austrians defended desperately. At last the latter were routed out. But they made a violent counter-attack and won back some of the ground. Whereupon General Cler hurled himself into the midst of the fray to urge on his men, but a moment afterwards his mare was seen galloping wildly back; he had been killed. And his troops fell back. Meanwhile MacMahon's guns had been silenced. A request for reinforcements was sent to the Emperor, who was at San Martino. But the rest of the troops were a long way off and could advance only across the marshy ground by narrow paths. " Hold firm and bar the way ! " was the order sent out. And they held firm. At last, at half-past three, a brigade of light infantry and infantry of the line came to the rescue and were greeted with shouts of joy by the Grenadiers and the Zouaves. It was high time; Gyulai was telegraphing the news of his success and Austrian reinforcements were also coming up. They were driven back, and Wimpffen advanced even beyond the canal.

What had MacMahon, who should long since have mastered the Austrian right and occupied Magenta, been doing all this time? Espinasse, his divisional commander, had lost his way, wandering eastward and getting separated from the other division under La Motterouge. It was imperative to bring all the troops together, and MacMahon led his forces back to allow the two columns to join up again. He himself galloped off to join Espinasse and led him back west. At last he re-formed the line of attack, and at about half-past four his guns began firing again, menacing Magenta.

At that moment Gyulai launched another counter-attack

184

against the French right, between the canal and the Ticino, and furious fighting took place round the few houses of Ponte Vecchio, a hamlet eight hundred yards south of the Ponte Nuovo. Fortunately Canrobert and Vinoy came up in time with reinforcements and hurled themselves into the fray. Canrobert, surrounded by Austrian cavalry, defended himself sword in hand. Meanwhile, at six o'clock in the evening, Espinasse and La Motterouge attacked Magenta and dispersed the Austrian sharpshooters hidden in the vines and mulberry bushes. Here Espinasse was killed, but his Zouaves pushed on and were soon afterwards joined by the troops under La Motterouge. In spite of heavy losses the town was captured, and MacMahon was given the Marshal's baton and the title of Duke of Magenta. The Austrians retreated in a southerly direction under the fire of forty guns.

As for the Emperor, he had not seen much of the operations. Official historians afterwards lauded his calmness and serenity. But P. de la Gorce describes it as a state of horrified stupefaction. All he did was to tell the Guards to stand firm and the reinforcements to hurry up. He had no means of communication with MacMahon, and, in the absence of news, thought of retreating. And he was the last to hear of the victory. It was not he who had won it, but his soldiers, and his leaders, generals and marshals, who fought in the thick of the fight like junior subalterns. Moreover, it was only a partial victory. The various bodies of troops entered the battle one after the other, and on neither side had the whole army been engaged : 48,000 French had fought in detail against 62,000 Austrians, and all through the night fresh divisions had come up to reinforce both sides. On the morning of the 5th of June, Trochu fell in with the Austrians and it seemed as though the battle would start afresh. But Gyulai decided to retreat, leaving the road open to Milan. That same day the Emperor went over the field of battle and saw with his own eyes what war was really like—the heaps of bodies, the wounded lying groaning or dying on the ground, some of them being operated on where they were, the surgeon cutting into the quivering flesh of an arm or a leg, while the victim ground the pipe between his teeth to prevent himself from screaming. And he was upset at

185

the sight of all this suffering; he did not possess his uncle's heart of steel. After all, war had been the latter's calling. Seven hundred dead and 3,000 wounded—losses amounting to 10 per cent.—seem but little to us, but they were enough to stir the heart of any man not incapable of feeling pity.

Milan was listening to the roar of the battle. During the night a messenger arrived on horseback with the news : " They are beaten ! " And the next day the Austrians **Entry into Milan.** fled and Italian flags appeared in the windows. On the 8th of June the Emperor entered the town with Victor Emmanuel at his side. He was not given a reception, because he arrived at eight o'clock in the morning, earlier than he was expected; there were only a few people about and the decoration of the streets had not been completed. But in the afternoon he was given an ovation; flowers were strewn under his horse's hoofs and palms and flags were waved as he passed. On the following day another battle was fought about nine miles south-east of Milan. Baraguay d'Hilliers and Bazaine drove the Austrian rear-guard out of Melegnano, the old Marignano, after a bloody conflict which cost the French a thousand men. The people of Milan sent out carriages to fetch back the wounded, and many an idyll arose between these valiant heroes and the fair nurses who looked after them.

From Milan the Emperor published a proclamation " to the Italians," begging them, in somewhat sorry style, to unite " towards one end, the liberation of their country," and to flock to the standards of Victor Emmanuel. He declared that he had no wish to impose his own will, all he wanted was to hold the enemy at bay and secure order at home : " My army will do nothing to hamper the expression of your legitimate wishes." Tuscany had already politely dismissed her Grand Duke, and an envoy from Piedmont had been appointed special commissioner in the name of Victor Emmanuel. It was even rumoured that Tuscany was going to be handed over to Prince Napoleon, but the tale was speedily denied. The respective rulers of Parma and Modena were holding themselves in readiness to take their departure, while agitation was growing in the Romagna, and especially at Bologna and

186

Ravenna. It really seemed as though the war were to be the war of liberation desired by Victor Emmanuel and Cavour. But the Emperor still continued to be subjected to adverse influences. Those who had openly declared their disapproval of the war wanted to see it quickly ended and circumscribed in its results. The Catholics were perturbed by the disturbances which were menacing the temporal power of the Pope in the Papal States. The Empress, who was very religious, was won over to their side; moreover, she feared the perils of war for her imperial husband, and also possibly the blandishments of the noble ladies of Italy. Business men were agitating for peace, and were supported by Walewski and even by Randon, who feared German intervention on the Rhine and was furious at being kept in complete ignorance of what was taking place in Italy. He was not even sent a list of casualties and was unable to give people any information about the fate of members of their family.

But, in spite of the brilliant successes that had been gained, the two armies had not yet faced each other in a great battle. However much the Emperor may have been hesitating, it was still too early to call a halt. The Austrians were retreating, abandoning all the right bank of the Po, evacuating Ptacenza, Bologna, Ravenna and Ferrara, and even abandoning Cremona on the left bank; they only came to a stand across the Chiese, south of the Lago di Garda, before the famous Quadrilateral—the fortresses of Peschiera, Mantua, Legnago and Verona —which was regarded as impregnable. Here they concentrated and reorganised their forces under the orders of the young Emperor Francis Joseph, who had arrived in person to take over the command. His army was 160,000 strong, and it was hoped that there would be a turn in fortune's wheel. Nevertheless, the Austrians were far from confident. The little towns of Lonato and Castiglione, through which they passed, whose names had been made famous by the first Bonaparte in August 1796, once more boded no good for the future. The Franco-Piedmontese troops naturally followed hard on the heels of the Austrians, viâ Brescia. They were subjected to long and difficult marches, under a blazing June sun amid clouds of dust; the roads were blocked with men and baggage, the columns became entangled with each other, and there were stampedes at every brook and stream. Coffee and provisions did not always arrive in time. As there was a shortage of bread and biscuits, an attempt was made to give the troops a maize ration for making " polenta." It was a grave mistake. Wherever he may be, a man will forget everything except his native language and the food of his own country. Trochu protested, the soldiers threw away their mess of maize, dubbed the officer in charge of supplies the Duke of Polenta, and went off foraging to see whether they could not find something more substantial.

On the 23rd of June the army, which had advanced from Brescia, had crossed the Chiese; the Austrians were said to be the other side of the Mincio. In the morning the aeronaut Godard went up in a captive balloon, but all he could see were a few troopers north of Solferino. But during the afternoon some Austrians returned and hurled themselves upon the French outposts. This attack was regarded as being merely a reconnoitring movement on the part of the enemy. It seemed incredible that, after having fallen back beyond the Mincio, the Austrians should have changed their plans, and have crossed the river again and marched forward once more in the direction of the Chiese. On the night of the 23rd both sides were buried in peaceful slumbers, while the red glow of the midsummer fires lighted by the peasants shone from the neighbouring heights. On the following day, these two blind armies, advancing towards each other, were to meet face to face and engage in a general conflict which nobody or almost nobody on either side had been able to foresee.

The country south of the Lago de Garda is a plain covered with mulberry bushes and broken up by screens of trees, but **Solferino.** drier and more stony than the Magenta district. In a semicircle round the lake a chaplet of hills stands out from the plain, most conspicuous among them a height near Solferino, covered with black cypresses, another on which stands the cemetery, and lastly a hill surmounted by a high tower, the *Spia d'Italia*, the *Spy of Italy*, from which the Austrians seemed to keep watch and ward over their Italian subjects.

188

THE ITALIAN WAR

On the morning of the 24th of June, the Franco-Sardinian forces, 140,000 strong, set out in an east-south-easterly direction. On the left, that is to say, to the north, starting from Lonato, were the Piedmontese, whose extreme left was resting on the Lago di Garda. Next came Baraguay d'Hilliers marching towards the hills of Solferino; MacMahon from Castiglione followed the Mantua road which runs south of Solferino; and lastly, on the right, to the south, Niel advanced towards the village of Medole. MacMahon was the first to fall in with the Austrians to the south of Solferino. Soon Niel too joined the fray and captured Medole. Then Baraguay d'Hilliers, who had been the only one on the preceding evening to foresee the possibility of this encounter, ordered Forey and Ladmirault to advance to the hills before Solferino. Lastly, to the north, the progress of the Piedmontese was arrested by the Austrians under Benedeck. Thus, when the Emperor arrived at Castiglione at eight o'clock in the morning, he found that there were three or four distinct engagements going on along a ten-mile front.

Naturally the centre of interest was Solferino, which occupied a commanding position in the enemy's centre. It was here the winning blow must be struck. Napoleon III sent his Guards out to support Baraguay d'Hilliers. Forey, Ladmirault and Bazaine had a difficult task before them. The Austrian guns hidden among the cypresses were deadly, and the Austrian infantry had found effective cover behind the crenellated walls of the cemetery. At the same time, on the left, the Piedmontese had been held in check by Benedeck at the hill of San Martino, and forced to retreat to the edge of the lake. On the right, Niel, with his divisional commanders, Luzy, Vinoy and Failly, was fighting on his own account before Medole without making any headway. He was afraid of being turned on his right wing and called for help from Canrobert and his reserve corps under Trochu and Bourbaki. Furious fighting continued throughout the afternoon, with assault after assault and one cavalry charge after another. Niel, who was afterwards promoted Marshal, accused Canrobert of having failed to give him sufficient support and of having wasted time keeping a look-out on the right for a danger that did not exist.

189

THE SECOND EMPIRE

In the end the Emperor was forced to intervene to prevent the two men from fighting a duel.

Thus on both wings the situation remained undecided, and it became more and more evident that it was in the centre, at Solferino, that the matter would be settled. A first attack on the village failed, a second succeeded. After artillery preparation, Forey captured the Cypress hill. The cemetery was stormed, and at two o'clock the tricolour was floating over the *Spia d'Italia*. MacMahon advanced in his turn, attacked the hills south of Solferino, in front of Cavriana, failing at first, and then, pushing forward step by step, with heavy losses, menaced Cavriana, the headquarters of Francis Joseph, and entered it at half-past four. The day had been hot and heavy, and for some hours the sky had been overcast. And now the storm that had been brewing burst out with all the characteristic fury of tempests in the Alpine regions; there was an avalanche of rain and hail and the thunder silenced the guns. In the evening, when the storm had died down, the Austrians retreated all along the line, except to the north at San Martino, which Benedeck evacuated only after dark. The French, according to P. de la Gorce, " either too tired or in too great confusion," possibly both, did not trouble to send the cavalry in pursuit of the enemy, but left them in peace during the night and the following day to cross the Mincio at their leisure on bridges of boats which they broke up behind them.

From Cavriana the Emperor telegraphed to the Empress at St. Cloud : " Great battle, great victory." He was wrong; it was a frontal encounter between two armies on the march, three distinct and completely unconnected battles, devoid of any tactical idea and lacking any of the manœuvres which the first Bonaparte used to plan with the lightning flash of genius, and which suddenly overwhelmed the enemy, forcing them to flight and disaster. Like Magenta, Solferino presented the picturesque spectacle peculiar to the wars of the period and which so rarely occurs in modern warfare—the French Marshals and Generals hurled themselves into the thick of the fray to urge on their men, and had on occasion to draw their swords to defend themselves in the hand-to-hand fighting.

190

THE ITALIAN WAR

The standard, like the commander, was in the forefront of the battle, and the fighting went on round the eagles as well as round the guns. A battle was still a piece of Épinal ware in crude colours—the infantry in white gaiters, red trousers, blue coats with the corners of the skirt turned up, red epaulettes, red caps with square peaks and narrow crowns; the Zouaves with green turbans round their red chechias, blue jackets with red braid and pockets faced with red, white, yellow or blue according to the regiment, a wide light blue sash under a black belt with a brass buckle, baggy red breeches piped with blue, yellow leggings with black borders, white gaiters, and a blue cape rolled up on their packs. And along the firing line the *cantinière* would make her way, in her red-and-blue dress, with the keg of brandy slung over her shoulder, attending to the wounded until they could be picked up by the ambulance protected by the red flag. Many of the combatants were soldiers by profession who had fought in Africa, and these jolly devils with their long moustaches and bushy beards knew their job. The Prussian Headquarters Staff dubbed them " willing fellows, independent, capable of initiative and of acting on their own." Sometimes, like the Zouaves at Palestro, they rushed to the assault of their own accord, dragging their colonel along with them. But their leaders relied on the courage of their men, knowing that they would know how to " get out of a mess," whether it were a matter of stealing a chicken in a village to make soup, or of capturing a redoubt, and after a battle they were always liberally rewarded, not only by the presentation of the military medal, but even with the Legion of Honour.

This theory of " getting out of a mess," was a semi-official doctrine. *L'Echo de la Guerre,* a history of the campaign which was published in parts in 1859 under the auspices of the *Siècle,* wrote quite seriously—and ingenuously—without demur on the part of the authorities : " The conditions of warfare have changed. In the old days the leaders used to prepare their plan of battle, they played hide and seek with each other, and at last, after groping for a long while, they met on ground which had long been the object of their study. . . . But now . . . there are no longer any strategic combinations

191

capable of resisting the unforeseen. Modern weapons of war prevent fighting according to plan. After the first volley there is a bayonet charge and the guns are captured before they have been reloaded. . . . All that is required is impetuosity—it is a matter of temperament and individual courage." But war had not yet become that colossal machine which occasionally seems to have escaped beyond the control of its leader. At Solferino, from the hill whence Napoleon III was watching the struggle, a large part of the battlefield was visible, and more particularly the Cypress hill and the *Spia d'Italia*, which can be recognised in Meissonier's picture in the Louvre. But all strategic and tactical science was scorned. To rely on the devil-may-care dash of the trooper was all very well against Arabs in Algeria, or against Austrian Generals paralysed by fear of defeat. But it led to a rude awakening eleven years later, when it was a matter of meeting Prussian Generals who knew their job. Who in 1859, however, could foresee such a turn of events? After Solferino the French army was in the eyes of everybody, or of almost everybody, the first army in the world.

The losses had been extremely heavy on both sides; the French had 12,000 men put out of action, of whom 1,600 had been killed; the Piedmontese 5,000, including 700 dead, and the Austrians 22,000. There was a shortage of doctors, ambulances and drugs. Wounded men died of gangrene on the spot where they had fallen. On the 26th of June, Castiglione was crowded with stretchers, when a rumour ran through the town : " The Austrians are coming back." A terrible panic ensued; the Italians burnt the French flags, and the auxiliary guards of the ambulance column, who were civilians, turned the wagons over into the ditches in order to make their escape more quickly (P. de la Gorce). Brescia provided 6,000 beds. " Brescia has a population of 40,000," observed the Mayor, " which means there are 40,000 beds." The wives, daughters and mothers of the wounded hurried over from France. Sometimes they arrived too late. It was to this confusion and suffering that the Society for the Succour of the Wounded in War owed its origin.

Meanwhile the army did not advance, but remained where

it was by the Mincio. The Austrians took advantage of the respite to retire behind the Adige and re-form between Verona and Legnago. The French followed, reinforced by the troops under Prince Napoleon, which came up by stages from Florence. Siege guns were arriving in preparation for the attack on the two towns of Peschiera and Mantua, which the Austrians had left in their rear surrounded by the enemy. A French squadron was menacing Venice. A great battle was expected for the 7th of July. On the morning of the 7th the whole **Sudden Armistice.** army was deployed ready for action. But suddenly at one o'clock on the same day the field telegraph transmitted to all the army commanders a message from the Emperor which fell like a bolt from the blue : " There is an armistice between the Emperor of Austria and myself."

In thus putting a sudden stop to the conflict Napoleon III was moved by various considerations. His visit to the battle-field of Solferino had stirred him deeply; he had been moved quite as much if not more than after Magenta. He was already sick and tired of this butchery, and had given up all thought of provoking fresh massacres or embarking upon the possibly interminable siege of the Quadrilateral Fortresses. Moreover, numerous cases of typhus had been reported in the army and there were 25,000 sick in the hospitals and infirmaries. He was also disquieted by the excitement in Italy; Parma, Modena and the Romagna were in a state of revolution, and Victor Emmanuel was sending his Commissaries everywhere—in France the general opinion was that he was opening his mouth too wide. On the very day that the battle of Solferino was fought, the *Moniteur* wrote : " [It is said] that Piedmont, without consulting the wishes of the peoples or of the Great Powers, is counting on uniting the whole of Italy into a single State with the help of the French armies. Such conjectures are utterly without foundation. . . . The dictatorship [of the King of Sardinia] is a purely temporary office which . . . in no way prejudices future developments." This boded no good for the forthcoming settlements. In any case the illogicality of a despotic system of Government posing as the champion of Liberalism was all too patent. Furthermore, Germany was becoming more and more anxious. Prussia, naturally pleased to see Austria beaten, was beginning to be jealous of the French successes. She had mobilised her forces and was talking of concentrating 250,000 men on the Rhine. And Randon was reluctant to take away troops from the Rhine to provide the reinforcements which Vaillant was demanding. Russia also was urging France to open negotiations for peace.

At one time the Emperor had thought of asking England to act as mediator, and of having Lombardy handed over to Piedmont and Venetia and Modena to an Archduke. The Liberal Government in London, under Palmerston and Lord John Russell, was in sympathy with the idea of Italian liberation. Indeed Palmerston would have liked to go even further. Austria, on the other hand, would not willingly abandon Venetia, which she still held, even in favour of an Austrian Archduke. It was at this juncture that Fleury was sent to the Emperor Francis Joseph at Verona and that the armistice was concluded. Napoleon III hastened to reassure the Sardinians, who were already becoming anxious, declaring that an armistice did not mean peace and that Austria would certainly not accept the extremely hard terms he would demand. The *Moniteur* spoke in the same strain. Nevertheless, on the morning of the 11th of July, the two Emperors met in the village of Villafranca, just as Napoleon and Alexander had met at Tilsit. The interview was marked by ex-

Meeting at Villafranca. treme courtesy. Napoleon III, who was the victor and the elder of the two—he was fifty-one at the time—showed the greatest consideration for his vanquished foe, the young Emperor of twenty-nine. It was strange that these two men, who were not even separated from each other by a generation, should have thus met face to face, when the one died so long ago and the other so recently that they seem to have lived in two different centuries. Nothing could afford better proof of the swift changes that take place in history within the brief compass of ordinary human existence.

The two men talked, were agreeably impressed by each other and soon reached an agreement. Francis Joseph consented to give up Lombardy, that is to say, he consented

Pre-liminaries. to present it, not to Piedmont, but to France, who was to hand it over to Piedmont. He insisted upon this tribute to his pride, declaring that he had been

194

defeated only by the French, and that as a matter of fact Benedeck had beaten the Piedmontese at Solferino. He was to keep Venetia, where he would introduce important reforms. An Italian Confederation was to be created under the presidency of the Pope, who would also be called upon to consent to reforms of a Liberal nature in the Papal States. The Dukes of Tuscany and Modena were to return, but were not to be allowed to use force to regain their thrones. The two Emperors did not even trouble to have a report drawn up of their conversation. In the afternoon Napoleon III dictated the preliminary draft which Prince Napoleon was to take to Verona and which would eventually be converted into a regular treaty at Zurich. Certain points which had not been raised in the morning were hotly discussed, the Emperor Francis Joseph insisting upon retaining the fortified Lombard towns of Peschiera and Mantua, which were on the Venetian frontier and which his garrisons still held. They had also forgotten to mention Parma in the morning. But as the afternoon passed by without their being able to reach a decision, it was arranged that nothing further should be mentioned in the preliminaries—a convenient way of shelving the difficulty which they had been unable to solve. Francis Joseph did not wish any mention to be made of the " wishes of the Italian peoples "; he was too deeply imbued with the idea of his own divine right to accept this revolutionary phrase. Napoleon III demanded constitutions for the Duchies, to which Francis Joseph replied that " it did not seem to him that France was governed any more constitutionally than Austria," thus maliciously putting his finger on the contradiction lying at the root of the imperial system and lurking in the heart of this dictator, who, outside his own country, set himself up as the champion of Liberalism, though Cæsarism, it is true, maintained that it derived its powers from the will of the nation.

It is better not to render a service than to do so by halves and thus disappoint hopes we ourselves have raised. Italy, as was only human, naturally forgot all she owed to France, and remembered only the aspirations which, through the fault of her ally, still remained unfulfilled. Gratitude is even more rare between nations than between individuals; but in Turin, gratitude, that is to say, if it ever existed at all, soon gave place to contempt and fury. There is a legal saw that to give with one hand and take with the other is no good. Where was Napoleon III's proclamation of May the 3rd saying that " Italy would be free as far as the Adriatic "? So Venice was to remain Austrian? Cavour, who scented danger, had rushed to headquarters. But he could not obtain access to Napo

Italian Disappoint- ment. leon. When he learnt of the preliminaries of Villa franca he sent in his resignation, and cursed the " treachery " of the Emperor. On the 15th of July, Napoleon III returned to Turin; in the windows his portrait had already been replaced by pictures of Orsini. He traversed the town under a strong escort. The procession was cheered, but the cries were intended only for Victor Emmanuel, who accompanied the Emperor. On the following morning he took his departure very early, applauded only by the police and their hirelings. On the 17th he was at St. Cloud.

Obviously he was far from pleased with his achievements. The dreamer tried to justify himself both to others and to

Return of the Emperor. his own conscience for not having carried out his original plans. On the 19th of July, at half-past eight in the evening, he received the representatives of the great Government bodies at St. Cloud—the Senate, the Legislative Body, and the Council of State—who came to congratulate him. According to the usual procedure, their three Excellencies, Troplong, Morny and Baroche, made speeches in the name of the Assemblies over which they presided. Almost their sole topic was the conclusion of hostilities. " French interests, which had demanded the war, to-day counsel peace," declared Troplong, extolling " that heroic moderation which belongs only to noble natures," and reminding his hearers that Scipio, after Zama, refused to raze Carthage to the ground. He congratulated the Emperor on his foresight " in the face of unjustifiable jealousies "—this was for the benefit of the other nations of Europe, who were perturbed by the French successes—" and of wild claims and revolutionary passions "— this for the agitators in Central Italy. " The greatest of all victories," declared Morny, speaking in similar strain, " is the victory that you have won over yourself through the marvellous moderation that characterises you." Morny had been too hostile to the war not to be sincere now. Baroche also extolled that " wisdom which, on the flood-tide of success, had known how to call a halt as soon as the interests as well as the feelings of France might have suffered from what seemed likely to be the future nature and developments of the war "— a transparent allusion to the anxiety created in the French Catholic Party by the agitation against the Pope in the Romagna.

The Emperor replied by " explaining the motive for his conduct "—it was here that the shoe pinched. He reminded his audience that after Solferino he would have had to embark upon " a long and fruitless period of siege warfare," conducted under the menacing eye of all Europe, " ever ready to dispute our successes or to exaggerate our failures." It was necessary for them openly and everywhere to " draw strength from the support of the revolution," in other words, by an extraordinary paradox, through the triumph of those Liberal and Nationalist ideas in whose name Orsini had attempted to assassinate him in 1858. " As soon as the fate of my country seemed likely to be placed in peril, I made peace." He protested, however, that the efforts and sacrifices had not been made in vain; that the King of Piedmont, the erstwhile " Alpine guardian " of France, had been delivered from invasion and that the bounds of his kingdom had been widened : " The idea of Italian unity has been accepted by those who were most hostile to it. And all the sovereigns of the peninsula at last understand the imperative necessity of granting salutary reforms." Thus, at the very moment when he had halted mid-stream in the prosecution of a policy of liberation which he declared had now become undesirable, he still tried to belaud its results; indeed he was driven to do so, if he wished to justify the slaughter and suffering of Magenta and Solferino, the 6,000 dead and 15,000 wounded during the campaign. It is here that the hazy, undecided and inconsequent nature of the Emperor's mind becomes abundantly clear.

In the first flush of victory these political mistakes for a time passed unnoticed. The *Siècle* alone deplored the fact that Venice had remained Austrian, and the journal was given

THE SECOND EMPIRE

the usual warning. But with the restoration of peace, confidence returned; in a few days Government securities rose five francs, which was the main consideration. On Sunday,

The Troops March Past. the 14th of August, the eve of the Emperor's birthday, the army from Italy collected at the Bastille during the morning and marched through the boulevards; the Emperor with his escort rode at the head, next came the able-bodied wounded, the Imperial Guard with Marshal Regnault de Saint Jean d'Angély, together with the flags and guns captured from the enemy, followed by the four corps with their Marshals, Baraguay d'Hilliers, MacMahon and his Turcos, who were tremendously popular, Canrobert, and Niel. All along the route, " which was decorated with Venetian masts, triumphal arches, columns and trophies," the crowd cheered the troops and threw flowers to them. On the Place Vendôme the Emperor halted; on the great balcony of the Ministry of Justice, in a box hung with red velvet, were the Empress, the Prince Imperial, the Princess Mathilde, together with members of the imperial family and the Ministers. In the square itself there were tiers of seats for the Government bodies and the authorities. The torn and tattered colours were cheered to the echo. Each standard-bearer came forward and presented his colours to the Emperor, who handed them to one of his Cent Gardes. In the evening the Generals were entertained at a banquet in the *Salle des États* at the Louvre. The Emperor modestly attributed " the greater part " of the victory to his Generals, who had " made his command easy," because, " filled with sacred fire, they had constantly set the example of duty and contempt for death." This was in keeping with the doctrine of the period, that the leader should share the risks of battle with his men. " May the memory of the obstacles overcome," he added, " the dangers survived, and the mistakes made, often return to your minds, for, in the case of every warrior, memory is knowledge."

Thus the intoxicating fumes of glory did not prevent him from perceiving some of the shortcomings in the military organisation of which the country was so proud. But would he ever have the strength of will to carry out the necessary reforms? He distributed the first silver medals commemorat-
198

ing the campaign, struck in his image, with a red-and-white-striped ribbon, and on the reverse the names of the six victories—Montebello, Palestro, Turbigo, Magenta, Marignano and Solferino. On the following day full and unqualified amnesty was granted to all those who had been sentenced for political crimes and misdemeanours, or had fallen under the ban of the regulations for public safety. Soon a reduction in the strength of the army was announced and everything was peace and joy.

Nevertheless, the difficulties of the Italian question were not yet settled. Cavour, it is true, had resigned and Victor Emmanuel was recalling his Commissaries from **Italy's Difficulties.** Modena, Bologna, Florence and even Parma, thus acquiescing in the note published in the *Moniteur* of the 24th of June and the counsels of the Emperor. But in all four States the Piedmontese Commissary left an enthusiastic party behind who were anxious for union with Piedmont. The Italian Confederation, mentioned at Villafranca, was not enough. As for the dispossessed Princes, they had been forbidden to act in any way contrary to the wishes of their peoples—and the latter did not want them back. Envoys set out from the four States for St. Cloud with the object of winning the sympathy of the Emperor. Walewski, at the Quai d'Orsay, gave them a far from hearty welcome, insisting upon abiding by the preliminaries of Villafranca. Napoleon III, on the other hand, was friendly. Turin sent him Count Arese, the old friend of his youth and of his exile, who, in 1836, after the Strassburg escapade, had gone before him to New York to give him a surprise welcome when he landed on the distant shores of America. Arese was given hospitality at St. Cloud itself, but the Emperor did not conceal from him that he was not prepared to look favourably upon the ambitions of Piedmont or the aspirations of Central Italy. He gave way only in the case of Parma, to whose union with Piedmont he consented. No mention had been made of Parma at Villafranca, and thus the Emperor's hands were not tied. But neither Modena, Tuscany nor above all the Romagna was to become Piedmontese territory, and French envoys were sent to Florence to stir up public opinion in favour of the Princes who had been driven out. But they succeeded only in irritating the Italian patriots against France and did not prevent Tuscany from voting her annexation to Sardinia on the 29th of August. Modena, Parma and Bologna quickly followed suit. Arese, who had returned to Turin, hastened back to France and joined the Emperor in the Pyrenees.

Napoleon III was beginning to get tired of Italian affairs. Arese submitted to him the draft of the speech which Victor **Central Italy and Piedmont.** Emmanuel intended to make to the delegates of the four States who were going to inform him of the results of the vote. The Emperor was already wavering, but declared he would accept their decision only on condition that the rest of Europe also gave its consent. But after a visit from Prince Metternich, the new Austrian Ambassador, he published in the *Moniteur* of the 9th of September a note deciding against the union of Central Italy to Piedmont. It is true that he also repeated that the Austrians were not to be restored by force of arms. Thus he continued trying to give with one hand and take with the other, dreaming of the establishment of a more Liberal system in Italy and of a confederation under the presidency of the Pope, but still endeavouring to avoid the creation of a united kingdom with Piedmont at the head, which would become a menace to France on the one side and to the Papacy on the other. Having failed to foresee the inevitable consequences of the policy he had chosen, he once again found himself in the position of the sorcerer's apprentice, at his wits' end to know how to stop the flood he had himself foolishly let loose.

Moreover, whatever was arranged, it was impossible to prevent the " Roman question " from being raised. If Bologna, **The Roman Question.** which was a Papal city, went over to Piedmont, it would mean the dismemberment of the temporal domain of the Pope; if, on the other hand, the Romagna had been evacuated by the Austrian troops in occupation, it had been owing to the menace of the French army. Thus, willy nilly, it was Napoleon III who had to shoulder the responsibility of this dismemberment. The French Catholics, hitherto so friendly to the Imperial Government, gave free rein to their perturbation and adopted a threatening attitude. They maintained that the Catholic religion

signy, " would you allow France to hold both Dover and Calais,
the entry and the exit of the tunnel? But we want to have
one of the two exits of the future Mont Cenis tunnel." England
referred the matter to Europe. Berlin, like London, lodged
a protest, affecting to fear that the Emperor would shortly
claim the right bank of the Rhine for France as well. But
Napoleon III met the King of Prussia at Baden and reassured
him on that score. Austria remained indifferent. Switzerland, Belgium and the Netherlands were perturbed by this
policy of annexation, which was becoming more and more
blatant. Switzerland more particularly had cause for anxiety.
The two Savoy *arrondissements* of Chablais and Faucigny,
which were on her frontiers, had been neutral since 1815, and
Switzerland had had her eye on them. She was therefore
horrified at the thought of seeing the French red breeches
there, and even more upset by the idea of the French customs
officers who would close the country to goods from Geneva.
Geneva even talked of opposing the annexation by force of
arms, and the Swiss Government formally demanded the
annexation by Switzerland of the two *arrondissements*. Whereupon the French Government, provoked by the demonstrations
at Chambéry, made a verbal promise to Berne to hand over
Chablais and Faucigny. Swiss agents immediately made
their appearance at Thonon and Bonneville " to educate "
public opinion. They inundated the district with pamphlets
pointing out that it would be intolerable to come under French
rule; they would be crippled by taxation, they would be forced
to root up their vineyards to prevent them from competing
with French wines, and their sons would be taken for the
army and sent out to be killed in China—as a matter of
fact there was fighting in China at the time. At this juncture
it seemed likely that Chablais and Faucigny would harmoni-
ously round off the map of Switzerland between Geneva and
Valais and that both sides of the Lake of Geneva would be
Swiss.

With the view of reassuring Europe, Napoleon III declared
that, as far as he was concerned, there was no question of
aggrandisement " in the name of nationalistic ideas or of natural
frontiers "; he had no desire for conquest, all he wanted was

a guarantee, a rectification of frontier. The consent of the people would, of course, be asked, but it was not in response to the popular will that the French would enter Chambéry and Nice. The Emperor was afraid of monarchical Europe, and hesitated to upset it by this fresh blow struck at the *status quo* established by the treaties of 1815, and he did everything in his power to palliate the significance of the annexation. As Ch. Seignobos observes, out of fear he publicly denied his most cherished convictions—national sovereignty and the self-determination of peoples. He was not the man to defy Europe, the truth being that in Italy, behind the factitious glory he had won, he had perceived the real weaknesses of his army. Why was he not as determined as he was clear-sighted?

Cavour tried to keep Nice, or at least to make it a neutral province. But the Emperor sent him his political representative, Benedetti, who stood firm. On the 24th of March, Cavour gave way. Possibly he was not so sorry as he tried to make it appear. " Henceforward we are accomplices," he whispered to the French *chargé d'affaires*. And, indeed, France had now been paid, and Cavour would in future, as far as France was concerned, have all the liberty he wanted to further his ambitious designs.

Meanwhile a campaign had been inaugurated in Savoy to protest against the dismemberment of the country and demand the annexation of the whole district, including Chablais and Faucigny, to France. By way of securing a neutral zone a compromise was suggested. In 1815 the district of Gex, which was also adjacent to Geneva and separated from France by the Jura, had been placed outside the jurisdiction of the French customs. Why not give Thonon and Bonneville, which were contiguous to Geneva, similar customs immunity, which would enable them to maintain their economic relations with the geographical centre of the country? This solution was immediately agreed to by the French Government, which was only too ready to be freed from its verbal promise to Switzerland. Napoleon III protested that he could not " force the will of the peoples." French agents as well as engineers arrived in Savoy, and embankments, roads and plans for railways became the only topics discussed. Everybody was dreaming of the golden age. Better still, it had already dawned. The agents of the Empire sold their wares very cheaply, below cost price, in fact—it was a small sacrifice made by the imperial Government with the object of securing the sympathies of the people. On the 22nd and 23rd of April the people of Savoy were summoned to vote by communes, with the tricolour and the parish priest at their head. The result was 130,000 *Ayes* in favour of annexation, and 235 *Nays*. The country was almost unanimously in favour of annexation. As for Nice, her reply was just as decisive: 15,000 *Ayes* to 160 *Nays*. At one time Napoleon III had had qualms with regard to these plebiscites; but they were without foundation. The Liberals, and even the Democrats, had been won over by the promises of prosperity dangled before their eyes, and by the solution whereby Chablais and Faucigny were made free zones, a solution destined to have results in the distant future, for the question was reopened after the Great War.

Owing to constant vacillation and recantation, France had not succeeded in gaining the friendship of a great nation beyond the Alps; nay, worse, she had helped to found the fortunes of a new country which might one day be a menace to her. But for the moment, at all events, this country was less of a menace than Austria. The Italian venture had secured for France a stronger frontier and three new departments, two in Savoy and the third—the Alpes-Maritimes—consisting of Nice and the *arrondissement* of Grasse, which had been severed from the Var district. It is only fair to place these solid gains to the credit of the Second Empire. Those who had laid down their lives at Magenta and Solferino had not died altogether in vain.

CHAPTER VI

TOWARDS THE LIBERAL EMPIRE

Further progress on the part of Piedmont—the annexation of Naples. The Roman question. French troops defend Rome against their former allies. Lamoricière and the Papal Zouaves. Entry of the Piedmontese into the Papal States. Castelfidardo (18th of September, 1860). Indignation of the Catholics against the Emperor. Dreams of Free Trade and Anglomania. First efforts against the protectionist tradition. Michel Chevalier and Richard Cobden. Secret negotiations. Letter to Fould of the 15th of January, 1860. Protests. Anglo-French Treaty of the 23rd of January, 1860. Hostility of the industrialists to the *régime*. A Liberal measure—the decree of the 24th of November, 1860—revives political life. Morny's policy. Resistance on the part of the " absolutists." First debates—the Roman question in the Senate and the Legislative Body; Prince Napoleon, Keller. The Five. Ollivier prepared for a rally. Plans for a Liberal Empire. The Catholics against the Empire—incidents and scandals. Monseigneur Pie. The Government conflict with the Society of St. Vincent de Paul. Economic crisis. Fould Minister of Finance. No more supplementary supplies. Efficacious control of the Legislative Body. The Roman question again. Recognition of the Kingdom of Italy. Incidents with Piedmont. The Emperor alienates himself from Piedmont and approaches Rome with a view to the elections of 1863. The Republican Party—the irreconcilables; the Five; the " Young Liberals." Difficulty of concerted action. The Marie Committee—the Liberal Union against the *régime*. Legitimists, Catholics, Independents, Liberals—Prévost-Paradol. Persigny against the Opposition. Official candidature, pressure on the part of the Government. Elections of the 30th and 31st of May. Success of the Opposition in Paris, and of the Government in the provinces. Nevertheless a blow for the *régime*. Fall of Persigny. Morny and Ollivier. Thiers and the indispensable liberties. Victor Duruy Minister of Education. Special education. Compulsory elementary education and the education of girls. Awakening of the working classes. The printers and the Palais Royal. The workmen's visit to London. Letter of the 17th of February, 1864. Workers' Unions allowed. Ollivier to the fore. Republican agitation. The Encyclical *Quanta Cura* and the Syllabus of the errors of the Age. Is it to be Liberalism? The death of Morny interrupts its development.

THE annexation of Savoy and Nice was not sufficient to regain the sympathies of the Catholics, who, like the Pope, felt the loss of the Romagna deeply and laid the blame on Napoleon III. Moreover, the union of Bologna with Pied-

210

mont was merely the first step in the dismemberment of the Papal States. "Italy," declared Victor Emmanuel at the opening of his new Parliament on the 2nd of April, 1860, "must be the Italy of the Italians." And in a single year, Piedmont, the nucleus of the great nation of the future, had increased her territory by the inclusion of Milan, Parma, Modena, Florence and Bologna. She still lacked Venice, Naples and Rome. Venice remained in the keeping of the Austrian white coats, and it was necessary to await a favourable opportunity. In the Kingdom of Naples just at this moment, April 1860, an insurrection had broken out at Palermo against the young King Francis II. At the beginning of May, Garibaldi, who had been held in check and publicly disavowed by Cavour, set sail from Genoa for Sicily with his "Thousand," landed at Marsala, captured Palermo, and menaced the King of Naples, who appealed in vain to Napoleon III. Thouvenel suggested that the English should prevent Garibaldi from crossing the Straits of Messina, but London pleaded the doctrine of non-intervention, and Paris let the matter slide—another vain

Annexation of Naples. attempt to arrest or retard the inevitable course of events which France herself was responsible for having set in motion. Garibaldi crossed over to Calabria, and on September 6th, Francis II left Naples for Gaeta. Thus ended the Kingdom of the Two Sicilies. The new Italy had acquired Naples and Palermo.

Rome remained, or rather that portion of the Papal States which had been separated from the Romagna; with Umbria and the Marches, the domain of the Pope still stretched from east to west of the peninsula, from Ostia to Ancona, and this strip of territory separated Victor Emmanuel from his new possessions in the south. Moreover, how was it possible for the new Italy to be complete without the historic capital of the great Empire of the ancient world? Thus the "Roman question," which was raised as soon as the Romagna had been annexed to Piedmont, pressed ever more urgently for solution. And it was destined to increase the hostility of the Catholic forces in France against Napoleon III, "the author of all the trouble"; so much so indeed that these far-away happenings in Italy really helped to mould .

The Roman Question.

events within the French Empire itself. On the Paris boule-vards a toy symbolising this imbroglio was sold under the name of the " Roman question "; it consisted of a confused jumble of little triangles with a ring entangled among them which had to be extricated.

The situation in Rome was paradoxical. The tricolour floated over the Castle of St. Angelo and yet the city was being menaced by Piedmont, who was an ally of France. Ever since 1849 French troops had been in occupation of the city, ready to defend it against the invader, and the invader whom the Vatican now had to fear was the *bersagliere* who had fought side by side with France at Palestro and Solferino. Thus the march of events proved how illogical had been the wavering policy of Napoleon, which in 1849 had crushed those who were dream-ing of a Roman Republic and a Great Italy, and in 1859 had helped the founders of the new Italy. Moreover, the French troops were not defending the whole of the Papal States, but only Rome and the Roman Campagna, while from time to time the forthcoming departure of the troops in occupation was announced. The Vatican was anxious to defend the Marches and Umbria, and eventually Rome herself, alone and unaided.

At this juncture, the Secretary of State, Cardinal Antonelli, who was prudent and diplomatic, was superseded by a bellicose

Lamoricière. prelate, Monseigneur de Mérode, who had been a Belgian officer and had fought in Algeria; and it was decided to make preparations for war. The French Catholics sent donations of money—the first payment of Peter's pence—and looked round for a leader. A Frenchman was chosen, Lamoricière, an old African General, who had been out of a job ever since the *coup d'état* of December, of which he had been one of the victims. Such a choice was not calcu-lated to please Napoleon III; but if he found objections to raise against it, would he have the strength of will to oppose it? Monseigneur de Mérode, moreover, was far from dis-pleased at emancipating himself in this way from the yoke of the Power that had been occupying Rome. With the title of Minister of Arms—a curious appellation for a Minister of Christ, but the authorities had not dared to say Minister of

War—he set to work like a Julian II to reorganise the pontifical forces with the help of Lamoricière. Lamoricière was to hit the revolution on the head " like a mad dog," and to lead a crusade against it similar to the old crusades against Islam. Recruits were raised from every quarter—from Austria, Switzerland and Ireland; the help of French officers who had resigned their commissions was enlisted, as was also that of the old royalist nobility, Legitimists, whose very names, like that of Monsieur de Charette, prevented them from rallying to the Empire and urged them, since they could not die for their King, to fight for their God. Soon from Anjou, Vendée and Brittany, bands of young volunteers flocked, all animated by the same spirit. At first they **The Papal Zouaves.** were dubbed the *Sharpshooters* and afterwards the *Papal Zouaves*. The Duc de Gramont, Napoleon III's Ambassador at the Vatican, considered this a unique opportunity for withdrawing the French troops, and on Cavour giving his promise not to attack the Marches, it was arranged that the army of occupation should return to France by units during the course of the summer of 1860.

But just at this moment Garibaldi entered Naples, and the situation immediately changed. The old revolutionary had **Garibaldi.** no intention of stopping at this, but wanted to march with his red shirts to Rome. Cavour was perturbed by the repeated successes of this free-lance. Though he was anxious to secure Italian unity, he wanted it to be established under the constitutional rule of Victor Emmanuel and not in the shape of the anarchical republic of which Garibaldi dreamt. It was therefore imperative to forestall the hero of the *Thousand* in the Papal States, and to occupy the Marches and Umbria in order to establish order in those districts; moreover, it was a good excuse to cut off another slice from the Papal domain. But for this the support of the Emperor was necessary. As it happened he was paying a visit to Savoy at the moment, and Cialdini and Farini were sent to join him at Chambéry to prove to him that the road must at all costs be barred to Garibaldi. Disturbances had already broken out at Ancona, Perugia and Spoleto. Revolution was menacing. Would he give his permission for the Piedmontese to enter the Marches and Umbria and restore order?

213

What was the Emperor's reply? He certainly did not forbid it. "The Emperor has sanctioned everything," wrote Cavour in a letter of this date. "Apparently he was delighted at the thought of seeing Lamoricière get into a scrape. . . . He said that the diplomatic world would protest loudly and that he would find himself in a difficult position, but that he would put forward the idea of a Congress." All this was not as unlikely as might be supposed. There was an element of conspiracy about the venture which was not altogether displeasing to Napoleon III, and the idea of the trick to be played on that old knave of a Lamoricière also appealed to him. Moreover, his contempt for the diplomatists was quite characteristic of the man, as well as the idea of a Congress, a solemn farce for setting them off one against the other. Later on, in answer to a suggestion made by Cialdini, the Emperor was supposed to have answered: "*Fatte, ma fatte presto.*" This "act quickly" was also very characteristic; Europe must be faced with the accomplished fact. Had not the Emperor written, or caused to be written, in the pamphlet *Le Pape et le Congrès*, that the smaller the domain of the Pope, the greater his authority would be? Moreover, it was understood that operations would be strictly limited to the Marches and Umbria, that Rome would not be involved; and the Emperor, still indulging in dreams of a new Italy, refused to see that step by step they would inevitably approach the obstacle of Rome herself, who, with Venice, would soon be the only foreign stronghold left in a united Italy.

Strong in the support of Napoleon III, who had just set out for Algeria, Cavour sent the Piedmontese troops into Umbria **Piedmont** and the Marches to prevent Lamoricière's foreign **enters the** mercenaries "from smothering every manifesta- **Papal States.** tion of national feeling in Italian blood." Thouvenel telegraphed to the Emperor suggesting that France should publicly protest and threaten Turin with a rupture of diplomatic relations. The Emperor did not go as far as that, but contented himself with saying to Victor Emmanuel: "If it is true that without legitimate reason Your Majesty's troops are entering the Papal States, I shall be obliged to oppose you. . . ." Monseigneur de Mérode, ever impetuous, and

214

doubtless anxious to encourage Lamoricière, translated this into "The Emperor will oppose by force of arms." The French Minister was recalled from Piedmont, but a secretary was left as *chargé d'affaires*. All this gave the impression of being a prearranged farce. "France is showing her teeth, but I am not certain that they are not false teeth," somebody declared. Nobody was taken in and the Emperor's *complicity* with Piedmont was quite clear. Lamoricière wanted to hurl himself on Ancona and entrench himself there. But on the 18th of September he and his handful of men ran into the Piedmontese under Cialdini at Castelfidardo, a few miles from Ancona. General de Pimodan's sharpshooters heroically allowed themselves to be killed. The rest of the little army disbanded and laid down their arms. Lamoricière made an attempt to defend Ancona, but was obliged to capitulate there himself a few days later. Umbria and the Marches were lost to the Pope.

Castel-fidardo.

The "martyrs" of Castelfidardo were mourned in France. Monseigneur Dupanloup pronounced their funeral oration in Orleans cathedral: "All that is honourable, pure and glorious here below rests upon you with the blessing of God." At the foot of the pulpit sat old Berryer, his eyes full of tears. The feeling in the Catholic salons of the faubourg when the tale of the *Fatte presto* was told may be imagined. Later on Monseigneur Dupanloup declared that on the day of the ceremony at Orleans "he was choking with all he was not allowed to say." Henceforward the gulf between the Catholics and the Empire was too wide to be bridged. The Emperor took the Piedmontese to task, but *molto amorevolmente*. Thouvenel, who was skilled in modelling his conduct according to the Emperor's wishes, considered that intervention was now out of the question. "The pontiff is respected," he observed of the Pope, "but the sovereign is not popular." And after much wavering, the Government decided to be led by Cavour and pushed to its logical conclusion the policy outlined in the famous pamphlet *Le Pape et le Congrès*: they were of opinion that the Pope should be content with the city of Rome. And the rest of Europe acquiesced. But the French bishops and devout

Catholic Indignation.

Catholics could not forgive Napoleon III for what they regarded as an act of treachery.

Thus by giving way to his sympathy with the idea of Italian unity and realising his grandiose dreams of new nationalities, **Free Trade and Anglomania.** the Emperor stirred up against him many people who had hitherto been his staunchest supporters. And in that same year, 1860, he also succeeded in rousing further hostility in a very different sphere through his passionate advocacy of Free Trade and his Anglomania. In the economic world, as in the world of religion, his airy schemes were opposed to certain established interests and provoked lively opposition. This political clumsiness, this incapacity to foresee results, this simple-minded hope of being able to hold within bounds an issue that he had himself let loose, and to guide a movement which he himself had created, this over-confident optimism of a blind and generous theorist, this love of utopias and chimeras—all this was both heart-rending and seductive, and explains why the *régime* was at once treated with great tolerance and exposed to the severest strictures. There was something of the " enlightened despot " about this " forty-eightish " Emperor. The pity of it is that those crowned dreamers who sincerely desire the welfare of their people, more often than not bring down all manner of disasters on their subjects even if they themselves escape. In any case, Napoleon III light-heartedly provoked the choler of numberless industrialists who had hitherto linked their prosperity with the fate of the Empire. Here again his airy theories were to cost him many a steadfast supporter.

France was protectionist by tradition. Colbert, Napoleon and Louis Philippe—a strange trio to be mentioned in one **Campaign against Protection.** breath—had been inspired by the same doctrine in this respect; it was essential for French industry to be protected against foreign competition by means of a whole system of prohibitive tariffs or high duties. But political economists had for many years been preaching the gospel of Free Trade. The creation of railways and great steamship companies was leading to an increase of trade between the various countries. Was this trade still to be

216

TOWARDS THE LIBERAL EMPIRE

hampered by excessive or prohibitive customs duties? Was it not illogical to have trains and fast ships at one's disposal and then to see the merchandise they bore held up at the frontiers by a Chinese wall of tariffs? As early as 1852 negotiations had already been opened with England with a view to reducing customs duties. In 1853, when the harvest was bad, everything had gone up in price, and it was thought wise to reduce the duties on cereals, cattle and meat, so that the imports might compensate for the shortage in French produce and lower prices. Similarly, between 1853 and 1855 the duties on coal, iron, steel and cast-iron goods and machinery were reduced. And, as had been proved by the Exhibition of 1855, French industry was just as flourishing. In 1856, at the Congress of Paris, Napoleon III informed the English of an impending reform in the direction of Free Trade. But the ironmasters and mill owners of the Legislative Body, fearing English competition, were very much perturbed by the idea. At Rouen and Elbeuf, Lille, Roubaix and Tourcoing an "era of calamity" was prophesied. And confronted by this opposition, the Government, who did not yet feel in a position to defy the industrialists, withdrew their proposal.

But the Emperor had not abandoned his ideas. His friend, Michel Chevalier, an old St. Simonian, and Professor of Political **Michel Chevalier.** Economy at the Collège de France, was giving lectures there in favour of Free Trade. He also contributed articles in the same strain to the *Débats*. Moreover, he was President of the General Council of Hérault, where there was no fear of competition on the part of foreign wines and there was a demand for the mutual abolition of customs barriers all round so that France might sell her wines to England. In the summer of 1859, Chevalier met Richard Cobden, the head of the Manchester School and the apostle **Cobden.** of Free Trade, at a Congress held at Bradford. He also interviewed Mr. Gladstone, at that time Chancellor of the Exchequer, as a result of which Cobden visited Paris on a semi-official mission, though to prevent a scare the utmost secrecy was preserved. He was received at St. Cloud and dazzled the Emperor by depicting the advantages of Free Trade in glowing colours—the nations would mingle in friendly intercourse and there would be universal peace. Above all Cobden reminded the Emperor of Sir Robert Peel, the man who had been responsible for reducing the duty on corn; and the inscription on his statue declaring that he had alleviated the lot of the working and suffering masses by lowering the price of prime necessities. This touched the heart of Napoleon III more than anything. For he sincerely desired the welfare of his people and was anxious to do all he could towards the *extinction of pauperism,* a subject which he had studied long ago in his prison at Ham. Thus the Emperor was won over. And he was the more readily converted since the first country with which the principle of Free Trade could be applied was England—an excellent opportunity of strengthening the bonds between that country and France, which had been somewhat strained since Orsini's crime and the Italian war.

Resistance on the part of the Legislative Body was only to be expected. But by virtue of a *senatus consultum* of 1852, **Secret Negotiations.** the Emperor had the right to sign treaties of commerce himself and introduce the changes in customs tariffs arranged for in such treaties without referring to the Legislative Body. Thus it was sufficient to draw up *in camera* a treaty with England to be able to apply the principles of Free Trade without let or hindrance with France's most important customer and source of supply. And negotiations were opened between Cobden and the English Ambassador in Paris on the one hand and Baroche, who was *ad interim* in charge of Foreign Affairs, and Rouher, the Minister of Commerce, on the other. The latter kept the matter dark from the officials in his own department, as well as from Magne, the Minister of Finance, who was known to be a protectionist and who would have had something to say on any matter affecting the customs. The affair had all the appearances of a conspiracy. It was only early in January 1860 that the English Press got wind of it. Whereupon the *Constitutionnel,* which had hitherto been protectionist, sang the praises of Free Trade, and, on the 15th of January, the *Moniteur* published a programme letter addressed by the Emperor to Fould, the Minister of State: " There is only

218

one universal system of sound political economy which, by laying the foundations of national wealth, can spread comfort **The** among the working classes. . . ." This universal **Emperor's** system was based upon the abolition of prohibitive **Letter.** tariffs, the establishment of moderate duties, and the conclusion of commercial treaties.   But, by way of compensation, industry would be provided with better weapons for fighting foreign competition :   " In order to encourage manufactures, all the raw materials—wool, cotton, etc.—indispensable to industry must be free of duty."   Furthermore, the construction of canals, roads and railways would be speeded up and an attempt made " to reduce tariffs by encouraging legitimate rivalry between the canals and the railways," and industry would be lent " the capital for perfecting its plant "—in short, an entire programme was drawn up for boldly encouraging French industry so that French manufactured goods, stuffs and cloths would be able to compete on equal terms with foreign industries.

This letter, which was meant to be reassuring, made a great stir in the industrial world.   Four hundred manufacturers **Protests.** came to Paris from Flanders, Picardy, Normandy and Alsace and in vain solicited an audience of the Emperor.   All they could do was to draw up a vehement address which the Press had the courage to publish :   " We are going to be condemned without having been granted a hearing. . . ."   Nevertheless, the Anglo-French treaty was signed on the 23rd of January, 1860.   It was to hold good for ten years, its main idea being the entire abolition of all prohibitive tariffs.   Customs duties were not to exceed a maximum of 30 per cent. *ad valorem* on goods imported from England **Anglo-** (25 per cent. after October 1864); these included **French** cottons, textile fabrics, iron, cast-iron and steel **Treaty.** goods, machines and tools.   The duty on coal was reduced by 50 per cent.   In return England lowered the duties on French wines and brandies, silk goods, dresses and millinery, and abolished them altogether on silks and fancy goods. Furthermore, both countries were to give the other the advantage " of any lowering of tariff granted to another Power "— this was the most-favoured-nation clause.

219

The treaty was clearly intended to facilitate commercial intercourse between France and England, but it did not establish Free Trade—very far from it. Neverthe- **Discontent** less, the industrialists were extremely irritated **of the In-** by this lowering of the protective tariffs, and their **dustrialists.** discontent became evident when the Legislative Body was called upon to ratify the abolition of the duties on woollen and cotton goods. The measure was introduced by Pouyer-Quertier, a Rouen manufacturer. He naturally supported the Bill, which was favourable to industry. But he seized the opportunity to make a fundamental attack on Free Trade and demanded that the duties on English goods should be fixed as near as possible to the maximum provided for, which " was really a protectionist measure." Other deputies complained that the Government had taken action without consulting the Legislative Body, and declared that the measure would lead to a fall in wages, to unemployment and ruin. Baroche replied by quoting Thiers : " Any industry that has reached its full development should not be protected." And he proceeded to assure the Assembly that the duties would not be fixed until an inquiry had been made into the cost price of similar articles in both countries. In practice the duties fixed by the conventions subsequently made with England did not exceed 20 per cent. for cutlery, 10 to 15 per cent. for cottons and textiles, articles against which the tariffs had hitherto been prohibitive. The Government confined the entry of English goods to certain ports, to prevent " dumping." As a matter of fact the English sent over their surplus rubbish at a low price. " Do they take us for Hottentots ? " exclaimed the French working people. " They are really too stupid if they think we are going to buy that sort of thing." But the fact remains that large numbers of French manufacturers were obliged to lower their prices. They found themselves in difficulties and blamed Napoleon III, with the result that the Empire suffered a still further loss of support.

In January 1860 Sir Charles Greville wrote in his Diary, that for the Emperor to defy both the clerical party and the protectionists he must have extraordinary faith in his own prestige, and that it would be interesting to see whether the event would justify his audacity. And it did indeed seem rash for the Government to turn both the Church and the industrial world, the two bulwarks of the *régime*, against it at the same time. A dictatorship, however absolute, is nevertheless dependent upon public opinion. Did the Emperor really imagine that his prestige would be sufficient to make up for the loss of these invaluable supports which he had so light-heartedly alienated? Apparently not. For it was in 1860 that a decree was suddenly promulgated which was to remain famous as the Decree of the 24th of November. By this decree the Address, that is to say, the reply drawn up by the Legislative

The Decree of November 24th. Body (or by the Senate) to the Speech from the Throne at the opening of the session, and which had been abolished in 1852, was again to be allowed. The purpose of this Address was to give the deputies the opportunity of discussing and criticising each paragraph of the Speech from the Throne; in short, of interpellating the Government on its general policy. The decree also arranged that the Government Commissioners should give the deputies all the explanations necessary in connection with the Bills put before them. And the Legislative Body was to have the right of debating these Bills *in camera* before appointing the Commission charged with the task of examining them. This facilitated the right of amendment. Furthermore, Ministers without portfolios, who were members of the Ministerial Council, and not only Councillors of State, might defend Government Bills before the Chambers. Lastly, the Press, which ever since 1852 had been allowed to publish only an extremely short report of the debates, would in future every evening receive a detailed report, and the *Officiel* of the following day would publish a verbatim shorthand report. Thus the public would be kept directly informed of what took place at the great political debates and would no longer depend upon vague hearsay. The doors of the Palais Royal, which had been shut since 1852, were also thrown open to the public.

This decree fell like a bolt from the blue. A Parliamentary system was, it is true, still very far from being established, and

Revival of Political Life. that docile assembly, the Legislative Body, was not by any means prepared to overthrow Ministries. Nevertheless, the right to debate the Address, the presence of Ministers at the debates, the publication of the discussions in detail, marked the return to a public life which had well-nigh been forgotten. Everybody was thunderstruck. The extreme Bonapartists, who "grumbled and growled" against the decree, regarded it as a dangerous sign of weakness, and talked about the *crime of the 24th of November ;* they were supported by polemical Liberals like Prévost-Paradol, whom a daring pamphlet had that very year cost three months' imprisonment. "The powers of the Chamber are so radically changed," he wrote in the *Débats,* "that it is no longer recognisable." The aged Guizot prophesied that "through this door standing half open to the Liberals, the revolutionaries would one day make their entry." While Proudhon declared that "the Empire had made a half-turn to the Left."

This "thunderbolt," this first change in the direction of a more Liberal system, was accounted for in a variety of different ways. Whatever the right explanation may have been, it was certainly something very different from the free and unsolicited sign of "good-will" that Émile Ollivier held it to be, or a "signal proof of confidence in the State Assemblies," as it was described in the preamble to the decree. How could these docile bodies, appointed by the Government itself and elected on the principle of official candidature, fail to command its confidence? There were far profounder reasons for the promulgation of the decree. The man behind it was the instigator of the *coup d'état* which had established the *régime*—Morny himself. Did he not, on the day after the decree was promulgated, say to Ollivier, "Well, I hope you are satisfied now?" Morny was the only statesman in the imperial Government, the only man capable of taking long views. But what did he see all about him in 1860? An army covered with glory, it is true, but the shortcomings of which were now becoming all too apparent; Catholics wounded in their respect for the Pope by the Emperor's Italian policy; industrialists who considered that their interests had been sacrificed by the commercial treaty with England; and Liberal journalists irritated by the thousand and one restrictions that hampered their activities. "The time has come," wrote the Duc de Gramont at this juncture, "for the Emperor to release his person of the burden of dis-

Morny's Policy.

222

content which his policy must inevitably engender." And doubtless Morny was well aware of all this. Was not the restoration of a certain amount of political activity to the Legislative Body and the publication of the debates on matters of vital national interest the best means of regaining the support of public opinion and winning back the sympathies of the country which were so necessary for the duration and perpetuation of the Empire? Morny had never imagined that the day of personal rule could be prolonged indefinitely, but had always been of opinion that when once it had been firmly established by " high-handed " methods, it would be obliged to slacken rein a little and allow the beast to take breath.

" The lasting and durable establishment of political liberty is the crown of every civilised society," he declared. A little later he added : " A Government that lacks control and criticism is like a ship without ballast. Absence of contradiction sometimes blinds and misleads those in power and does not inspire confidence in the country." The *régime* had imposed its will on France throughout eight years of dictatorial rule; it had now become necessary for it to become merged in the country by means of a clever transformation, making it form a single corporate whole with the nation. The Emperor was already growing old and suffering from bladder trouble. Morny, who was far-sighted, must at this time have been in constant dread of a catastrophe, and anxious to secure the throne for the boy of four who might one day be left an orphan. The personal rule of the Emperor must be transmuted into a national Government which would inspire the sympathy of the majority by entering, circumspectly, of course, upon the path of Liberalism.

The decree was followed by other measures tending in the same direction. Baroche, Billault and Magne were made Ministers without portfolios. Fould, who did not approve of reform, was replaced at the Ministry of Finance by Forcade, a half-brother of St. Arnaud on his mother's side. Persigny returned to the Ministry of the Interior and instructed his Prefects to " show deference to any honourable and distinguished members of the old Governments." He cancelled the warnings that had been sent out to the newspapers and authorised Nefftzer, of the *Presse*, to found a new Opposition journal, the *Temps*. The change had become clearly defined. But for the moment it went no further, and soon those in the Government who believed in the doctrine of the " high hand " felt the need of stopping it altogether. " The decree of November has said its last word," Billault shortly afterwards declared in the Legislative Body, " . . . it has granted France all the concessions of which she is worthy, and she can claim nothing further." Thus he was still drawing distinctions between the *régime* and the country, instead of understanding, like Morny, that they should become incorporated in each other. And it was not long before Persigny began to issue warnings against the Press. The *Débats* was cautioned for having " shaken faith in the strength and durability of our institutions," and others were treated in the same way. He made his Prefects draw up lists of dangerous men, " Republicans, Orleanists and Legitimists," and have warrants ready signed in advance for their arrest. And he had a private document by the Duc de Broglie, entitled *Vues sur le gouvernement de la France*, seized. Thus an isolated decree was not sufficient to change the imperial policy and the habits of the Government and the police. But at least it had the effect of allowing the Opposition to make its voice heard and to start undermining the edifice founded on the 2nd of December.

It was, of course, the everlasting Roman question which in March 1861 provided the subject for the debate on the first Address. In the Senate Prince Napoleon, in the name of " the spirit of modernity," made a violent attack on the Marquis de la Rochejacquelin, who, true to his name, had defended the temporal power of the Pope. The Marquis's speech had " clearly emanated from a holy council of Legitimists and clerics." But Napoleon III " represented popular right as opposed to divine right "; Cæsarism made a point of differentiating itself from the absolute monarchy of the Bourbons. " There has been talk," added the Prince, " of sympathy with Francis II." Francis II, besieged and bombarded in Gaeta, had refused to embark on board one of the French ships which Napoleon III, doubtless

The Roman Question.

224

moved by qualms of remorse, had sent to fetch him, and had been finally obliged to capitulate. "Do not let us confound **Prince** sympathy with pity. Our sympathy is reserved **Napoleon.** for the glorious cause of Italian freedom. For the ex-King of the Two Sicilies we can feel only pity." A violent attack on the Bourbons, of whom Francis II was doubtless the last to wear a crown, followed, and also of Lamoricière and his "bands," of Monseigneur de Mérode, of the new "Coblentz" formed by the *émigrés* in Rome, and of the Papacy, that "crystallisation of the Middle Ages." In conclusion, the Prince invited the Pope to abandon even Rome and retire to "some place from which he could dominate the whole world without being dependent upon anybody."

This intervention, bold though it was, had certainly been engineered by the Government. This is proved by the fact that the *Moniteur des Communes* published the text of the speech, while the Emperor wrote to the Prince to congratulate him on his "noble and patriotic sentiments," and the police seized a pamphlet in which the Duc d'Aumale had had the temerity to defend the Bourbons. Cavour also complimented the Prince. "Your Highness's speech has done for the temporal power of the Pope what Solferino did for the rule of Austria." The Government openly took sides against the temporal power of the Pope and in favour of the complete establishment of Italian unity without troubling about the opposition of the French Catholics. The Senate, however, was not so firmly convinced, for shortly afterwards, out of 139 votes, 61 were in favour of the temporal power. In the Legislative Body several Catholic deputies likewise came forward in favour of the Pope. One speaker, named Keller, who had never been **Keller.** heard of before and immediately relapsed into obscurity again, revelled in an hour of glorious oratory. If France had allowed Piedmont free rein, he declared, it was because she had started back in horror "before the Revolution incarnate in Orsini. . . . The struggle was the struggle of 1848 over again between the Catholic faith and the revolutionary faith. . . . You, who have had the temerity to reopen this conflict without understanding its significance, who are you and what do you want? Are you

Q

revolutionaries? Are you Conservatives? Or are you merely spectators of the struggle? Up till now you are none of these things. . . ." This amounted to boldly putting the Emperor with his back to the wall, and pointing out the illogicality, the vacillation and the weaknesses of his Italian policy, and, worse still, the innate contradiction of Cæsarism, the despotism which maintained that it was founded upon the sovereignty of the people. As Billault observed, the violence of the debate proved "how fast matters had moved in a week." On the following day Prévost-Paradol wrote : "Salute the old Chamber of 1857; she is dead as a doornail and we shall never see her again."

Political life was reviving. After a silence of eight years these first signs of movement stirred the country deeply. Students flocked in crowds to the Palais Bourbon, hoping to find seats in the galleries, and the attendants were already beginning to fear disturbances, another 15th of May. The session lasted five months, as long as it used to do under Louis Philippe. The Opposition under the *Five* seized the opportunity presented by the debate on the Address to criticise the

The Five. *régime* as a whole. Jules Favre attacked the laws of public safety and other measures of an exceptional nature which were contrary to the principles of '89, the principles which were said to form the basis of the Constitution of 1852. He also demanded greater freedom for the Press and a less farcical procedure in the conduct of the general elections. Ernest Picard criticised the rebuilding of Paris under Haussmann's administration, and the crying abuses of expropriation and speculation. But on the 14th of March, 1861, an extremely significant incident occurred. Émile Ollivier had demanded the abolition of the preliminary authorisation required for the publication of newspapers and the establishment of the system of trial by jury for Press misdemeanours. In his peroration he addressed himself directly to the Emperor : "Sire," he declared, "when a ruler is every day . . . acclaimed by thirty-five millions of subjects, when he has the world at his feet . . . there is still one ineffable joy left for him to taste—the joy of courageously initiating a great people into the mysteries of freedom. . . . And I hereby

226

declare, I who am a Republican, that such a day would win the whole-hearted approval of the vast majority and secure their support." Morny cleverly had the words, "I who am a Republican," deleted from the report, and Ollivier did not protest. It was another deputy who demanded an explanation from Morny. The President very reasonably adduced the moderation of Ollivier's speech as his justification. "When Monsieur Ollivier was declaring that he would rally to the support of the Government in spite of his previous Republican convictions it was surely not a right or suitable moment" to call him to order by virtue of his oath of allegiance to the Emperor. These words and this conciliatory attitude combined with the decree of the 24th of November shed a clear light on Morny's game. He obviously hoped, by means of Liberal reforms, to see a strong moderate party come into being of which Ollivier, abandoning the *Five*, would be the leader. He already envisaged that Liberal Empire which in his eyes constituted the final consolidation of the *régime*. But he died too soon to see it realised, too soon to be able to support it and—who knows?—perhaps defend it against wind and tide.

But the goal was still far distant. The Catholic Opposition in the Legislative Body as well as in the Senate was still very **The** strong. An amendment by Jules Favre demanding **Catholic** the abandonment of the Pope and the withdrawal **Opposition.** of the army of occupation received only five votes. And there were 91 votes to 126, that is to say, a significant minority, demanding that the accusation brought against the Pope of having offered resistance to wise counsels should be deleted from the Address. The Government, it is true, carried its point, but it now found itself faced by a Catholic Opposition which was going to turn the new semi-Liberal system to account in order to raise serious difficulties. Doubtless the Government still had certain weapons at its disposal. Had not its present opponents been elected as official candidates? "We shall have our own back at the elections," was the threat held out by Persigny over the head of one of the Catholic deputies who had played a leading part in the struggle. The Government had no intention of leaving public opinion alone; it still proposed to guide it—to prevent a surprise. The Government, and the Government alone, had the right to direct and interpret the popular will on which it maintained that it was based.

This petty warfare between the Empire and the Catholics, the Prefect and the Bishop, continued throughout 1861. Country **Mon-** clergy who in their sermons failed to moderate their **seigneur** language on the Roman question were prose-**Pie.** cuted or the payment of their stipends was forgotten. In the north, Belgian priests were driven out and religious communities broken up. Much capital was made out of young Jewesses being kidnapped and converted by force, and the scandalous debauching of youth by clerics. Officials who sent their children to the Bons Pères were denounced, while the Government virtually ostracised Monseigneur Pie, Bishop of Poitiers, who was particularly hostile to the Emperor on the subject of the Roman question, comparing Napoleon III to Pontius Pilate. A certain cavalry colonel boasted of having defied the ban placed upon the Bishop, and the Emperor himself, who was in Biarritz at the time, ordered his Minister of War to " reprimand the colonel severely for having dashed up on horseback at the head of his subordinate officers to the Bishop's house." This was reminiscent of the docket system of unhappy memory. Victor de Laprade, a Catholic, and Professor at the Faculté des Lettres at Lyons, who was regarded in certain circles as a poet because he wrote in verse, was dismissed from his post because in the *Muses d'État* he had had his say on the subject of the semi-official Press. It is true that the authorities also stopped an ex-seminarist who had called Jesus Christ " a peerless man " from lecturing at the Collège de France; this was Ernest Renan. The fact that the clergy were in evil odour was no reason for leaving religion defenceless.

The tiniest little incident was sufficient to give rise to a scandal. The Prefect of Ile-et-Vilaine had appointed a lay teacher contrary to the wishes of the municipal council of the commune, who had asked for a cleric. There was a protest from the Archbishop, a petition to the Senate and interminable debates—a regular storm in a teacup. The struggle had its comic side. Monseigneur Pie, Bishop of Poitiers, who

228

was in the habit of compromising cavalry colonels, unearthed the name of a certain Gicquel, "a Catholic and Royalist son of Brittany," who had met a glorious death at Castelfidardo. And in the ancient church of Sainte Radegonde he pronounced a panegyric on this pious and virtuous soldier of the Pope who had always paid every man what he owed. And he promised to raise an imperishable monument to his name. Whereupon it was discovered that the said Gicquel was not dead and was nothing but a vulgar swindler. He had discovered an ingenious way of securing board and lodging. He would go to a priest and tell him that he was a Protestant but harassed by doubt, and thus secured hospitality until he was converted and baptised, whereupon he would go to another priest and repeat the process. At Poitiers he had been enrolled in the service of the Pope; he duly received the Bishop's blessing and with his enlistment bounty in his pocket he went off and enjoyed himself in low haunts. In Rome he had not run any very great risks, except of being court-martialled, and had not even played an active part at Castelfidardo. But after the fight he passed himself off as having been badly wounded and pretended that he was Lamoricière's aide-de-camp, thus exploiting the sympathy of right-minded people. He ended his career in a reformatory; but the imperial attorney, and after him the Government Press, took a mischievous delight in recalling the pompous panegyric of the unfortunate Bishop.

There were also incidents of a more serious nature. The Society of St. Vincent de Paul, founded by Ozanam in 1833 with the object of visiting the poor, had grown by leaps and bounds. In France it had over 1,500 centres engaged in good works or social welfare activities—befriending young apprentices, providing economic stoves, founding libraries, helping the poor to get married, giving medical assistance, opening clothing clubs and rent funds. It was controlled by a central council in Paris, with central and local councils in the provinces. Though the whole organisation was public and above-board, it infringed the regulations regarding associations. And although the members of the Society played no part in politics, some of their number were inevitably involved in the struggle against

The Society of St. Vincent de Paul.

the Empire. It was even rumoured that at a lottery held at one of the centres the place of honour had been occupied by a bust of the Comte de Chambord.

A meeting of thirty centres held at Lusignan, in Monseigneur Pie's diocese, also caused a great stir. The semi-official journals talked about the *birth of another Vendée*, and Persigny, who was Minister of the Interior at the time, felt obliged to take action. He ordered his Prefects to forbid all committee or council meetings, since the Society was an unauthorised association and partook of the nature of a secret society. The central council was to be allowed to continue its activities only if the Emperor himself chose its President. But the authorities were determined to appear to be acting quite impartially between the Church and her enemies, between Ozanam and the philosophers of the eighteenth century; and at the same time as proceedings were taken against the Society of St. Vincent de Paul they also attacked Freemasonry, which was likewise guilty of infringing the regulations against associations. This classing of the two together was extremely distasteful to the Catholics. The Society, moreover, which had branches abroad, was an international body and accordingly refused to have its head appointed by the Emperor, while the Freemasons accepted the new chief, Marshal Magnan, placed at their head by imperial decree. This conflict and this settlement with the Freemasons served to alienate the Catholics even further from the *régime*.

But there was another trouble which was perhaps even more serious for the Empire—trade was bad. The Americans of the Southern States, engaged in civil war, were **Economic** no longer sending France all the cotton she had **Crisis.** been in the habit of receiving, and it was even feared that supplies might cease altogether. Moreover, the fatal 1st of October, 1861, the date on which the ill-omened commercial treaty would come into full operation, was looming menacingly on the horizon, and the manufacturers, convinced beforehand that they would find it impossible to struggle against English competition, were closing their factories. Lastly, the harvest had been bad and it would be necessary to make heavy purchases of foreign corn. It happened too

230

that the country's savings were almost exhausted at this time owing to various foreign loans, and more especially the Italian loan which had been floated on the Paris market with the support of the Government. There was a shortage of money and the Bank of France raised its rate of discount to 6 per cent. The *Revue des Deux Mondes* denounced the mistakes that had been made—expenditure had been extravagant and too many public works had been undertaken. Monsieur Haussmann was too expensive a luxury. And from economic questions they naturally turned to politics : " No Government can be financially sound which is not under the rigorous control of the representative Assemblies and the vigilant censorship of a free Press." No proper Budget could be framed without the intervention of the Chambers and of the newspapers. . . .

The *Revue*, which was then in its infancy, enjoyed the privilege, at that time almost unique, of being paid serious attention. The Tuileries began to get alarmed. For the sake of example, a warning was issued against the *Revue*.
But at the same time the Emperor hurled one of the unexpected thunderbolts so characteristic of him, but which were none the less disconcerting. On the 15th of November, a month after the *Revue* had raised the alarm, the *Moniteur* published a long Memorandum by Fould, the banker, who had suddenly been made Minister of Finance, with plenary powers over all fresh expenditure. Napoleon III thought he had found the right man to deal with the situation. At heart, Fould agreed with the *Revue des Deux Mondes*. All the trouble was caused by the supplementary Bills of Supply which were granted every year as necessity arose, and which the Legislative Body was called upon to pass when the money had already been spent perhaps eighteen months previously. It was owing to this that between 1851 and 1858 expenditure, which had been largely met by loans, had exceeded receipts by 2,400 million francs (£98,000,000), an enormous sum for the period. The departments and towns followed the example of the State, borrowing money in the same way and eating corn in the blade. It was imperative to put a stop to this system of supplementary supplies, to strengthen the control exercised by the Legislative

Fould.

231

Body without making it too powerful, and when it was not sitting, to meet unforeseen expenses by means of diverting part of the funds voted for one Government department to the use of another. In this way at least the sum-total of expenditure estimated would not be exceeded. Not only would this method result in the balancing of the Budget by giving the Emperor an excuse for evading the endless demands for help and subsidies which he received from every part of the country, where it had become customary to regard him as the universal benefactor and philanthropist, but it would also serve to calm the fears of Europe, where rumours were constantly in circulation regarding the secret sources of supply and the mysterious armaments of the militarist and bellicose French Empire. With the return of security, general prosperity would also revive.

All these ideas, especially the last, were put forward with the object of pleasing the Emperor, who, at this time, was sincerely anxious to perfect the Constitution. A **Reforms.** *senatus consultum* of the 31st of December, 1861, abolished the system of supplementary supplies—other sources of supply would have to be arranged by law—confirmed the right to divert monies from one Government department to another, and gave the Legislative Body the power to vote the Budget, not by departments, as had been arranged in 1852, but by sections. Thus parliamentary control would be more efficacious and the balancing of the Budget better secured. This reform put the finishing touch to the decree of the 24th of November, 1860, by granting new powers to the deputies. From this moment the Cæsarian dictatorship seemed to have lost faith in itself and to be instinctively trying to regain its footing by placing greater reliance upon the support of the country. But, after all, it was much ado about nothing. For a few months later a decree was issued by which the Government once more arrogated to itself the right to " amend " the Budget, and amended Budgets meant that the Government need not be limited to mere diversion of monies, but could revive the ill-omened system of supplementary supplies. The reason for this step was to be found in the fact that money was required for the " grand schemes of the *régime*," and

232

especially for the Mexican venture, and it was more convenient to take it without asking. It was by such behaviour that the *régime* slowly but surely undermined its strength.

The Roman question still remained unsolved, and Cavour had died on the 6th of June, 1861, leaving to others the task of achieving Italian unity. In the March before **The Roman Question.** his death he had emphasised the fact that " without Rome as the capital of Italy, it was impossible for Italy to be formed." And shortly after his death, Napoleon III, not without considerable hesitation, had decided to recognise that Kingdom of Italy, which the Pope insisted on calling the " Kingdom of Piedmont." The Empress, always extremely hostile to her husband's Italian policy, had risen from her seat and left the room in the middle of a council meeting, rather than sanction the recognition of the new State by her presence. But the Emperor insisted upon leaving his forces in Rome as long as Victor Emmanuel was not reconciled with the Pope and the latter remained exposed to the menace of invasion. Arese came to Paris with the object of securing the withdrawal of the French troops, but his visit was fruitless. **Incidents with Piedmont.** Incidents occurred with Piedmont, who declared that she would never cede Sardinia to France— as a matter of fact France had never asked for it; in Naples the Piedmontese shot brigands and the supporters of the dethroned Bourbon King indiscriminately, which aroused great indignation in France, and this was met by a complaint from the Piedmontese in Rome to the effect that French officers were giving their support to members of the Bourbon party who had sought refuge there from Naples. Nigra, the Italian Ambassador in Paris, sympathised both with the Emperor and the Empress. But he was shunned in order to avoid tackling the Roman question. Piedmont hoped that the Emperor would ask the Pope to give up Rome in return for money and guarantees. But the Emperor made no reply.

The fact was that at the Tuileries his Italian policy was by no means acceptable to everybody. The Empress was not the only person to condemn it; she was supported by Randon,

Magne, and Walewski, who together with the whole of the Catholic Party wanted the French to remain in Rome. The Emperor, who was personally in favour of evacuation, as usual found his only support in Prince Napoleon, Persigny, Morny, the Republicans—the latter, it is true, going even further and wanting Rome to be the capital of Italy—and his Minister Thouvenel. In the end he tried to persuade the Pope either to accept the arrangement suggested by Piedmont, or at all events to come to some agreement, a *modus vivendi*—Italy and the Church were each to recognise the territory actually held by the other. The Pope would keep Rome under the guarantee of the Powers and would be granted a civil list to compensate him for the loss of his provinces. He, on his side, was to grant Liberal institutions to the States he still held. But the Vatican categorically refused to grant any such recognition of the " spoliations " to which it had been subjected. And Napoleon III continued to waver between the Catholics and the " Italianissimi."

But an incident occurred which threw him into the arms of the Catholics. Garibaldi made an attempt against Rome which was accompanied by gross abuse of the Emperor of the French; he was stopped in Calabria by the Piedmontese forces. Thouvenel, who was too " Italian," had to be replaced, and the Empress proposed Walewski. But Persigny and Morny protested. " You allow your wife to lead you by the nose just as I do," Persigny remarked in a fine sally, " but I at least compromise only my fortune." And Morny, who was undoubtedly in favour of Liberalism, pointed out the danger of giving way to these " representatives of the old *régimes*." In the end the Emperor recalled Drouyn de Lhuys, who had played no part in public life for seven years, a diplomat who upheld the old traditions, the advocate of *rapprochement* with Austria, and the opponent of territorial changes and of the new Italy. " We shall be de-Italianised for some time now," wrote Viel-Castel at the time. Arese again hastened to Paris to try to arrange matters. But for the moment Napoleon III, having developed a sudden passion for history, was interested only in his forthcoming book, *La Vie de César*. And, more important still, the Government was anxious to conciliate the clergy, and there was no more talk of evacuating Rome—the elections were approaching.

In 1863 a new Legislative Body would have to be elected, and the revival of political life which had been going on for some years indicated that the elections would be more lively than they had been in 1857. The Parties were awaking out of their long sleep.

On the Left there were still the men of 1848, Marie, Crémieux, Carnot and Garnier-Pagès, though they were old and half **The** forgotten. There was more talk about the exiles, **Re-** of Victor Hugo, who from his retreat in Jersey **publicans.** " was still defying Sulla "; of Ledru-Rollin, Louis Blanc and Schoelcher, who had sought refuge in London; of Barbès, in Holland, and of Edgar Quinet and Charras in Switzerland. The sonorous verses of *Les Châtiments* were learnt by heart, and the pamphlets which were surreptitiously circulated, making violent attacks on the Emperor, *Les Propos de Labienus* and *Dialogue entre Machiavel et Montesquieu*, were eagerly devoured. People quoted Tacitus, who had also anathematised the imperial " monsters " Nero and Tiberius, and recited Juvenal, while a French composition by a man named Richard, a competitor in the *Concours Générale*, was passed from hand to hand. He had succeeded in raising a fine scandal. The subject set was a panegyric on the late King Jerome, but Richard, in glowing verse, had sung the praises of Garibaldi and Mazzini and poured abuse upon the *coup d'état*. The Emperor was extremely unpopular and his enemies took a delight in blackening his reputation. They were destined to be the irreconcilables who never forgave the *Five* for having sworn allegiance to the Empire or admitted that such a humiliation was a fair price to pay in 1863 for the right of sitting in the Legislative Body and carrying on the good fight there.

The *Five*, for their part, continued the struggle by supporting amendments to the Address, a proceeding which had been **The Five.** permitted since the 24th of November, 1860, and demanded " a genuine return to a free system of Government." The Press, they declared, should " cease to be a monopoly under the control of a secret censorship," and

235

Press misdemeanours ought no longer to be summarily dealt with by the magistrates, whose profession it was to repress, but should be tried by jury at the assizes. The "elections should be conducted by the electors and not by the Prefects," the "right to hold meetings" was demanded, and "the communes were to have the appointment of the municipal authorities." They complained that the decree of 1860 had been mere "eye-wash," and that although the word "liberty" constantly figured in official speeches, the Government nevertheless continued "to forbid all intellectual activity and free discussion. . . ." Doubtless these amendments were regarded as rubbish by the majority, who contemptuously threw them out. But to be able to propose them and support them in public was already a great advance.

Lastly, there were the "Young Liberals," all of them lawyers, who in private showed but little consideration for their elders —"old greybeards, old bonzes and boobies. . . ." **The Young "Liberals."** They were loyal readers of the *Temps*, which at that time supported the Left, and haunted the public gallery of the Palais Bourbon, where there were only eighteen seats. They were ironically dubbed the "audience of the Legislative Body." Most conspicuous among them were Hérold, Floquet, Jules Ferry and Léon Gambetta. They brought out an electoral manual which explained to the reader all the formalities he would have to go through to have his name put on the electoral registers—in spite of the difficulties that the Mayors appointed by the Emperor were only too ready to raise.

The Republicans embarked upon a vigorous campaign in preparation for the elections. They counted on Paris, which in 1857 had already voted for the Left. But what could they expect from the provincial towns and the country districts where every elector voted under the eye of the Prefect, the sub-Prefect or the constable? Garnier-Pagès set out on a tour at the end of 1862 and visited over sixty towns in France. He conjured the Republicans not to abstain from voting but, on the contrary, to put up a fight wherever they could raise a candidate. Meanwhile all kinds of plans were laid in Paris, but it was difficult to make headway. Abstention at all events was not to be feared; with the exception of Proudhon, the members of the Opposition were determined to vote. But there were too many candidates, and ambitious aspirants met in rivalry which threatened to imperil the victory of the cause and to play into the hands of the official candidates.

The first incident that occurred was between the *Five*, who, supported by the *Presse* and the *Temps*, considered themselves masters in their own house, and Havin, of the *Siècle*, who had his eye on Picard's seat. From the provinces, Garnier-Pagès suggested that the Republicans should appoint a committee to choose their candidates. But how was this committee itself to be chosen? Carnot organised an election by means of militants, but failed; he would have liked to see the men of '48 on the committee, but the electors of the committee, although they had placed him at the head, had shown but little enthusiasm for the "greybeards," including Garnier-Pagès—the workers had not forgotten the June insurrection.

In the end Marie, on his own authority, formed a committee in conjunction with Garnier-Pagès, Carnot, Crémieux, Jules **Marie's Committee.** Simon, Corbon, Henri Martin and some of the younger generation, chief among them Jules Ferry, Floquet, Hérold and Hérisson, for whom room was made. It was this committee that chose the nine Opposition candidates for the Seine department—Favre, Ollivier, Picard, Darimon (of the *Five*), Havin of the *Siècle* (who, though a Republican in Paris, was Bonapartist in his own province of Normandy), Guéroult of *l'Opinion Nationale* (a friend of Prince Napoleon), Jules Simon, a moderate Republican, a Professor who had been dismissed from his post in 1852 for refusing to take the oath, Pelletan, and lastly Laboulaye, a Liberal on the *Débats*, who was soon to be outshone by Thiers. After various vicissitudes the Republicans accepted Thiers, who, though not a democrat, was in ill odour at the Tuileries. **The Liberal Union.** This resulted in a sort of coalition, a block or cartel, a *Liberal Union* against the Empire, founded on a tacit though somewhat frail alliance between the Republicans and the old Orleanists.

On the extreme Right the Opposition consisted of Legitimists, who, since the raising of the Roman question, had been joined by some of the Catholics. But the Pretender, the Comte de Chambord, continued to forbid his followers to take any part in politics, in spite of the protests of Falloux and Berryer, who in the end presented themselves as candidates in spite of his prohibition. They were supported by the *pure Catholics*, the defenders of the Holy See who had voted against the Government. Persigny had made up his mind that at the coming elections he would make some of them feel the full weight of his enmity, more especially Keller, who had once waxed so eloquent on the Roman question. They presented themselves as Independent candidates, which was extremely displeasing to the *Moniteur*, for officially even the candidates who were most strongly supported by the Prefects were independent. And they did all they could to win the votes of malcontents of any description —Catholics vexed by the Roman question or industrialists embittered by the commercial treaty. Lastly, there were the Liberals, the majority being Orleanists, and all without exception upholders of parliamentary institutions, focussed mainly round the *Académie ;* with such men as Guizot, Broglie, Rémusat, Vitet, St.-Marc Girardin, Montalembert, Monseigneur Dupanloup, Odilon Barrot, Duvergier de Haurranne, Dufaure, Laboulaye, and Thiers among their number. Several, in addition to Thiers, presented themselves as candidates— Rémusat, Dufaure, St. Marc Girardin, Casimir Périer, Cornélis de Witt (Guizot's son-in-law), Montalembert and Barrot. In spite of all the talent displayed by Prévost-Paradol, the great journalist of the *Débats*, who led the attack on the Government by means of a campaign of irony, allusion and innuendo, they were not strong enough to guide public opinion again. And in the end the Tuileries prosecuted this " general secretary of the old Parties," who occasionally went a little too far. He also contributed to the *Courrier du Dimanche*, a little weekly journal with a modest, homely title, which, in the struggle against the Empire, P. de la Gorce compares to a fire-ship used in naval battles to run alongside the large vessels and sink with them. His audacity resulted in the issue of the two preliminary warnings against him, whereupon he exercised greater prudence in order to

The Opposition.

Prévost-Paradol.

238

escape the third, which would have silenced him for good. An armistice followed which cancelled the two first penalties, and the *Courrier* returned to its mad attacks. But these satires from the pen of a literary light were read only by a small and select circle and could have no influence on the masses. Nevertheless, Prévost-Paradol presented himself for election both in the Dordogne and the Seine districts.

Such was the host of opponents Persigny had to be prepared to face. This friend in adversity had been covered with honours

Persigny. by the Emperor; he was a senator, Grand Cross of the Legion of Honour, Member of the Privy Council, and erstwhile Ambassador in London; for the last three years he had again and again been appointed to the Ministry of the Interior. He was a curious mixture, at once despotic and Liberal, an autocrat and an Anglomaniac, ambitious and disinterested. There was also a touch of the Jacobin in this old non-commissioned officer. And he succeeded in making himself detested by everybody, from Morny to the Empress. Hard and crushing, he was certainly becoming impossible, and the Emperor himself was growing tired of his remonstrances. " Persigny," he said to him one day, " I can't think why you're so cross ! " And the latter replied like Alcestis, " And I can't think, Sire, why you are not ! " Possibly the churl really knew what he was doing when he anathematised weaknesses and scandals, but he was not endowed with the capacity so necessary for the ordinary man of getting on with other people, nor had he the genius which secures toleration even for the most odious brutalities.

Persigny wanted to enter upon the conflict with drums beating. On the 8th of May he sent a circular to his Prefects in

Official Candidature. which he once again set forth the principle of official candidature. He reminded them of the achievements of the Empire, which had "restored moral, political and religious order, doubled real estate, increased the fortune of the nation by seven or eight milliard francs (£320,000,000), augmented the public revenue by 300 million francs (£12,000,000), intersected the whole country with roads and railways, and last, but not least, restored to French foreign policy the influence it had lost." The work could never have been accomplished and could not be continued without the trust and confidence of the country. If all the Parties had been attached, as they were in England, to the fundamental institutions of the nation, the Government could have stood outside the fray. But in France, " after so many upheavals," there were factions which " were nothing but a coalition of hostility, rancour and spite opposed to the glories of the Empire. . . . They called upon the name of Liberty only to turn it against the State. . . . To be free, it was necessary for the electors to be enlightened by the Prefect. And in order that the good faith of the people might not be led astray by verbal subtleties and equivocal professions of faith, the Prefects were boldly to designate, as they had done at previous elections, those candidates in whom the Government felt the greatest confidence . . . men whole-heartedly and disinterestedly devoted to the imperial dynasty and to French institutions." And thus the all-wise and benevolent Empire not only poured forth its blessings in the shape of railways, it also took the trouble to protect the poor dear elector against the snares of the wicked. Was not such solicitude touching? It must be a stony heart indeed that could wax indignant against it !

In practice the Government had recourse to the old tried methods—committees and meetings were forbidden, suspect journals were cautioned and threatened with sup-

Government Campaign. pression, a campaign was conducted on behalf of the official candidates in the provinces by newspapers approved by the Prefect, which, owing to having the monopoly of judicial announcements, were the only ones that could survive, and strict rules and regulations were made with regard to the printing of circulars and hawking. Furthermore, a decree was promulgated whereby the divisions were ingeniously cut up; they were no longer areas corresponding with the *arrondissements*, but consisted of groups of 35,000 inhabitants. A canton that was suspect would be taken away from a certain Opposition candidate and merged in a Bonapartist department, while an official candidate whose seat was threatened was helped by the addition of a canton in which full reliance could be placed. The large towns, which were always dangerous, were deliberately cut up into small sections,

240

each of which was allocated to a rural area which "voted rightly."

The Prefects set to work in good earnest. On their tours of inspection round their districts they had already presented the official candidates. And they returned accompanied by engineers from the Department of Roads and Bridges and surveyors, armed with the apparatus for pegging out the sites of the future railways under the excited eyes of the people, who had no difficulty in understanding this "word to the wise." The candidate for Nîmes, a local man who had made his pile in Egypt, promised to provide his faithful town with water, and on the eve of the elections laid the foundation stone of the aqueduct. But there was such a scandal that he was twice disqualified, though he was also twice re-elected. Men caught poaching were let off and informed by the gendarmes that they owed their pardon to the Emperor himself. In Corrèze, the Minister of Public Works came down and promised all kinds of wonders and was saluted by the Prefect as "the Colbert of the nineteenth century." In other places the agent of the Opposition candidate was arrested and his circulars were lost in the post. Officials, mayors, retailers of wine and tobacco, school inspectors, justices of the peace and gendarmes all had to come forward as one man in support of the official candidate. And last, but not least, Persigny charged full tilt against Thiers, the representative of a system "which replaced the fruitful bustle of action by the sterile agitation of speech, which for eighteen years had produced nothing but impotence at home and weakness abroad, and, founded on insurrection, carried on amid the uproar of insurrection, had gone down in insurrection." But was all this agitation as skilful as it seemed? Merimée, a friend of the Empire, expressed his doubts about it when he wrote: "Persigny is like a coachman pulling at the reins and striking out right and left with his whip."

Voting was to take place on Sunday and Monday, the 30th and 31st of May. The 30th was *Grand Prix* day, the first *Grand Prix de Paris*, and the crowd went to see the race at Longchamps, which Morny had founded, and then watched the fine carriages driving down the Champs Élysées. But on the evening of the 31st this

The Elections.

same crowd feverishly read the result of the election in Paris, round the very gas lamps which the ungrateful creatures owed to the munificence of the *régime*. That night the city was swept by a wave of joy—the Government had been beaten all along the line. The nine Opposition candidates, that is to say, eight Republicans and Thiers, had been returned (one of them, it is true, had reached only the ballot stage, but was sufficiently high up to stand a good chance in the second round, which as a matter of fact he got through safely). The poll had been light; out of 326,000 on the registers, only 175,000 voted, but of these, 153,000 were for the Opposition, and 22,000 for the Government. Revenge for the 2nd of December and the restoration of the Republic were already being hailed. . . . Paris, the brain of France, who from the very beginning had been hostile to the Empire, was clearly irreconcilable.

But France did not follow the lead set by Paris. In the provinces only a few Republicans were returned in the towns—

The Third Party. Hénon, Glais-Bizoin, Dorian and Marie. The representatives of the *old Parties*, Barrot, Rémusat, St.-Marc Girardin, Dufaure, Casimir Périer, Prévost-Paradol and Montalembert, failed. With Berryer and a few "Independents," elected in spite of Persigny, the Opposition of the Right and the Left combined held only 32 seats in a Chamber of 282 deputies. What could these two little groups, 17 Republicans or Liberals, and 15 Catholics of the Left Centre, afterwards called the Third Party, do against the body of 250 deputies who were true to the *régime?* Nothing, or next to nothing!

True! But for these victories to have been won in spite of the system of official candidature was surely something of a triumph. Furthermore, the way Paris and the large towns had voted produced a certain impression. "Paris is not France," declared the rural districts. But it was none the less significant that even the capital, where the Emperor was in residence, where the army on its return from war was acclaimed and the Cent Gardes round their Master were the cynosure of all eyes, refused to rally to the hero of the 2nd of December. And when the sum-total of Opposition votes came to be reckoned, it was found to reach 2,000,000

242

against the 6,000,000 for the Empire—that is to say, out of 10,000,000 altogether. Even Persigny, though he publicly proclaimed his satisfaction at the victory, was bound to see that, somehow or other, universal suffrage had been "caught napping" by this coalition of Parties that supported previous systems of government, and which had come into being for the first time in ten years. These elections undoubtedly constituted a blow at the *régime*, and they were well aware of it in the Tuileries. The Emperor, by dismissing the man who had organised the struggle and had failed to win success, himself proved that the publicists who were proclaiming their victory were right. Persigny lost his office, and by way of compensation was given a Duke's coronet, or, as Merimée puts it, "he was embalmed." The salons did not shed a tear over his departure; it was declared that "in making Persigny a Duke, the Emperor's object was to put a stop to the legal investigations into his title of Count, which was held to be somewhat dubious. . . ."

Fall of Persigny.

The fall of Persigny was the signal for a change of personnel. Walewski went with him. They had both stood for autocracy and the "high hand." Morny, who hated them and had been largely responsible for their disgrace, tried ever more assiduously to set the *régime* on a firm constitutional basis. He feared the future, anxiously watching the revival of political life and the workers awaking from the long sleep into which they had been plunged since June '48. Above all he perceived the dangers of a foreign policy entirely dependent upon the caprices and visions of the Master. Thus it was small wonder that, in his powerful position as President of the Legislative Body and the organiser of the *coup d'état*, he should have sent for Émile Ollivier, the blushing Republican adversary who was ready to rally to the Empire. Thus he pursued his policy of setting the *régime* more firmly on the basis of public support, even at the expense of inevitable concessions. He read Ollivier a note he had sent to the Emperor which was significant : "The elections have left only two forces facing each other, the Empire and Democracy. . . . It is time to give . . . if not full immediate political liberty, at least civil liberty, and to study social problems. It has become urgent

Morny.

for the Emperor to cease springing surprises upon the country and leaving his councillors in complete ignorance regarding his foreign policy." Morny was clearly of opinion that if the Empire was to last it must make up its mind to be resolutely Liberal. And he made this perfectly plain at the opening of the new Assembly when he welcomed the old parliamentary lights, Thiers and Berryer, and when he declared that "liberty could be peaceably established only by agreement between a Liberal sovereign and a moderate Assembly." Unfortunately he had not two years to live and died too soon to see the *régime* of which he had dreamt. The man who was destined to become very powerful, but who had neither the versatility nor views of a statesman, was Rouher, who, on the death of Billault in that same year 1863, became Minister of State entrusted with the task of representing the Emperor in the Chambers (the Ministers without portfolios of 1860 having been abolished), and of more or less playing the part of President of the Council, a President who did not need to stand in fear of being thrown out of office by a vote of lack of confidence. For it would be a mistake to suppose that this "movement" of 1863 was "a hammer stroke from the Left" against the Emperor. It was merely a question of having somebody reliable—and eloquent— to reply to the old leaders who were returning to public life— Thiers and Berryer, and to the Republican Opposition, which had become three times as large as it had been.

At the beginning of 1864, Berryer drew up the financial balance sheet of the *régime*, pointing out that in twelve years **Thiers' "In-** almost three milliard francs (£120,000,000) had been **dispensable** raised by means of loans, and condemning the system **Liberties."** of supplementary supplies, which had been revived, and expensive expeditions to distant parts. Whereupon Thiers took up the cudgels. Apparently this meant the revival of parliamentarism, he declared; and he proceeded to enumerate "the five indispensable liberties"—*individual liberty;* the law of public safety must be repealed; *liberty of the Press;* and the abolition of the system of warnings. "What can you do?" he asked. "The peoples to-day would prefer to ruin their cause themselves rather than allow others to manage it well on their behalf." This showed that he was far from convinced

244

of the desirability of allowing public opinion to control politics
and that he was announcing a fact rather than enunciating
a principle. Next came *electoral liberty;* all attempt to guide
the so-called all-powerful system of universal suffrage must
be abandoned, or, in plain language, a stop must be put to
official candidature; *liberty of the deputy*, that is to say, the
control of affairs by the Legislative Body; and, lastly, *liberty
of the majority*, which, as the interpreters of public opinion,
should guide the policy of the country by appointing the Ministers responsible to it. This amounted to insisting upon the
Empire, which had been founded on force and confirmed after
the event by the plebiscite and the system of official candidature, returning to the old parliamentary system based upon
the representation of the people and on " legality." Thiers
had the logic of circumstances on his side—the country was
waking up and it had become imperative to listen to it. On
that condition he declared himself ready to rally to the Empire.
And he ended his speech on a note of menace; if these liberties
were not granted to the country, some day perhaps it would
" insist " upon them. But his eloquence aroused no echo;
neither the majority nor the Emperor had any desire for a
return to the parliamentary system, and Rouher openly said
so. The time had not yet come.

For the fact remained that in 1864 the *régime* still felt itself
firmly established. The harvest had been good, industry was
suffering less than had been expected from the commercial
treaty, and the cotton crisis was blowing over. The police were
well organised; they had succeeded in arresting four Italians in
the nick of time. They were veterans belonging to Garibaldi's
Thousand, who had come from Lugano, and were discovered
in possession of eight bombs, revolvers and daggers. They
had planned to kill the Emperor because he was preventing
the establishment of Italian unity, and declared that they
were the agents of Mazzini, the revolutionary who had sought
refuge in London. The latter, however, swore by all the gods
that he had had nothing whatever to do with the matter. A
sop was also given to the Catholics, allies whose loss was still
a sore point, in the shape of forcing Ernest Renan to resign
his Chair at the Collège de France. In 1863 he had been guilty

of publishing his *Vie de Jésus*, from which " he eliminated the miraculous element," and had irritated the Church all the more by the love and respect he showed for the " noble initiator " whom he had deprived of his halo. In his own way he had made a divinity once more of the person he claimed to regard as a mere man. The Emperor himself, in a public letter to the Bishop of Arras, took sides against the sacrilege. Lastly, the all-powerful will of the Master was made manifest in the University.

Ever since 1863 the Minister of Education had been a certain Monsieur Duruy. He was Professor of History at the Lycée Saint Louis, wrote manuals and treatises on Roman history and was living in semi-obscurity, " working like an ox patiently ploughing the furrow," when a marvellous piece of good fortune befell him. Somebody recommended him to the Emperor, who was working at his *Vie de César* and bringing all the ardour of the amateur to bear upon his task. Duruy was summoned to the Tuileries, where his very awkwardness won him approval; " it was the delightful awkwardness which princes find such a pleasant respite from the attitude of the Court " (P. de la Gorce). His opinion of Cæsar, whose destruction of that Roman Republic which had become nothing but a " bloodstained shadow " he regarded as admirable, also delighted the Emperor. Napoleon III flattered himself that he resembled Cæsar, and that he too had put an end to a *régime* that was no more than a shadow. And in the twinkling of an eye the insignificant little Professor became Inspector of the University, Inspector-General and Minister—the University was going to be ruled by a University man.

Victor Duruy.

He endeavoured to reform it, and set to work by means of decrees, resolutions and circulars to such good purpose that he very quickly made his mark on public opinion, though, while some regarded him as a great Minister, others held him to be a misguided busybody. As a matter of fact he accomplished a very great work. In the domain of secondary education he revived the Philosophy course, which, before he came into office, had been reduced to the inoffensive Logic course, and created the Modern History and Modern Language courses.

246

Instead of the " bifurcation " which, as soon as they had finished
their grammatical studies, used to divide the students into two
sections, " Literature " and " Science," he arranged, in addition
**Special
Education.** to the old Classical course, which prepared men
for the liberal professions, a vocational or special
course, in which Latin was not included, intended
for those who wished to embark upon industrial, commercial
or agricultural careers. It was an attractive idea; there
would be fewer bad scholars and more good business men;
the instruction provided would be adapted to the requirements
of the particular districts, English being taught along the
Channel coast, German in the east, Italian in the Alps and
Spanish in the Pyrenees, while in seaports geography and
trade would be studied, the mysteries of silk-making would
be unveiled in Lyons, and of wool and cotton in Normandy,
and in the north and in Alsace laboratories, factories, agricultural institutions, etc., would be visited.

But it did not meet with much success; the bourgeoisie
did not think much of this second-grade education. In the
**Elementary
Education.** domain of higher education Duruy founded new
Chairs and Faculties, creating the Political Economy
course at the *École de Droit de Paris*, founding the
École Pratique des Hautes Études, and doing all he could to
equip laboratories and libraries. For subsidising elementary
education he demanded contributions from the municipalities,
from the General Councils and private persons, and succeeded
in getting them, devoting the proceeds to building schools,
extending the courses for adults, and supplying teachers with
any apparatus they lacked. And he even dared to suggest
in a report published in the *Moniteur* that elementary education
should be free and compulsory. This won him great popularity
with the Opposition, but gave rise to virulent attacks on the
part of the Conservatives as well as of Parieu, the Vice-President
of the Council of State, who inveighed against him in the Legislative Body itself—a united policy being as yet non-existent
in the Councils of the Government.

And, as a matter of fact, the Emperor was not prepared to
follow his Minister to the bitter end. After having declared
in his Speech from the Throne in February 1865 that " in a

country which practised universal suffrage every citizen should know how to read and write," he retreated a step; the usual words : " Seen and approved by the Emperor," were absent from the report in the *Moniteur*. Worse still, the public were informed by a note that the report was merely a personal expression of opinion on the part of the Minister, and Duruy demanded the withdrawal of this note in vain. Meanwhile, the aged Guizot protested in the columns of the *Débats* against this " coercion brought to bear on paternal authority," this " tyrannical demand " on the part of the State " by which parents would be forced either to send their children to the State schools in which they did not believe, or else to submit to the Government inspectors entering their homes to make sure that the children were securing the benefits of elementary education." The Catholics were even more hostile to this " layman " who privately confessed to being " a free-thinker to the backbone," and they trembled for the *loi Falloux*, which they held so dear. They were even more hostile later on when Duruy arranged public courses of lectures for girls to be delivered by the masters in the boys' *lycées*, and

Education of Girls. thus tried to deprive the Church of a branch of education of which she then enjoyed the monopoly. Girls, declared Dupanloup, used to be brought up in the lap of the Church. And this provided the Catholics with a yet further cause for deserting the *régime* and turning away from that strange Emperor who was at once a supporter of law and order and a democrat, capable of condemning a Renan and at the same time supporting a Duruy. As a matter of fact, in this he was true to the real Napoleonic tradition, which stood for the restoration of authority while opposing the *ancien régime*, and for upholding the Throne while maintaining certain Jacobin sentiments.

A fresh danger threatened the Empire about this period. Morny, who was clear-sighted, declared that it was high time

Awakening of the Working Classes. to study social problems. The working-man, after having been silenced for ten years by the bloodshed of June '48, had just woken up. In 1859 the faubourgs had cheered the Emperor as he was setting out for Italy to take part in the war which was to set a people free from the yoke of Conservative Austria. In 1861, Prince Napoleon, who lived in the Palais Royal, held consultations with some printers, and had anonymous pamphlets published which were immediately dubbed "the Palais Royal pamphlets." In them the Emperor, the sincere friend of the people, a Free Trader with the object of making life less hard for the poor, the man who owed his power to the plebiscite, that is to say, to universal suffrage, was contrasted with the bourgeoisie who had shot down the masses in June '48. The bourgeoisie were Protectionists from self-interest, and in 1850 had dared to limit the right of suffrage. Prince Napoleon's Cæsarism was also true to the democratic and egalitarian tradition of the Bonapartes. In October 1861, certain St. Simonians—showing how profound an influence St. Simon's ideas had exercised—Arlès Dufour, a big Lyons manufacturer, in the *Progrès de Lyon*, and Guéroult, the director of the Paris newspaper *l'Opinion Nationale*, and a friend of Prince Napoleon, suggested, with the approval of the *Temps*, that a party of working men should go to London, as they had done in 1851, to visit the International Exhibition about to be held there, and study English industrial methods. But it was insisted—and herein lay the novelty of the proposal—that the men should be chosen by their comrades and not appointed by their employers, and that the expenses of their visit should be paid by subscriptions raised among the workers themselves. One man, a bronze-worker, insisted that the initiative should come " from below . . . and should not be due to the patronage of the authorities and the manufacturers," declaring that there was only one way of inspiring confidence in the workers and preventing them from feeling that they were being " directed, guided and fettered," and that was to say to them : " You are free; organise yourselves, and arrange your own affairs; we shall not put any difficulties in your way."

This idea was subsequently developed by Corbon, a workingman who had been a member of the Constituent Assembly. He declared that the workers were in favour of the " corporative idea " and the creation of a Chamber of Syndics such as their employers possessed, whose object it would be to keep up wages. Thus both theorists and workers agreed in demand-

ing the right of association for the latter, a right which at this
time was labouring under a twofold ban: since the Revolution
of '89 the formation of societies and coalitions, and consequently
the right to strike, had been forbidden, while since the reaction
of '48 any kind of association or gathering had been prohibited.
The Emperor, who had always been in sympathy with the
theories of St. Simon and sincerely desired the welfare of his
people, allowed himself to be persuaded. Furthermore, the
Government and the city of Paris each gave a donation of
20,000 francs (£800), which was added to the 13,000 francs (£520)
Workers' raised by subscription. During May and June 1862
Visit to the workers in the various trades elected the delegates
London. to attend the London Exhibition. The latter met
their English comrades and envied their high wages, their
fifty-five hours working week and their clean and sanitary
workshops. Did not the English owe all this to the liberty
secured by the Trade Unions? And at this first international
meeting there was already talk of "the union of the workers
of the world," and discussions as to how "the countries could be
kept in touch with one another." But the delegates returned
to Paris above all convinced of the advantages of Trade Unions
to confront the employers: "The relations between the isolated
worker offering his services," one of them declared, "and the
capitalist body which bargains for them are manifestly unfair."

Moreover, it was at this juncture that the breach occurred
between the workers who owed allegiance to the Palais Royal
and Prince Napoleon and the Republican workers who relied
more on liberty than on a benevolent Cæsarism for the realisation of their dreams. But, on the other hand, these Republican
workers had no wish to come to an understanding with the
men of '48. The June massacres could never be expiated,
and after them it had become impossible to bridge the gulf
between the Liberal bourgeoisie and the working classes. At
the elections of 1863, the workers, who did not trust lawyers
or journalists to espouse their cause in the Legislative Body,
sent one of their own number, a printer named Blanc, to demand
the right of association and the creation of Chambers of Syndics.
But he met with no success. At the time of the bye-elections
of 1864, when Carnot and Garnier-Pagès ousted their Labour
250

competitors, one of whom was Tolain, there appeared in *l'Opinion Nationale* of the 17th of February a letter signed by sixty men belonging to the art-workers', printing, building and tailoring
The trades, which aroused but little attention at the
Workers' time, but which we now know was the first manifesto
Letter. issued by the working classes in France : " Universal suffrage has given us the political majority, but it still remains for us to win social emancipation. . . . The equality secured by law does not exist socially and has still to be put into practice. Those who have neither education nor capital and are unable to offer resistance by the exercise of free corporate action [an allusion to the right to strike] are bound to be crushed beneath the heel of capital. . . . What we want is a Chamber of Syndics composed exclusively of workers elected by universal suffrage, a Labour Assembly." These workers had not yet read Proudhon or Karl Marx—they were soon to discover them— and life alone had taught them these new doctrines.

The idea of the freedom of Labour was " in the air " and Morny had been quick to feel it. Moreover, custom had outstripped the law, and workers were no longer prosecuted for going on strike. In 1862 there was a printers' strike to secure higher wages. According to the laws in force at the time they ought to have been prosecuted and punished, but public opinion was on their side and supported their counsel, the great Berryer, and the Emperor immediately pardoned them. Clearly the law against workers' unions, coalitions and strikes was out of date, and Morny on this occasion once more approached Émile Ollivier with a view to " extending civil liberties " and putting an end to the onerous rules and regulations to which the working classes were subjected. It also provided him with an opportunity of ingratiating himself with Napoleon III : " The Emperor is good," he declared, " and loves the people."

But the matter was not so simple as it seemed. Cornudet, the Councillor of State entrusted with the task of presenting
Workers' the Bill, did not slur over the danger of strikes.
Unions. Morny actually had the hardihood to suggest that Émile Ollivier himself should be appointed to draw up the Bill, an unheard-of proposal, for ever since the foundation

of the Empire no Opposition deputy had ever been charged with such a function. Morny was met with resistance on the part of Rouher, who was not at all inclined to favour this gradual movement towards a Liberal Empire, which he regarded as weak and misguided. But in the end Morny, by means of clever wire-pulling, had his way and secured the appointment of Ollivier by the Legislative Body. Ollivier recast the Bill. Strikes were no longer to be illegal and unions of both masters and men might be formed. But, on the other hand, the Government authorities could intervene if a strike were accompanied by violence or carried on by means of fraudulent manœuvres, or if serious attacks were made on the liberty to work. The Bill, which was eventually carried by a large majority, was opposed on the one hand by Conservative industrialists, among them Seydoux, Pouyer-Quertier and Wendel, who feared the activities of the ringleaders, the "engineers of strikes," and were also afraid that the refusal to work on the part of a few skilled workmen might force a whole mill to close down, and on the other by deputies of the Left, like Jules Simon and Jules Favre, who considered the Bill inadequate and the "liberty" it granted illusory, since it did not concede the right of association or of holding meetings, and it was always open to the magistrates, however justifiable a strike might be, to discover fraudulent manœuvres which were liable to prosecution.

On this occasion, Ollivier separated himself from his old friends of the Left, saying that he did not wish "to refuse a progressive measure because it was incomplete," and **Ollivier.** added : " I do not look a gift horse in the mouth. . . . To-day we have the coalitions law, to-morrow we shall get the associations law." In the eyes of the little group of Republicans this was clearly a defection to the enemy. "He has gone over heart and soul," declared Garnier-Pagès. "In politics there are two schools," was Jules Favre's haughty reply to Ollivier, "the school of principle and the school of expediency. The latter creates nothing, and we belong to the former." This amounted to condemning the "opportunism" of Ollivier in the name of sacred "principles," and anathematising his "treachery." And indeed, as the framer

252

of a Bill put forward by the Council of State, attacked alike by the Right and the Left, Ollivier was already cutting the figure of a Government man.

In the spring of 1864 everything seemed ready for the Liberal Empire, although the *régime* was still capable of defending itself against too virulent attacks. For instance, **Republican Agitation.** it prosecuted and fined thirteen members of the Republican Electoral Committee who in view of the bye-elections of March 1864 had formed an association of over twenty persons. The trial of the Thirteen brought before the public, and above all before the younger generation in the Schools, the names of Ferry and Gambetta, who were Republicans like the men of '48, but, in addition, atheists, Positivists and materialists. They no longer invoked the name of Christ in their speeches; they were not only unbelievers but also anti-clerical. It was at this time that a slogan invented by a journalist named Peyrat became all the rage : " Clericalism is the enemy ! " In the *Quartier Latin,* where the students were just the age when young men are as a rule violently " agin the Government," whatever it may be, the Empire was held in abhorrence and its adversaries were acclaimed. Professors who stood too high in Court favour were " ragged," while the spicy innuendoes of Liberal-minded masters were loudly applauded. They sang " The lion of the *Quartier Latin !* " " No, youth is not dead. . . . The young lion has roared." They read little rags of newspapers which for lack of funds to pay the deposit could not touch politics but professed to deal only with literature, philosophy and social questions, ardently discussing God, morality and society. Among them was *La Jeune France,* edited by Vermorel, the future member of the Commune; *Le Travail,* to which in 1862 two men of the extreme Left contributed, Méline and Clemenceau, who belauded not only '89 but even '93; and the *Rive Gauche* under Longuet, who, full of Proudhon's ideas, wanted to abolish the allocation of public monies to the Church and the Army, and condemned the men of '48 for being afraid of Socialism. Young Republicans and Socialists here met on common ground. They constituted a new danger which soon became formidable, but which a Morny might have been capable of warding off at the

253

same time as he gave the country the Liberal institutions it desired.

Towards the end of 1864 and the beginning of 1865 it seemed likely that Liberal reforms would be introduced. And it **The** seemed all the more probable because between **Encyclical** the Church and the Empire, between the Catholics, *Quanta* who believed in Conservatism and authority, and *Cura.* Napoleon III, the gulf had been made even wider by the famous *Quanta Cura*, " the encyclical letter of His Holiness Pope Pius, by Divine Providence Ninth of the name, to all the patriarchs, primates, Archbishops and Bishops in grace and communion with the Apostolic See " (December the 8th, 1864). In it the Pope denounced all manner of " evil opinions and doctrines," more especially the following :—" that Governments should draw no distinction between the true religion and false faiths," that " liberty of conscience and worship is the right of every man," and that citizens " have the right to full liberty for the open and public expression of their opinions " (the liberty of damnation as the Encyclical called it); that " the will of the people constitutes the supreme law, independent of all right, divine or human, and that in the domain of politics, the *de facto* is likewise *de jure* "; that " the rights of parents over children, especially the right to educate and instruct, springs from and is dependent upon the civil law " (the Encyclical denounced these " errors," it is difficult to see exactly why, as communistic and socialistic, adding, an attempt is being made " to take education out of the hands of the Church with the object of defiling and debasing the tender and sensitive souls of the young by means of the most pernicious errors and every description of vice "); and " that the authority of the Church is subordinate to the civil authority."

The Encyclical was made all the worse by the addition of the *Syllabus*, a summary of the " errors of our age " already **The** pointed out by the Pope in his speeches and en- **Syllabus.** cyclicals, in which he condemned all rationalism and Liberalism. It transpired that these " evil opinions and doctrines . . . denounced, proscribed and condemned " by the Pope were the very principles upon which, in most countries, modern society and public law were founded.

254

TOWARDS THE LIBERAL EMPIRE

How could Napoleon III, who boasted of being the heir of '89, who was Emperor by virtue of the *fait accompli* of the 2nd of December and of the " will of the people," acquiesce in a denunciation which even a King by divine right would have found difficulty in accepting? Furthermore, many magistrates and officials were Gallicans and could not bring themselves to allow that a foreign Power, even if it was of divine origin, should arrogate to itself the right of dictating to the Government of a State, and especially a Napoleonic State. The Government too forbade the Bishops to publish the anathemas just pronounced by the Pope. But many of them disobeyed from the pulpit, and the Emperor retaliated by appointing Prince Napoleon, who was known to be anti-clerical, Vice-President of the Privy Council and allowing Duruy to publish his famous report in the *Moniteur*. At the beginning of 1865

Death of Morny. everything seemed to point in the direction of Liberalism, and it looked as though Morny could take active steps and lay the foundations of the new *régime*. Unfortunately the *Nabab*, depicted by Alphonse Daudet, had burnt the candle at both ends. He died on the 10th of March, 1865, and his death was destined to retard the success of Ollivier and the advent of the Liberal Empire.

CHAPTER VII

COLONIAL EXPEDITIONS

No premeditated plan of imperialism. The policy of prestige. *Algeria :* its conquest completed. The Emperor's sympathy with the Arabs. *Senegal :* Faidherbe *versus* El Hadj Omar. *New Caledonia :* transfer of the convict prisons which had hitherto existed in the naval bases. Cochin-China and Cambodia : Saïgon (1859); cession of Cochin-China by the King of Annam. Protectorate over Cambodia. *China :* missionaries and merchants. Demonstration of 1857–58. Defeat at Taku (1859). Cousin Montauban's expedition (1860) : Taku, Palikao, the Summer Palace, Pekin. *Syria :* Druses *versus* Maronites. Massacres of 1860. Damascus (July). Beaufort d'Hautpoul's expedition. Concessions by the Turks. The English perturbed by the prolonged presence of the French. Order in Syria. *Mexico :* Miramon *versus* Juarez. Foreign loans. Dream of a Latin Empire in Mexico. Convention of London (1861) and the action of the English, the Spaniards and the French. The Jecker-Morny Loan. France breaks with her allies. Lorencez and Almonte. Defeat at Puebla (5th of May, 1862). Retreat. Forey besieges and takes Puebla (1863). Entry into Mexico City. Bazaine, Commander-in-Chief. The Empire of Maximilian (1864). The hornet's nest of Mexico. Incidents and difficulties. Repatriation decided upon in 1866.

THE Second Empire sent out her soldiers and planted the French flag in every continent. But this does not mean that she had any comprehensive and premeditated plan of colonial expansion or of imperialistic conquest. The Government of Napoleon III, however, seized every opportunity that offered for pursuing a policy of prestige through-
Colonial Policy. out the world. France regarded herself as the first Power in Europe, ceding pride of place to none, not even to the ancient realm of England, who as it happened was her ally, or to Russia and Austria, the former beaten at Sebastopol and the latter at Solferino. Thus it was incumbent on her to appear in any part of the world from which a call came. And calls were not lacking.

In Algeria, Napoleon III had received from the hands of

256

Louis Philippe a country three-quarters conquered and in process of being pacified. The Moors and the Jews swarm-

Algeria. ing in the white streets of the towns, the Arabs galloping across the plains or lurking in their grey tents in the depths of the valleys, were acquiescing in the rule of their new masters. The only people who still remained to be conquered were the Kabyles in their fortified villages on the mountain sides, the horsemen of the desert and the agricultural tribes of the southern oases. In 1849, after a siege of fifty days, the oasis of Zaatcha had been taken, and the oasis of Mzab had also been occupied. In 1851 St. Arnaud made an expedition into Little Kabylie, where he won his promotion to divisional commander, a necessary step towards the high honours held in store for him by the Prince President. The Empire, which was naturally inclined to activity, if only for the sake of humouring the army, which was its chief support, took in hand the task of completing the conquest of Algeria. The Republic of '48 had tried to free the country from military rule, and had granted 50,000 settlers citizen rights, and created three departments which were represented in the Assembly in the same way as French departments. Large sums of money had also been spent in establishing fresh settlers, un-employed working-men, who were provided with houses, land, ploughs and grain for sowing. Twenty thousand were settled in this way, but only 10,000 remained. The Empire put an end to the representation of the country in the Assembly and naturally restored full power to the army, whose first thought was to fight. In 1852 Pélissier and his Zouaves took the towers of Laghouat by storm. In 1854 Ouargla, Touggourt and the oasis of Oued Rhir were reduced to subjection. Lastly, Randon had roads made round Great Kabylie, and in 1857, with 35,000 men, he surrounded the mountain district, conquered the tribes one after the other, captured a prophetess named Fathma, who incited the Kabyles to resistance, and in the end forced the chiefs of the Kabyles in their turn to submit to the yoke of France. Their institutions were respected, the French contenting themselves with levying a war tax and building Fort Napoleon (now Fort National) in the heart of the hills. The year 1857 marked the completion of the conquest. But the work of colonisation was continued, villages were built, the cultivation of corn was encouraged by allowing the grain to enter France free of duty, the vine was introduced and the European population steadily increased.

Henceforward France had her foot firmly planted in the colony. The Emperor took a lively interest in Algeria and set to work to organise the Civil Service, making his cousin, Prince Napoleon, "Minister for Algeria and the Colonies," creating General Councils in the three departments and appointing Prefects. However, it soon had to return to a military government under Pélissier, only to re-establish a civil government at the beginning of 1870 and restore the power of the Prefects—a distressing series of changes, though natural enough, since France was as yet inexperienced in the art of colonisation. Napoleon III paid a personal visit to Algiers in 1860, and wanted to grant autonomy to the fine Arab race with their chivalrous chiefs and splendid horsemen, and to regard Algeria not as a colony but as an Arab kingdom. "I am as much **The Emperor and the Arabs.** the Emperor of the Arabs as the Emperor of the French," he declared. He also wanted to secure the Arab douars in possession of their common lands, which amounted to siding with them against the settlers, who were all " on the make " and lodged a protest. In any case his dreams were premature. The Ouled-Sidi-Cheik rebelled in 1864 in the south of the province of Oran, massacred a whole body of troops and laid waste some villages. The Kabyles also rose up, and it took a year's fighting to subdue the insurgents. Nevertheless, the Emperor persisted in his plans for granting autonomy to the Arabs. Did they not constitute a nation worthy of support whose existence should be guaranteed on the same terms as that of United Italy? But his dreams vanished in smoke; locusts, famine and cholera devastated the colony during the last years of the Empire. But at least the European population increased in spite of these disasters, and the new railways were destined to advance the prosperity of these lands of the future.

In Senegal France possessed in 1848 only a few isolated trading stations, where traders bought gum arabic and earth-nuts, which the *inhabitants*, half-castes descended from French fathers and the daughters of the black chieftains, used to go

Senegal. inland to collect. The Moorish chiefs were paid royalties and *customs*, which were of course quite arbitrary. And all around there were bellicose and hostile tribes, Moorish horsemen and Peuhl shepherds, a white Mahommedan race, negro settlers who worshipped fetiches, and " Toucouleurs "—Peuhl and negro half-castes—who owed allegiance to the prophet El Hadj Omar. The French traders asked the Emperor for military garrisons to protect them, and declared that in future they would pay a fixed duty instead of the *customs*. Faidherbe, an officer in the Engineers, inspired

Faidherbe. their confidence, and in 1855 they succeeded in having him appointed Governor. Faidherbe remained in the country for ten years. With a few infantry companies, some native Senegalese sharpshooters, and a small flotilla he undertook to conquer a territory larger than France. In the first place he had to defend the port of St. Louis itself against thousands of assailants. Whereupon he turned to El Hadj Omar and the Moors, who had all the soldier's contempt for the white man—" They are only traders "—and refused to admit that these vile merchants knew how to fight. Hostilities lasted for years. In 1856 Faidherbe went up the Senegal River as far as Medine above Kayes, a distance of over 550 miles from St. Louis, that is to say, as far as from Dunkerque to Perpignan, and built a small fort there armed with four guns. In April of the following year, Omar, with thousands of horsemen, attacked the fort, which was defended by a handful of men, most of them natives, under the command of a mulatto named Holle. Holle repulsed two assaults and was besieged for weeks; it was a matter of being able to hold out until July, which was the rainy season, when the river rose and would enable Faidherbe to come up with reinforcements. Food ran short and the garrison were reduced to eating raw earth-nuts. They had only two cartridges left apiece when Faidherbe arrived and drove back Omar. But for a few subsequent expeditions, this was the final episode in the struggle, and Faidherbe, who was at once an administrator and a soldier, set to work as best he could, and almost

without help from the mother country, to organise the colony
he had created. He even sent Mage, the naval lieutenant, to
negotiate a commercial treaty with Omar's son, and made
plans for gaining a footing at Bamako, on the Upper Niger,
thus outlining the future region of French West Africa. All
the honour of the achievement belongs to Faidherbe alone,
and is in no way shared by the Empire, which ignored or misunderstood the significance of the enterprise.

The Emperor, who was a humanitarian and an Anglo-maniac,
wanted France, like England, to deport her criminals and give
New them an opportunity of making good in some distant
Convict land where they could start life afresh on virgin
Settle- soil. In 1852 he did away with the convict prisons
ments. at the naval bases, and thenceforward convicts were
sent to Guiana and the Iles du Salut. Later on, in 1854, he
had New Caledonia seized, where French missionaries had
already been established, and founded a new convict settlement
there. High hopes were founded on these colonial peniten-
tiaries—far too high, no doubt.

Moreover, France found herself inveigled into the conquest
of Cochin-China and into establishing a protectorate over
Cambodia. French missionaries and traders were
Cochin- already in Indo-China, managing as best they
China. could without guarantees of any sort. A commercial treaty was concluded with the King of Siam, and French
traders in Bangkok were granted the requisite facilities for
carrying on their business, acquiring real estate and practising
their religion, and they had to pay to Siam only three per cent.
on the merchandise they imported. On the other hand, the
King of Annam refused to allow the Christians freedom of
worship. In 1858 a French fleet came up and bombarded
Tourane and menaced Hué, but dysentery, fever and cholera
obliged the forces that had gone ashore to retreat. Whereupon it was decided to retire between five and six hundred
miles south and ascend the delta of the Mekong; and in 1859
Saïgon, the rice emporium of Annam, was taken. But the
French, deterred by the thought of the expenses that colonisation would involve, had no intention of remaining there. All
260

they wanted was to extract from the King of Annam an indemnity and guarantees similar to those which had been obtained from the King of Siam. But they negotiated in vain, and the little garrison in Saïgon resisted a year's siege on the part of the Annamites. It was then suggested that the administration of Cochin-China should be placed in the hands of natives under the control of French naval officers, and the latter communicated with the Annamite Mandarins by means of Catholic natives, pupils of the missionaries, with whom they spoke Latin. But the Annamites rebelled and the French had to take full control once more. At last, in 1862, force of circumstances drove Admiral Bonnard to extract a treaty from the King of Annam whereby Cochin-China was handed over to France.

Shortly afterwards, Doudart de Lagrée went to Cambodia, and Norodon, King of Cambodia, was forced to accept a French
Cambodia. protectorate, Doudart holding his revolver at the head of the Siamese Resident, who, by virtue of a secret treaty, was trying to establish a Siamese protectorate over the country. Finally, after considerable hesitation and plans for evacuation, it was decided to remain where Fate had led, and to place the administration of the new colony in the hands of naval officers, who were to make their career there, with the assistance of Annamite soldiers and interpreters.

To the west of Saïgon, the conquest of Cochin-China was completed in 1867, after a rebellion had taken place. From that time forward the colony more than paid its way, although a few years previously Napoleon III had wanted to evacuate it for purposes of economy. It was the French naval officers who had forced his hand, and this initiative on the part of subordinates, similar to the spirit of enterprise displayed by Faidherbe, won France a new territory which was larger than the mother country and destined to be a source of great wealth.

The protection of traders and Catholic missions also led Napoleon III to intervene in China. Ever since 1844 the
China. French had by treaty been given the right of possessing commercial houses, churches, cemeteries, schools and hospitals in five Chinese ports—Canton, Amoy,

Fou-Tcheou, Ning-Po and Shanghai. But, by agreement with the English, they wanted to be allowed to send representatives to Pekin itself, with a view to securing better guarantees; for the guarantees granted by the treaty were far from satisfactory. In 1855, Chapdelaine, a French missionary, had been tortured and put to death, and in 1856 an English boat had been captured at Canton by the Chinese authorities; the English had bombarded the forts and the Chinese had set fire to the European factories. Whereupon it was decided to make an Anglo-French naval demonstration, the French insisting upon appearing side by side with the English, who were already cutting off the lion's share for themselves in China.

The two fleets bombarded Canton in 1857, and then, sailing north to the Gulf of Pechihli, forced the defences at the mouths of the Pei-ho without fighting in 1858, and reached Tientsin, the port of Pekin. The Chinese Government gave way and promised all the guarantees demanded for the missionaries and merchants. "China is at last opening her arms to Christianity," the French Ambassador telegraphed to Paris, "the true source of all civilisation, and to the industry and commerce of the Western nations," thus ingenuously classing missionaries and merchants, the Gospel and sales registers in the same category. The treaty was to be ratified in Pekin, the sacred city.

But when the diplomatists reached the mouths of the Pei-ho in 1859 on their way to Pekin, they encountered fresh
Taku. defences; although the forts of Taku were silent and deserted, they seemed to be armed, and the river was obstructed by barbed wire, beams and chains. The French and English gunboats were hurled against the barriers. Suddenly the Chinese unmasked their batteries and opened a bombardment from both banks. The flotilla had to retreat with 450 men put out of action. This happened the very day after the battle of Solferino. Paris and London agreed to punish this " outrageous violation of the rules of international law." A force of 8,000 volunteers was raised in France and put under the command of Cousin Montauban, an " African " cavalry General. This worthy man knew what to say when

262

he addressed his troops; no doubt he had made a close study of Napoleon's proclamations: "When you return to the mother country you will tell your fellow-citizens with pride that you have borne the national standard into lands where immortal Rome at the height of her glory never dreamt of penetrating with her legions." At all events he knew how to prepare the expedition down to the smallest detail.

Cousin Montauban.

The troops left Toulon in December 1859 and sailed to the distant shores of China viâ Teneriffe and the Cape. The Suez Canal had not yet been cut, and they did not reach their destination until May. Montauban went ahead viâ Egypt, landing at Alexandria and embarking again at Suez and reaching Shanghai in two months. After a fruitless ultimatum sent to the Chinese the Anglo-French forces landed in August 1860, without striking a blow, on the flat muddy coast near the Pei-ho. Montauban, in spite of his sixty-four years, was the first to jump into the water to reach the shore. Amid the cheers of the troops the colours of the two countries were planted in the ground. A few days later the first of the four forts of Taku was attacked. As soon as the Chinese guns had been silenced by the French artillery, the infantry assaulted, clearing the ditches, pulling down the bamboo palisades, scaling the walls by means of ladders brought up by coolies, and after sanguinary hand-to-hand fighting, driving out the Chinese, who had had but little experience of fire-arms and defended themselves with pikes, arrows and stones. The three other forts fell without any defence being offered. The defeat of June 1859 was avenged.

The Allies then pushed on to Tientsin. The Europeans, the "Barbarians" on whose heads a price had been put by the Chinese General, Sang-ko-lin-sin, were calm and confident. But Sang-ko-lin-sin had been deprived by imperial edict of "his aigrette of three peacocks' feathers and the blue Manchu banner" of Commander-in-Chief for having lost Taku. Negotiations were opened, but the Allies were met at every step by the duplicity of the Chinese, who were trying to gain time until the winter, when the Barbarians would be forced to retire. The first Chinese envoy was obliged to confess that he had not been given plenary powers, and as the Allies continued their march towards Pekin they were met by a " little Mandarin with a blue button," who informed them that the first envoy had been disavowed. He was followed by one Mandarin after another, all of whom did their best to stop the progress of the Europeans. The latter eventually agreed to halt at about six or seven hours' march from Pekin, and a small body of French and English delegates, one of whom was an English interpreter, went forward to negotiate. Lively discussions followed, more especially in connection with the demands of the English and French Ambassadors, who insisted upon being given audience by the Emperor in Pekin to prove that their countries were the equals of the Chinese Empire. In the end the envoys were seized by some Tartar horsemen and others by the Chinese mob, and thrown into prison. Only one or two, who had been wounded, were able to rejoin the army and raise the alarm, whereupon it was decided to advance and try to rescue the hostages. At Changkiawang Allied forces succeeded in breaking through the Tartar hordes almost without loss. On the 21st of September a body of 800 French troops attacked the Chinese defences on the Palikao bridge outside

Palikao. Pekin. The infantry stopped the charges of the Tartar cavalry, who in the end turned tail and fled, whereupon the infantry and chasseurs stormed the bridge, which was defended by chieftains waving gold-embroidered flags, soldiers armed with matchlocks and bows, and gunners who did not know how to lay their wooden guns and culverins. The position was soon taken. The French had twenty men put out of action and had put to flight between forty and sixty thousand Chinese. Montauban, ever mindful of antiquity, conjured up visions of " the victories constantly won by a handful of Roman soldiers over the barbarian hordes."

Another " little Mandarin with a silver knob and a hat on his head " now came to negotiate. But he said nothing about returning the hostages, of whose fate he knew nothing. In a note which had reached the army, the English interpreter had written in Chinese that he was being well treated. But in the flourishes of his signature he added : " All this is dictated." The Allies then skirted Pekin, and to the north reached

264

COLONIAL EXPEDITIONS

the Summer Palace of the Emperor, almost without striking
a blow.   All the Emperor's treasures were stored here, in
The   kiosks and pagodas in the middle of the gardens
Summer   —jewels, silks, embroideries, crystals, porcelains,
Palace.   precious stones, incense, candelabras and golden
statues.   Montauban, in conjunction with the English, began
to make an inventory of all these treasures, ear-marking the
most precious objects for their rulers' museums—and the
generals and departmental chiefs.   But suddenly there was a
rumour that the Chinese were pillaging the palace, whereupon
the Allied soldiers fell upon the treasures and began to sack
the place.   " There was so much that they did not know where
to begin, taking, discarding and taking again, scattering their
booty along the road, draping themselves in the silks amid
the jibes of their comrades; it was not so much pillage as
wholesale squander and waste " (P. de la Gorce).   Meanwhile
some of the hostages, and among them the interpreter, succeeded
in reaching the camp after days of excruciating suffering and
torture.   But others, some score of them, were brought back
in coffins, " very nice coffins," a Chinaman had assured the
Allies.

On the 13th of October French troops occupied one of the
gates of Pekin without striking a blow, surrounded by an
Pekin.   inquisitive swarming crowd held off by the whips
of the Chinese police.   The English Ambassador
had the Summer Palace consigned to the flames by way of
retaliation for the deaths of the hostages, among whom there
had been a correspondent of the *Times*.   Thus on the one side
there had been murders, and on the other pillage and incen-
diarism.   But at least the war was over, and the Europeans
were treated as equals by the Chinese, who granted concessions
for the future.   The ratification of the Treaty of 1858 was
demanded, the free entry of the French and English Ambassadors into Pekin, apologies on the part of China for the surprise
attack of 1859, the throwing open of fresh ports and of Tientsin
to foreign trade, guarantees for merchants and missionaries,
war indemnities and reparations.   And the old cathedral of
Pekin, built long ago by the Portuguese and since abandoned,
was once more opened for worship.   Whereupon, in order to

escape the winter, the French troops left Pekin in November and returned to France, taking with them all they had been able to keep of the treasures of the Summer Palace. The soldiers were also presented with a medal with a beautiful yellow ribbon ornamented with Chinese characters in green. Montauban was made a Senator and Comte de Palikao—a title which afforded a good target for rhymsters and lampoonists. He was not taken seriously and the Legislative Body protested when the Emperor wanted them to vote him a gratuity, and the Commission, of which Monsieur de Jouvenel was chairman, threw out the Bill. " Only degenerate nations haggle over the means of expressing their gratitude," the Emperor wrote to the deputies. But he no longer showed the energy of the dictator, but merely the bitterness of impotence. Thus ended this venture undertaken for the sake of prestige, this " punitive " expedition which at least helped to open up China to Europe.

Circumstances also conduced to make France intervene in Syria, where two races, the Maronites and the Druses, were
Syria. at loggerheads under Turkish rule. The Maronites were Christians, affiliated to the Church of Rome although they had their own special liturgical rules and allowed their priests to marry. They were the traditional protégés of France who had established religious communities and convents in the country. The Druses were heretical Mussulmans. They were on good terms with the Turks, more especially with Kourchid, the Pasha of Beirut. Moreover, they naturally turned for support to England, the only other Power capable at that time of facing France on equal terms. The
Druses Maronites and Druses were constantly massacring
versus one another. It will be remembered that at the
Maronites. Congress of Paris in 1856, the Sultan had promised to safeguard the privileges granted to the Christians. Such a firman could serve only to embolden the Maronites and irritate the Druses and the Turks, and fights between the two races grew more and more frequent. The French consul at Beirut naturally laid the blame on the Mussulmans, while the English consul accused the Christian Committee of inciting
266

the Maronites to demand independence. In the spring of 1860 the Druses attacked the Maronites, and on more than one occasion, with the help of Turkish irregulars, known as Bashibazouks, and occasionally even with the connivance of regulars and of the Turkish population, they massacred the Christians. The men, who were incapable of defending themselves, were put to the sword, old men and children had their throats cut, the wounded were put out of their misery, women were tortured to force them to give up their money and jewels, young girls and youths were violated, towns, villages and hamlets were pillaged, cattle were driven off and houses were sacked and burnt. Particularly tragic scenes occurred at Saida, the Sidon of the Old Testament, Hasbeiya and Deir-el-Kamr, a few hours distant from Beirut. Altogether there were 6,000 victims in the Lebanon district. The trouble spread as far as Damascus, the great city of Syria, where it was no longer Maronites and Druses, but 20,000 Christians, many of them rich, not to say extremely wealthy, who were confronted by 130,000 Turks. On the 9th of July the Mussulmans hurled themselves upon the Christian quarter, and the Bashibazouks and Turkish police, far from stopping them, joined their ranks. Achmet, the Governor, did not interfere. They attacked the houses of the rich, the consulates, and the churches where the **Massacre of Christians.** Christians had sought refuge. The massacre lasted for three days and there were 5,000 victims. Abd-el-Kader, the erstwhile foe of France in Algeria, who had been set free by the Emperor, was living in retirement in Damascus. He threw open his palace to the Christians and saved fifteen hundred.

The news of the first massacres caused great excitement in Paris. France regarded herself as the traditional protector of these Christians who were being done to death, and the voice of public opinion was raised demanding vengeance. Moreover, it afforded the *régime* an opportunity of perhaps regaining the sympathies of the Catholics, those Catholics who had not forgiven the Emperor the blows he had struck against the temporal power of the Pope. It was suggested that a European Commission of Inquiry should be sent to Syria, and one or two battleships were despatched to Beirut. After the

Damascus massacre it was decided to intervene. But the English were perturbed. They were jealous of French influence in Syria, and were afraid that if once the French forces were installed in Beirut they would not want to leave. The Napoleon who had just annexed Savoy and Nice was perhaps dreaming of conquering Syria, just as the first Bonaparte had conquered Egypt, and was in any case menacing the road to India. In Paris everything was done to reassure London. The expedition would have no other object than that of helping the Sultan to restore the public peace; Napoleon III would be the mandatory (already!) of the European Powers in Syria. The occupation would not last longer than six months. Six thousand men set out from Toulon under the command of General de Beaufort d'Hautpoul, and arrived in Syria at the end of August 1860.

Expedition to Syria.

Here they were met by a perfectly novel situation. Constantinople, in order to take the wind out of the sails of the French expedition, which was sufficiently mortifying to Turkish pride, had decided to take the first step and punish, or make a show of punishing, the culprits. Fuad Pasha was sent to Syria with plenary powers. He went to Damascus, had a few dozen Turks shot or hanged, sent 500 to prison or into exile, and presented Abd-el-Kader with the Order of Medjida at the very moment when the Grand Cordon of the Legion of Honour reached him from Paris. As for the Governor, Achmet, he was tried *in camera* and secretly executed—which led to the rumour that as a matter of fact he had been extricated from the unfortunate affair.

When Fuad arrived at Beirut the French were encamped in the pine woods round the town, protecting themselves as best they could against the heat. They made a military expedition to the Lebanon district while the Turks allowed the Druses to escape to the south. Some of the Maronites took the opportunity of the presence of the French to murder some of the Druses, which naturally led to trouble with the English. At the request of the European Commission of Inquiry, which had at last assembled, Fuad condemned to death eleven Druse chieftains, who apparently managed to escape execution, sentenced Kourchid, the ex-Pasha of Beirut, to imprisonment for life—it would be easy enough to set him free later on—and had a few hundred Druses arrested. But the English, in spite of the horror of the recent massacres, instinctively sided with the Druses, and blamed the Bishops for having denounced them, declaring that thirst for vengeance was contrary to the spirit of the Gospels. A fund was opened for compensating the victims, who in addition received help from the French religious bodies and from French and English charities.

Meanwhile the months slipped by, and in January 1861 the English requested Paris to recall the forces that had gone ashore. But nothing had yet been settled, and **Jealousy of England.** this would have meant the possibility of fresh massacres. England, however, was afraid that the Emperor intended to remain in Beirut just as he had remained in Rome ever since 1849. And the *Saturday Review* declared that it was not for nothing that *Partant pour la Syrie* was the national anthem of the Napoleonic dynasty, that the conquest of Syria and Egypt was the favourite idea of the Napoleonic mind, and that the Syrian plot was the remains of the old spirit of aggression inherent in the military despotism of the Bonapartes. Paris set too much store by the English alliance not to dispel these suspicions, and contented herself with prolonging the occupation only until the 5th of June, 1861, when the battle squadrons were to be allowed to cast anchor off the coast of Syria.

Lastly, the Druses who had been arrested were banished to Tripoli, and quite inadequate help was doled out to the Maronites and the Christians in Damascus. Turkey, **Order in Syria.** who lacked funds for her own officers and soldiers, was by no means anxious to spend money on " dogs of Christians." At the beginning of June the French troops returned to Beirut and embarked once more. But at least they had succeeded in securing the reorganisation of the administration in the Lebanon district. Hitherto there had been two Governors there (kaimakhans), one a Druse and the other a Maronite. It was decided to put the district into the hands of a single chief, either a native or a foreigner, to be appointed by the Sultan and independent of the Pashas of Beirut and Damascus. The first Governor was an Armenian

Catholic. And thenceforward order reigned in Syria. The French expedition had put an end to the massacres. Furthermore, the *Comité des Écoles d'Orient* of Paris collected three million francs (£120,000) by subscription, which Abbé Lavigerie himself distributed in Beirut and the Lebanon district; and French religious orders gave shelter to the children made orphans by the massacres. Could France have gone further and have founded a French protectorate over Syria at this time? It would, of course, have meant alienating England for ever. The Second Empire had so much to answer for in connection with other adventures that it must be credited with the extreme prudence it displayed, at least in the case of Syria.

It was in America that the Second Empire pursued the most fantastic as well as the most dangerous of all its adventures **Mexico.** in distant lands. Civil war was, as usual, raging in Mexico. Two parties were fighting for power: the Conservatives, that is to say, the clergy and the large land-owners, who, led by young General Miramon (it was possible in Mexico to be a General at the age of twenty-six), aimed at establishing a strong centralised Government, like the Spanish Government, under a powerful king or emperor, and the Liberals, federalist Republicans, like the Americans, and anti-clerical, with the lawyer Juarez at their head, who wanted the State to confiscate the property of the Church. Europeans, English, Spaniards and French, who had come to Mexico in fairly large numbers to make their fortunes, received blows from both sides in the struggle; there were requisitions and forced loans, farms or *haciendas* were burnt, convoys carrying silver from the mines to the coast were robbed, and private individuals were cast into prison or murdered. The immigrants called upon their native countries to demand compensation. But in the anarchy that reigned in Mexico how was payment to be secured? It was necessary to employ force. As early as 1858 France had sent a flotilla to Vera Cruz, and in 1860 Paris, London and Madrid dteermined to put an end to the matter by despatching a strong naval expedition to secure the regular payment in future of all debts to foreigners.

COLONIAL EXPEDITIONS

But the authorities in Paris tried to take a longer view. When Louis Napoleon was a prisoner at Ham he had studied Central America, and dreamt of a canal joining the Atlantic to the Pacific and a " new Constantinople " to be built between Anglo-Saxon North America and Latin America. And the time seemed to have come for the old theorist of " forty-eight " to realise his dreams. Saligny, the French Minister in Mexico, supported the Conservatives. Moreover, rich Mexicans, who had sought refuge in France, had the ear of the Tuileries and above all of the Empress, whose native language they spoke. Ought not France to help them? It was a favourable opportunity; Juarez and the Liberals were backed by the United States, but the latter were themselves distracted by the civil war between North and South, and were for the time being quite powerless. It was imperative to turn the situation to account to help the Conservatives and found a centralised Latin and Catholic Empire in Mexico, thus putting a spoke in the wheel of the North American Puritans and democrats, those " Yankee pork-butchers " as Merimée dubbed them, who were in such ill odour at the Tuileries. Already the Emperor's mind, as usual full of visions and schemes, was drawing an ideal map of the New World—on the Canadian frontier the northern States of America, a purely Anglo-Saxon confederation kept within strict bounds; in the south, a con-

Dream of a Latin Empire. federation including the slave-holding States at present in revolt against the North, inhabited by planters, some of whom were of Latin race and Catholics, who cultivated cotton by means of slave labour; and still further south a purely Latin Empire of Mexico in which French influence would be paramount. Dreams—reveries! Already he had his eye on Maximilian, the brother of Francis Joseph, as the head of this Empire, hoping, as he had done ever since Villafranca, that he would be able to regain the sympathy of Austria and thus perhaps win Venice for Italy without striking a blow.

At the beginning of 1861, Juarez, the Liberal, defeated Miramon and entered Mexico City. Saligny, who was on the spot, renewed his demands for intervention every time Europeans were exposed to fresh brutalities. Juarez, who

THE SECOND EMPIRE

was in want of money, suspended the payment of interest due to foreign creditors for two years. Europe became excited. Clearly it was high time to take action, to bombard the ports, seize the customs and pay their own people. London had no wish to go any further or to meddle with the internal affairs of Mexico. Madrid dreamt, possibly quite vaguely, of reconquering her lost colony or at least regaining some influence there by installing—who knows?—a Bourbon on the throne. But Paris was of opinion that the hour had come for the realisation of her grand schemes.

The three Governments signed an agreement in London on the 31st of October, 1861, by virtue of which they undertook "not to exercise in the internal affairs of **Convention of London.** Mexico any influence calculated to undermine the right of the Mexican nation to choose and set up its own form of Government." But, on the other hand, the signatories were authorised, in addition to seizing the fortresses along the coast, to allow "their troops to carry out all such operations as might be necessary for the realisation of the end specified (an extremely unfortunate expression), and above all for securing the safety of the foreigners resident in the country. As usually happens in the case of international treaties, each party to it interpreted the convention as it pleased, London having no desire to penetrate beyond the coast, Paris dreaming of pushing on to Mexico City, and Madrid wavering between the two. Moreover, Vice-Admiral Jurien de la Gravière, who was in command of the French expeditionary force, had only 2,500 men at his disposal. This was a large force compared with the 700 Englishmen under Dunlop, but **Prim.** insignificant by the side of the 6,000 Spaniards under the daring and ambitious General Prim, whose head was possibly filled with visions of a kingdom to be won for himself out of the venture.

The three fleets arrived separately at Vera Cruz in December 1861 and January 1862, and the town was occupied without resistance being offered. But it was not long before disagreements arose between the Allies regarding the interpretation to be put on the Convention of London. And an even graver incident occurred when the enormous sum claimed by France

272

became known, which made the total demanded by the Allies amount to the entire revenue of Mexico for two years. France wanted to force Mexico to repay her debt to a certain Swiss banker named Jecker, who in 1859 had lent a few millions to Miramon, and by sharp dealing, which almost amounted to **The Jecker-** usury, had placed Mexico in the position of owing **Morny** him a sum nominally amounting to 75 millions. **Loan.** Jecker had gone bankrupt. His creditors were chiefly French, and their only security was this Mexican debt. But above all it was rumoured that Jecker had a powerful patron—the Duc de Morny himself, who was to receive 30 per cent. of anything Jecker managed to recover. Thus usury and wire-pulling were entangled in the vague dreams of the Emperor and served to push the French soldiers and sailors towards Mexico, where the bullets of Juarez' troops were awaiting them, and also an even more formidable foe—the *vomito negro*, or yellow fever, which in summer rages in the marshes of the tropical districts along the coast.

Saligny had led his countrymen to suppose that they would be hailed as liberators and that all the Conservatives would rise up against Juarez immediately the French force arrived. But nobody raised a finger and the weeks slipped by. The summer, with its rain and mosquitoes, was approaching, and already there were numerous cases of dysentery. It was impossible to remain at Vera Cruz; the troops must either embark again or penetrate beyond the zone of tropical heat and reach the nearest heights of the Mexican plateau, where the climate was temperate and healthier for Europeans. Prim and one of Juarez' Ministers came to an agreement at Soledad on the 19th of February, 1862, whereby the Allied troops were to be allowed to advance as far as Córdoba, Orizaba and Tehuacan, towns which were situated beyond the torrid zone, and stay there as long as negotiations regarding the settlement of the debt were being carried on. The Allies, on their side, undertook to respect the independence and integrity of the Republic of Mexico, which some of them in their heart of hearts had been hoping to overthrow.

Communications between the leaders of the expedition and their respective Governments were far from easy. The trans-

T

atlantic cable had not yet been laid and telegrams had to be sent by boat, viâ New Orleans, the headquarters of a regular service of liners. When the news of the Convention of Soledad reached Paris at the beginning of April, the Government hastened to disavow it. It was impossible to confirm an act recognising the independence of the Republic under Juarez. And it was decided to grant plenary powers to Saligny and to confine Jurien de la Gravière to the command of his flotilla. But London and Madrid approved of the Convention. This proved the death-blow of the alliance, which had already been shaken by various disagreements. The French, for instance, had sent reinforcements of 4,000 men, under General de Lorencez, at which the English and Spaniards had taken umbrage; rumours were current in Europe to the effect that the Crown had been offered to Maximilian; and above all London absolutely refused to acknowledge the Jecker debt. The alliance was also broken in Mexico at the same time. Almonte, one of the Conservative leaders, had just disembarked at Vera Cruz. He had been Miramon's Minister in Paris and had ingratiated himself with the Emperor. It was Napoleon III himself who had persuaded him to return to Mexico in order to hasten on the Conservative movement which Saligny was always announcing but which was still being awaited. Naturally Juarez, supported by Dunlop and Prim, protested against the landing of this exiled rebel; it was clearly contrary to the spirit of the Convention of Soledad. But Almonte reached Córdoba under the protection of French infantry, and it was clear that France wanted to intervene in the internal affairs of Mexico. The English and Spaniards immediately took ship, and at the same moment Jurien de la Gravière learnt of his degradation. The result was that about the middle of April 1862 Lorencez found himself alone in Córdoba with his 6,000. Before him lay the Mexican plateau defended by the Juarists, and behind him the marshes haunted by the spectre of yellow fever.

The Allies Disagree.

Won over by Saligny's arguments, he made up his mind to act, to break with Juarez and to advance; it was imperative at all costs to flee from the *vomito negro*. The murder of one or two soldiers, and alleged menaces made by Mexicans against sick men left behind in their lines,

Lorencez.

served as an excuse for repudiating the Convention of Soledad, by which French troops were not to remain in the temperate zone after the negotiations on the subject of the debt had terminated. A proclamation was issued telling the Mexicans that the only aim of the French was " to inspire the honest elements in the country, that is to say, nine-tenths of the population, with the courage to make known their wishes." Whereupon Lorencez marched on Orizaba. He entered it after a short struggle and was joined by a few Mexican horsemen. They were a disorderly body, followed by women and heavy baggage; but what matter? These first recruits gave earnest of others to follow. Moreover, were not French troops invincible? Lorencez imagined he had already won the victory, and wrote to the Minister for War a letter which sheds considerable light on his illusions and his simplicity. " We are so far superior to the Mexicans (under Juarez) both as regards race, organisation, discipline, morality and loftiness of feeling, that I beg Your Excellency to be so good as to inform the Emperor that, at the head of my 6,000 soldiers, I am now the master of Mexico." This was written at the end of April. On the 5th of May he reached Guadalupe, which protected Puebla from Los Angeles, the City of Angels, the last

Puebla. obstacle on the road to Mexico City. It was an extremely strong position, similar to Mont Valérien, which dominates Paris. Lorencez decided to storm the place. The artillery opened fire, but from a distance of over 2,000 yards, which was a long way for that period, and made but little impression on the Mexican defences. No matter! The Zouaves and chasseurs rushed forward to the assault, crossed the ditches and scaled the walls with the help of improvised ladders. Roblet, the bugler, hoisted himself up on to the parapet and blew the call to charge. But the French fell beneath the fire of the Mexicans, and a torrential downpour of rain ended the struggle. The French had 500 men put out of action, a twelfth of their force, and Lorencez beat a retreat, while the Mexicans proclaimed the victory of their troops over " the finest soldiers in the world." And, indeed, a handful of badly-armed Indians had stopped the French army, which regarded itself, and was regarded by the rest of the world, as the best of its day.

On the 1st of June, the *Patrie*, a semi-official journal, wrote : " Our troops are advancing triumphantly across Mexico," and added that they would shortly enter Mexico City. The truth had not yet reached Paris, but it did not take long to do so. On the 15th of June the *Moniteur* announced the defeat at Puebla. On the 26th of June Jules Favre denounced the expedition in the Legislative Body, and even dared to refer to the Jecker bonds. Morny, who was presiding, did not move a muscle. He was a good actor. Although they had no love for him, the majority listened to Jules Favre. Meanwhile the Emperor was personally endeavouring to set matters right. He studied the map of Mexico, superintended the arrangements with regard to the clothing, headgear and rations of the reinforcements that were to be sent out, and give orders that, with a view to escaping the ravages of yellow fever, not more than a week was to be spent in crossing the torrid zone. Twenty-three thousand men were despatched during the course of the summer, under the command of Forey, who was given plenary powers.

Meanwhile Lorencez beat a retreat with his wounded, keeping his Mexican horsemen in hand, and reached Orizaba once more **Retreat.** on the 18th of May. Here he fortified his position. But how was he to exist? The convoys from Vera Cruz, which had to come by very bad roads, were frequently attacked by Mexican guerilla bands or decimated by yellow fever. The men had to be rationed. Moreover, Lorencez had quarrelled with Almonte and Saligny ; he accused the latter of having deceived him regarding the real feeling of the country and he refused to see him. Meanwhile the Juarists were becoming menacing. One night they occupied a steep hill overlooking Orizaba, which Lorencez had omitted to guard. Fortunately that same night a company of infantry managed to reach the top of the hill, which was almost perpendicular, surprised the Mexicans and captured the position at the point of the bayonet, putting 2,000 of the enemy to flight. The army was saved, but it still had to hold out for some weeks.

At last, in September, the first reinforcements arrived, though some of the units were immediately decimated by yellow fever. Forey followed with the bulk of his forces and Lorencez

276

COLONIAL EXPEDITIONS

returned to France. Forey had 27,000 under his command. But he refused to risk another venture *à la* Lorencez, and

Forey. intended to take his time before acting. Months slipped by, and Paris began to grow impatient. At last, in March 1863, Forey advanced. Puebla constituted a formidable obstacle, with strong forts, barricades in the town, and every block of houses and convents constituting a fortress. The 20,000 Mexicans who were defending the town were exultant at the recollection of the victory of 1862 and over Favre's speech, copies of which were distributed to them. Forey surrounded the town with his two divisions, under Bazaine and Douay, and at the end of March, after six days spent in digging trenches at a distance of about 600 yards from the salient of the fort, and three days' bombardment, captured Fort St. Xavier. But further advance was checked by blocks of houses—" *cadres.*" They were captured one by one, but there were said to be 158 of them. Was it going to be another siege of Saragossa? Mining operations were attempted, but solid rock was soon reached. And the loss in men was heavy. At one time the idea of raising the siege and marching on Mexico City was entertained. But it would have been madness to leave the enemy in the rear. On the 25th of April the convent of St. Inez was attacked; it was surrounded by walls, railings, abattis and network. After springing a mine and bombarding the place for three hours, the Zouaves rushed forward to the attack. They got into difficulties in the minor defence works and in the end were repulsed. The soldiers and even the officers began to tire of this street-fighting. What was the good of it? they asked themselves. They were even more embittered by the telegrams from Paris. On the 25th of April a telegram from the Emperor announced that they would meet with no resistance at Puebla or at Mexico City! But on the 8th of May, Bazaine inflicted a decisive defeat at St. Lorenzo, near Puebla, on a Mexican force that had come to the rescue. " It was a pretty little battle," declared Margueritte, at that time a Lieutenant-Colonel, if, that is to say, a battle can be regarded as pretty by anybody except a soldier. In Puebla the besieged were losing heart. On the 17th of May they destroyed their weapons and the town capitulated

277

after a siege of sixty-one days. Unfortunately at this very moment the Danjou Company of the Foreign Legion was **Fall of Puebla.** surprised and massacred on the road from Vera Cruz. Only one man was able to make his escape —as always happens in such cases—and lived to tell the tale.

In spite of their success, the situation of the French thus hazarding their lives in the heart of Mexico, with far from reliable means of communication, was extremely perilous. Nevertheless, on the 10th of June, without striking a blow, Forey entered Mexico City, whence Juarez had fled. The inhabitants received him with open arms. The Conservatives **Entry into Mexico City.** at last showed their faces, and the crowd, with the cowardice common to all crowds, rallied to the support of the victor. On the 10th of July, a junta of the leading men was formed, consisting in the first place of members chosen by Forey and Almonte, additional members being subsequently appointed by the former. This junta decided to offer the Crown of Mexico to Maximilian. Forey, who in war was slow to act, had been somewhat precipitate in the realm of politics. The Government in Paris was already talking of curtailing the expenses, which it regarded as excessive. " How much longer shall we be dragged into sending fresh troops to Mexico?" demanded Randon; and he was supported by Fleury and the Legislative Body. Nothing further was said about Maximilian. Saligny was in disgrace. But, with the slowness of telegraphic communications, how could Paris and Mexico possibly have acted in concert? Suddenly Forey himself was recalled and presented with the Marshal's baton to compensate him for his fall from **Bazaine.** favour, and Bazaine was appointed to take his place—Bazaine, the hero of San Lorenzo. He understood the soldier, he was clever and wily and quick to win popularity in the army, and his sudden rise resembled that of General Nivelle during the Great War. His was to be the task of founding the Empire of Maximilian.

Bazaine had 34,000 men. After a short period of hesitation, Paris had decided to support Maximilian, provided he was accepted by the vote of the country. The French victories were
278

celebrated, and a new medal was struck with a white ribbon on which two red and green stripes formed a St. Andrew's Cross, surmounted by the black Mexican eagle holding a symbolic green serpent in its beak—the last medal presented by the Empire, the last reflection of glory. Bazaine decided to take action and sent Castagny and Douay at the head of two columns towards the west of Mexico City. A swift and daring march brought them to the town of Guadalajara in January 1864. In every town that was taken, the leading citizens, willy nilly, accepted the Empire of Maximilian, and Napoleon III was obliged to be satisfied with this pseudo-plebiscite. Juarez was lying low. These successes closed the mouths of the croakers in Paris, silenced Thiers and Berryer, who, on the 26th of January, 1864, had adopted a prophetic tone, emphasising the expense and endless complications which the support **The** of Maximilian would entail. In March the *Moniteur* **Emperor** announced that the pacification of Mexico was **Maximilian.** complete, and the Minister Duruy forthwith despatched a scientific commission, as the First Consul had done in the case of Egypt. Maximilian made preparations to set out with his wife, Charlotte of Belgium, and all eyes were sympathetically turned on this Emperor of thirty-two.

Napoleon III now signed in conjunction with him the Convention known as the Convention of Miramar, Maximilian's residence near Trieste, which arranged for the reduction and recall of the French expeditionary force as soon as Maximilian had organised his own national army. A minimum of 20,000 men was guaranteed until 1867, and the maintenance of the Foreign Legion until 1873. Maximilian, for his part, undertook to indemnify all French subjects for any damage they might have suffered and to pay all the expenses of the expedition. The total amounted to a sum representing the entire revenue of Mexico for several years, and there seemed little likelihood of Maximilian ever being able to pay it. But the Government wanted to satisfy the Legislative Body. At the last moment Maximilian almost refused the crown which Mexican delegates had come to offer him; his brother Francis Joseph insisted upon his definite renunciation of all right to the throne of Austria, and he refused to give his consent. Where-

279

upon Napoleon III despatched General Frossard to him to persuade him to agree. At last, on the 10th of April, 1864, he gave way and on the 14th he set sail, escorted by a French ship. On the 15th Napoleon informed Fould that there would shortly be a reduction in taxation owing to the " happy settlement of Mexican affairs."

This settlement, however, was further off than had been hoped. After an enthusiastic reception, Maximilian soon **Mexico a** found himself confronted by all manner of diffi-**Hornet's** culties both political and military. It is true that **Nest.** the French forces were meeting with success both to the north, as far as Monterey and Matamoros, on the frontier of the United States, and in the south, against Porfirio Diaz, in the direction of Oaxaca, which Bazaine, who had been made a Marshal, had himself captured in February 1865. But this period of triumph was immediately followed by difficulties, especially on the Pacific coast, where soldiers and Juarists massacred each other, as well as in the north and even in the neighbourhood of Mexico City, where insurrection once more broke out. And as soon as the French forces evacuated the town, the Juarists entered it, and shot without quarter all those who had sided with the French. The latter retaliated in the same way. Every fortnight it was announced that peace had been restored, but the public were no longer to be deceived. " Juarez is still fleeing, as he has been doing for such a long time past," declared the *Débats* ironically. Were the French ever going to get out of this " hornet's nest of Mexico "?

Furthermore, Mexico was torn in two by a serious religious question. The Liberals a short time previously had nationalised **Religious** and sold the property of the clergy, and the Con-**Difficulties.** servatives wanted to take away these domains from their new owners and restore them to the Church. Forey and Bazaine had already encountered many difficulties in these bitter struggles in which the basest appetites were mingled with spiritual interests. Napoleon III was of course not in favour of the return of the national property and regarded it as " an arbitrary measure opposed to modern civilisation." And Maximilian in his turn entered into conflict

280

with the Nuncio. Such squabbles did not tend to strengthen his authority.

Even more serious were the financial difficulties. The Budget could not be made to balance, the expenditure amount-

Financial Difficulties. ing to 200 millions and the receipts to 80. A Mexican Finance Committee had been created in Paris, with Monsieur de Germiny, the honorary Governor of the Bank of France, as its President. In 1864 a Mexican loan was floated which was not fully subscribed and brought in only 50 millions in new money. In 1865 further debentures at 6 per cent. were issued, on behalf of which Rouher and a certain deputy named Corta made enthusiastic speeches in the Legislative Body. The latter, who had just returned from Mexico, gave a glowing account of his visit. The loan was a success. It was not officially guaranteed, but sub-scriptions could be paid in at public offices. Nevertheless, it was not sufficient to set matters straight. And the Legis-lative Body continued to complain of the mad expenditure which it was called upon to control eighteen months after it had been incurred.

Moreover, various incidents arose. Bazaine, who was Com-mander-in-Chief, could not agree with Maximilian, the political

American Opposition. head of the State, while the superior army officers maintained that they ought to take precedence of the Prefects, as they did in France. There were also incidents with the United States, who regarded the French intervention in Mexico with a far from friendly eye and officially applied the epithet of " honourable " to a transaction whereby arms and munitions were sold to the enemies of France, the Juarists of Matamoros. Washington also sided with the " native Republican Government founded by the Mexican people." Napoleon III was far from popular. He had shown his deep sympathy with the South, and his obvious desire for the United States to be split up into two distinct Confeder-ations, while he had also facilitated the settlement in Mexico of Southerners who had been defeated, The United States Government also refused to recognise Maximilian and his foreign crown, although Drouyn de Lhuys offered to withdraw the French troops if they did so. And frontier incidents grew more and more frequent at Matamoros, where American gunners were in charge of the Juarist guns.

At the beginning of 1866 the French Press insistently urged evacuation; St.-Marc Girardin in the *Débats* and Forcade in **Recall of** the *Revue des Deux Mondes* declaring that an end **the French** should be put to this " gigantic folly." The Emperor **Troops.** replied that the evacuation would shortly take place, as Maximilian had not paid his debts, and he wrote instructing Bazaine that if Maximilian raised any difficulty, he was to organise before he took his departure a Republican Government which would undertake " to pay most of the debts due to France." He was trying to save what he could from the wreck. Baron Saillard presented himself to Maximilian to tell him the news, but the latter refused to believe it. Had not the Emperor promised to help him until the country had been completely pacified? Nevertheless, he tried to create a Mexican army. Unfortunately funds were lacking, in spite of the loans advanced by Bazaine, who had married a Mexican and become reconciled with Maximilian. Meanwhile Paris had decided to recall the troops in three batches during 1866 and 1867. Almonte rushed to Paris from Mexico; but all in vain. The political sky in Europe was far too overcast at the moment for evacuation not to be insisted upon. It was hoped that Maximilian would be persuaded to abdicate; the Juarists were everywhere regaining the upper hand. But the Empress Charlotte, determined to hold firm, set out for Europe on the 8th of July, 1866, with the object of persuading Napoleon III to continue his support. Alas! three days previously Prussia had won the victory of Sadowa, and this disturbance of the balance of power in Europe nullified every effort on the part of Charlotte.

CHAPTER VIII

THE THUNDERBOLT OF SADOWA

The growing menace of Germany under Bismarck. Poland ; the insurrection of 1863. Russo-Prussian agreement. French public opinion on the side of the insurgents. Notes to Russia. Failure of plans for a Congress. The impotent Empire. Denmark ; the conflict over Schleswig, " German territory " and Danish property. The succession of 1863. The war of 1864 ; France allows Denmark to be crushed. French impotence. The Roman question ; Convention of September 1864. " We evacuate Rome, but Italy must respect the Holy See." Italy covets Rome. To gain possession of Venetia she approaches Prussia. *Rapprochement* between Prussia and France ; Bismarck at Biarritz (1865). A Hohenzollern at Bucharest. Dreams of annexations in Rhineland. Thiers' speech of the 3rd of May, 1866. The Austro-Prussian War ; Sadowa (3rd of July). Astonishment of Europe. Napoleon III meditates intervention but withdraws. Demands for " Gratuities " ; the left bank of the Rhine, Belgium. Optimism of the circular of the 16th of September, 1866. The Luxemburg incident (1867). The International Exhibition of 1867. Festivals and visits from foreign potentates. " Maximilian has been shot." A shadow spreads. Interview between Napoleon and Francis Joseph at Salzburg. Black clouds on the horizon. Incidents with Italy. Fresh expedition to Rome against Garibaldi ; Mentana (3rd of November, 1867). End of the friendship between France and Italy. Plans for military reform. Opposition. Niel. The Law of the 14th of January, 1868. The *Garde Mobile*. Inadequate reform.

THE gradual evolution towards a more Liberal system of Government was due not so much to the strength of will of a Morny, who was soon to make his exit, or the half-formulated desires of an Ollivier, as to the long series of difficulties and disasters encountered by the Empire abroad. The day of lucky adventures, brilliant wars and triumphal entries was over. French soldiers were no longer fighting and winning facile victories under the eyes of all Europe. Diplomatists were talking, negotiating and in the end failing. The fact was that a man of might, a new figure, had just made his appearance in Europe and before long was to talk to Napoleon as an equal

THE SECOND EMPIRE

—Graf von Bismarck-Schoenhausen, Minister of the King of Prussia since September 1862. Before his advent France enjoyed a position of uncontested if somewhat factitious prestige on the Continent, even compared with the insular might of England, who was already almost outside the pale of Europe. But a new Power was rising to menace and before long to conquer her, and that was Germany.

For the moment Germany was still a confederation under the suzerainty of Austria, but at the beginning of the century she **Germany.** had begun to wake up to the idea of German unity. The French Revolution had already been responsible for abolishing a number of petty principalities both secular and religious, while Napoleon had inspired a national hatred which, for every German, had become a common article of faith. And the heart and soul of this hatred had been Prussia, vanquished at Jena, but triumphant at Leipzig and Waterloo. One of the combatants of 1813 had become King of Prussia in 1861—William I. He was sixty-three, but was still full of vigour and ambition. " It is not the destiny of Prussia to be content to live in the enjoyment of what she already possesses," he declared ; and in Bismarck he found the Minister he required to impose his will upon Austria, his suzerain in Germany, and on France, his ancestral foe in the west.

Bismarck entered upon the scene at the beginning of 1863 in connection with Polish affairs. In the treaties of 1815 the **Poland.** Poles had been promised " national institutions." In 1861 they had not yet received them. Who would help them ? France was the traditional friend of martyred Poland, but she confined herself to Platonic hopes for the realisation of Polish nationality. " God is too high up in the sky and France is too far away," declared a certain Polish hero. And she was now even further away, since Napoleon III, who had drawn nearer to the Tsar after the Crimea, was anxious to retain his friendship. Relying upon themselves alone, the Poles held demonstrations in Warsaw against the Russians who massacred them or sent them into exile. In January 1863 the police laid hands on all the young Polish patriots to enrol them in the army of the Tsar. This gave the signal for insurrection, and badly armed bodies of men hurried into the woods and

284

menaced the Russians. Bismarck did not hesitate. Prussia also had her Polish element which at any moment might rebel. He foresaw that public opinion in Europe would be on the side of the insurgents against the Tsar. What a unique opportunity to secure the friendship of Alexander II by immediately ranging Prussia on his side at the risk of upsetting public opinion in **Russo-** Europe! On the 8th of February a Convention **Prussian** was signed between Prussia and Russia, by which **Agreement.** the armies of the two countries were to help each other against rebellious subjects, if necessary with the right of crossing their own frontiers.

In Paris, Drouyn de Lhuys and the Emperor were extremely perturbed by this " sudden resolution " on the part of Prussia. In vain did they urge Vienna and London to lodge a common protest. The fact was that public opinion in France was becoming more and more hostile to the Tsar and friendly to Poland, the nation in mourning. Ever since 1861 the Government had been endeavouring to hold this feeling in check, though it was not always successful. Any demonstration on the part of France in favour of the rebels in Warsaw was likely to incur the displeasure of the Tsar and to menace the alliance. With England suspicious, Italy disappointed in her hopes, Austria but lately hostile and Prussia cold and furthermore a second-rate Power, Russia was the only ally on whom France could rely. The semi-official Press took their cue from the *Moniteur*, who " discouraged hopes on the part of Poland which might perhaps be impossible of realisation," or from Billault, who condemned " these insurrectionary passions." But public opinion made itself felt notwithstanding.

Thousands of petitions reached the Senate on behalf of the martyrs, though they did not actually go so far as to demand war against the Tsar. In the Senate itself Prince Napoleon intervened : " I do not want war," he declared, " but neither do I want peace." What could be done ? Through semi-official channels the Government brought pressure to bear upon the Tsar to prevail upon him to grant concessions, the only possible solution, and let it be understood that Prince Napoleon did not represent its sentiments. But the negotiations in St. Petersburg were fruitless. And public opinion was becoming more and more pressing. The leaders of the Polish bands were lauded to the skies and subscriptions were opened on their behalf. As P. de la Gorce remarks, the cause of Poland aroused sympathy in every quarter—from the Catholics, the democrats, the revolutionaries and the salons. " The *Siècle* used the same language as the *Monde*, the clergy as the University, the *Académie* as the Faubourg St. Antoine, and, strange and incredible as it might seem, and unprecedented since the beginning of the reign, on the Polish question the Empress and Prince Napoleon were of the same opinion." In the end the Emperor gave way and " did something."

This " something " consisted of a Note to Russia, which was presented to the Tsar at the same time as a Note from England and Notes from Austria, Italy, Spain, etc. Thus **Notes to Russia.** France supported the other nations in Europe in appealing to the treaties of 1815 and remonstrating on behalf of Poland, while Prussia, of course, took care to have no hand in the matter. William I assured the Tsar of his support in case of war, and in return begged for the help of Russia in the event of Napoleon III, that disturber of the peace, making an attack on the Rhine. As this first overture had no result, a second was made. Paris, London and Vienna simultaneously demanded an amnesty for Poland, together with a system of national representation, a Polish administration, liberty of conscience, the Polish language to be the official language of the country and the recruiting of a regular army. Meanwhile people were killing each other in Poland and Lithuania, and the *Siècle* demanded a plebiscite on the question of intervention. Russia replied to the " six points " by a plea in bar. It was Europe herself who was encouraging the insurgents by continually presenting Notes and prolonging the rebellion. Further remonstrances met with no better success. At last, in November 1863, the Emperor sent out invitations to a Congress which was not only to settle the Polish question but also to recast the map of Europe by rescinding the Treaties of Vienna, which on nearly every point had been " destroyed, modified or menaced—hence the existence of unregulated duties, illegal rights and unbridled pretensions." And thus the ideologist, the theorist and the " man of forty-eight " reappeared in the

286

Emperor, who, still misled in regard to his real power, once again dreamt of being the arbiter of Europe. A clean sweep was to be made of everything, and under his auspices a new, harmonious and well-balanced world was to be built up.

But he soon sang another tune. Prussia expressed polite indifference; Austria, with an anxious eye on Venice, and Russia, little disposed to give way on the Polish question, asked for further particulars; while England categorically refused. How could she accept such a proposal emanating from a Bonaparte of whose visions and adventures she stood in constant fear? Above all, how could the English spirit, which flourishes on fact and experience alone, lend its support to a theoretical and chimerical reconstruction of Europe? The **The Impotent Empire.** dreamer of the Tuileries did not insist. Meanwhile the Tsar succeeded in crushing the Polish insurrection, and the only result of the episode, as far as the Empire was concerned, was that its prestige was lowered and that it stood convicted of impotence in the eyes of Europe. Its vague and fruitless efforts to satisfy public opinion in France had resulted only in alienating Russia, while Bismarck had seized the opportunity to win in St. Petersburg a firm and enduring friendship which was to stand Prussia in good stead in the future.

It was not long before the Danish question was raised, which ended in a fresh defeat for the Emperor and another victory **Denmark.** for Bismarck. An ancient feud separated Denmark and Germany. The Duchies of Schleswig, Holstein and Lauenburg, to the south of Jutland, formed part of the domain of the King of Denmark. Holstein and Lauenburg, the population of which was German, were ruled by Denmark, though they were members of the Germanic Confederation and enjoyed a sort of autonomy. Schleswig, on the other hand, was in no way connected with the Confederation. But German patriotism declared that Schleswig was German territory like Holstein, and wanted to place it in the same position. As a matter of fact, quite apart from "historic rights," a great many Germans were settled in Schleswig. In 1848 there had been a war between Denmark and Germany, and peace had been signed in London in 1852, under the guarantee of the

Powers, especially France. On the death of the King of Denmark in 1863 the whole question was reopened. His successor was Christian IX, as had been arranged in London. But a **The Duke** certain Duke of Augestenburg, who in return for a **of Auges-** lump sum had " given his word of honour as a **tenburg.** prince " to renounce all his rights in the Duchies both for himself and his heirs, at the time when peace was signed in London had the effrontery to claim them for his son, and to write to Napoleon III appealing to the principle of nationality. From Paris Napoleon III sent a reply to the Duke, his cousin, couched in fairly favourable terms, and referring to oppressed nations in connection with the Duchies, adding that " Denmark had possibly been guilty of doing Germany an injustice." Thus, in the name of beautiful theories, he was perhaps somewhat light-heartedly overlooking the guarantee given in London in 1852.

The Duke of Augestenburg had Germany on his side, and Saxon and Hanoverian troops occupied Holstein without striking a blow. Meanwhile General Fleury had arrived in Copenhagen from Paris to offer his congratulations once more to the King of Denmark, but with instructions to be extremely reticent regarding the Danish question; he was to let it be understood that in case of war between Denmark and Germany, France would not intervene on the side of Denmark. Napoleon III was still smarting from the blow of his abortive Congress with which Europe would have nothing to do, and was sulking. Moreover, he was not interested in Denmark.

On his way back Fleury met Bismarck in Berlin, and doubtless allowed him to guess that his master was utterly indifferent regarding the Danish question. Bismarck, who saw clearly ahead, dropped the words, " left bank of the Rhine," in the course of the interview. Was it not the dream of the Revolution and of Napoleon to make the Rhine the north-east frontier of France? This was the first temptation of the devil, but for the nonce the Emperor resisted it. As a matter of fact the offer was put forward as a feeler, for the militaristic ambitions of Bonapartist policy were extremely disquieting to Prussia in connection with her Rhineland territories. At all events nothing was to be feared for the moment. And at the beginning of

THE THUNDERBOLT OF SADOWA

1864, when Bismarck and Austria called upon Denmark to grant Schleswig a certain measure of autonomy, France did not interfere. Prussian militarism was to be given its baptism of fire and the Generals could not contain themselves for joy. " Just fancy, my dear General," Manteuffel observed to Fleury, " I am General of a division and I have never seen fire ! " whilst von Roon declared that right had nothing to do with the matter, that it was a question of might, " and we have the might." These observations acquire a peculiar significance in the light of 1870; at Sedan the Empire may possibly to some extent have paid the penalty of its culpable indifference with regard to Denmark in 1864, and its silence in face of a violation of right. Immanent justice? Who can tell?

The Prussians and Austrians accordingly invaded Schleswig-Holstein and penetrated, without much difficulty, as far as Jutland. The Danes offered resistance only at Düppel and Fredericia. Meanwhile England, the traditional friend of Denmark, insisted that a European Conference should be held in London to settle the conflict. It was now England's turn to press France to take action, and the turn of France to pay her back in her own coin and hesitate to follow her, just as England had failed to follow France in connection with the Polish question. In April 1864 the Emperor made a significant pronouncement : " We have received a serious rebuff from Russia in connection with Poland, and unless we can right that, it is impossible for us to stand another from Germany in connection with Denmark. It would expose us to contempt and derision. *Moreover, I am not prepared for war.*" This showed extraordinary perception on the part of a man whose head the facile victories in Italy and fortunate ventures outside Europe had not turned; this Bonaparte did not trust his army, though that army, apart from the Mexican muddle, still enjoyed an untarnished reputation and regarded itself as the first in the world.

At this juncture Düppel and shortly afterwards Fredericia fell. A conference met in London but proved abortive. Napoleon III, as a matter of fact, suggested that a plebiscite should be taken in Schleswig, but once again refused to intervene or to arbitrate, in the end urging Denmark to acquiesce in the

War of 1864.

u   289

loss of Schleswig. Hostilities had again broken out, and the
Germans had reached the north of Jutland. All that remained
to Denmark were the two islands of Fünen and Zealand. She
gave way and abandoned the whole of Lauenburg and Schleswig-
Holstein to Prussia and Austria. Napoleon III had been
obliged to allow Bismarck to try his hand and Prussia to sharpen
her claws in violation of every right. Later on France was to
pay the price for this weakness.

The everlasting Roman question had not yet been settled,
but in the autumn of 1864 it was hoped that a solution had
been found. If the Emperor had failed in connec-
The Roman tion with Poland and Denmark, he flattered himself
Question. that, thanks to the victories of 1859, he was still
master in Italy. And he was all the more annoyed that the
Roman question should remain unsettled. Rome was still
occupied by French troops, who were apparently defending the
Pope against the ambitions of Piedmont, although the latter
was the ally of France. It was high time to put an end to this
ridiculous situation, which only reflected the policy full of contradictions which the Emperor had pursued in Italy for the
last fifteen years, protecting the Papacy in Rome against the
revolution in favour of Italian unity, but everywhere else supporting this revolution. Napoleon III himself secured the sign-
Convention ing of the Convention of the 15th of September
of Septem- 1864 whereby France undertook to evacuate Rome
ber 1864. within two years; meanwhile the Papal army was
to be reorganised, and Italy promised not to attack the existing
Papal States, and even to defend them against external aggression. Most important of all, a supplementary protocol arranged
for the transference of the capital of the new kingdom. The
Emperor and Drouyn de Lhuys were of opinion that if Victor
Emmanuel left Turin and made Florence his headquarters he
would give the best possible proof that Italy had given up all
pretension to Rome and provide the surest guarantee for the
Holy See.

Was it a solution? It was hardly even a postponement of
the problem and satisfied nobody. In the first place the Pope,
who had been left out of all the negotiations, declared that it
was " quite impossible for him to place the slightest trust in
290

the word or the signature of Piedmont." Public opinion in Italy was also disappointed and indignant, and Garibaldi, who refused to allow the new kingdom to renounce Rome as capital, published a violent letter against the Emperor. " We are not renouncing Rome," declared a parliamentary commission sitting in Turin, " we are merely renouncing getting there by force." In the Tuileries these demonstrations aroused great excitement and fresh assurances were demanded from Piedmont. " The transference of the capital is not merely temporary. . . . Rome can be united to Italy only with the consent of France. . . ." All in vain ! " The aspirations of a country," replied the Italian Government, " constitute a matter for the national conscience and can never become the subject of discussion between two Governments." Thus Italy was from that moment resolved to secure complete unification without the help of Napoleon III, and if necessary against his wishes. At all events the Roman question became for the time being of secondary importance, and Italy turned her eyes to the other Italian province which she still lacked—Venetia. She was thus naturally led to a *rapprochement* with the Power which had come out

Italy and Russia. of the Polish and Danish embroglios with flying colours and was becoming a menace to Austria. It was Prussia who was to help her to regain Venetia and drive out the white coats and the military bands that played on the Piazza San Marco. Europe already foresaw war between Austria and Prussia, and at the end of 1863 Napoleon III had told Italy that this would provide a favourable opportunity for her; under cover of the crisis she could obtain Venetia from Austria, who by way of compensation would annex Roumania.

Prussia also made advances to France; the ancestral foe of Austria might well be her friend. And Napoleon III was

France and Prussia. friendly rather than otherwise to this little state, which with its population of 18,000,000 did not seem formidable. It was he who in 1856 had secured her admission to the Congress of Paris. In 1860 he had met in Baden the man who was destined to become King of Prussia and had been extremely cordial to him. In 1861 he had welcomed him to Compiègne, where William had won all hearts.

The army gave a most friendly reception to the Prussian officers who came to watch the manœuvres at the camp of Châlons or operations in Mexico; how could these men who came to learn from the "first army in the world" be anything but well received? In 1864 General von Roon, the Prussian Minister for War, came in person to the Châlons camp, visited Nancy, went on to the military port of Cherbourg, discussed artillery with the Emperor, and on taking his departure received the Grand Cordon of the Legion of Honour from the hands of the little Prince Imperial. In the light of Sedan this episode assumes an almost tragic complexion. Public opinion in France was already prepared to accept the idea of German unity, the logical conclusion of the theory of independent nationalities. "We do not fear a kingdom of 26,000,000 Italians," said Edmond About; "so why should we fear 32,000,000 Germans on our eastern frontier?"

As for Bismarck, he was well known in Paris, where he had been Prussian Ambassador before being made Prime Minister.

Bismarck. He had returned to Paris in 1864, where he had the reputation of being full of life and vitality and extremely witty. He also knew how to listen to the advice he was kindly proffered. Persigny, for instance, told him not to neglect his army, but always to keep it in good trim. Such simplicity raises a smile. But was there anybody at that period who was sufficiently well aware of the power of Prussia to be able to foretell the future? Bismarck himself at that time had more ambition than self-confidence. Lastly, Count von der Goltz, the new Prussian Ambassador in Paris, had succeeded in winning the confidence of the Emperor and ingratiating himself with the Empress, whose beauty he admired. He had the entrée to the Tuileries and would often pay a visit to the Master without the intervention of his Ministers.

Nevertheless, there was a rift in the lute between the two countries. Von der Goltz was already dreaming of a Franco-Prussian alliance against Austria, but Bismarck was trying to moderate his enthusiasm. However much the sympathies of the Court might have been on the side of Prussia, there was also a party more inclined to favour Austria. It was made up of those who had disapproved of the Italian venture, who defended the Holy See and supported tradition against all suggestions for recasting the map of Europe; among them was Drouyn de Lhuys at the Quai d'Orsay. Thus it was necessary to go warily; a false step might lead to offers of alliance being conveyed to Vienna, or at least a promise of neutrality. "The Emperor is well aware," declared Bismarck, "that France cannot be an ally who can stick to Prussia through thick and thin, or *vice versâ*. France would turn against us as soon as her interests demanded it, and we should do the same when occasion arose."

In October 1865 Bismarck insisted upon going in person to Biarritz to interview the Emperor. He completely won the heart of Merimée. "He is a great and extremely **Bismarck at** cultured German," the latter declared, "and any-**Biarritz.** thing but a fool. He seems absolutely lacking in *Gemüth* but is full of wit." At first Bismarck found the atmosphere far from favourable. After having almost come to a rupture, Austria and Prussia, by the Convention of Gastein, had reached an understanding with regard to sharing the government of Schleswig-Holstein. This *rapprochement* had perturbed France. And the convention had outraged public opinion; the inhabitants of the Duchies had not been consulted and the rights of the Germanic Confederation and of the Duke of Augustenburg had been entirely overlooked. In a circular to his diplomatic representative, Napoleon had protested against this Convention, which "violated treaties, legality, the laws of succession, the principle of nationalities and the will of the people," and which had "no foundation except might, and no justification beyond the mutual convenience of the two signatories."

One of the first questions put by Napoleon III to Bismarck was to ask him whether at Gastein he had not in some shape or form guaranteed to leave Austria in possession of Venetia. Thus it was for Italy that the Emperor of the French still reserved the warmest corner of his heart. And Bismarck did not forget it. Who could tell? Possibly the offer of Venice would provide a surer means of winning over Napoleon III than the Rhineland provinces. Bismarck went as far as to unmask his ambitions. "The interests of the Tuileries can best be served," he declared, "by supporting the national mission of

Prussia; Prussia, on the other hand, wretched and abandoned, would be driven to seeking in central and northern Europe for allies against her powerful neighbour in the west." The Emperor vaguely acquiesced and they discussed other matters—Holstein, and the plague of cholera that was devastating the south of France at the time, and for the stamping out of which Europe ought to present a united demand to the Porte, insisting that measures should be taken to stop the spread of the scourge from Mecca. They also talked about Roumania, which might compensate Austria for the loss of Venetia. But these conversations did not result in any treaty. " We must not force circumstances," the Emperor declared; " they must arise of their own accord, and then we can make our plans accordingly." The sentiments thus expressed were characteristic of his fatalistic nature though quite alien to Bismarck, who must have drawn the remark down upon his head by allowing his eagerness to guide and dominate events to appear too obvious to Napoleon III. And this doubtless accounted for the fact that on leaving his future victim Bismarck declared that his was " a great but misunderstood intellect." The contempt which, in his heart of hearts, the man of iron still felt for the dreamer, the giant for the invalid, can easily be imagined. Henceforward he was in a position to take the measure of his possible adversary. Nevertheless he represented a Power which it was still necessary to humour; what would Prussia do if, fully occupied as she was with Austria, she was taken in the rear by 300,000 men on the Rhine?

Shortly afterwards, in February 1866, a revolution broke out in Bucharest, and the Italians thought the moment had come to realise the plan conceived by Napoleon, and prevail upon Austria to give up Venetia in return for Roumania. But the Emperor had at last understood that Austria would never voluntarily consent to such an exchange, and he came to an agreement with Prussia whereby Prince Charles of Hohenzollern-Sigmaringen was to be given the Crown of Roumania.

Roumania. While Drouyn de Lhuys refrained from tendering any advice to Italy, Napoleon III urged the Italian Government in Florence to make an alliance with Prussia, although he himself refused to be a third party to it, and recommended Italy not to take the initiative in declaring war. He hoped that the menace of this alliance would be enough to induce Austria to acquiesce. With this object in view, Italy despatched General Govone to Berlin, and Benedetti, the French Ambassador, who had been left in the dark, gravely informed the Quai d'Orsay that Govone had arrived on a special mission which had really been arranged in Paris. After innumerable difficulties—for up to the last Bismarck suspected that he was being tricked and was afraid that Italy would negotiate directly with Austria on the Venetian question—an alliance was at last concluded between Prussia and Italy on the 8th of April, 1866, for three months only.

But, as Bismarck remarked, " all these arrangements were valid only if France so desired; if she were to show ill-will, nothing could be done." And France was the Emperor. " I am the only man who knows what the foreign policy of France is going to be," he informed von der Goltz, recommending him to ignore newspaper opinions even when they were formulated by a Minister. The last illusion of greatness ! During March and April 1866, Metternich, the Austrian Ambassador, on the one hand, and von der Goltz and Nigra on the other, fought to obtain the Emperor's support. To von der Goltz, Napoleon III talked vaguely of " compensation," and the ceding to France of the old frontier of 1814, with Landau and Sarrelouis. " Ah ! if only you had a Savoy ! " he exclaimed. As a matter of fact, if this was an allusion to annexations in Rhineland it was animated less by personal passion and desire for aggrandisement than by a desire to satisfy French public opinion. And he was torn in two between his various advisers; for while Metternich was supported by Drouyn de Lhuys, von der Goltz and Nigra had Benedetti on their side. Moreover, the unfortunate Drouyn de Lhuys often knew less than Benedetti about the policy of his master, who dealt with the Ambassadors direct. All this incoherence was calculated to disquiet Bismarck, who could only interpret it as sharp play and, in spite of his contempt for Napoleon III, could not possibly have imagined the existence of such anarchy and weakness. In his heart of hearts the Emperor was counting upon intervening as arbiter between the two parties at the end of the Austro-Prussian War, and laying down the law to them.   If Prussia were to gain the upper hand she would no doubt have the hegemony in northern Germany, but south of the Maine, Bavaria would dominate the southern states.   A most felicitous arrangement this, of two Germanies balancing each other without menacing the security of France; thus it was all to the advantage of the latter to remain neutral.

But, in addition to the Emperor, there was also France herself to be reckoned with.   On the 3rd of May the Legislative **Thiers' Speech.** Body met in grand session, and Thiers made a speech of dramatic intensity, declaring that right, which had been trampled underfoot in connection with the Danish question, must be defended.   " These fair Duchies," he exclaimed, " were seized in the name of the Germanic Confederation, or, as we say to-day, in the name of the German Fatherland;   and then they were kept.   In the end, after having seized them with the help of Austria, Austria is bidden to let them go on pain of a declaration of war."   And waxing prophetic, he pointed out the danger of a more powerful Prussia allied with Italy.   " It would be the revival of the old alliance between Austria and Spain, the Empire of Charles V over again."   Lastly, he condemned the policy of compensations.   " It would be shameful conduct on the part of France to consent to receive a solatium at the expense of her greatness, which would be dishonourably compromised in the near future." And he concluded by condemning the Italo-Prussian alliance and demanding that Prussia, or at all events Italy, should be restrained in her warlike proclivities.   At the end of his speech he was overwhelmed by congratulations on every side, and this member of the Opposition met with unheard-of success with the majority.   Sybel, the German historian, afterwards wrote that Thiers on that day was the soul incarnate of his country.

But to the Emperor the speech was a source of pain and annoyance.   On the 6th of May he replied to Thiers at Auxerre, declaring " that he detested the treaties of 1815 which certain persons were trying to make the basis of French foreign policy." This was a clear pronouncement against the traditional Conservative policy of Drouyn de Lhuys and in favour of a continuation of the Italian policy of the years 1858 and 1859. The visionary had not abandoned his dreams of a reconstructed

Europe and an entirely new map which he himself was to draw. Nevertheless, at this very moment he was still hesitating. Austria had put forward an offer to buy the neutrality of France and Italy by presenting Venetia to Napoleon III, who was to hand it over to Italy; she was counting on defeating Prussia and compensating herself for the loss of Venetia by taking back Silesia, which Frederick II had wrested from Maria Theresa. But Italy was bound to Prussia and could not free herself; moreover, she disliked the idea of receiving Venetia from the hands of a third party instead of conquering it by force of arms.

Bismarck, who quickly got wind of these intrigues, replied by secretly offering to enter into an alliance with Vienna, to divide Germany into two Confederations and—already !—to conquer Alsace. These proposals, however, met with no better success. Whereupon Napoleon, believing that he could settle everything without having recourse to war, again put forward the idea of a Congress at which he would once more act the part of arbiter. But on the 3rd of June Austria refused to agree to it, except on condition that none of the Powers should seek aggrandisement. This amounted to a refusal, since it was impossible to settle the Venetian question. Nothing could now prevent war except a word from Napoleon III. But Bismarck was still tempting him, hinting at rectifications of the frontier on the Moselle and in Luxemburg. Moreover, unknown to Florence, Paris had just secured from Vienna a promise that in the event of an Austrian victory, Venetia would be handed over as the price of French neutrality. On the 12th of June Napoleon announced that he would maintain an attitude of vigilant **The Austro-** neutrality. On the 16th hostilities were opened **Prussian** between Austria on the one hand and Prussia and **War.** Italy on the other. " I am in the Emperor's hands," observed William to Benedetti, " and am counting upon his loyalty." And Prussia withdrew all her troops from the Rhine frontier. The campaign was very short and allowed France no time to intervene even had she desired to do so. On the 24th of June the Italians suffered a reverse at Custezza; on the 3rd of July the Prussians inflicted a crushing defeat upon the Austrians at Sadowa.

THE SECOND EMPIRE

The news burst upon Europe like a thunderbolt. All the prophets and advice-mongers were stupefied. What? An Empire of 25 millions had been defeated in a few hours by a monarchy of 18 million souls, by an army of conscripts, who had seen little service and had never been under fire, a sort of " National Guard," as P. de la Gorce puts it, by that Prussian needle-rifle about which nobody had a good word to say, because it was much too complicated for use in war—its range was too small, and above all it required too many cartridges? The whole of Europe was expecting an Austrian victory, or at all events a long war; after all, the Austrians had not fought so badly at Magenta and Solferino, and it was for this reason that Napoleon III had dreamed of intervening as mediator and as the sovereign arbiter between two exhausted combatants.

Sadowa.

And, in spite of everything, he made an attempt to play the part he had mapped out for himself. He did not want to follow the lead of Russia, who, even before Sadowa and in spite of her sympathy with Bismarck, had launched the idea of a Congress. He wanted to reserve the benefits of intervention for himself alone. At the request of Austria, who was ready to cede Venetia, he offered Prussia and Italy to act as mediator. For some hours the Tuileries and all Paris were under the impression that Sadowa had been a triumph for French policy, and La Valette, the Minister of the Interior, had the public buildings illuminated to celebrate the surrender of Venetia, with the result that on the 6th of July there was a rise of four francs in Government securities. But as early as the 5th of July the initiated knew the truth, and at a grand council held at the Tuileries, two rival policies struggled for supremacy. Drouyn de Lhuys, the advocate of alliance with Austria, Duruy, Randon and the Empress demanded immediate mobilisation on the Rhine, the convocation of the Legislative Body and the adoption of a threatening attitude towards Prussia, at the moment engaged in the depths of Bohemia, to prevent her from delivering a final blow to her foe. Prince Napoleon, on the other hand (who incidentally was not present at the council), Rouher, Persigny and La Valette were passionately hostile to Austria, La Valette reminding the Emperor that he himself was respon-

298

sible for the alliance between Prussia and Italy. Was he going to be a turncoat? Moreover, was France ready to fight? Had not Mexico depleted a number of barracks and arsenals? Napoleon wavered between the two opposing parties. All night long the *Moniteur* was expecting orders for mobilisation and for the summoning of the deputies to be issued from the Emperor's cabinet. But he waited in vain. La Valette and the pacifists carried the day.

King William was very much annoyed by the offer of mediation, and public opinion in Berlin agreed with him. Out of prudence Bismarck accepted the offer and consented to an armistice, but only on condition that he reached a preliminary agreement with Italy and fixed the terms of peace in advance; this meant securing delay. Meanwhile the Prussian army pushed on and menaced Vienna, while Italy was far from pleased by the idea of receiving Venetia from the hands of a third party. She wanted to conquer it herself and thus wipe out the defeat of Custezza; and as a matter of fact her troops were at the very moment entering Venetian territory. Furthermore, she demanded the Italian Tyrol, and portraits of Orsini, who had been made a hero for his attempt to assassinate Napoleon, once more appeared in the shop windows in Italy. The Emperor sent Benedetti to the headquarters of King William himself to urge the Prussians to accept an armistice. After various fruitless overtures, Benedetti succeeded in extorting from Bismarck, who still feared French intervention, a half-hearted acceptance on condition that Prussia should be allowed to form a North German Confederation and to annex the Rhine provinces to the kingdom of Prussia. But Paris was unable to exploit this last favourable opportunity.

For in Paris dire confusion reigned. Drouyn de Lhuys and Randon would not admit defeat and returned to the charge on **Confusion in Paris.** behalf of Austria, that is to say, against Prussia, pointing out the danger of German unity. " Really you make me shudder ! " exclaimed the Empress when the Prince of Reuss discussed the strength of Prussia with her. " You are becoming so powerful that we run the risk of seeing you before Paris some day. One night I shall go to bed a Frenchwoman and wake up in the morning a Prussian ! "

No doubt, as is frequently the case, a tone of banter concealed fears that were only too real. Prince Napoleon, for his part, urged the Emperor to continue his policy of supporting the principle of nationality and not to bind himself to the " Austrian corpse."

The Emperor still hesitated. He was suffering agonies from stone. And he felt so much alone in his own Palace of the Tuileries ! Morny, who might have guided and perhaps saved him, was no longer there; Walewski and Rouher were incapable of taking his place. He was no longer merely a dreamer and a weakling, he was also an invalid with nobody upon whose advice to rely. When he was addressed he did not reply, but seemed to be stupefied by irresolution and suffering. He was wavering. Little by little he allowed himself to be won over by the arguments of Prussia. After all, the growth of Prussia dealt a fresh blow to the hateful treaties of 1815, and by realising German unity she was continuing the work of Napoleon I himself. He dreamt of two Germanies, one in the north under the hegemony of Prussia, the other south of the Maine and independent. A sudden foolish outburst of patriotism led him at the same time to dream of " compensations " for France with a view to maintaining the balance of power in the face of Prussian aggrandisement, and he also clung to the integrity of Austria, with the exception of Venetia. " The Emperor seems to have lost his bearings entirely," declared von der Goltz, King William's Ambassador, who saw him nearly every day. On the 12th of July he cancelled his visit to Nancy, where the centenary of the union of Lorraine to France was being celebrated. Count von Beust, who had come on a special mission from Vienna to ask him once again to mobilise on the Rhine, received a reply which throws light on the whole situation, a reply which he had already made in 1864 at the time of the Danish crisis : " I am not ready for war." Weak and worn out, he consented in the end to the annexations which Prussia was announcing her intention of making in northern Germany. Drouyn de Lhuys had lost the game and was in despair. " All that remains for us is to weep," he declared. And indeed it was during this fatal month of July 1866 that Napoleon III decided the fate of France and of his own throne. From that moment Sedan was inevitable.

Meanwhile Bismarck was making peace with Austria, refraining from imposing conditions that were too hard and would have made her irreconcilable, and refusing to deprive her of any territory; possibly this might also have been due to French intervention. He confined himself to cutting Austria off from Germany. This was the moment tactlessly chosen in Paris by Drouyn de Lhuys to demand compensations, or "*gratuities*," as Bismarck contemptuously referred to them later on, "innkeepers' bills." Drouyn insisted that "it was only right and seemly to grant the French Empire compensations calculated, in some measure, to increase her defensive power." He was well aware of the danger of this sudden brilliant rise of Prussia, but he set to work a little bit too late to ward it off. The Emperor was crippled with pain and taking the cure at Vichy. He seemed quite incapable of thinking or discussing anything.

The Peace Terms.

Thus at the beginning of August France requested Prussia to hand over the left bank of the Rhine as far as and including Mainz. Bismarck firmly, though, in spite of what he said about the matter later, without any display of violence, refused to surrender an inch of German territory and talked about bringing his forces to the Rhine. He was quite rightly determined to exploit the fatal mistake just made by the dreamer and visionary; for to dare to make such a demand showed an entire misunderstanding of German patriotism. Bismarck was clever enough to get the matter discussed with a correspondent of the *Siècle* who had been following the campaign, and the latter, who was a good journalist, hastened to send the news to his editor, who published it on the 10th of August. The effect it produced in Germany and throughout Europe when the German newspapers repeated it may be imagined. Clearly this man of fine phrases, this defender of nationalities, was nothing but a conqueror like the others, but more hypocritical. In Russia the news alienated the Tsar and Gortschakoff, who were inclined to act in concert with France, and made them reject any idea of a Congress, drawing them definitely towards Berlin. Lastly, Bismarck pointed out the danger to South Germany, where France was a menace to Hesse and Bavaria, to whom certain districts on the left bank

"Gratuities."

of the Rhine belonged. Against this French menace the natural shield was Prussia; and Wurtemberg, Baden and Bavaria, who were officially independent, formed a secret alliance with Prussia and accepted her leadership in case of war. This took place before the signature of the Peace of Prague between **Peace of Prague.** Austria and Prussia, in which, at the request of Napoleon, a clause was inserted declaring that " the southern states were free to form a German union enjoying the benefits of an independent national existence." In the midst of the embroglio Drouys de Lhuys was reduced to sending in his resignation.

These were dark days for Napoleon III. He had returned from Vichy weaker than ever without having been able to **The European Charlotte.** finish his cure. On the 11th of August a spectre appeared at St. Cloud—Charlotte, Empress of Mexico, had come, though all in vain, to beg France to save her husband. She had arrived in Paris two days previously from St. Nazaire. There was nobody to welcome her at the Gare d'Austerlitz and she was obliged to drive to the Grand Hotel in a cab. On the following day Eugénie received her and did her best to be kind to her. Cowed by the consequences of his weakness, Napoleon III tried to avoid giving her an audience. Charlotte, however, forced her way in, and made a violent attack on Bazaine; but she merely found herself confronted by the arguments of the Emperor : " It is impossible for me to give Mexico another penny or another man." And she continued to talk in the air while he sat cold and tongue-tied. In vain did she appeal one after the other to Drouyn de Lhuys, Rouher, Randon and Fould. In the end she failed and left Paris in despair. She made her way to Rome, to the Vatican, where she showed the first signs of the mental derangement which before long was to deprive her of her reason.

The public was as yet unaware of these tragedies and tribulations—the Government was trying to save its face. On this very same day of August, at the prize-giving for the Concours Général, Drouyn de Lhuys, who had already sent in his resignation, referred to the Emperor " as the tutelary genius hovering above the storm clouds," while at the festival of the 15th of August, Baroche boasted of " the moral ascendancy of the

Emperor." Both men were no doubt sincere. The illusion of greatness was to fade only with the advent of disaster.

But the idea of " compensations " had not yet been abandoned, and at this juncture a Danish agent named Hausen, **Hausen.** who was *persona grata* at both the French and Prussian Courts, was despatched to Berlin. He was entrusted with the task of proposing to Bismarck the formation of a neutral buffer state on the left bank of the Rhine, a purely German state, it is true, under a Hohenzollern Prince. Persigny was responsible for the idea. But Hausen did not even succeed in reaching Bismarck; he saw only subordinate officials and was met by constant refusals. They talked about the annexation of Saxony by Prussia and compensations for Saxony on the Rhine. Hausen telegraphed to Paris in a cipher couched in terms of comic opera : " The House of Berlin is vaguely talking of taking the Dresden china in exchange for the Rhine wine." And there the matter ended.

Finally, having failed to secure either annexations on the Rhine or the formation of a neutral state, France fell back **Belgium.** upon Belgium. On various occasions Bismarck had tried to turn the envious eyes of the Empire away from this country, " where French was spoken," and which was a natural extension of French territory. But Napoleon III was deeply concerned about satisfying and reassuring French public opinion by means of territorial aggrandisement. And this dreamer and visionary, who occasionally also played the part of a miniature Machiavelli, set to work to perpetrate what we cannot help regarding as a villainy. It is true that he himself declared there was no such thing as a Belgian nation, and doubtless imagined that France could easily absorb and assimilate Belgium. And indeed Belgium had not as yet enjoyed forty years of independent existence, and it might well be supposed that so young a country, which had not passed through the furnace of war and invasion, had not reached self-consciousness. Benedetti was accordingly instructed to demand from Bismarck the surrender of Landau, Sarrebrück and Sarrelouis, which would restore the frontiers of 1814—" paltry old towns " which France reclaimed merely on principle—and above all to secure his support with regard to the surrender of Luxemburg and eventually, by means of a secret treaty, the annexation of Belgium. It was well known that this mad and fantastic idea would be likely to perturb England, but it was hoped that the offer to make Antwerp a free city would act as a sop—as though London could possibly agree to such a combination, or to the menace of a nominally free city on the Belgian coast surrounded by French territory and subjected to strict supervision on the part of France. Benedetti, in conjunction with Rouher, drew up with Bismarck the plan for a secret treaty; the Emperor was to recognise the recent acquisitions made by Prussia and to accept the federal union " of the Confederation of the North with the South German States," while the King of Prussia was to undertake to facilitate the acquisition of Luxemburg by France and would give armed support to the Emperor " in the event of his being forced by circumstances to allow his troops to enter Belgium or to conquer it." And the two sovereigns entered upon an offensive and defensive alliance. Bismarck folded up the document. Following in the footsteps of Frederick II, he had secured " something in writing," something which might serve him in good stead in the future. Meanwhile peace had been definitely signed between Prussia and Austria, and at the end of August Bismarck suddenly turned the cold shoulder on Benedetti, and the negotiations were broken off. They were never to be reopened, and Paris, weak and powerless, did not insist. But Benedetti's scrap of paper was destined to appear again and to be used as a formidable weapon against France.

Meanwhile in Paris the authorities continued officially to adopt a tone of resolute optimism. Drouyn de Lhuys, who **An** had lost the game and sent in his resignation, was **Optimistic** replaced by Monsieur de Moustier, the French **Circular.** Ambassador in Constantinople. While awaiting his return, La Valette was temporarily installed at the Quai d'Orsay. On the 16th of September 1866 he sent a circular to all the French agents in which the Emperor's style could be clearly discerned, for Napoleon III was better and must have helped to draw it up. The circular declared that " public opinion was wavering between joy at seeing the end of the treaties of 1815 and fear that the power of Prussia might attain undue

304

proportions." But it drew a reassuring picture of a new and harmonious Europe; the old coalition of 1815 against the France of Napoleon had been broken up. The great Powers had been restored their full measure of independence. Doubtless the peoples were uniting in large bodies and petty states were tending to disappear, but there was nothing in the distribution of power in Europe to disquiet France. "France with Algeria will soon have 40 million inhabitants; Germany 37; Austria 35; Italy 26," and, "in spite of a certain ill-considered hastiness and momentary unfairness, Italy by her principles, her interests and her ideas is bound to the nation that has poured out its blood for her." What optimism! For at that very moment Italy was deeply hurt at receiving Venetia from the hands of General Leboeuf, a French Commissary, and in order to prevent unpleasant incidents and insults, the latter was obliged to hand over his powers in a Venice hotel instead of in the Ducal Palace.

In conclusion, the circular declared that it was only the moderation of the Emperor that had saved France from war and that the nations had won autonomy without France having lost anything of her greatness and prestige. Thus everything was for the best in the best of all possible Empires, although one disturbing little sentence on the necessity of " perfecting the military organisation " of the country managed to slip into the circular. It was necessary to make the best of a bad job, and the *fait accompli* had to be accepted, or apparently accepted. " Reasonable resignation," declares P. de la Gorce. Yes, if it had been sincere. But in spite of all these proud assurances, the menace remained. In vain did the Court hold its usual revelries at Biarritz and Compiègne; a shadow seemed to hover over all its pleasures. And this was not due to the cholera. The plague was on the wane, and the Empress, who had bravely visited Amiens when the epidemic was at its height, had regained a certain popularity there. Nor was it due to the poor harvest or the bad news from Mexico. But one day the Press announced that Monsieur de Chassepot had received a decoration for having invented a rifle which was apparently superior to the needle-rifle; another day an article written by Louis Napoleon in Ham in 1843, in which he recom-

x

mended the adoption by France of the military organisation of
Prussia, was unearthed from the *Progrès du Pas-de-Calais;*
while at Compiègne, during the autumn of 1866, the guests
included a more than usually large proportion of Generals, with
whom the Emperor discussed plans of military reform. Henceforward absolute security was and could not fail to be a thing
of the past.

At the beginning of 1867 a fresh crisis broke out in connection
with the compensations which, in spite of the circular of Sep-
Luxemburg. tember 1866, France had not yet given up all hope
of receiving. " Ah ! if only you had a Savoy ! "
the Emperor had exclaimed to von der Goltz only a year previously. Well, by dint of a persevering search this Savoy had
at last been discovered in the Grand-duchy of Luxemburg, a
state which, though independent, was bound by certain ties to
Holland and to Germany and was under the guarantee of
Europe. And as a matter of fact before 1866 Luxemburg, with
its 200,000 inhabitants, was semi-autonomous, though under
the nominal rule of the King of the Netherlands, and was
also a member of the Germanic Confederation and of the
German *Zollverein.* Ever since 1815 Luxemburg had been one
of the strongholds that kept watch and ward over France and
was occupied by a Prussian garrison. But in 1866 Luxemburg
had not been admitted into the new Confederation of Northern
Germany. Moreover, at the beginning of 1867, Holland, who
since the rise of Prussia feared for her own independence,
inquired semi-officially of France what her attitude would be
in case of a conflict between Holland and Prussia. Paris
immediately seized the opportunity. The *King Grand-duke* was
offered compensation, and it was suggested to Holland that in
order to secure the support of France she should hand over
Luxemburg, since it was the anomalous position of the Grand-
duchy which was likely to give rise to the difficulties with
Prussia of which The Hague stood in fear. A French official
was sent to Luxemburg, ostensibly on private family business,
to glean information regarding the wishes of the people. Moustier
was already of opinion that " by gracefully accepting the union
of the Grand-duchy with France, the Berlin Cabinet would
imagine it had brought off a shrewd political move and would
306

be pleased to give France a moral and material triumph which, by bringing the two countries into closer touch with each other, would contribute to the peace of Europe."

But The Hague had no confidence whatever in the goodwill of Berlin or in friendly relations between the two countries. And it was perfectly right. On the 14th of March, Thiers, in a speech delivered in the Legislative Body on the subject of foreign policy and the Prussian menace, had condemned the principle of nationalities as " fatal, chimerical and puerile. . . . There are no more mistakes left to be made ! " he exclaimed. Rouher replied by confessing that the Tuileries had been torn by " patriotic qualms " after Sadowa, but pointed out that the old Germanic Confederation, which, with Austria and Prussia combined, had a population of 75 millions, had been replaced by a Germany divided into three—Prussia north of the Maine, South Germany and Austria. Surely it was in the interests of France to have to deal with these three separate groups rather than with a single whole? " No mistake has been made ! " he exclaimed in conclusion. But at this very moment Bismarck announced to the world the existence of the treaties of alliance binding Wurtemberg, Baden, Hesse-Darmstadt and Bavaria to Prussia in case of war, and published the details. Thus two of the three divisions would be welded together as soon as hostilities were opened, and it became evident that France and Prussia were not so intimately bound as the Government had tried to imply. The Hague, in agreeing to the surrender of Luxemburg, felt it incumbent upon her to inform Berlin.

Bismarck, who was semi-officially following the affair, did not care a straw about Luxemburg, but he would have liked the negotiations to be carried on officially without his being consulted so that he might be confronted by a *fait accompli*. But the Venerable Master of the Masonic Lodge in Luxemburg informed certain Prussian journalists, whereupon there was a fine hulla-baloo in the German Press. Was Luxemburg, which was " German territory " and still a member of the *Zollverein*, going to be abandoned? Was the Prussian garrison going to evacuate the fortress before the French army, like vanquished troops in the face of their conquerors? Bismarck pretended to be over-whelmed by public opinion, although at a word from him the journalists could have been silenced. And Bernstorff, his Minister in London, inquired of the Foreign Office what the attitude of England would be in case of a Franco-Prussian war. Nevertheless, on the 1st of April, after having received Benedetti's assurance that nothing definite had been signed between France and Holland, and having given him to understand that signature would inevitably mean war, Bismarck made an extremely moderate speech in the Reichstag, declaring that he was anxious to respect both Prussian honour and French susceptibilities. In the end The Hague became frightened by the German demonstrations and, after representations on the part of the Prussian Minister, refused to abandon Luxemburg.

Whereupon Monsieur de Moustier, by coolly beating a diplomatic " retreat," as P. de la Gorce calls it, which was a marvel of skill, succeeded in avoiding both " humiliation and war." He forestalled all debate in the Chambers by reading to the Palais Bourbon and the Senate a brief declaration which the Empress had regarded as too cut and dried, but which he had not altered—he wanted to avoid inflaming national feeling in any way. Benedetti was instructed to see as little as possible of Bismarck, and last but not least, Moustier proposed a deal— France would renounce all claim to Luxemburg provided Prussia evacuated the fortress, which was a permanent menace to France, and where Prussia was the mandatory of the old Germanic Confederation which no longer existed. He secured the support of England and Austria for this proposition, and Beust, the Viennese Minister, who disliked Bismarck, even put forward the idea of handing Luxemburg over to Belgium, in return for which the latter would surrender Marienburg and Philippeville to France, who had lost these towns in 1815. But Napoleon III did not expect so much; the support of Austria was quite sufficient for him. And it was all the more valuable seeing that Bismarck was at this very moment offering to make an alliance with Austria, evidently directed against France, who was to be " made to see reason." At one moment war was again feared; the military authorities in Berlin reported that France was increasing her forces and her war material. Queen Victoria wrote a personal letter to William begging him to keep the peace. In the end Bismarck gave way to the solicitations of Austria and England, who were also supported by Russia, on condition that the demand for evacuation came **The Con-** from Holland and not from France, and that Lux- **ference of** emburg should be made a neutral state under the **London.** guarantee of Europe. St. Petersburg suggested a European Conference, which met in London on the 7th of May.

At the eleventh hour there was some fear that the conflagration might burst out again. The Prussian Staff were disquieted by the activities of Marshal Niel, who, in January 1867, had taken the place of Randon at the Ministry of War; stores were being piled up, men on leave were being recalled, and rifles were being manufactured. " Nothing would be more agreeable to us," wrote Moltke in May 1867, " than a war, which despite every effort was found to be inevitable." Thus a conflict seemed to him unavoidable, and he was even of opinion that it was in the interests of Prussia to hasten its outbreak in order to forestall the French preparations. Bismarck lodged a protest against the purchase of horses by France in Hungary. Moustier retorted by reporting similar purchases by Prussia in Poland, Hungary and Ireland. Whereupon the Prussian army set feverishly to work to repair and furnish with guns that very fortress of Luxemburg the evacuation of which was being discussed. But in spite of everything the Conference of London resulted on the 11th of May in an agreement being reached that Luxemburg should be neutralised and the fortress evacuated. Thus in the end the result was a diplomatic success for France, who was at last able to turn her undivided attention to the great event of the moment—the International Exhibition.

It had been opened on the 1st of April in the midst of menaces of war in cold and rainy spring weather. The exhibits, of course, **The Inter-** were not ready. With the advent of May the sun **national** made its appearance, peace seemed assured, and the **Exhibition** preparations were completed. There were 52,000 **of 1867.** exhibitors as compared with the 24,000 of 1855. The Exhibition building was placed in the Champ de Mars in the middle of an open space reserved for it; it consisted of a huge oval, one-storied gallery between the Seine and the *École Militaire*, to which concentric galleries were joined by means of corridors radiating from the centre. The outer gallery, which was the longest, was set apart for machinery, next came raw materials, clothing, furniture, the liberal arts and, last of all, in the centre, the fine arts and the history of Labour. The radiating corridors separated the exhibits of the various countries from one another. Thus the visitor could, by following either a gallery or a corridor, study a certain commodity in all the countries of the world, or learn to know the full range of commodities produced by any particular country.

There were plenty of novelties to admire—steam engines, gas or compressed-air engines, mine-borers, railway carriages and signals, aluminium, petroleum oils, and carbolic acid, which was destined to be widely used as a disinfectant in the case of cholera. The cotton industry had suffered owing to the American Civil War, and the silk industry was languishing owing to silkworm disease and a tendency to greater simplicity in dress and the abolition of the crinoline; nevertheless, there were some extremely beautiful plain silks. The woollen goods produced by Rheims, Amiens, Roubaix, Elbeuf and Sedan were greatly admired, as were also the Brussels and Auvergne lace and the Swiss embroideries. The furniture consisted chiefly of slavish copies of the old styles, except in the case of easy-chairs for smoking-rooms and gardens, and rocking-chairs which came from America. Some of the galleries were reserved for cheap goods for the poorer classes, and were marked with their prices— " zinc candlesticks, plated dish-covers, bedsteads in white wood, wall-papers at 15 centimes, layettes at 15 francs, wicker cradles, and cardboard dolls " (P. de la Gorce). There were also workmen's dwellings exhibited in the enclosure, one of them being shown by the Emperor himself, who was ever a philanthropist. Here too were huge Krupp guns cheek by jowl with French guns, field kitchens and ambulance wagons. The associated Protestant missions displayed Indian idols, African fetiches, and the costumes and weapons of all manner of tribes. The gallery devoted to the history of Labour had every sort of exhibit, from chipped flints to eighteenth-century fans. Lastly, the exhibition of Fine Arts included works executed since the 1st of January, 1855; masterpieces that had stood the test of time were hung in close proximity to sham masterpieces long since forgotten—Rousseau, Corot, Millet and Flandrin might be

310

seen side by side with Gérôme, Cabanel, Breton and Meissonier; Falguière, and Carpeaux by the side of Guillaume and Crauk.

But the main attraction of the Exhibition was not the Exhibition itself but the enclosure in which it stood, or, as we should

An International Fair. call it to-day, the amusement park, a sort of travelling show on a gigantic scale, an international fair. There were Russians with their Ukrainian horses behind an *isba* (hut), Arabs under tents, Mexicans on Aztec tombs, Tunisian cafés, Chinese women in their pagoda, Egyptians in their temple, and numbers of Turks; brass-ware, fancy cakes, sausages and potted meats, photographic studies—more or less of a novelty for the masses—balls, musical cafés, and lotteries all beckoned for custom, while women in light attire, masquerading in Bavarian or Dutch dress, offered food and drink, and love into the bargain. A little further Bibles were being distributed and sermons preached in French, English and German. Lastly, in a more peaceful corner of the garden, away from the hullabaloo of the fair, people sat and listened to waltzes by Strauss and Métra by the side of miniature lakes or banks of flowers.

The Exhibition was visited by illustrious foreigners—the King and Queen of the Belgians, the Queen of Portugal, the Grand-Duchess Marie of Russia, Prince Oscar of Sweden, the Prince of Wales—afterwards Edward VII—and a Japanese Prince. On the 1st of June the Tsar Alexander arrived, and care was taken that the Boulevard Sébastopol did not figure in the official itinerary. The Tsar met with a cold reception outside the Gare du Nord—the people had not forgotten Poland—but was cheered in the wealthy quarters; he alighted at the Élysée, and that same evening was present at a performance of *La Grande-Duchesse de Gérolstein* at the Variétés. On the following day, as he went about paying various official visits, he heard cries of *Vive la Pologne!* fairly often, more especially at the Palais de Justice, when he thought the shouts of " Clear out ! " addressed to the demonstrators, were meant for him. These incidents were regrettable. On the 4th of June King William, an affable old gentleman, arrived accompanied by Bismarck in the uniform of an officer of the Landwehr cuirassiers. They were well received by the crowd all along the route from the Gare du Nord to the Pavillon de Marsan, where the King was to stay. On the 6th of June they were shown the army at Longchamp—35,000 men under Canrobert. The two sovereigns were escorted by the Cent Gardes "resplendent as mythic deities." William was most affectionate to the little Prince Imperial, who had just left a sick bed and was limping a little. During the march past they were filled with admiration of the infantry, with their bearded sappers in busbies and white aprons, their gigantic plumed drum-majors, their red-skirted *cantinières*, their *serre-file* non-commissioned officers with the stripes on their sleeves, their picked companies, grenadiers with red epaulettes, and light infantry with yellow epaulettes. Even greater was their admiration for the cavalry—carabineers with breastplates ornamented with a gilded sun, lancers in chapskas, dragoons in green with white fronts, guides with their aiguillettes and sabretaches. The Crimean, Italian, Chinese and Mexican colours were saluted. But all too soon, and partly through the activities of that stiff cuirassier who was looking on stern and unmoved, this empty glory was to vanish in smoke.

On the way back an incident occurred which was far more distressing than those of which the Tsar had already had to **Attempt on** complain. In the Bois, at the cross-roads formed **the Tsar's** by the Rue de la Vierge and the Rue des Réservoirs, **Life.** a man tried to shoot Alexander, who was in Napoleon's carriage. One of the Emperor's equerries spurred forward his horse in time, and the animal received the bullet in its nostrils. "We have been under fire together, so we are now brothers-in-arms," observed Napoleon III to the Tsar. At such moments the Emperor was never at a loss for an apt remark. "Our lives are in the hands of God," replied the Tsar. The would-be murderer was of course a Pole; his name was Berezowski, and he wanted to avenge his country.

The incident did not put a stop to the round of festivities—a ball at the Russian Embassy, a ball at the Hôtel de Ville, a **Festivities.** ball at the Tuileries. Meanwhile Bismarck was meeting with great success in official salons; his wit was winning all hearts. He talked to Rouher and Persigny, assuring them that the South German States had no wish to join the Northern Confederation, and even had the effrontery to tell them what he would have done had he been in the

Emperor's shoes—he would have made a close alliance with Prussia before Sadowa. Failing this he would have encouraged Prussia after her victory to keep an Austrian province in order to perpetuate discord between the two German Powers. Meanwhile Paris was a huge hostelry, the Subura of the modern world. Even the little hotels on the left bank were invaded by foreigners, and the students, clerks and shop-assistants, who were driven out by the rise in the price of rooms, held meetings to protest. There were hilarious suppers at the *Café Anglais* and the *Grand 16*. By way of entertainment there was *L'Africaine* at the Opéra, *Hernani*, *Le Lion Amoureux* or Ponsard's *Galilée*, *Le Gendre de Monsieur Poirier* and *Mademoiselle de la Seiglière* at the Français, *La Famille Benoîton* at the Vaudeville, and at the Gymnase *Les Idées de Madame Aubray*, in which the younger Dumas presented the sequel to his *Dame aux Camélias*. But more popular than any of these were the comic operas by Meilhac and Halévy with music by Offenbach. They constituted the triumph of the Variétés, where *La Belle Hélène* and *Barbe-Bleue* were followed by *La Grande-Duchesse*. All Europe flocked to applaud Hortense Schneider in the part of the Grand Duchess and to laugh at the misfortunes of General Boum. The Tsar took his departure on the 11th of June and King William on the 14th. But another potentate arrived, the Sultan himself, who had left Constantinople because he too

Death of Maximilian. wanted to "attend the Carnival of Venice." The festivities were to have been continued, when on the morning of June the 30th a terrible piece of news was made known : "The Emperor Maximilian has been shot."

Almost a year had passed by since Charlotte had left Mexico on her vain mission of endeavouring to secure the help of France. At that time Bazaine had already begun to evacuate the towns at some distance from Mexico City and to bring back his troops to the centre. There was constant friction between him and Maximilian, who protested against these evacuations, complaining that he was never informed about them in time and was unable to warn his officials to flee and make their escape from the Juarists. At one moment Maximilian tried fresh tactics, proposing that Bazaine should declare a state of siege for the purpose of placing the power in the

313

hands of the French army and increasing the responsibility of France. And he appointed two French Generals to Ministerial posts. But Bazaine refused to proclaim a state of siege and ordered the two Generals to resign; he was careful not to allow himself to be caught in the wheel in this way. In the autumn General Castelnau, Napoleon III's aide-de-camp, arrived, armed with plenary powers, even over the Marshal. He had received instructions to liquidate the whole matter as best he could; it was becoming far too expensive. The Mexican customs were bringing in less and less revenue, although the French wanted to collect half by force. No dividends were paid on the loans, not even debentures were met. The 6 per cent. loan of 1864 stood at 27 francs, and the debentures of 1865 at 160. Between Maximilian and Bazaine and between Bazaine and his subordinates (one of whom, Douay, was thoroughly exasperated with him), Castelnau was to act as arbitrator, and he had been instructed to bring back the troops to Europe, all the troops, even the Foreign Legion, as well as Maximilian himself.

But he had a far from easy task. Bazaine was by no means anxious to return. He had married a Mexican, who was expecting a child, and had important private affairs to settle in Mexico. Possibly too he was nursing a hope that if he ejected Maximilian he might carve out an Empire for himself as Bernadotte had done. Maximilian, for his part, was meditating abdication, but on the perfidious advice of Bazaine, who promised to prolong the stay of the French army, and in spite of Castelnau's summons, he decided to remain. In the end further grave incidents (Bazaine set free a man who had been arrested by one of Maximilian's subordinates and stopped the publication of a Mexican newspaper) brought about a complete rupture between Maximilian and the French in January 1867. On the 5th of February, Bazaine left Mexico after having damped the supplies of powder, broken up any projectiles that could not be carried away, sold his horses for a song, and ordered all Frenchmen, even those bound by personal ties to Maximilian, to leave Mexico on pain of being deprived of their nationality. The one thought in the minds of the officers was to get back to Paris; one of them had actually reserved a stage-box at the Variétés, for *La Bell Hélène* on the 1st of May. On the 11th of March, Bazaine

314

set sail from Vera Cruz with the last of the troops. In a few months Maximilian was surrounded by the Juarists, couped up in Queretaro, captured by treachery on the 15th of May, tried by court-martial on the 13th of June, condemned to death, and after a delay of three days—" still further torture "—shot on the 19th.

When the news reached Paris and was confirmed at the beginning of July, " a dark cloud hung over everything " (P. de la Gorce). The festivals, reviews and banquets **A Shadow** were all cancelled; the Sultan was forgotten. On **Spreads.** the 9th of July, in the Legislative Body, Thiers made out the balance-sheet of the adventure; it had cost France 6,000 men killed and 600 million francs at their present-day value (about £5,000,000). And he pointed the moral, demanding a more effective parliamentary control of the life of the nation. The Minister for War replied with the official emphasis which, in such circumstances, is the same under every Government : " Our soldiers do not count the number of the enemy before the fight; after the fight, they do not count their dead." " No ! " interrupted the aged Berryer, " but here in France there are mothers, daughters and wives who have counted them."

Misfortunes never come singly; the harvest was bad in France and even worse in Algeria, where a plague of cholera also broke out. There was talk of war, and at the Palais Bourbon an Army Bill to provide for a huge force of 800,000 men was debated; the German menace was growing. Bismarck had just united north and south Germany in a single customs union. When the French diplomats reminded him that by the Treaty of Prague northern Schleswig was to have been restored to Denmark, Bismarck had them categorically informed through the Press that the matter was nothing whatever to do with France, and Moustier at once protested that he had had no intention of " wounding the susceptibilities of a neighbouring friendly Power." Berezowski, who was defended at the assizes by Emmanuel Arago, was condemned by the jury only to penal servitude for life, which vexed the Tsar, who would have liked a sentence of capital punishment, enabling him to play the magnanimous part of begging for the reprieve of his assailant.

France was alone, terribly alone, in Europe. The Tuileries felt this, and Napoleon III accordingly determined to respond to von Beust's solicitations and draw closer to the **Isolation of** country vanquished at Sadowa. The Emperor and **France.** Empress accordingly met Francis Joseph at Salzburg to convey to him their condolences on the death of his brother Maximilian. They stopped at Augsburg, where Napoleon III wanted to revisit the streets and houses of his childhood. On the 18th of August they arrived at Salzburg. Napoleon III had not met Francis Joseph since Villafranca. At the foot of the wooded hills and the grey walls of the citadel, on the banks of the turbulent grey-green waters of the Salzbach, in the little town where between river and mountain cluster **The** the old houses, each one of which claims to have **Salzburg** been " Mozart's house," they amicably discussed **Meeting.** the European situation. But no alliance was concluded; it was merely agreed to avoid all friction with Prussia and any demonstration " calculated to arouse the susceptibilities of the German spirit." This did not prevent the *Allgemeine Deutsche Zeitung* and the *Kreuzzeitung* from regarding this Austro-French *rapprochement* as a sign of hostility to the North German Confederation. And Bismarck let it be known that German affairs were not the concern of other nations.

The prestige of the French Empire in Europe was certainly very different from what it had once been. Napoleon III **Black** harboured no illusions on the matter and publicly **Clouds** confessed as much in a speech he made at Lille, **on the** when he had a sudden access of frankness not **Horizon.** uncommon with him. " Black clouds have arisen to darken our horizon," he declared. The expression became all the rage, more so than its author may perhaps have wished. In vain did he end by the customary appeal to confidence in " the wisdom and patriotism of the Government " for the warding off of " imaginary fears "; the public remembered only the " black clouds," which it found extremely disquieting. On the 23rd of October Francis Joseph came to Paris to return the Salzburg visit, and went to the Exhibition, which was on the point of closing. He talked of peace at the banquet at the Hôtel de

Ville, but, as had been the case at Salzburg, no formal alliance was concluded.

Only one country remained from which France could expect, if not a tribute of friendship, at all events some sign of gratitude —Italy. But the Roman question, the everlasting

Italy.   Roman question, was to separate France from this last remaining country and leave her henceforth alone in the middle of a jealous, indifferent or hostile Europe. Following upon the Convention of 1864, efforts had been made in various quarters to bring about a reconciliation between the Pope and the King of the new Italy. Persigny had gone to Rome and solemnly published a *Letter* in which he declared that ancient Rome would " bury Victor Emmanuel beneath the whole weight of history " if he dared to enter. He suggested that Rome should be a free city in the kingdom of Italy. Spain proposed to France that the Catholic Powers should take concerted action on behalf of the Pope. The scheme, which would have been most displeasing to the Italians, ended in smoke. The time was approaching when the last French soldiers were due to leave Rome. By way of compensation Napoleon III raised a legion of volunteers at Antibes who set sail to take the place of the regulars. " Never," declared the Emperor at the time, " never shall I allow Italy to violate the territory of the Holy See."

But in Florence, ever since Venetia had been won, all thoughts were concentrated on Rome, and the Government was well aware that France was no longer the indispensable ally of yore, since Italy owed the acquisition of Venetia to the Prussian alliance. Napoleon despatched Fleury to Florence in November 1866 with instructions to " remind Italy of her plighted word " and to prevail upon the King to give strict adherence to the Convention of 1864. Fleury met with a cool reception. " So far, no insults," he noted with satisfaction; nevertheless, he could not prevent the King from referring to " national aspirations " in his speech to Parliament. But in Paris his mission was regarded as a success. In December 1866 the last French battalions left Rome without any incident occurring.

Before long Garibaldi and his men revived the agitation against the Pope, and Paris remonstrated in vain with Piedmont.

Florence retaliated by protesting against the official support accorded to the legion from Antibes. There was a brief truce, but in September 1867 Garibaldi presented himself **Garibaldi at Geneva.** at Geneva in his red shirt and grey felt hat, at the same time as the anarchist Bakunin, to speak at the Peace Congress and demand that henceforward a permanent international Congress should settle all international disputes. Thus the famous prophet, fifty years before it met, preached the Gospel of the League of Nations on the very spot where it was afterwards to hold its sessions. On his return from Geneva he was on the point of marching on Rome, when the Italian Government, at the instigation of Paris, had him arrested. His arrest infuriated public opinion in Italy and the Government fell. Whereupon bands of Garibaldi's followers entered the Papal States.

Armand, the French representative in Rome, did his utmost to denounce the obvious complicity of the Florentine Government, which was counting on a rising in Rome itself for the opportunity of intervening, and was providing the Garibaldians with arms and money. Whereupon Napoleon displayed an energy of which Florence no longer believed him capable. He concentrated troops at Toulon for the purpose of himself defending the Pope in the last resort. Moustier, Niel and the Catholics were urging him to take action. Prince Napoleon, La Valette, Minister of the Interior, and Rouher, it is true, were bringing pressure to bear in a contrary direction; they were anxious to save what survived of the Italian friendship to counterbalance the Prussian peril. In the end, after innumerable tergiversations and counter-orders, and in spite of all the representations of Nigra, the Italian Ambassador, the party in favour **Expedition to Rome.** of intervention carried the day and " a second Roman expedition " was decided upon. The fact was that Garibaldi, carelessly guarded, had escaped and had set off triumphantly from Florence itself, to attack Rome, while his followers were endeavouring to organise acts of violence in the Holy City itself. The French squadron sailed, came back and set out again on the 26th of October. This time Gueydon, who was in command, determined to avoid further counter-manding, took it upon himself not to answer the semaphore signals from the coast. Garibaldi, who had reached the gates of Rome, hesitated. On the 30th of October the French were in Rome.

Victor Emmanuel had done all in his power to forestall this new expedition to Rome, promising to put a stop to the recruiting activities and the departure of the Garibaldians, and issuing proclamations. But it was too late, and he thereupon made up his mind to enter the Papal States at the same time as the French, " to maintain order." Were the allies of Solferino going to kill one another? Both sides tried to prevent untoward incidents. Moreover, the Papal troops hastened to settle the matter as quickly as possible. On the morning of the 3rd of **Mentana.** November they set out to attack Garibaldi in the direction of Mentana, a few hours' march from Rome. They were supported by 200 Frenchmen. The Papal troops opened the attack, approached the walls of Mentana, found themselves in difficulties and at the end of the day appealed to the French to stop a counter-attack on the part of the Garibaldians. The *chassepot* rifles were here used for the first time in battle, and their accuracy and long range, which had previously been extolled, wrought havoc among the insurgents. The next morning the white flag was flying over the village and the Garibaldians disbanded, and on the following day Victor Emmanuel's forces evacuated the territory they had invaded.

The last remnant of the Pope's temporal power had been saved—for the time being. And General de Failly, who was in command of the expedition, wrote in his report : " The *chassepots* have done marvels." In Paris Moustier hesitated to allow the phrase to appear in the *Moniteur*, but Niel insisted upon its being published. It was imperative for the French army to have confidence in the weapon with which it was not as yet familiar; moreover, it was a warning for the neighbour beyond the Rhine. Unfortunately the word, which did not have the effect of frightening Prussia, wounded Italy to the core; never would she forgive France the bloody conflict which had stopped the advance of the heroes of Italian unity who wanted Rome as capital. And the matter was only aggravated by the fact that Rouher, replying to Thiers in the Legislative Body and

going one further, exclaimed, amid the applause of the majority :
" Never shall Italy lay hold of Rome. Never will France allow
such violence to be done to her honour, not to mention the
Catholic cause." " The Pope is saved," observed Thiers on the
following day to Monseigneur Dupanloup.

As a matter of fact, Napoleon III was far too vacillating
ever to adopt so uncompromising an attitude, and after congratulating Rouher, he added with a smile : " In politics the
word *never* must not be used." He was once again hovering
between the Catholics and the *Italianissimi*, between the
Empress, who said : " I am in favour of Italian independence,
which is the work of France, and not of Italian unity, which is
the work of the Revolution," and Prince Napoleon, who wanted
the work of Magenta and Solferino to be completed—the endless
contradiction which was to help to kill the *régime*. For in the
day of trial France was destined to be abandoned by everybody,
even by the only country who might have been her ally—
Italy. Disappointed in her hope of securing Rome, Italy would
not forgive the word *never*. " We will teach him what *Never*
means ! " exclaimed Victor Emmanuel, growling with vexation.
All hope of a Franco-Italian alliance was at an end.

Isolated in Europe, Napoleon III, faced by the Prussian
peril which he was afraid of visualising too clearly, was more
than ever convinced of the need of a strong army.
Military Reform. Was the French army still the first in the world, as
it prided itself on being? It will be remembered
that the Italian victories had not blinded the Emperor to the
disorder and imperfections in the military organisation of the
country, and that at the height of his triumph he had alluded
to the necessity for reform. Since then the Mexican imbroglio
had again called attention to the urgent need for these reforms.
Last, but not least, the facile success of the Prussians at Sadowa
over an adversary whom France had experienced considerable
difficulty in defeating at Magenta and Solferino—that sudden
knock-out, as we should say to-day, of a party in the game
whom France had beaten on points—was calculated to rouse
anxiety and inspire dark forebodings. If ever the enemy across
the Rhine were roused he would certainly prove far more
formidable than the white-coats of Francis Joseph.

THE THUNDERBOLT OF SADOWA

France knew what Prussian organisation was, but before Sadowa she regarded it with a touch of contempt, as nothing **The** more than a " National Guard brought to perfec-**Prussian** tion " (P. de la Gorce). But since 1866 it had been **System.** referred to with the greatest respect. In Prussia all men capable of bearing arms were compelled to undergo a term of three years' military service. After this they went into the Reserve, and then into the *Landwehr*, both of which were efficiently organised according to districts. The French system, founded in 1832, was very different. Every Frenchman " drew lots at the age of twenty-one," and according as to whether he drew a lucky or an unlucky number, a high or a low one, he either had to do seven years' service or **The French** was free of all obligation. Rich men who had drawn **System.** an unlucky number could get themselves " relieved " by paying a fine to the Government. Thus an army was formed consisting of veterans and men who had re-enlisted; for at the end of seven years a great many men remained in the service, which seemed a sound concern but was necessarily limited in numbers.

It was the question of numbers which frightened all thinking men when they contemplated the huge mass of the Prussian army. As the Emperor observed on the 14th of February, 1867, at the opening of the Chambers : " The power of a nation depends upon the number of men she can put under arms." He accordingly seriously entertained the idea of adopting the Prussian system, which, as a matter of fact, he had praised in newspaper articles during the time of his imprisonment at Ham. In this he was supported by Prince Napoleon, who, like a good democrat, was in favour of universal compulsory military service. He was also supported by some of the Generals, including Ducrot and Trochu, whose anonymous pamphlet, *L'armée française en 1867*, in which he had severely criticised the army of veterans and adopted a pessimistic tone, had created something of a scandal. But against him he had **Opposition.** most of the soldiers who owed allegiance to old Randon and were convinced that the existing system alone was sound, and who had confidence only in the veteran on the active list, a resourceful fellow full of initiative, and were suspicious of reservists, "those floating masses" who would never be roped in; quality, they maintained, was better than quantity.

Thiers, who had made a special study of military history and consequently considered himself something of a soldier, supported them. But Rouher maintained that public opinion was expecting a reduction rather than an increase in military expenditure. How could the dangers of war be recognised at this period of understandings between the nations, Peace Congresses, and international exhibitions, when sovereigns were paying each other friendly visits and falling upon one another's necks? And indeed when the *Moniteur* informed the country that it was necessary to have an army of 800,000 men—an enormous figure for the time—compulsory service for all, either on the active list or in the reserve, with instructional periods, and proposed to create a militia, protests were raised in all directions. So the poor would no longer have a chance of escaping conscription by drawing a lucky number, and the rich would no longer be relieved! There were lively discussions all over the country, in the Legislative Body and at the Ministry of War.

In order to carry out the reform Napoleon III had replaced the aged Randon by Marshal Niel, whose military knowledge, **Niel.** determination, authority and character the Government loudly proclaimed, and who in the Crimea and in Italy had refused to make allowances for mistakes committed by his colleagues or his superiors. Niel had a struggle in the Legislative Body and experienced considerable difficulty in winning the day. In the first place he was opposed by the extreme Left, Jules Simon and his friends, who extolled the Swiss militia system, with musketry courses in the schools, instructional periods and rifle practice on Sundays. Niel was obliged to inaugurate a regular Press campaign against his opponents, who had no wish to fortify the Government by strengthening the army. Prévost-Paradol alone, though he attacked the Government, defended the suggested reform with a clear-sightedness all too rare. But even the Bonapartist majority, accustomed as it was to docility, felt that the country in the background hated this reform. The Empire no longer possessed the authority it had enjoyed during its palmy days.

322

THE THUNDERBOLT OF SADOWA

To gain his end Niel was obliged to make more than one concession and to palliate some of the hardships of his original scheme.

At last, on the 14th of January, 1868, it was decided not to establish universal military service; the system of lucky numbers was maintained, but the unlucky numbers were to be called upon to do five years' service on the active list and four in the reserve. The rich were still to be allowed to buy themselves out. But all men capable of bearing arms were theoretically to belong to the *Garde Mobile* (militia), though it was stipulated that instructional periods for this body were not to exceed a fortnight a year, that the recruits were not to be shut up in barracks, but were to be allowed to go home every night, and that they were not to be under military discipline or subject to army regulations. The idea had been to have a *Landwehr* like the Prussians, and all that had been accomplished was to form an exceedingly second-rate militia. Would this reform suffice? The country was running the risk of having to pay heavily for the weakness of the Government—and the blind egoism of the electors.

The Garde Mobile.

CHAPTER IX

THE LIBERAL EMPIRE

Rouher, the supporter of autocracy, has all the power in 1865. Opposition of the Third Party; the Republicans. Current of free thought. First successes of the International. Letter to Rouher of the 19th of January, 1867; fresh Liberal reforms though modified in their scope. Anxiety, strikes, menaces—" giving and taking away." Press Law of the 9th of March, 1868. Law of the 25th of March, 1868, concerning meetings. Revival of opposition; *La Lanterne*. Atheism. Actions against the International. The meetings of 1868–69. References to the 2nd of December. Actions against Delescluze; Gambetta's speech for the defence (14th of November, 1868). The Emperor tired out. The Empress. Depletion of the imperial staff. Elections of 1869. Official candidature *versus* the Liberal Union and the advanced Republicans. Gambetta and the Programme of Belleville. Elections of the 23rd–24th of May. Progress of the Opposition. Demonstrations in Paris. Massacre of La Ricamarie. The Emperor meditates resistance. He gives way to the demand for Liberal measures (12th of July–8th of September). End of the Rouher Government. Revolutionary agitation. The massacre of Aubin. Threat of disturbances in Paris. Conversation with Ollivier. Ministry of the 2nd of January, 1870. Idyllic beginnings. The Pierre Bonaparte affair. Police measures and Liberal measures. Political attacks. Reform of the Senate. Plebiscite of the 8th of May. Fresh success for the Empire in the rural districts.

THE death of Morny meant the inevitable postponement of the Liberal Government of which he had dreamt and of which the decree of the 24th of November, 1860, had been regarded as the herald. But in vain did Ollivier, on the 27th of March, 1865, a few days after Morny's death, appeal to the memory of the statesman with whom he had so to speak joined forces, declaring that the sound policy was not to resist but to give way in time, and concluding by saying that he would support the Government, though his vote would not imply whole-hearted agreement but merely express a hope. For several years to come, however, his advances were destined to

be fruitless. This became abundantly evident during the debate
on the Address, when without much hope of success the fifteen
Republicans of the Legislative Body demanded " a free Press,
responsible Ministers, and the Government of the communes by
magistrates chosen by the people." They were the only members who refrained from voting the Address, as against a majority
of 249 who remained faithful, and in reply to them the Emperor
observed that France feared " excess of liberty much more
than excess of power."

In the spring of this same year Napoleon III paid a visit to
Algeria, and during his absence the Empress acted as Regent
The and presided over the Cabinet. " The Spaniard "
Emperor had the reputation of not being enamoured of Liberal
in Algeria. ideas, and the active part she was temporarily called
upon to play increased her influence. The shrewder minds
about her were all the more anxious to please her, since the
Emperor's ill-health seemed to indicate the possibility of the
establishment of a regular regency in the near future. She did
not like Prince Napoleon, whom she regarded as
Prince too much of a Liberal and anti-clerical. And at this
Napoleon. very moment he was guilty of an act of indiscretion.
On the 15th of May, when he was unveiling a monument to
Napoleon I at Ajaccio, he let himself go, and inveighed against
dictatorship and the temporal power of the Pope, that "mediæval
fortress." In a letter addressed to the Empress from Algiers,
which was published in the *Moniteur*, the Emperor disowned
his cousin, whereupon the Prince, who was Vice-President of
the Privy Council, sent in his resignation. This was a further
blow for the advocates of a Liberal Government. Henceforward
Rouher, who believed in despotism, remained in sole command
by the side of the Empress. As Minister of State,
Rouher. charged with the task of representing the Government in the Chambers, he was practically Prime Minister. At
the Ministry of the Interior he had a man of his own choosing,
La Valette. Parieu implored the Emperor to put a stop to
the " frittering away of the capital of authority " which had
been begun in 1860, and in September the *Moniteur* denied
that there was to be any immediate change either " in the
staff or the arrangements of the Government." In November

325

the Privy Council threw out two Bills which had been dear to the heart of Morny—those giving the Legislative Body the right of interpellation and Ministers the right to be present at parliamentary sessions. Darimon, it is true, was given a decoration, and Ollivier was invited to dinner, everything being done to win over these erstwhile opponents, who, as a matter of fact, were only too ready to be won; but the Empire was apparently determined to maintain its reputation of being a strong and despotic system of government. Nevertheless, it was during this very period, 1865 and 1866, that, whether secretly or openly, the Opposition gathered fresh force in all directions.

In the first place there gradually came into being in the Legislative Body the little group constituting the Third Party, made up of Independents and members of the old parties who at the elections of 1863 had presented themselves in opposition to the official candidates. It was joined by Protectionists, still irritated by the effects of the Commercial Treaty of 1860, and above all by Catholics. In vain did Napoleon persist in forbidding the Italians to enter Rome. The Catholics could not forgive him for having allowed, nay, actually compassed the siege of the Papacy by a united and menacing nation which would never lay down its arms until it had won back its historic capital.

The Third Party.

At the beginning of 1866, during the debate on the Address, Independents, Protectionists and Catholics agreed in declaring that " France, devoted though she was to the dynasty which secured law and order, was no less devoted to liberty," and called upon the Emperor " to allow the natural developments of the great Act of 1860 to continue." Buffet, a Catholic Orleanist and a Liberal to boot, supported the amendment and demanded the carrying out of the reforms which Morny had planned—the right of interpellation and the presence of Ministers in the Legislative Body—as well as more Liberal regulations for the Press. Rouher again condemned this attempt to return to a parliamentary system. He felt it would inevitably destroy the original character of the Empire, which had been founded on the plebiscite and was the direct creation of universal suffrage. The amendment of the 42—signed by 42 deputies—secured

63 votes to 206.   It was a small number, and yet, in a sense, it
was not; almost a quarter of the Legislative Body were demanding reforms.   The Empire felt this and threw out some
ballast by allowing the deputies the right of consider-
**Con-
cessions.** ing amendments even when they had not been accepted by the Commission and by the Council of State, and
by no longer limiting the session to a maximum of three months
(a maximum which, as a matter of fact, had always been exceeded
since 1860), and lastly by increasing the salaries of the deputies,
which in future were to be 12,500 francs (£500) for the ordinary
annual session and 2,500 per month (£100) for the extraordinary
session.   But it was pointed out that " the Constitution remained
above all controversy."   As a matter of fact, the opposition of
Buffet and of the Third Party was not formidable, and the
Government was well aware that one or two changes of detail
would suffice to close their mouths.

The Opposition of the seventeen Republicans in the Legislative Body was not dangerous either.   In 1866, as in 1865,
they made unsuccessful demands for the liberty of
**The Re-
publicans.** the Press and of elections, the right to hold meetings,
municipal freedom, and the responsibility of officials
(the latter at that time could be prosecuted only on the authority
of the Government).   Moreover, these heroes of '48, or those
who were worthy of being their comrades, men like Jules Favre,
Garnier-Pagès, Pelletan, Marie, Picard and Jules Simon, supporters of law and order, members of the bourgeoisie and
deists, were being gradually supplanted outside Parliament by
the younger generation, Republicans who declared themselves
irreconcilable, anti-clericals, atheists and Radicals, who were
deeply concerned with social problems, men like Jules Ferry,
Gambetta, Floquet and Brisson.   They were extremely critical
of the *greybeards* of '48, dubbing Ledru-Rollin a " fashion-plate
Danton."   Moreover, they had no love for the two great newspapers of the Left, *l'Opinion Nationale* under Guéroult, whom
they regarded as being the creature of Prince Napoleon, and
the *Siècle* under Havin, who, they declared, was merely an
accomplice of the Government, taking his orders from the
Tuileries and providing just the modicum of opposition the
latter desired.

But there were two factors which came into being at this time and which were destined to make the Republican Opposition veer even further to the Left—

Free-thought. Free-thought on the one hand and the International on the other.

The progress made in the various sciences, the discoveries of Leverrier in the realm of astronomy, of Foucault in physics, of Berthelot in chemistry, of Claude Bernard and Pasteur in biology, whatever the personal convictions of these scientists may have been, served to strengthen the influence already exercised by the doctrine of Auguste Comte, with its suspicious attitude towards all revelation and metaphysics. The Taines and the Renans set themselves up as champions of a materialistic and determinist philosophy, in which there was no room for God, or at all events for the God of the churches. People were reading Darwin, the French translation of whose works was published in 1862, and commentaries were issued on the German materialists, Moleschott, Büchner and Virchow. In *Les Jeunes*, *Candide*, *La Rive Gauche* and *Le Courier Français* there were articles by Protot, Tridon, Vermorel and Jules Vallès, atheists and future members of the Commune, who, moreover, at the time of the Austro-Prussian War, suggested that there should be " a strike of the peoples against war," declaring that nationality and native country were mere words. A congress met at Liége, where the younger generation had an opportunity of speaking out what they had long been thinking in their hearts. " Science," they declared, " does not deny God; she goes one better, she makes him unnecessary." The University felt obliged to take severe measures against seven Paris students who had gone to speak at Liége. By way of retaliation (in December 1865) the professors who had condemned the students and excluded them from the Faculty were " mobbed."

It was at this time too that the *Société Internationale des Libres Penseurs* was founded in Paris with the object of refusing all religious sacraments both for themselves and everybody

The International. connected with them. They zealously attended all funerals conducted with civil rites—the funerals of Proudhon and Bixio in 1865, for instance. Before long the *Siècle* under Havin, anxious not to remain idle, opened a sub-

328

scription for the purpose of putting up a statue to Voltaire in Paris. At the end of 1866 Jean Macé founded his *Ligue de l'enseignement*, the object of which was strictly secular. The literature of the day reflected nothing but doubt, " scientific " materialism and despair. It was during these years that after *Salammbô*, Flaubert wrote his heart-rending *Éducation Sentimentale*, that Zola published his first essays and the Goncourts their realistic novels, which presented a striking contrast to the works of the idealist Octave Feuillet. Leconte de Lisle in powerful verse gave expression to his pessimism and his belief in nothingness. Against the danger of this spirit of irreligion, which was becoming evident in all directions, and which the Pope had already denounced in his Encyclical *Quanta Cura*, the Church took up the cudgels, and in 1866 Monseigneur Dupanloup, in a pamphlet entitled *L'Athéisme et le Péril Social*, declared that religion and Society were intimately connected and that the growth of unbelief constituted a menace to political order itself. And, as a matter of fact, nearly all the atheists helped to swell the ranks of the party opposed to the Government.

The International, which had just come into being, gradually increased in numbers. At its first meeting French and English working-men had gathered together in London at the time of the International Exhibition of 1862, and the French delegates had been filled with admiration for the power exercised by the **French** English Trade Unions, which succeeded in keeping **Workers in** up and even increasing the rate of wages. In 1863 **London.** another delegation of French working-men had gone to London to arrange for concerted action between themselves and English workers on behalf of the Polish insurgents.

On the 28th of September, 1864, a further meeting was held in London in connection with Polish affairs, when certain English working-men and political refugees, among them the German Karl Marx, founded the *International Association of Workers*. Three Frenchmen were present, one of whom was Tolain the metal-chaser, the Labour representative, who in that same year had been an unsuccessful candidate at the bye-elections. He read an address in which, referring to Poland, he declared that the peoples must be freed—freed both politically and economically; the masses, he said, were raising their heads " against tyranny in the sphere of politics and privilege in the sphere of economics." He reminded his hearers of the progress in industry, machinery and Free Trade : " Capital is being concentrated and organised in powerful financial and industrial companies. If we are not careful, this power, which has nothing to counterbalance it, will soon exercise the rule of a despot "—the power of the " princes of finance and the aristocracy of industry. . . . Owing to division of labour the worker is nothing more than a mechanical agent." And he conjured the workers to unite, trade by trade, and country by country; without such solidarity between them, " industrial servitude would be set up more implacable and more disastrous for humanity than the slavery destroyed by our fathers during the great days of the French Revolution." Without such solidarity humanity would be divided " into two classes—an ignorant, half-starved proletariate, and plethoric, bow-bellied mandarins."

The considerations upon which the regulations of the new Association were based, and which secured the representation of every country within the fold of the International, re-echoed Tolain's address by enunciating idealist principles which proved that the old spirit of '48 was not yet dead : " The basis of conduct towards every man is truth, justice and morality. . . . No rights without duties; no duties without rights. . . . The emancipation of the workers should be the task of the workers themselves. . . . This economic emancipation is the great goal towards which all political action should be subjected *as a means*." These three last words, which appeared in the original English—the London representatives did not wish to abandon the political struggle which would help to shake off the yoke of Capital—these three words disappeared in the translation. Were they forgotten or deliberately omitted ? At all events Tolain and his friends regarded this truncated phrase as expressing obvious approval of their most profound belief—that the form of Government was of little importance, that the Republic was not necessary for " emancipation," and that it was Capital rather than the Empire that had to be opposed. The worker had had enough of rushing into revolutions and allowing himself to be killed on the barricades in order to defend or found a bourgeois Republic which would only make of him what he was under any system—the slave of the rich.

Thus, during these first years, the International was not a direct menace to the Empire; indeed the Republicans and Revolutionaries, like Vermorel, Jules Vallès and Tridon, who, in his *Candide*, a journal founded in 1865, extolled the memory of Hébert and brute force, " the queen of the barricades," as well as the disciples of Blanqui, who flocked to hear the master speak (though shortly after his return to France he was imprisoned in Sainte Pélagie, having been arrested by the police in November 1866 in the Café de la Renaissance), and more especially the young Blanquists of the bourgeoisie, the " unclassed," that " secret ferment which silently worked upon the mass "—these one and all accused Tolain of carrying on the tradition of the " printers " of the Palais Royal and of being in league with the Emperor to divert the forces of Labour into the channels of a sort of Bonapartist Socialism.

At all events, during the first years the International was not dangerous; in France it numbered barely 500 members, who paid a subscription of a penny a week. The Paris branch used to meet in a small room on the first floor of a dingy house looking out on a courtyard, Number 44 Rue des Gravilliers, in the heart of the old working-class quarter of Paris, near the Rue du Temple. Could they possibly constitute a menace— this handful of dreamers, brought up on Proudhon, who believed that one day the workers' associations, forming free unions for the purpose of common production, would raise their heads in the face of Capital and in the end take its place with the help of co-operation and " mutualism " between the societies in each country and between one country and another? Moreover, the statutes were regularly deposited with the Minister of the Interior and the Prefecture of Police. Members of the bourgeoisie like Henri Martin and Jules Simon were members. But at the first International Congress, held at Geneva in September 1866, the Tolains and the Fribourgs met with lively resistance on the part of the Blanquists as well as of Marx, who, instead of Proudhonian dreams to be realised in some far-distant future, demanded an immediate strike and a class war. And very soon the " co-operators " were outnumbered by the revolutionaries.

Nevertheless, at the end of 1866 the International did not yet constitute a menace. Moreover, neither the dawn of the free-thought movement nor the quasi-bureaucratic opposition of the Republicans in the Legislative Body nor the more " dynastic " opposition of the Third Party placed the Empire in jeopardy. Yet, at the beginning of 1867 we find the Empire " throwing out ballast "—the metaphor is appropriate, for this was the period of great ascents in spherical balloons—and promising reforms of a Liberal nature. This was due to the fact that the *régime* had received a terrible blow abroad—the battle of Sadowa. For some years past Napoleon III had been unfortunate in his foreign policy; there was the defeat of Puebla in 1862, the failure in connection with Poland in 1863 and Denmark in 1864, the collapse of the Empire of Mexico in 1865 and 1866, followed, in the summer of 1866, by the thunderbolt of Sadowa. France, taken aback, saw a new Power rise up menacing before her eyes whom, by her tactless demand for " gratuities," she succeeded only in alienating still further. The Emperor, ill at ease, and also tortured by his bladder trouble, was disposed to do what all military leaders have done when their star was on the wane—he meditated throwing up the reins. In the face of the menace from abroad he instinctively sought about him for fresh support in public opinion.

On the 19th of January, 1867, he wrote to Rouher with characteristic abruptness, informing him that constitutional reforms were to be introduced and that he intended " to allow the institutions of the Empire to develop to the full extent of their capacity, as well as to concede a further increase of public liberty, without, however, compromising the power conferred upon him by the nation." The Address was to be replaced by " a judiciously regulated right of interpellation." All the Ministers, and not only the Minister of State, were to be allowed to attend the Legislative Body and the Senate as " special delegates " for any particular debate. But they were still to be responsible to the head of the State alone. Lastly, a Press law was promised which would release newspapers from the jurisdiction of the Prefects and place

Letter to Rouher.

332

ever since 1860 the Government had ceased to prosecute " veiled attacks and allusions " and had winked its eye at " the skilful wording of monstrous statements." The truth was that it was afraid of the publicity given to parliamentary debates and the scandal to which severe repressive measures would give rise both in the Legislative Body and among the general public. Nevertheless, the Bill retained unmodified certain regulations already in existence; every copy of a newspaper was still to pay stamp duty, which was reduced by a fraction from 21 francs 60 to 18 francs (from six to five centimes a copy) on a subscription of 42 francs for a Paris journal. It is true that Press misdemeanours were to be brought to trial and were no longer to be summarily dealt with by the " iron hand " of the Government without defence or right of appeal; henceforward they would be brought before the police courts and tried by magistrates anxious to please the Government, while the definition of misdemeanours was sufficiently vague to be dangerous—" false or erroneous news," incitement to hatred or contempt of the Government. " The publication of information regarding the private life of an individual " also constituted a misdemeanour. Monsieur de Guilloutet, an obscure deputy representing the Landes district, who had been responsible for inserting this clause in the Bill, immediately sprang to fame, though doubtless in a way he had little expected; his name had something ridiculous about it which led people to poke fun at him, and the Press raised many a laugh over Guilloutet's amendment. It was also necessary to give notice of the creation of a new journal and to pay a deposit. Only the official reports of parliamentary proceedings might be published, and, as a matter of fact, at this very moment the law was taking proceedings against " superfluous reports, parallel cases and suchlike " which the newspapers had dared to print.

Naturally the Bill displeased everybody—the advocates of resistance, like Rouher, who were of opinion that too much had **Discontent** been conceded, and the Opposition, who regarded it **with the** as inadequate. On the 31st of January, 1868, Granier **Press Law.** de Cassagnac, the editor in chief of the *Pays* and deputy for Gers, who was more Bonapartist than the Emperor, made a fundamental attack on the law whereby the Government

z

" was itself placing weapons in the hands of its opponents."
He met with such success among the majority that the Emperor
meditated withdrawing the Bill.   They hesitated and talked,
and Baroche, the Keeper of the Seals, defended the Bill without
overmuch conviction.   Rouher, who was opposed to it, offered
to resign, but in the end he was persuaded to remain in office,
and, doing as he was bid, constituted himself the advocate of
the law he had been anxious to oppose.   Reminding his hearers
of " the engagement entered into before the whole country "
on the 19th of January, 1867, he said : " We are no longer
living in the days when the country's peril gave birth to the
Empire.   Since 1852 four million fresh names have been added
to the electoral lists."   These young men " do not remember
what we remember, nor have they been through the experiences
we have been through; they are entering the arena with fresh
enthusiasm and demanding a wider liberty.   Do not let us
stop them; let us try, not to hold them back, but to guide
them."   Thus the question was stated with perfect clarity.   In
order to satisfy the demands of those whom the memories of
June '48 no longer terrified, was the Empire going to become
Liberal?   In the end, on the 9th of March, the majority gave
their support to Rouher, though much against the grain.   Had
they not been assured at one moment that the Emperor had
confessed " that he would bear no grudge against those who
voted against the Bill "?   All this wavering, hesitation and
uncertainty bore witness to the weakness of the *régime*.   The
man who in 1851 and 1852 had seized full power was now weak
and helpless.   And he had not succeeded in surrounding himself
by a body of leaders and statesmen, but was exhausting himself,
between the attacks of his malady, in a vain attempt to improve
the institutions which he doubtless knew full well were already
tottering to their fall.

In connection with the law on the right to hold meetings we
find the Emperor once again forcing the hand of his majority
The Law and pushing through the new Liberal measure by
concerning which he hoped to consolidate his throne.   The con-
Meetings. cession, however, was trifling—meetings were to be
allowed only for the discussion of agricultural, industrial, scientific and literary questions.   Political and religious subjects
338

were forbidden. Political meetings were sanctioned only at election times for a limited period of ten days, and then not within five days of polling. All meetings were subjected to endless conditions; in the first place, seven persons had to be found in the commune willing to sign the declaration three days in advance, informing the Government that a meeting was going to be held. It had to take place in enclosed quarters, an official had to be present, and he had the power to break up any rowdy gathering or one which wandered from the subject specified; so much so, declared the Left, that it took a superintendent of police or a *garde champêtre* to decide the point at which industrial or agricultural topics merged into politics. The Prefect could adjourn and the Minister of the Interior forbid any meeting " calculated to disturb the peace or jeopardise public safety." Infringements of the law were to be tried in the police courts and were liable to punishment by imprisonment or by the loss of civic rights.

This Bill met with a similar reception to that accorded to the Press law; the Opposition felt that it merely placed restrictions on the pseudo-liberty to hold meetings, and twenty-two members of the Left voted against it. The majority, however, regarded the concessions as excessive. They already conjured up visions of the terrible Clubs of '48, and prophesied that these assemblies of tub-thumpers would foment civil war. Moreover, the right to hold political meetings at election times would lead to dreadful complications during the struggle, even for the official candidates. It was so convenient to be able to secure election by merely paying for drinks in the cabarets, and without making an appearance before the electors, those " individuals without a mandate," as Rouher contemptuously expressed it. In his explanatory statement, Chassaigne-Goyon was far from enthusiastic; and the reporter was even less so. But the Emperor held his ground, maintaining that " the state of public opinion and the ideals of the day forced him to try the experiment "; the law could always be rescinded if the attempt was unsuccessful. " The Emperor is providing the rods for his enemies to beat him with ! " declared some of the deputies. In the end the majority passively submitted and voted for the Bill (25th of March, 1868). In their eyes it afforded a further evidence of weakness; the Emperor, on the other hand, regarded it as another attempt to steady the tottering Government and to seek support in public opinion. As a matter of fact, these two laws on the Press and the right to hold meetings, timid measures though they may have been, were destined to enable the Opposition to level some heavy blows at the Empire. An iron-handed Government which has abolished liberty cannot retrace its footsteps; it must either hold firm or disappear; it is a question of brute force between it and its opponents, and when the kettle boils there is no safety-valve to prevent it from exploding. The price paid for dictatorship is that under it the people grow unaccustomed to the exercise of that liberty which alone can lead to moderation and prevent abuses.

And, as a matter of fact, these two Liberal laws of the beginning of 1868, and especially the Press law, had the immediate result of giving a further fillip to the Republican Opposition. Fresh newspapers were founded—the *Tribune* under Pelletan, the *Electeur Libre* under Picard, and the *Réveil* under Delescluze, the old exile of 1851 who had returned from Cayenne, a frigid, sarcastic enthusiast like Robespierre (P. de la Gorce), who dated his journal according to the revolutionary calendar and was more of a Jacobin than a Socialist. In the provinces there were *Le Peuple* (Marseilles), *L'Émancipation* (Toulouse) and *L'Indépendant du Midi* (Nîmes).

Revival of Opposition.

But the greatest success was achieved by the little bright red review of sixty 32mo pages, which from the 30th of May, 1868, appeared once a week. On its cover, printed in long white letters, was the title *La Lanterne*, by Henri Rochefort. Each number, which was dotted with small symbolic drawings (the mirror emerging from the well, the bell, etc.), contained a series of short news paragraphs and boulevard " jokes " arranged according to the seven days of the week that had just elapsed, and constituting so many little arrows aimed at " the light blue uniform of the satellites of the Government," and not even sparing crowned heads. The editor, Henri de Rochefort-Luçay, was a member of an old family and had at one time filled a sinecure's post at the Hôtel

" La Lanterne."

340

de Ville. After that he went in for comic opera, and was verse-writer and reporter to *Figaro*, where Villemessant discovered him and gave him his chance. Villemessant himself subsidised *La Lanterne*, which was a huge success. Although the price of the copies was high for the period (40 centimes, equivalent to 3 or 4 francs to-day), it was eagerly snatched up. 121,000 copies were sold of the first issue and fetched 2 francs apiece in some of the kiosks. For three months Rochefort amused Paris and the whole of France with his epigrams. The first number opened with the sentence : " According to the *Almanach Impérial*, France contains 36,000,000 subjects, without counting the subjects of discontent." It was full of sarcastic jokes. " I am a Bonapartist. . . . My hero is Napoleon II. Nobody will deny that he occupied the throne, since his successor bears the title of Napoleon III. What a reign, my friends, what a reign ! No taxes, no futile wars followed by war-levies, no distant expeditions costing 600,000,000 francs to get back 15 [an allusion to Mexico], no extravagant Civil List, no Ministers each filling five or six offices at 100,000 apiece. . . . Oh yes ! Napoleon II, I love and admire you with all my heart !—The army [an allusion to the Army Bill of 1868] takes Frenchmen away from agriculture to send them to defend our frontiers which nobody in the world is menacing.—Young men have been condemned at Toulon for singing ' To the cry *Vive la République ! le Vengeur* was sunk ! ' They were indeed guilty. People must not be allowed to remain in ignorance of the fact that the *Vengeur's* glorious fight took place under the First Empire and that the patriotic song which celebrated its sinking ended with these two lines : ' To the cry : *Vive la Reine Hortense ! le Vengeur* was sunk ! '—Queen Hortense is constantly being mentioned in official circles, but never, even from the lips of the most highly paid devotees, have I heard a good word for King Louis of Holland, her husband. . . . There is something here beyond my comprehension which clearly calls for a *communiqué*.—Dialogue in a café :—Waiter, *la France ?*—Certainly, sir, as soon as she is free.—Then I shall have a long time to wait ! "

The venture ended as might have been expected. In August *La Lanterne* was seized and Rochefort fled to Belgium, where he continued to produce his review, but in an even smaller form, printed on thin paper and without a cover. Henceforward he was a celebrity, and the *régime* remained, as it were, riddled with banderillas. This was serious, for in France at this period ridicule was a deadly weapon. And the sentences rained down on all the Opposition newspapers merely served to increase their circulation and power. Books also appeared which supplemented the action taken by the newspapers. Lanfrey, in his *Histoire de Napoléon I*, tried to deprive the Emperor of his halo, and the *Revue des Deux Mondes* sang his praises " for refusing to do sacrifice to a gigantic superstition." Erckmann and Chatrian published their Alsatian novels dealing with 1813, and applied themselves to depicting the sufferings of the obscure masses, " the reverse of the epic." The Tuileries were perturbed by these publications, which aimed at destroying the imperial legend, one of the mainstays of the *régime*, and at one time contemplated publishing in the *Petit Journal*, for the consumption of the masses, a Bonapartist war novel as an antidote. But they were perhaps aware that an " official " novel of this description would certainly not have had the success achieved by the detective story published in this same paper—*Monsieur Lecocq*, by Emile Gaboriau. It was issued with a great flourish of trumpets at the same time as *La Lanterne*, and secured a daily circulation of 300,000 for *Le Petit Journal*, an enormous number for the period.

Disquieting incidents became more and more frequent. At Bordeaux, Toulouse and Montauban the people rebelled against the attempted organisation of the *Garde Mobile*. At a bye-election in the Jura, Grévy defeated the official candidate by a crushing majority. In August, General Cavaignac's son, one of the prize-winners in the *Concours Général*, refused to go and receive his crown from the hands of the Prince Imperial, and his comrades at the Lycée Bonaparte greeted his action with murmurs of approval. The Empress wept with rage, although Duruy had promised her not to give any decorations that year to the professors of that particular Lycée. In the Senate, Sainte Beuve, who was ill and nearing his end, and whom the Catholics accused of having eaten meat on Good Friday in the company of Prince Napoleon, declared that " common sense consisted in the tendency to reduce belief in the super-natural to a minimum," demanding "full philosophic freedom of thought" and invoking "the boundless diocese of free thought" in the presence of the Cardinals who had seats in the Senate and who, in spite of the Roman troubles, supported the *régime*. On the Left, Favre, Cousin's successor at the Académie, was in evil odour because in his inaugural address he had called upon the name of "the God who revealed himself to the conscience by means of reason." In vain did Monseigneur des Loges, Bishop of Metz, condemn the *Ligue de l'enseignement* founded by Jean Macé; in vain did the Arch-bishop of Rouen protest against a medical dictionary which had dared to define man as "a mammal belonging to the order of primates"; in vain did the aged Guizot, the survivor of an epoch long since passed away, preach the union of all Christian sects against unbelief; atheism continued to spread, and its breath was far from favourable to the established system.

Atheism.

Furthermore, the International had developed to such an extent that it was ready to play a part in politics. In November 1867, by sending a pilgrimage to the tomb of Manin, one of the heroes of Italian independence, it had protested against the French intervention to save Rome. The Society, which had become an organ of class warfare and a weapon against the established system, was progressing by leaps and bounds. It had 3,000 members in Paris, and its propagandists were working the provinces. The Government was quite right to be perturbed, and in March 1868, in order to strike a blow at this "unauthorised association," it prosecuted and fined the office of the Paris section. Before these prosecutions Tolain and his friends had already resigned membership, but they were immediately replaced by more violent supporters—Varlin and Benoît Malon. The Government immediately took up the challenge and condemned the new commissaries to three months' imprisonment. In the prison of Sainte Pélagie they met some Blanquists who had been sentenced "for forming a secret society," and fell under their influence. The third Congress of the International, which met at Brussels in September 1868, categorically demanded a return to a collectivist state of society, and the formation of

Progress of the Inter-national.

" companies of industrial and agricultural workers " for the working of quarries, mines, collieries, railways, roads, canals and forests, and even arable land. The Congress also demanded guarantees for the protection of Labour against the encroachments of machinery. " We want no more Governments," exclaimed the President of the Congress, " for Governments crush us beneath a burden of taxation; we want no more armies, for armies massacre us; we want no more religion, for religion stifles the intellect." And fresh adherents flocked to swell the ranks of the International. During the last days of the Empire it boasted of 200,000 members in France, of whom Paris accounted for 70,000, and from the year 1868 it became the centre of violent opposition to the *régime*.

Moreover, the law on the right to hold meetings, in spite of all the restrictions it placed on liberty of speech, especially in **A Period of** the realm of politics and religion, nevertheless gave **Meetings.** free scope for countless demonstrations against the Empire. The great period for meetings was the winter of 1868–69. On one side of the scale were the leaders of culture, and at the other the revolutionaries. In the fashionable quarters Favre, Simon, Passy, Pelletan, Laboulaye, Léon Say, St.-Marc Girardin and Broglie discoursed on great subjects— progress, duty, the family, a man's love for his profession, and by allusions and innuendoes waged a sort of academic guerilla war against the Government. On the other hand, throughout Paris, but particularly in the working-class quarters, the masses flocked to the dance halls and gymnasiums, where, in one quarter or another, every class of society was represented; in one place the " paletots " of the bourgeoisie standing out conspicuous, in another the " blouses " of the workers, every man still wearing the uniform of his calling. As political subjects were forbidden, these orators also gave dissertations on the " great questions " of philosophy—the training and education of children, women's work, heredity, divorce, unemployment, the wage-earner and the struggle of man against Nature. Attacks were made on the Jesuits, free love was advocated, the divorce law, which had not yet been passed, being dubbed an " Orleanist expedient." Meanwhile, at the end of the bench an individual sat in solitary state as though he were in quarantine

THE LIBERAL EMPIRE

—the superintendent of police. He had no gendarmes with him, and would therefore have been unable to break up the meeting, although the law gave him the right to do so. All he could do was to make a note of subversive statements for the purpose of future prosecutions. And Heaven knows he was provided with sufficient material!

The discussion of " great questions " naturally led to references to politics and religion. " Religion is bound up with the political system beneath the yoke of which we are bowing. . . . I am a Radical Socialist and demand the abolition of this Empire founded on assassination and perjury." The Emperor was stigmatised under the name of Tiberius, Caligula or Heliogabalus. The dressmakers and milliners who worked themselves to death to produce corsets and hats for the Empress were held up as objects of pity and commiseration. The memory of the " great ancestors " of revolution, Hébert and Robespierre and their like, was celebrated in this year LXXVII of the French Republic. Even the September massacres were extolled, and the President of one meeting called to order a speaker who imagined he could make exceptions and had " dared to insult one of our great revolutionary dates." The Moderates, the greybeards of '48, Jules Favre, that *old marmot* of a Garnier-Pagès and *fat little* Picard came in for some rough handling. And unknown men sprang to the fore—Napoleon Gaillard, Peyrouton, Ferré, Duval, Ranvier, and above all Raoul Rigault, future members of the Commune. After allowing things to take their course, the Government decided to adopt measures, and several orators were imprisoned and meetings became few and far between.

One of the references which produced the most effect at these meetings was the " second of December." A book had just been published which reminded the public of the way in which the *régime* had originated, and awoke memories which for over sixteen years had lain dormant. It was entitled, *Paris en Décembre 1851. Étude historique sur le Coup d'État.* The author was Eugène Ténot, the editor of the *Siècle.* He had already written another work, which was published at the beginning of 1866—*La Province en Decembre 1851.* In it he set out to prove, in contradistinction to the official historio-

345

graphers, that at the time of the *coup d'état* the Republican Opposition in the country districts had been a genuine political movement, and not a mere demagogic peasant upheaval or a revolt on the part of thieves and malefactors against social order. In *Paris* he described the events of the first days of December 1851, and in venturing upon such dangerous ground, it required only the most elementary caution to make him limit his treatise to a strict statement of fact without attempting to weigh or judge what had taken place. The slightest invective, or even the use of an epithet, would have landed him in a prosecution. Thus his book resembled a police statement or military report, cold, objective and passionless. But its effect on public opinion was all the greater. And the *coup d'état* appeared in its real light as a surprise attack made by a handful of adventurers who had the army on their side; above all, the public learnt that success had been due to the brutal shooting on the boulevards which had brought Paris to her knees. The spring-board of the *régime* had consisted of the heaps of bodies on the Boulevard Montmartre and the Boulevard Poissonnière, innocent victims, carpenters and bailiffs' clerks, servants and gentlemen of independent means, dress-makers and shop assistants all lying pell-mell together. Ténot ended his book with a list of their names, and hatred of the Empire increased the more.

This work also brought into the limelight the figure of Baudin, the deputy who had allowed himself to be killed on the barricade in the Faubourg St. Antoine " for 25 francs a day."

Baudin. On the eve of All Souls' Day the *Réveil* under Delescluze reminded its readers of Baudin, who had been buried in the cemetery of Montmartre. On the 2nd of November some Republicans, among them Quentin, Gaillard and his son, and Peyrouton, went to find the martyr's tomb; it was deserted and they had some difficulty in discovering it. They gathered round it, and some other pilgrims who had come to pay their respects at Cavagnac's grave joined them, whereupon two or three orators proceeded to make speeches in praise of Baudin's memory. There were shouts of " *Vive la Liberté!* " and even of " *Vive la République!* " which led the newspapers to decide upon opening a subscription to raise a monument to the hero.

346

THE LIBERAL EMPIRE

Delescluze was, of course, one of the number, and was supported by Peyrat of *L'Avenir National*, Challemel-Lacour of the *Revue Politique*, and Hébrard of the *Temps*, who had been responsible for the idea. The subscription did not meet with much success, and the demonstration against the *régime* looked as though it was going to hang fire, when Pinard, Minister of the Interior, in spite of the remonstrances of Rouher and Baroche, was foolish enough to prosecute Quentin, the two Gaillards, Pey-

Delescluze. routon, Challemel-Lacour and Delescluze. The semi-official Press supported the Minister, expressing approval of these prosecutions of "persons who were manœuvring at home with the object of disturbing the public peace"—a belated echo of the law against suspects of 1858 which was supposed to have been abolished. Thus the Government itself shed a lustre upon the affair which those who had engineered it had never expected.

Delescluze chose as his counsel the young Gambetta, a Republican, a passionate opponent of the Empire and an enthusiastic reader of Hugo and Tacitus. On the 14th of Novem-

Gambetta's Speech. ber, Gambetta, drowning both the President and the attorney in the torrent of his eloquence, made a speech in defence of Delescluze which amounted to a violent arraignment of the Government, and which above all poured anathema on its origin. In thundering accents he hurled epithets and denunciations against it which Ténot had never dared to put into print, and asserted and proclaimed aloud what had been in the mind of every Republican on reading *Paris en Décembre 1851.* " Is it really possible," he demanded, " that in any nation, in the bosom of any civilised nation, there should come a moment when reasons of state or a *coup d'état* can, on pretext of the public safety, violate the law with impunity, overthrow the Constitution, and treat as criminals those who at the risk of their lives defend the right ? " And he arraigned the heroes of the *coup d'état :* " Yes," he exclaimed, " on the 2nd of December, about the person of a Pretender, there grouped themselves a body of men on whom France before that day had never set eyes, men devoid of talent, honour, rank and office, the sort of people who in every age are the accomplices of violence, the sort of people about whom

347

we can but say what Sallust said of the mob that surrounded Catiline, what Cæsar himself said in describing his accomplices, the refuse which is always to be found in well-ordered societies :

Aere alieno obruti et vitiis onusti,
Un tas d'hommes perdus de dettes et de crimes,[1]

as Corneille translated it. . . ." And he conjured up before the eyes of his listeners " the thinkers and the martyrs who in the name of outraged religion and wounded morality raise their voices in protest against right trampled beneath the heel of a soldier."

These men of December, these adventurers, claimed to have saved France. And he proceeded to expose the legend, declaring that all the men of light and leading who, if the country had really been in danger, would have rushed to her rescue, had been the first to fall victims to the act of violence—men like Changarnier, Cavaignac and Thiers. Finally, in his peroration he arraigned the supporters of the Empire : " Listen, for seventeen years now you have been the absolute, discretionary masters of France. . . . But your greatest condemnation, because it is the embodiment of your own remorse, is the fact that you have never dared to say, ' We shall celebrate the 2nd of December as a national anniversary and make it one of the solemn festivals of France.' You know very well that if you had attempted to do so the conscience of mankind would have rebelled. Well, this anniversary which you would have none of, we demand, we claim it as our own, we shall celebrate it always and without ceasing; year in year out it shall be the anniversary of our dead, until that day when France, once more the mistress of her fate, shall demand from you full public expiation in the name of liberty, equality and fraternity ! " The Opposition newspapers published the speech in full; it shook the country and made Gambetta famous in a night. Yet another blow, a terrific blow, had been levelled against the Empire.

How did the Empire defend itself against this rising tide of unpopularity ? It struck out blindly right and left; but what **The** it lacked was a guiding will. The Emperor's health **Emperor** was becoming worse and worse, but he still insisted **tired out.** upon governing. He was worn out before he was old. In the middle of the month of July 1868 he had a fire

[1] A crowd of men foundering in debt and crime.

348

lighted in the Council chamber. His lined cadaverous countenance was that of a man tortured by an incurable disease. At his elbow the Empress, whose influence was increasing, meddled with politics on the pretext of preparing herself for an eventual regency. She had neither intellect nor education nor the calm composure which would have made her a true sovereign, and since her husband had been scandalously unfaithful to her, carrying on intrigues with *demi-mondaines*, she had ceased to be a wife. She was merely a mother, anxious for her son's throne, moved by the cares, the passions and the caprices of a woman, and a Spanish woman at that, which were hardly calculated to provide the Government with the balance it lacked.

The imperial personnel was also becoming depleted. In face of ever graver difficulties and menaces both at home and abroad, **Depletion of the Imperial Staff.** the members of the Emperor's staff grew embittered and vilified each other. Persigny, Fleury and Maupas opposed Rouher; Rouher was against Walewski, and La Valette against Drouyn de Lhuys. But in spite of wind and tide Rouher managed to keep St. Paul, one of his own creatures, as the political head of the Ministry of the Interior. He was the real Minister; Pinard, the nominal Minister, trying in vain to get his own way. And better still, at the bye-elections, Rouher had the candidates who favoured absolute rule supported by St. Paul, although the Emperor and Pinard would have liked to leave the field clear for the Liberal candidates. Pinard, however, soon fell, owing to the fact that he had apparently lacked presence of mind on the 3rd of December, 1868, when the Republicans, ignoring the menace of the police and the military, had organised a pilgrimage to the tomb of Baudin on the anniversary of his death. Lastly, Haussmann, the Prefect of the Seine, more autocratic and crushing than ever with so many years of seniority behind him, was impatient of the authority of the various Ministers of the Interior who came and went while he remained. This personnel lacked a master, and in the absence of a head, discord reigned and the Ministry was like a crate of crabs. Moreover, death demanded its toll, one after the other disappearing—Walewski, Moustier, and Troplong, President of the Senate, who on the 6th of March, 1869, was honoured by a funeral as magnificent as that of Morny himself. How were they to be replaced? The Emperor, who had no love for new faces, had kept his old staff. Moreover, where could their successors have been trained? As Conti, his First Secretary, wrote in 1868: " The stuff of which Ministers are made is growing more and more scarce. . . . We have not succeeded in creating a generation of politicians." The *régime* had insisted upon having its own creatures, deputies or senators on whom it could rely, and demanded a docility and servility to which only mediocre minds could consent. How could it possibly have been surrounded by statesmen? Will is a function which, like every other, dies when it is allowed to atrophy. Strength of mind was to be found only among those who had escaped the imprint of the Government, that is to say, among the enemies of the Empire.

Between the Opposition, which every day became more violent, and the *régime*, which was growing feebler and feebler, a fresh battle was to be fought; with 1869 the time **Elections of 1869.** for the elections once more came round. Rouher, relieved of Pinard's presence, was relying on the old methods of official candidature to keep the ground that had already been won. Forcade la Roquette, his new Minister of the Interior, provided official justification of the system by declaring that the Government confined itself " to consulting the heart of the people and guessing the name which the crowd itself was already murmuring." It was a spicy way of putting it, but we should like to feel sure that the words were uttered with a touch of irony. In vain did Jules Favre protest against this " single will which nominated the Ministers, the Senate, the Council of State and all the officials, and in addition wanted to nominate the deputies." But the Government stood firm, chose its candidates, again split up certain divisions to further its own interests, and called upon all its officials, even those who dealt with finance, actively to lend a helping hand to the men it wished to see returned. Clément Duvernois, a young and ambitious journalist, editor-in-chief of the *Peuple Français*, who was himself standing as an official candidate in the Hautes-Alpes, constituted himself the apostle of the democratic Empire, while a pamphlet, printed by the *Journal Officiel* and circulated by hundreds of thousands, extolled the advantages of the *régime*, its social undertakings—workmen's dwellings, co-operative con-

350

cerns, crèches, schools, orphanages, pensions, hostels and hospitals. On the other hand, the semi-official journals and one or two books, including a work by Vitu, did not fail to conjure up the " red spectre," to point to the danger of the Clubs, and the menace of a repetition of the June disturbances. And, in order to rekindle the enthusiasm of those who were wavering in the northern districts, the inflammatory writings of Delescluze and his *Réveil* were distributed from house to house.

In the departments, numerous opponents, Royalists or moderate Republicans, endeavoured to form a coalition against the official candidates, at least in the second round. **The Liberal Union.** They were known as the Liberal Union, and among its members Ernest Picard was to be found side by side with the Orleanists Rémusat and Prévost-Paradol, the *Débats* cheek by jowl with the *Gazette de France*. A few Legitimists, among them Falloux, also took their chance, while even Renan made an attempt to enter public life in the Seine-et-Marne district. In Paris and the large towns lively contest took place, not so much against the official c— beaten in advance, as between the mo— the extreme democrats. For men li— Darimon, who more or less sup— like Favre, Carn—

vacant seat in the Var district. Rochefort seemed certain to get the better of Jules Favre, that "smooth-tongued and embittered Isocrates," whom the police had on occasion to protect against the mob. Lastly, at Belleville, the aged Carnot found himself opposed by a candidate whose name had echoed far and wide—Gambetta, the "irreconcilable," who undertook not to enter into any compromise with the Empire. Gambetta invited his constituents to state their wishes in a *cahier*, as had been done in '89; and he replied by "swearing fidelity to the contract, and allegiance to the sovereign people."

The event had proved that the Opposition deputies could in six years lead their constituents from the right road and betray **The Belleville Programme.** them; consequently it was necessary for the deputy to be given a mandate, for the electors to formulate this mandate and for the mandate itself to be "imperative." And thus the famous "Belleville programme" came to be drawn up: "Individual liberty to be placed under ægis of the law. . . . Direct responsibility of officials (who re allowed to be prosecuted only on the cil of State). Liberty of the Press, duty, the deposit and the printer's meetings and associations. The ry education to be

took
candidates, who were
...derate Republicans and
...ke Ollivier, Guéroult and
...pported the Empire, and men
..., Carnot and Garnier-Pagès, bourgeois Republicans
of '48, had been ousted by new men—Gambetta, Ferry and
Rochefort, or exiles of '51, like Raspail or Bancel, who had
returned to France.

Epic duels took place in Paris. Against Guéroult, who was
accused of having entered into a pact with the Palais Royal
and Prince Napoleon, Jules Ferry won the day. He had already
gained popularity by the publication of a pamphlet the title of
which alone would have made its fortune—*Les comptes fantas-
tiques d'Haussmann*. This expression, which, if we may say so,
was a born catchword, was very neat, and all Paris had devoured
this violent criticism of the financial policy of the Prefect of
the Seine, whose expenditure was always greater than his assets,
but who cared not a straw, hoping that eventually he would
become " Minister of Paris." In another quarter, Bancel, who
had been exiled after the *coup d'état*, and was a natural orator,
defeated Ollivier, who was already taking steps to secure a

the æg...
before that time we...
authority of the Cour...
abolition of the stamp...
licence. . . . Freedom for ...
separation of Church and State. Elementar...
secular, free and compulsory . . . leading lights of the educational world to assist in admitting students to the higher classes. . . . Abolition of the *octrois*, large salaries and plural offices. . . . The election of all public officials. Abolition of standing armies, which were responsible for ruining the financial resources of a country and breeding hatred between the peoples. Economic reforms and social justice and equality." The last point was somewhat vague. But the rest of the programme was perfectly clear and in the political sphere resolutely revolutionary.

The elections were held on the 23rd and 24th of May. Merimée was afraid that they would prove " incredible." But

Result of the Elections. they were at once a victory and a defeat for the Government—a victory, since the Empire, thanks to the loyal vote of the rural masses, had a majority of deputies, upon whom it could rely, returned in its favour. The new Chamber would contain barely 30 Republicans and a slightly stronger Left Centre or Third Party. These two groups, even if they united—and was it possible for them to unite?—would find it impossible to make any headway against the solid mass of official deputies. But considered from the point of view, not of the number of deputies returned but the number of votes cast, the elections showed a distinct loss of popularity on the part of the *régime*, the Government candidates having secured less than four and a half million votes, that is to say, 900,000 less than in 1863, while the Opposition candidates had won 3,350,000, or 1,400,000 more than in 1863. And as 1863 had already given similar results as compared with 1857, the only conclusion to be drawn was that with the passing of the years the country was becoming more and more alienated from the Empire. Among the successful candidates were Bancel (who was returned both for Lyons and for Paris, Ollivier being defeated in the latter city and transferring his activities to the Var), Ferry, who ousted Guéroult, Gambetta, who was returned for Paris instead of Carnot and also for Marseilles, Esquiros and Raspail, all of them new men or returned exiles. But some of the old figures were also successful—Favre (against Rochefort), Garnier-Pagès, Picard, Simon, Pelletan and Grévy.

A few disturbances followed the elections. On the night of the ballot, the 7th of June, demonstrations were held in Paris in support of Rochefort, whose defeat the people refused to accept. And every evening, for several days afterwards, the demonstrations were renewed. Men in white blouses arrived from Belleville and invaded the boulevards singing the *Marseillaise* and shouting "*Vive Rochefort! Vive la République!*" They threw down the kiosks, burned the reactionary newspapers, and improvised barricades by overturning omnibuses and heaping up the paving-stones. The police took forcible measures, and scandal-mongers even declared that they intervened at the very beginning of the disturbances, and that the "white blouses" were its creatures—*agents provocateurs* in fact. Thus, even after these adverse elections, the Government was able to pose as the defender of law and order and, by once again conjuring up the spectre of the June disturbances, secure the sympathy of all "good citizens."

Demonstration in Paris.

A A

At the same time grave incidents occurred in the Black Country, near Saint Etienne, incidents which were certainly not engineered by the police. A strike broke out among the miners, possibly on orders circulated by agitators sent from outside the district. There were shouts of "*Vive la Rouge!*" and the *Marseillaise* was sung. Troops were rushed up, but they were greeted with cries of "*Vivent les militaires!* Down with the officers!" Women went up to the soldiers shouting: "Fire if you dare!" During the night of the 15th–16th of June a company of infantry **Massacre of** were bringing back to St. Etienne some demonstrators **La Rica-** who had tried to prevent the loading of coal, when **marie.** in a sunken road near La Ricamarie they were surrounded, insulted, threatened and stoned by a crowd of miners. The soldiers fired, and the mob fled helter-skelter. But they left behind them thirteen dead and nine wounded. The "catastrophe of La Ricamarie" could not fail to cast yet further gloom over the public mind.

At this juncture what attitude was the Emperor going to adopt? Was he going to give way to the current or resist it? Conflicting influences were brought to bear upon him. Rouher and the Empress still advocated resistance, while the survivors of the *coup d'état*, Maupas and Persigny—both of whom, it is true, were in partial disgrace—were in favour of changes of a Liberal nature. The Emperor ought to summon a new generation to his aid, wrote Persigny to Ollivier in an open letter: "As for the men of the 2nd of December like myself, our part **Hesitation** is played!" Thus the very founders of the dictator- **of the** ship were the first to vaunt a Liberal Empire—an **Emperor.** extraordinary change of front, which may to a certain extent be explained by the hatred felt by these men, who had been ousted from power, for Rouher, the man who still remained in office. At first it was believed that the Emperor would support Rouher. On the 16th of June he wrote in an open letter (a method much in vogue at the time): "Concessions of principle or the sacrifice of persons are always futile in the presence of popular movements; a self-respecting Government should refuse to give way either to pressure, to temptation or to riot." And he made Jérôme David, one of Rouher's creatures, Vice-President of the Legislative Body, and Grand Officer of the Legion of Honour. President Schneider, who was a Liberal, took this as an affront and sent in his resignation, whereupon the Emperor informed him through the medium of another open letter that the task that had been undertaken was to be carried out : " . . . the combination of a strong Government with sincerely Liberal institutions." This inconsistency and tergiversation showed that the Emperor was wavering.

In the Legislative Body, the Third Party decided to bring pressure to bear upon him as the " 42 " had done in 1866; and they drew up an interpellation declaring that the country wanted " to play a more active part in the direction of its own concerns," and demanded full ministerial responsibility from which even the Emperor was not to be excluded. Some of the official deputies lent their support to the Third Party, and the Bill of interpellation soon had 116 signatures. At one moment the Emperor thought of resisting. " You want to pull out the teeth and cut the claws of the old lion," he observed to Buffet, " and leave him only his fine mane." But he was growing old ; he was ill and tired out, and in the end he gave way.

On the 12th of July a message to the Legislative Body announced the inauguration of reforms, which were submitted
Reforms.   to the Senate and adopted on the 8th of September. The Legislative Body was to appoint its own board, it was to initiate legislation, and to be given an extended right of amendment (two privileges which had hitherto been reserved for the Council of State); it was also to have the right of interpellation and the right of giving its reasons for the order of the day. The Budget was to be voted by clauses. In short, the Legislative Body was to enjoy the prerogatives of a regular parliamentary assembly. The Senate was also to have the right of interpellation, and could send back the Bills passed by the Legislative Body for amendment or veto them, while its sessions were to be public. The Ministers might be members of the Chambers and could attend them on demand. The office of Minister of State was abolished. Ministers were to be " responsible," but only in cases of criminal behaviour; they were not to be responsible to Parliament, but were to be answerable to the Emperor alone. This was the last privilege that Cæsarism tried to preserve for itself in order to avoid falling into that parliamentary system of which for seventeen years

official doctrine had had nothing too bad to say. Moreover, it might well be asked how the right of interpellation enjoyed by the Chambers was to be reconciled with that authority over the Ministers which the Emperor could not bring himself to abandon. At all events the change was perfectly clear—the 12th of July continued the work of the 24th of November, 1860, and of the 19th of January, 1867. And it put **Fall of Rouher.** an end to the long reign of Rouher, whose name did not appear again in the new Ministry of the 17th of July. It doubtless revealed the fact that the Emperor was still hesitating, for in his choice of Ministers he did not take the trouble to consult the 116. But for Rouher, he kept his usual staff, Magne, Forcade, etc., and dismissed Duruy, an obvious concession to the Catholics and the party of resistance. Clearly the Empire was not light-heartedly resigning itself to becoming a parliamentary system, and in the Senate Prince Napoleon, not yet satisfied, in vain called upon the despotic Empire " to burn its boats."

Months of doubt and uncertainty followed. The festivities of the 15th of August held in celebration of the centenary of the birth of Napoleon I and the amnesty granted on this occasion left the public at large completely cold. The wavering between the policy of resistance and the adoption of a frankly Liberal **Revolution- ary Agita- tion.** policy was again increased in the autumn of 1869 by an outbreak of revolutionary agitation. The newspapers led the dance—the *Réveil*, under Deles- cluze, the *Marseillaise*, managed from Brussels by Rochefort, whose name was in itself a programme under the Empire, and the *Rappel*, founded on the 4th of May, under the auspices of Victor Hugo, by his two sons, in conjunction with Vacquerie and Meurice. The poet explained the title, in his usual style, by declaring that the new journal was " to beat the call to principle through the voice of conscience, to duty through the sense of right, to the past through history and to the future through logic—an illuminating and keen-edged journal at once a sword and a ray of light." One or two Socialist newspapers, the *Réforme*, under Vermorel, the *Travail* and the *Voix du Peuple*, had not as yet secured much of a circulation. But on the 6th of September, 1869, the International met at Bâle, and condemned the principle of private property even in land, which it declared should once more be shared in common. And the French delegates were so confident of revolution in the near future that they had the meeting of the next Congress fixed for the 5th of September, 1870, in "free Paris." On the 14th of September the Congress of Peace and Liberty opened at Lausanne, and Hugo, after announcing the gospel of eternal peace, except for the abolition of all tyranny by means of a war which was to be the last, hailed "the acceptance of the Republic and of Socialism."

On the 8th of October, at the Aubin mines in the Aveyron district, the military fired on strikers who were threatening, **The Massacre of Aubin.** insulting and throwing stones at the soldiers, and there were 14 killed and 20 wounded. Lebœuf, the Minister for War, who had succeeded Marshal Niel, presented a decoration to the officer who had given the order to fire. On the 10th of October, at the *Club des Folies-Belleville* in Paris, the police handled some demonstrators roughly after a meeting which one of their officers had just broken up. Meanwhile the Republican deputies were protesting against the delay on the part of the Government in convoking the Legislative Body. The old assembly had been dissolved on the 27th of April, and, but for an extraordinary session held in June to enable the new deputies to take their seats, the interval of six months allowed by the Constitution for the convoking of the new Assembly expired on the 26th of October. Kératry and Gambetta loudly declared that the representatives of the people ought to meet, come what might, on the 26th of October, in the Place de la Concorde, to march to the Palais Bourbon and take their seats. The Emperor replied by convoking the Legislative Body for the 29th of November.

This was regarded as a challenge. "Let the deputies of the Left do their duty!" urged the *Rappel*. "They will set forth a body of forty men from the Place de la Bastille; in the Place de la Concorde they will number 100,000." Whereupon, discretion proving the better part of valour, it beat a retreat. "The *chassepots* were ready, though well concealed," wrote Merimée; and what could be done against armed force? Even the *Rappel* observed that "energy should be tempered by prudence." Whereupon the revolutionaries, who were already counting upon an "insurrection" which was to lead to the social Revolution, broke with the deputies, whom they accused of treachery—clearly even these "irreconcilables" were compounding with the Empire. Some bye-elections took place in Paris at the end of November, and the Socialists, invoking the names of Ledru-Rollin, who was still in London, and of Barbès at The Hague, conducted a campaign against the "sworn" candidates, who, in order to have their candidature officially recognised, had sworn allegiance to the Empire. Nevertheless, Paris returned bourgeois Republicans—Emmanuel Arago, Crémieux and Glais-Bizoin. But, in addition, Roche**Rochefort** fort, who had come back from Brussels for the **Elected.** occasion, was also elected. He had been arrested and then released by order of the Emperor, and although he was a poor orator, he had won a brilliant success over his rival Carnot, thanks to the support of the faubourgs and his extraordinary popularity in Paris. This election was a slap in the face for the Emperor, and the whole world knew it.

This revolutionary agitation did not have upon Napoleon III the effect that might have been expected. Another man would have thought only of resistance, and would have placed himself once more on the side of Rouher. The Emperor, on the contrary, became more and more convinced that it was necessary to throw out ballast. For three months, through the medium of Duvernois, he had been communicating with Émile **Ollivier.** Ollivier, the man who seemed most capable of founding the Liberal Empire of which Morny had so long dreamt. The Emperor hesitated. Would he prove himself a statesman, this lawyer who was certainly a great orator, but had no experience of affairs, and seemed more capable of enthusiasm than of calm composure? Would he be reliable, this erstwhile Republican whom the Left regarded as a renegade, and the Right as a convert? But Ollivier proposed a programme that was seductive. He declared himself ready to "enter upon a hand-to-hand fight with the Revolution as Minister." On the night of the 31st of October, with the greatest secrecy, without his spectacles and smothered in a muffler, Ollivier presented himself at Compiègne, and Piétri, the Prefect of Police, conducted him to the Emperor by a hidden door—afraid of gossip in the Press and at Court. The Emperor thought at one moment of " annexing " Ollivier to the old Cabinet. But the latter refused to "insinuate" himself in this way among the Ministers still in office, and demanded a more fundamental change than mere " patchwork," insisting upon a Ministry chiefly composed of new men.

But where were they to be found ? The Legislative Body had just met and the parties had grouped themselves in it. Between the 80 " Arcadians " of the Right, the supporters of absolute rule, and the 30 or 40 Republicans of the Left, the two Centres constituted the majority—the Right Centre with 110 members, the Left with 40. To this latter group belonged the Orleanists, the men of the " old parties," the Buffets and the Darus, of whom Napoleon III was still suspicious. The two Centres, however, declared that they desired " the maintenance of the Empire based upon Liberal and parliamentary institutions." This loyalty was reassuring. They demanded a homogeneous responsible Ministry, the liberty of the Press and of elections (that is to say, the abolition of official candidature), trial by jury for Press cases, liberty for higher education (this was to please the Catholics), and an inquiry into the results of the commercial treaties (to satisfy the Protectionists). The Left Centre went further, demanding the election of the Mayors by the municipal councillors. After further hesitation and recoiling—at one moment it seemed likely that a coalition would be formed under Magne, who was certainly not one of the new men—and long negotiations, the Emperor at last decided to enter upon the path of parliamentarism and to dismiss his old staff. And he wrote to Ollivier asking him to tell him the names of " the men he regarded as capable of forming a homogeneous Cabinet with him, who would faithfully represent the majority in the Legislative Body and be resolved to carry out the *senatus consultum* of the 8th of September both in letter and in spirit."

On the 2nd of January, 1870, the Ministry of new men was formed. Except for the Minister of War and the Naval Minister, who retained their posts—the Emperor keeping the domain of national defence in his own hands—the Cabinet consisted of eight parliamentarians, six of whom belonged to the Right Centre and two, Buffet and Daru, to the Left. Ollivier was not President of the Council—none

The New Ministry.

was appointed—but Keeper of the Seals, though he had the right of precedence notwithstanding. On this date the Empire at last became definitely parliamentary, since, although the Emperor took care to keep up the fiction of choosing his own Ministers, and had asked Ollivier to *tell him the names of the men* whom he considered *capable* of forming a Cabinet, the Ministry was in point of fact chosen by Ollivier from among the majority in the elected Chamber, that is, in conformity with the wishes of the country.

Napoleon III was anxious that the experiment should be given a thorough trial; he presided over the Cabinet meetings but refrained from expressing any opinion. Only when the members disagreed did he give a casting vote. The police reports and diplomatic telegrams were all communicated to Ollivier, who found himself really treated as Prime Minister. But, stranger still, the Empress was no longer present at Council meetings. " The Ministers who enjoy the Emperor's confidence may rely upon my goodwill," she observed when the Cabinet was presented to her. The shade of difference between the two words was fairly obvious, but the main consideration was that she remained outside the Government.

The Ministry met with a cordial welcome, and the opening of 1870, that year of dismal memory for every Frenchman, was almost idyllic. Throughout the country there was confidence in the Emperor and his new staff, and the throne of the Prince Imperial seemed to have been secured. Catholics, Protectionists and members of the old parties smiled upon the new *régime ;* Guizot, Barrot and Duvergier de Hauranne once again attended ministerial receptions, while the Académie, now coquetting with the Government which but a little while back it was riddling with epigrams, elected Émile Ollivier. On the 7th of January, Daru, in the Senate, declared that he was ready to reply to all the interpellations : " We have signed programmes which we intend to carry out; we are men of honour ! " he exclaimed. At the same time, Haussmann, the last survivor of the old staff, the despotic Prefect accustomed to taking the high hand with the law, was superseded. And the Minister of the Interior advised the Prefects to avoid any exaggerated exercise of power and arbitrary conduct, and to treat the worthy members of all

360

parties with strict impartiality, while Ollivier preached goodwill
and clemency to his subordinates at the Ministry of Justice.
After long years of police restrictions, and of government by
the " iron hand," there was a regular recrudescence of confidence
and Liberalism. In vain did the Arcadians meet the Ministers
with black looks; in vain did Duvernois, furious at not having
been summoned to the Cabinet, attack the Government in his
Peuple Français. In vain too did Gambetta on the 10th of
January openly cross swords with Ollivier in the Legislative
Body, declaring that the established form of Government was
entirely incompatible with universal suffrage. " Between the
Republic of 1848 and the Republic of the future you are only a
bridge," he exclaimed, " and that bridge we shall cross." All
in vain! The majority did not take this flight of oratory any
more seriously than it had done the attacks by critics like
Duvernois.

But those in high places seldom enjoy an idyll for long. On
that same 10th of January an accident happened which almost
developed into a catastrophe. In the depths of
Auteuil there lived a poor relation of the Emperor,
Prince Pierre Bonaparte, son of Lucien, a cousin of
Napoleon III, who was kept at arm's length by the Tuileries.
Paschal Grousset, writing under a pseudonym in the *Revanche*,
and Rochefort in the *Marseillaise*, had attacked Napoleon I.
Like the loyal Corsican he was, the Prince roundly retaliated in
the columns of a Bastia newspaper. Grousset and Rochefort
despatched their seconds to him on the 10th. Grousset's
seconds, Ulrich de Fonvielle and Victor Noir, two contributors
to the *Marseillaise*, were the first to arrive upon the scene—
with pistols in their pockets; the Prince was known to have
a violent temper. They handed him Grousset's letter demanding satisfaction. The Prince had never heard of Grousset and
awaited Rochefort's seconds. He declared that his quarrel was
with Rochefort and not with his handiwork. Whereupon there
was a scuffle—nobody quite knew how it all happened—between
Victor Noir and the Prince, who gave back what he got. In
any case, the Prince, who also had his pistol in the pocket of
his dressing-gown, fired and hit Victor Noir; the latter fled,
staggered down the stairs and fell prostrate on the pavement,

**Pierre
Bonaparte.**

followed by Fonvielle, who left the room backwards, pistol in hand, having been twice shot at by the Prince. On the following day the *Marseillaise* appeared with black borders containing an article by Rochefort couched in the violent terms that were only to be expected : " I was weak enough to believe that it was possible for a Bonaparte not to be an assassin. . . . But in that family . . . violence and murder are customary and traditional. Victor Noir has been murdered by that bandit Pierre Napoleon Bonaparte. For eighteen years France has been in the blood-stained hands of these cut-throats, who, not satisfied with shooting Republicans in the streets, lure them into filthy traps in order to cut their throats at home. People of France, don't you think you have had enough ? "

The Government took immediate measures. It had Prince Pierre arrested—legally he was entitled to be tried before the High Court, which acquitted him in March—and at the same time it had the *Marseillaise* seized and Rochefort prosecuted. " We represent liberty," declared Ollivier on the 11th, " but if you force our hands, we shall use violence." Raspail retorted by comparing Pierre Bonaparte to a monstrous Tropmann about to be guillotined. On the 12th Victor Noir's funeral **Funeral of Victor Noir.** took place at Neuilly in the presence of 100,000 persons. Some members of Clubs wanted to divert the convoy to Paris, to the Père Lachaise, and harnessed themselves to the hearse, and Flourens hoped that the day of revolution had dawned at last. Delescluze and Rochefort had difficulty in dissuading them; the Champs Élysées were lined with troops, and the Emperor was in uniform ready for battle. In the end Victor Noir was buried in the cemetery of Neuilly and the revolution was once more postponed.

But disturbances still continued to take place—the International deciding to extend its activities in conjunction with Rochefort. At its behest Gambetta and Esquiros interpellated the Government on the subject of the intervention of the military at the Creusot works, where large bodies of troops had just intimidated 3,000 workmen on strike because an agitator, named Assi, had been dismissed. The Legislative Body voted that action should be taken against Rochefort, who, as a deputy, could be prosecuted only with the consent of his colleagues;

THE LIBERAL EMPIRE

whereupon the mob held demonstrations on the boulevards. At St. Mandé an appeal for the murder of the Emperor made by Félix Pyat, who had fled abroad, was read aloud and a toast was drunk to the " little bullet of freedom which the world was awaiting." Sentenced by default to six months' imprisonment for insulting the Emperor and incitement to civil war, Rochefort was arrested on the 7th of February just as he was arriving at a meeting. Flourens, who was presiding over the gathering, learnt the news, whereupon he proclaimed the revolution and had the police officer who tried to break up the meeting arrested. Barricades were flung up, but the police quickly got the upper hand. The Government had all the contributors to the *Marseillaise* arrested as well as a crowd of suspects, 450 persons in all.

Disturbances.

To maintain order Ollivier found himself obliged to return to the repressive measures of Rouher. It is true that at the same time he persevered in his Liberal policy, as he was anxious to carry out the programme of the Centre parties—an amnesty for Ledru-Rollin; the justices of the peace to be confined to the exercise of their judicial functions and not to meddle with politics; the liberty of the Press (except for attacks on the Emperor and incitement to rebellion); journalists to be allowed to comment on the proceedings in the Chambers; Press misdemeanours to be tried by jury; the courts to be independent of the Government; repeal of the Law of Public Safety and the appointment of grand commissions for the administrative reform of Paris; decentralisation and the freedom of higher education. Prévost-Paradol hailed this " recasting, in the sense of setting free, all the institutions created in France by the Revolution, the Consulate and the Empire." At the same time Daru, true to the old Gallican tradition, intervened at the Vatican Council to protest against the consequences of the new dogma of Papal Infallibility which was being proposed at the Council, and against this " consecration of the supreme authority of the Church over civil society." His protests, however, were destined to be fruitless.

Repressive Measures.

But such Liberalism as this was not sufficient to content the Left in the Legislative Body. The irreconcilables attacked

363

Ollivier in his most vulnerable point—was this " Liberal " going to continue the system of official candidature? It was a clever move, since it placed Ollivier on the horns of a dilemma, forcing him either to betray his Liberal principle by adhering to the methods of Rouher, or by renouncing the latter's methods to alienate the majority who owed their election to them. Ollivier was anxious to please everybody. He declared that the Government had the absolute right to designate the candidates it preferred, but he added, that for his own part he would remain neutral in the electoral struggle. The Right immediately voted against him—men like Pinard, Jérôme David and Clément Duvernois. And Favre, Ferry and Gambetta upheld this renegade from Republicanism, this convert to the other side ! But was it possible for the Ministry to carry on for long between the rancour of the Arcadians and the demands of the irreconcilables?

A fresh question soon arose which was destined to rouse all the political passions. In the new Liberal Empire the Senate **The Senate.** constituted an anachronism, a remnant of 1852. Could this assembly of high officials nominated by the Emperor still be allowed to exercise the sole right of deciding on matters of constitutional law, that is to say, on the very principles of the political organisation of the country? After the great increase that had taken place since 1860 in the power the nation was able to exercise over public affairs through the agency of the Legislative Body, was it logical to allow the continued existence by the side of this Assembly of " a perpetual non-elective Constituent Body," as P. de la Gorce calls it? A reform was imperative. The Emperor, as usual, replied through the medium of an open letter addressed to Ollivier on the 21st of March, in which he declared that he meant to reserve the right of appointing the senators, in spite of the theorists who wished at least fifty per cent. of them to be elected by the General Councils. But the province of constitutional law was to be limited to essentials, and the Senate was to share legislative power with the other Assembly. Above all, the Constitution thus reduced to fundamentals could not be modified except by plebiscite.

Whereupon a turning of the tables occurred which Ollivier

had failed to foresee. The Senate, who accepted this *diminutio capitis* with exceedingly bad grace, maintained that the reform was so fundamental that it necessitated an immediate appeal to the people—a fresh plebiscite was called for to modify the measures accepted by the plebiscite of 1852. And all the advocates of imperial despotism, men like Rouher, Magne and Jérôme David, immediately supported the idea; it afforded a unique opportunity for the Emperor once more to get into touch with the country, for Cæsarism to exploit its principle of appealing to the people; by so doing it would regain all its former strength, like Antæus touching mother earth.

It was a clever move—under pretence of asking the nation to express its approval of the recent Liberal reforms, a signal manifestation of loyalty and Bonapartism would be provoked. The Emperor, with the idea of consolidating his son's throne ever in mind, soon allowed himself to be convinced. And Ollivier was obliged to give in, although at first he looked with a far from friendly eye on the political agitation which must inevitably result, and was too much of a parliamentarian to relish this Bonapartist practice of appealing to the country. Naturally the Left (Grévy and Picard) lodged a protest on the 4th of April against the plebiscite, the weapon of despotism, and Gambetta, on the same day, pointed out the canker and inconsistency lying at the core of the *régime*—every plebiscite was bound to be misleading unless the Legislative Body discussed its terms with the object of fully enlightening public opinion. Moreover, what was the plebiscite? It was power put to the vote. Then what became of the hereditary principle, the dynastic principle? It was clear to all that Gambetta was referring to the glaring illogicality of the Emperor having his power confirmed by the popular vote while his son, the Prince Imperial, would shortly succeed to the throne and was preparing to reign as though he were the son of a king by divine right. " There is but one form of Government suitable for universal suffrage," he boldly declared, " and that is the republican form." Nevertheless, the majority, supported this time by the Right, followed Ollivier. But Buffet, an old parliamentarian, resigned his office rather than acquiesce in this plebiscite, this return to the " vagaries " of Cæsarism. And Daru quickly

THE SECOND EMPIRE

followed his example. They had requested the Emperor to save the prerogatives of Parliament by having recourse to a plebiscite dependent upon the consent of the Chambers being secured, but in vain !

On the 20th of April a *senatus consultum* was passed establishing the " Constitution of 1870." It summed up and codified **The Consti-** the various Liberal reforms introduced since 1860, **tution of** as well as defining the powers which the Emperor **1870.** still reserved to himself—the right of appealing to the French people, the right of appointing Ministers who, although " responsible," were dependent upon him alone and not upon the vote of the Chambers. Was this Constitution likely to prove lasting? What would have happened in case of a conflict between the elective Assembly and the Emperor's Ministers, that is to say, between the representatives of the country and the Master? Would the country have been faced with a series of dissolutions and plebiscites? The *régime* disappeared too soon for the matter to be put to the test.

On the 8th of May the French people were asked to vote *Yea* or *Nay* on the following proposition : " The people approves the Liberal reforms introduced into the Constitution **The** since 1860 by the Emperor with the help of the **Plebiscite.** great State bodies, and ratifies the *senatus consultum* of the 20th of April, 1870." In his proclamation the Emperor invited his people to ward off the menace of revolution, to place order and liberty upon a firm basis and to facilitate the transmission of the crown to his son. The question was cleverly put—the reforms were to be approved and at the same time, by ratifying the *senatus consultum*, the Empire was to be supported. In vain did the Left Centre demand that two separate urns should be used for the two questions. The Ministry, fearing indifference and abstention from voting, urged its officials to exercise " devouring activity " to make people vote, and vote rightly. A central committee on the plebiscite (the Right Centre and the Centre in favour of legality) was formed in Paris with the object of making the appeal to the people a success, a triumph; men like David, Pinard and Duvernois, helped by the clergy, were convinced that this fresh consecration of the Empire would prove so brilliant that it would leave the Liberal
366

THE LIBERAL EMPIRE

reforms in the shade, in spite of the fact that the plebiscite approved of them in the same breath. And under cover of this popularity it would doubtless be possible gradually to return to the principles of imperial despotism and escape from the " Orleanist and parliamentary rut," as the *Pays* put it. The Left Centre, from hatred of the revolutionaries, resigned itself to voting *Yea*—all except Thiers. The Legitimists and the Republicans, with the exception of Picard, who was a Moderate, were the only ones to decide on voting *Nay* or abstaining from voting altogether. The Republicans organised an anti-plebiscite committee, which declared that the new Constitution was merely the " ghost " of government of the people by the people.

They were supported by the advanced journals which had come into being almost everywhere in the provinces, and also by the International, which now had 245,000 members. It was continually fomenting strikes and had become a power. At public meetings the Government was violently attacked; Fonvielle, Lissagaray, Lefrançais Millière and Rigault all joining in the chorus of abuse. The plebiscite was to be the " Waterloo of the Empire." Anti-militarist propaganda was carried on in the purlieus of the barracks, for the army too was to vote, and the revolutionaries argued that if they won over the *chassepots* they would have won everything. In the end Ollivier was obliged to follow Rouher's example and arrest the leaders and prosecute the newspapers, while the police most opportunely unearthed a certain man named Beaury who had come from London armed with a revolver to kill the Emperor. The plot was discovered just in time once again to conjure up the spectre of revolution and anarchy and incite good citizens to vote as they should.

The result was that on the 8th of May, despite the official wording of the plebiscite, the people voted for or against the

Result of the Plebiscite. Empire. Once again the large towns voted against —in Paris and the Seine district there were 184,000 *Nays* and 83,000 abstentions to 138,000 *Yeas ;* while Lyons, Marseilles, Bordeaux and Toulouse followed suit. The Tuileries grew perturbed. But before long the results from the rural districts came in, and once again the country-folk saved

367

the *régime*. The total amounted to 7,359,000 *Yeas* to 1,572,000 *Nays* and 1,894,000 abstentions. It was a triumph for Napoleon III, who had repeated his success of 1852. Gambetta and Favre were filled with despair—the Empire was " stronger than ever." The Opposition of the Left was now split in two, Grévy and Gambetta insisting that the group should shut out all who were not Republicans and irreconcilable, Picard wanting to include the Orleanists and content themselves with a dynastic Opposition without attempting to " bring about a revolution." This division into a " closed Left " and an " open Left " was not calculated to strengthen the Opposition. At the same time, the Right, encouraged by the result of the plebiscite, regained confidence. The Emperor, it is true, protested that he would not deviate from the Liberal path he had traced out for himself, but Ollivier felt he could no longer trust him, and an inevitable return to the methods, the principles and possibly the personnel of imperial despotism was only to be expected.

Napoleon III was intoxicated by his triumph. " More than ever before can we look forward to the future without fear," he declared on the 21st of May. But two months later the war broke out which was to hurl the whole Empire, together with its personnel, its systems and its principles, into the abyss. The success of the plebiscite appears to us to-day in the light of the euphoria of the moribund.

CHAPTER X

DISASTER

D URING the years 1868 and 1869 the feeling of anxiety following upon Sadowa and the Luxemburg crisis still continued to oppress men's minds. Benedetti, the French Ambassador in Berlin, informed Paris that the two " sections " separated by the Maine were showing signs of joining again and that Prussia was in a position to unite the whole of Germany whenever she wished. Certain leading politicians like Ollivier, Prince Napoleon, Jules Simon and Jules Favre were

Fear of Prussia. of opinion that German unity should be accepted. Others, on the contrary, wanted to oppose it at all costs, even at the expense of war; among these latter were

Rouher, Thiers, Gambetta and the Staff of the army. In their eyes war with Prussia was inevitable. Prévost-Paradol foretold it in his *France Nouvelle*, which appeared in 1868, and even dared to envisage possible defeat : " It would be the grave of French greatness, and we should be reduced to living upon the glory of the past . . . and boring Europe with recollections of Louis XIV and Napoleon, just as Spain hurls the names of Philip II and Charles V in the faces of the indifferent chancelleries." Stoffel, the French military attaché in Berlin, sent report after report emphasising the formidable menace of the Prussian army, which numbered a million well-trained men, equipped with up-to-date guns and under the command of an excellent Staff. In the end the Ministry of War no longer took this prophet of evil seriously, regarding him as a " Prusso-maniac " hypnotised by Bismarck. But public opinion, vaguely aware of these menaces, remained nervous and anxious, and it only required a bellicose speech on the part of King William, one of those war harangues which are traditional with the Kings of Prussia, to give rise to a panic on the Bourse, leading to the sale of securities by the sheaf and an alarming slump in the market.

At the same time there was a further outbreak of incidents between the two countries. In 1867 Bismarck had reorganised the Customs Union, arranging that the four southern States should elect representatives by universal suffrage and send them to Berlin to confer with the Reichstag on economic questions. This " Customs Parliament " was the prototype of the German Parliament of the future. Paris became perturbed ; Bismarck was irritated, and Moustier told Benedetti to appease him, but to keep a loophole for the future by avoiding giving the impression " that he would in the end approve of the concentration of the whole of Germany under the ægis of Prussia." Moreover, the deputies elected by the South were chosen from the ranks of the opponents of Prussia—possibly the " section " beyond the Maine was not quite so ready to become united with the North after all !

The Zollverein.

A fresh incident occurred at the beginning of 1868. The little army of King George of Hanover, who had been despoiled of his States by Bismarck, had sought refuge in Alsace.

Berlin demanded the disbanding of this " Hanoverian legion,"
and France was obliged to see that it was done. " We might
The have avoided this little *insult*," observed Ducrot,
Hanoverian who was in command at Strassburg, " if from the
Legion. very beginning we had taken the line which has just
been forced upon us by Prussia."

Further incidents occurred in connection with Schleswig.
After the conquest of Schleswig by Prussia and after Sadowa,
Schleswig. France had arranged for Schleswig to be consulted
by plebiscite on the question of her annexation.
But Berlin had continually postponed the plebiscite, which
seemed likely to have awkward consequences. In 1867 a semi-
official application from Paris had already met with a far from
courteous reply from Prussia—France was told to mind her
own business. In 1868, as a Danish Minister had arrived in
Paris, the Berlin Press again fulminated against France, saying
she had no right to meddle with German policy and with
the relations between Denmark and Prussia. Thus at every
opportunity Prussian public opinion disputed the hegemony
which the French Empire still professed to exercise in Europe.

Everywhere Prussia disputed the leading part France felt
entitled to play. Between 1859 and 1862, Napoleon III, loyal
to his policy of supporting nationalities, had encouraged the
formation of Moldavia and Wallachia, principalities under the
suzerainty of Turkey, into a single state, and in 1866 had
supported the accession to the throne of a Prince of the Catholic
Prince branch of the House of Hohenzollern, a cousin of
Charles of the King of Prussia. Elected hereditary Prince of
Roumania. Roumania, Charles of Hohenzollern was thus released
from the hegemony of the Sultan and Roumania became really
independent. It was not long before Prussian influence ousted
that of France in Bucharest. Bratiano, a Liberal Minister,
who was already dreaming of annexing the Roumanians of
Transylvania, had many friends in Paris, among them Prince
Napoleon, who paid a visit to Bucharest and was loudly
Bratiano. acclaimed. As the Liberal intrigues in Transylvania
naturally perturbed the Hungarians, and as Bismarck
had joined sides with their Minister Andrassy against Austria,
Bismarck demanded and succeeded in securing the dismissal

371

of Bratiano (November 1868). This constituted an obvious defeat for French policy.

About this time too Bismarck also led the dance in a dispute between Turkey and Greece in connection with Crete. Greece

Crete. was trying to prevent the return to Crete of natives of the island who had sought refuge with her in order to escape the Turkish yoke. Turkey protested and broke off relations. Napoleon III, who was sick to death of these everlasting complications in the East, refused to intervene, and it was Bismarck who secured the convoking of a Conference, which at the beginning of 1869 forced Greece to give way. The Conference, it is true, met in Paris—a last purely formal acknowledgment of French hegemony; but as a matter of fact it was Prussia who held the strings of action.

A further incident occurred at the beginning of 1869 which brought the two countries once more face to face. The *Chemin*

The Grand *de Fer de l'Est* had acquired the Grand Luxemburg
Luxemburg line, a half-ruined Belgian company. The Tuileries
Railway. regarded this as a means for penetrating into Belgium and of preparing the way for the economic absorption of that country. Brussels was well aware of this, and the Belgian Government forbade any railway line to be ceded. This incensed Napoleon III and he interpreted it as a challenge. " Public opinion is persuaded," he wrote to Niel, the Minister for War, " that Belgium adopts this arrogant attitude only because she has Prussia behind her." And, since he had not renounced his dreams, he added : " The possession of Belgium would provide

Belgium. substantial compensation for us ; . . . Belgium opens the gates of Germany to us. A beaten Belgian army would easily be absorbed by ours." Although too much store should not be set by such *rapprochements* between nations from the historical point of view, one is inevitably reminded of the attitude of Germany towards Belgium in 1914. At one moment there was talk of war—Niel declared that he was ready. But in the end, after having in vain suggested a political alliance with Belgium, which was a neutral country, France gave way and did not insist. Belgium, who had been supported in this affair by Prussia and England, remained suspicious of France and rightly jealous of her own independence. And once again French policy met with defeat.

DISASTER

In this atmosphere of tension and menace it was imperative to have soldiers and allies. The soldiers were there—or were believed to be there. In his mind's eye Niel saw the work he had inaugurated already finished; the Emperor, who was himself drawing up a memorandum on the organisation of the army, reckoned he could count on almost 500,000 men. *Chassepots* were being manufactured, and the working of German guns was being studied in Belgium; it was acknowledged that they were superior to the French guns. At Meudon, in the utmost secrecy, experiments were being made in guns designed to fire ball cartridges, or mitrailleuses, which were expected to put an immediate stop to any enemy offensive. In the east the cadres of the *Garde Mobile* were being formed; Generals set off either officially or unofficially to reconnoitre the Rhineland with a view to the coming offensive; young officers studied strategy, topography and geography, and gave lectures or published books; a Commission was preparing the military transports on the railways, and an attempt was made to reform the General Staff and to foresee the part cavalry would have to play as intelligence and liaison troops, for in view of the quick-firing weapons of modern war any massed action on its part seemed likely to be impossible in future. And Niel was able to assure the Emperor that he had " the finest army in the world," and that the Ministry of War was ready prepared. The *Officiel* of April 1869 announced that in case of war an army of 750,000 men could be raised; it was calculated that 400,000 could be assembled in a week.

Vain illusions! The task had only just been begun and years would have been required to finish it. Niel died in harness in August 1869. His place was filled by Lebœuf, and the work undertaken by Niel necessarily slowed down. And how great was the opposition that had to be overcome! The old leaders clung to their routine, confident that when the great day came they would be able to pull through as they had done in Italy and in the Crimea. They had full confidence in the French defences on the Rhine and in the Vosges, at Strassburg and Metz. The Legislative Body haggled over the Bills of Supply, giving Niel five millions for his *Garde Mobile* instead of the fourteen millions for which he had asked, reducing the sums to be spent on the

Military Preparations.

Opposition.

THE SECOND EMPIRE

fortresses, the artillery and armaments, and discharging from twenty-five to fifty per cent. of the forces in order to mitigate the effects of the law of 1868. The country was dreaming of universal peace. The *Ligue Internationale de la Paix,* founded by Dollfus, Michel Chevalier and Frédéric Passy, protested against the system of armed peace which was ruining the nations. In vain was the centenary of Napoleon I celebrated in August 1869; the heart of the people was not in it, and Jules Janin in the *Débats,* and Littré in the *Revue Positiviste* coldly and dispassionately summed up the great man, recalling all the harm he had done and all the horrors of war. Émile de Girardin, it is true, was still demanding the left bank of the Rhine, even if necessary at the cost of " drenching Europe in blood." But his was more or less the voice of one crying in the wilderness.

Would this army, which was in process of reorganisation, have alliances to fall back upon when the crisis arrived? It was fondly hoped it would, and attempts at *rap-prochement* with Italy and Austria were made. In 1867 the meetings at Salzburg and Paris had testified to the reconciliation between the ancient foes of Solferino. The Duc de Gramont, the French Ambassador in Vienna, who was very popular in high Viennese society, noted with pleasure every incident that occurred between Vienna and Berlin, between von Beust and Bismarck, and did all in his power to bring about an alliance between France and Austria. He secured a promise that Austria would resist the annexation of Southern Germany by Prussia even by force of arms, and raised hopes of an alliance in the near future. Negotiations were opened between the two Courts through the medium of semi-official agents and sometimes even without the knowledge of the Ambassadors. But Austria insisted upon confining herself to a defensive alliance against any future attack on the part of Prussia.

General Türr, an aide-de-camp of Victor Emmanuel, a Hungarian by birth, whose wife was a Bonaparte, acted as connecting link between Florence, Vienna and Paris. In 1869 Rouher drew up with his own hand a plan for an offensive and defensive alliance. Vienna, however, did not want to go to these lengths, and suggested that the three

Austria.

Italy.

374

DISASTER

countries should promise to support one another in the maintenance of peace, and the safeguarding of their territories, and should undertake not to enter into secret negotiations with a third party. This plan for a Triple Alliance was extremely limited in scope, but, modest though it was, it never came to anything. Italy, in fact, demanded that France should evacuate Rome and promise never to intervene there again, and Napoleon III, anxious to please the Catholic Party, firmly refused. The negotiations ended in a mere exchange of autograph letters between the sovereigns concerned, in which they supported the principle of a Triple Alliance which should present "a formidable barrier to unjust pretensions" (an obvious allusion to Prussia's designs on Southern Germany), and entered, albeit somewhat vaguely, into definite undertakings with regard to the Austrian plan of a Triple Alliance. In fact these letters merely amounted to a promise to arrange a treaty, but did not in themselves constitute a treaty. But the Tuileries imagined that they "might, at a given moment, serve as the basis for the drawing up of a treaty which would only require signature." There is nothing more dangerous than semi-engagements which, without binding anybody, give a false sense of security.

Austria and Italy were the only two possible allies. Russia, since the Polish disturbances and the Tsar's visit to Paris, was **Russia.** veering towards Berlin. Alexander, it is true, treated the French Ambassador, Fleury, the Emperor's confidant, with great friendliness, but at the same time he exchanged decorations with the King of Prussia, and reminded him of 1814, when the armies of both countries had fought against another Bonaparte. Paris had no illusions on this score. "Do not forget that all you say is repeated in Berlin," was the warning sent to Fleury. The only means of winning over Russia would have been to revise the Treaty of Paris; but Napoleon III did not wish to sacrifice the advantages he had gained by his war in the Crimea.

England, who was becoming ever more and more absorbed in her colonies, was living in her splendid isolation, somewhat **England.** contemptuous of Europe, ever unsettled and on the verge of war. Nevertheless, at the beginning of 1870 she felt called upon to intervene. Daru, the Minister for Foreign Affairs in Ollivier's Cabinet, wanted to preserve the

peace and the *status quo* in Europe—"not to raise questions
and to stifle those that did arise." Animated by this spirit,
he advised Fleury, who had received instructions to interest the
Tsar in Schleswig, to drop the matter. Ollivier on his side
constantly reiterated that "there was no German question."
And finally this same Cabinet, averse though it was to adventure
of any sort, felt it must respond to the desire for peace which
was animating France at the time, and revived the idea of
disarmament which had already been put forward in vain in
1863 and 1867. The English Foreign Minister, Lord Clarendon,
who was a friend of the Emperor, was captivated by the idea,
and undertook to bring pressure to bear in Berlin by making it
known that France, in order to set the example, intended to
reduce the contingent she was going to call up from the 1870
class by 10,000 men. But he was met by a categorical *non
possumus* from Bismarck.

Thus it became necessary to return to the plans for alliances,
and the idea of an alliance with Austria was again discussed.
The Archduke Albert, the brother of Francis Joseph, the victor
of Custozza, came to Paris in March, and was welcomed as a
friend by the Generals and the Emperor. Whereupon in May
the Emperor confided his grandiose dreams to Marshal Lebœuf,
and Generals Frossard, Lebrun and Jarras. He conjured up
visions of an army trapping the Prussian forces on the Sarre,
another army marching into Bavaria to join the Austrians,
while the Italians debouched from the Tyrol and the French
fleet sailed into the North Sea to incite Denmark against the
common foe. Dreams, chimeras! The Emperor had been
informed by the Archduke Albert himself that Austria would
require six weeks before she could be ready for war, and Prussia
would certainly profit by the delay to steal a march upon her
adversaries and be on the Rhine within a fortnight. Finally,
this council of war was obliged to come to the conclusion that
the French army could not hold out for six weeks by itself
Austria wants Peace. against the forces of Northern Germany. Shortly
afterwards (in June) Lebrun was sent to Vienna to
continue the negotiations with the Archduke. But
no progress was made. Moreover, Francis Joseph, who
granted Lebrun an audience, told him, "I want peace, and I
376

should make war only if I were forced to do so." He could intervene only if the French army were to appear in Southern Germany in the guise of liberator. Thus all this diplomatic labour had resulted merely in attempted alliances and plans for common action, when a crisis supervened which was more alarming than any that had yet occurred and was destined to precipitate the Franco-Prussian War, which people in the end had ceased to fear because they had been expecting it for too long.

Ever since the revolution of 1868 had driven out Queen Isabella, Spain, which was being ruled by Marshal Prim, had **Spain.** been looking for a King. As a possible candidate mention was made of Leopold of Hohenzollern, the brother of Prince Charles of Roumania, who was a distant connection of the King of Prussia by a common ancestry dating back to the thirteenth century. He was an officer in the Prussian army and a son of the Prince Antony who had acted as Prime Minister to King William. In March 1869 Paris had been extremely perturbed by the rumour, and Benedetti, the French Ambassador, had discussed the matter with one of Bismarck's colleagues, who had assured him that the suggestion was entirely without foundation. In May Benedetti had had an interview with Bismarck himself, who showed but little enthusiasm for the candidature, but refrained from giving Benedetti the assurance the latter demanded, that is to say, an undertaking on the part of King William never to allow Prince Leopold to accept the throne of Spain.

That Bismarck had deliberately engineered every detail of the Hohenzollern candidature, fully aware of what the results of **The Hohen-** his Machiavellian conduct would be, is hardly likely. **zollern** The politician exploits rather than creates circum- **Candidature.** stances, and Bismarck saw in this matter, which was not due to his initiative, a means of playing a trick on France, by placing a Prussian Prince on the throne of Spain, and thus menacing her Pyrenees frontier, even at the risk of throwing down the gauntlet to French national sentiment. In March 1870 a secret council was held in Berlin which decided that it was " the duty of a patriotic Prussian " for the Hohenzollern

THE SECOND EMPIRE

Prince to accept the Spanish crown. But Bismarck advised Prim to address himself not to the Prussian Government but to Prince Antony in his private capacity; thus it would be a family affair and France would have no excuse for interference. At the end of June Leopold accepted the offer, and King William did not protest. Prim, who expected opposition on the part of France, would have liked to keep the matter secret until he was able to announce the news himself to Napoleon III at Vichy, and prevail upon him to accept it. But an indiscretion on the part of the Madrid Press made the affair common property on the 2nd of July. On Sunday the 3rd Paris knew it.

The Minister for Foreign Affairs at this time was the Duc d'Agénor de Gramont, who had once been Ambassador in Vienna. The Emperor had appointed him to the **The Duc de** office at the end of May—without overmuch enthu- **Gramont.** siasm. " It does not matter whom we appoint," he had observed, " since we have made up our minds to do nothing." This spoke volumes regarding his weariness and lassitude. Gramont was an aristocrat of the first water whose device was *Gratia Dei sum id quod sum.* Ollivier described this diplomatist as " being quick as an arrow to see things," which was apparently meant as a compliment. He returned from Vienna to the Quai d'Orsay imbued with Viennese feelings of hatred for Prussia. Bismarck gave him his own back by calling him the stupidest man in Europe—*ein Rindvieh.* Haughty and choleric, he was imbued with a mystic spirit of patriotism. " I decided on war," he afterwards observed, " with full confidence of victory. . . . I believed in the greatness of my country, in her strength, and her warlike prowess with almost as much faith as I believe in my holy religion." Such mysticism may be excellent in a soldier who is called upon only to allow himself to be killed; but it runs the risk of being dangerous in a Minister upon whom peace and war and the future of a great nation depend. Gramont, it is true, was not the master; but who had he above him? Ollivier? A weakling. The Emperor? An invalid whom the doctors had examined on the 3rd of July with the result that they recommended him to have an operation.

From the very beginning Gramont allowed his rage to have full play. " The acceptance [of the crown of Spain]," he

378

DISASTER

declared to the English Ambassador on the 5th, "attacks our interests and wounds our pride. It is impossible for us to acquiesce in a combination which, in case of war with Prussia, would force us to waste an army corps on the Spanish frontier. No sacrifice is too great to prevent such a plan. If
Threat of War. Prussia insists," he added, "it means war." Had not Lebœuf promised to mobilise 250,000 to 350,000 men in a fortnight, as well as 120,000 men of the *Garde Mobile*? On the same day the crowd began to get excited, St. Cloud talked of war with obvious satisfaction, and there was a fall in Government securities. On the 6th Cochery interpellated the Government in the Legislative Body, and Gramont read a declaration which still rings out like a battle-cry. "It is impossible," he declared, "for us to allow a foreign Power to place one of its Princes on the throne of Charles V and thereby upset the present balance of power in Europe to the detriment of France and the peril of her interests and her honour. To prevent this eventuality we count both on the wisdom of the German people and the friendship of Spain. But if it should turn out otherwise, strong in your support, gentlemen, and in that of the nation, we shall know how to fulfil our duty without hesitation or weakness."

He was cheered to the echo, especially by the Bonapartists of the extreme Right, who were already counting upon war to renew the prestige of the *régime* and mark a return to the traditions of despotism. Meanwhile Thiers, who had not been present, had arrived and was informed of Gramont's declaration. "But it is madness," he exclaimed, and conjured Ollivier to put on the brake. Ollivier made a speech declaring that "while the Government would only have peace with honour, it was passionately desirous of peace." But it was too late! Gramont's menacing declaration had already been telegraphed far and wide. That evening and the following day the whole Press, with the exception of the *Temps* and the *Débats*, was bellicose, not to say violent; the most vehement newspapers being the *Peuple Français* under Duvernois, the *Pays* under Granier de Cassagnac, and the *Liberté* under Émile de Girardin. Demonstrations were held on the boulevards, and the mob even dared to sing the *Marseillaise*, which had once been a revolutionary song, but had again become an expression of patriotism. Pacifists were hooted and hissed and those in favour of war greeted with cheers.

The Government thereupon decided to approach King William himself in his capacity as head of the House of Hohenzollern, **Benedetti** and Benedetti was sent to Ems, where the King **and King** was taking a cure. Benedetti was entrusted with **William.** the formal mission of prevailing upon the King to *revoke* the acceptance of the Hohenzollern Prince—" Otherwise it means war." Gramont was anxious at all costs to force Prussia, whom he hated, to make a public recantation. On the 9th of July Benedetti saw the King and instinctively toned down Gramont's demands. The King replied that for the time being he was speaking merely as head of the family, that he was leaving the Prince free to accept or to refuse without bringing any pressure to bear upon him, and that he had put himself in touch with Prince Antony and informed him of the excitement raised in France by the candidature; he added that he had been hurt by " the almost provocative tone " of Gramont's declaration. In the end he kept Benedetti to dinner.

On the 10th, Gramont growing impatient—he had expected on the previous day to begin preparations for making war within a fortnight and thus avoid being forestalled by Prussia as Austria had been in 1866—Gramont insisted that Benedetti should secure an immediate definite reply from the King himself : " Public opinion is tense with excitement and is getting out of hand in all directions, and we are counting the hours." On the 11th Benedetti again saw the King, who showed some irritation at his persistence and declared that he too was taking precautions, but added that he was expecting the reply of the Hohenzollern Prince within a few hours. His aim was to leave the latter apparently free to make whatever decision he pleased and thus to be solely responsible if his acceptance was withdrawn; for any concession on the part of the King of Prussia would have been galling to German public opinion. Such, at all events, was Benedetti's interpretation of his attitude, and he was probably right. As a matter of fact the King had prevailed upon Prince Antony to persuade his son to refuse. At the same time Napoleon III was adopting a similar course through the medium of the Paris agent of Charles of Roumania. On the evening of the 11th, Gramont, still in a state of great excitement, reproached Benedetti for showing lack of determination : "We call upon the King to forbid the Hohenzollern Prince to persist in his candidature. In the absence of a definite reply to-morrow we shall interpret silence or ambiguity as a refusal to satisfy our demand."

At midday on the 12th, when the arrival of the Emperor from St. Cloud at the Tuileries was interpreted by everybody **The Candidature Withdrawn.** as a sign of war, Paris was informed through the Spanish Ambassador that Prince Antony, in the name of his son, had withdrawn the acceptance. Ollivier, radiant with joy, announced the news in the Palais Bourbon. Speculators jumped into cabs and rushed to the Bourse, and the 3 per cents rose from 67 to 70 francs. Apparently it was going to be peace, the peace that the country in its heart of hearts desired, as was proved, in spite of the excitement in Paris, by the reports of the provincial Prefects. The Emperor, who had been following the crisis " with mournful eyes," also expressed his approval. " Public opinion would have preferred war," he said. " The country will be disappointed. But it cannot be helped ! "

But the Government had failed to take into account the attitude of Bonapartist Chauvinists—deputies and journalists— **The Chauvinists.** who regarded the concession as worthless since it had not come from the King of Prussia himself. They made fun of *Father Antony's* telegram, and Duvernois wanted to interpellate the Cabinet " as to what guarantees it had secured or hoped to secure to avoid a recurrence of complications with Prussia." Gramont, still anxious to gain a diplomatic victory over Prussia, had already asked Benedetti to secure confirmation of the fact that the King " supported the renunciation," and in order not to be outdone by Duvernois, once more put forward the fatal idea of guarantees. And the situation was again critical. Gramont saw the Prussian Ambassador, Herr von Werther, and gave him the rough draft of a letter which King William might address to the Emperor to smooth matters over : " In authorising Prince Leopold to accept the crown of Spain, the King had no intention of attacking either

381

the interests or the dignity of the French nation. His Majesty associates himself with the renunciation of Prince Leopold of Hohenzollern and expresses his desire that all cause for mis-understanding between his own Government and that of the Emperor should be henceforward removed." This amounted to dictating to the King the confession of his withdrawal. Everybody knew that Gramont hated Prussia, but they did not know that his hatred went to such lengths ! And it must be confessed that the Gallic cock has never deserved the reputa-tion for overweening conceit and foolish vanity more than it did at this juncture.

On the evening of the 12th Gramont had an audience with the Emperor at St. Cloud at which neither Ollivier nor the Cabinet was present. He did everything in his power to secure his support. The Empress intervened to the same effect, still convinced that a victorious war would consolidate her son's throne. The Emperor allowed himself to be persuaded, and at seven o'clock Gramont telegraphed to Benedetti : " Apparently it is necessary for the King of Prussia to support [the renun-ciation], and to give us the assurance that he will not authorise such a candidature again. Please go to the King immediately and ask him for this declaration, which he cannot refuse if he really has nothing to hide. In spite of the renunciation which has now been made known, the public excitement is so great that we do not know whether we can keep it in check." That same evening the *Marseillaise* was hummed on the boulevards, and drunken brawlers shouted " To Berlin ! " Ollivier, who was informed of Gramont's action late in the evening, was terrified and had a second telegram sent : " Emphasise the fact that we are not seeking a pretext for war." A futile palliation. The harm had been done !

On the 13th of July, Benedetti, determined not to be exposed to further reproaches from Gramont, entered the peaceful Park of Ems. Surrounded by " bathers " he met the King, and communicated Gramont's demands to him, emphasising his request in what the King regarded as " an almost impertinent tone." William refused to enter into any " engagement which was to have no limit and was to apply in all circumstances," but he added that his cousins

Benedetti at Ems.

382

were honourable men, who, if they had withdrawn their candidature, were certainly not nursing any secret intention of reviving it at some later date, and that as far as he himself was concerned the matter had been the occasion of far too much annoyance for him to be tempted to reopen it. And he dismissed Benedetti, without any sign of discourtesy, promising to send for him again when he had heard from Prince Antony. Shortly afterwards he received from Paris the rough draft of the letter given by Gramont to Werther and was extremely indignant : " So I am expected to adopt the attitude of a repentant sinner ! . . . They have made up their minds to provoke us at all costs." Meanwhile Bismarck in Berlin had begged him to stop this irregular method of negotiation, and to return to the usual channels—that is to say, to send all communications in future through Berlin. The King sent his aide-de-camp to Benedetti and made him return again twice in reply to demands for an audience, telling him to inform Benedetti that he had received confirmation of the renunciation and had given his consent to it, but that he could not reopen the discussion regarding assurances for the future and considered the incident closed. On the following day, in the station from which he was to take the train to Berlin, he took a friendly farewell of the French Ambassador.

It was at this juncture that Bismarck appeared upon the scene. On the very evening of the 13th he received from Abeken, one of his own creatures whom he had placed in the King's immediate circle, a telegram informing him of what had taken place at Ems during the day. On the previous evening he had believed, like everybody else, that peace had been secured, and had informed his wife that he would be returning to the country. But the fresh demands from France had revived the crisis, and he felt this might possibly provide the opportunity for opening the flood-gates for the war which in his heart of hearts he had long been desiring. But, in order to carry the whole of Germany with him, it was necessary for France, " the hereditary foe," openly to appear in the light of aggressor. At the end of his telegram Abeken added : " His Majesty leaves it to your Excellency to decide if this fresh demand on the part of Benedetti

The Ems Telegram.

and the refusal with which it was met should be communicated to the Ambassadors and the newspapers." Bismarck, who happened to have Moltke and Roon with him, was convinced that it was in the interests of Prussia to precipitate hostilities. And he summed up what had taken place at Ems as he thought fit. " The news of the renunciation of the Crown Prince of Hohenzollern has been officially communicated to the Imperial French Government by the Royal Government of Spain. Since then the French Ambassador has addressed to His Majesty the King at Ems a request to authorise him to telegraph to Paris that His Majesty the King undertakes for ever and a day not to allow the candidature to be revived. Whereupon, His Majesty the King refused to receive the Ambassador again, and informed him through his aide-de-camp that he had nothing further to communicate to him." And Bismarck observed that in Paris this statement " would be like a red rag to the Gallic bull." Had he " falsified " Abeken's telegram? The telegram had never been made public and he was at liberty to give whatever form he wished to his *communiqué*. But at all events this *communiqué* was misleading to the point of mendacity, and gave the impression that the King had not seen Benedetti and had curtly refused to grant him an audience, meeting the French demand for guarantees with an insult.

On that same 13th of July, while Benedetti was having his meeting with the King in the park at Ems, the Cabinet was sitting at St. Cloud. They were informed of the decisions of the previous evening, which had been reached without their knowledge. Some of the members, including Parieu, were astonished and filled with anxiety. If Bismarck wanted war he had been provided with the best possible pretext by the demand for guarantees for the future. The majority, however, approved of the instructions that had been sent to Benedetti, but, at the same time, it was decided to postpone the calling up of the Reservists which Lebœuf was demanding. And as the English Government was exhorting the French Government to be reasonable it was decided, whatever might be the result of Benedetti's demands, to regard the incident as closed.

But matters had already gone beyond control and Paris was still a prey to war fever. In the Legislative Body Jérôme

384

David wanted to interpellate the Cabinet regarding the "ridiculous dragging out of the negotiations with Prussia" and
"the attacks on the dignity of the nation." And
Excitement Lebœuf plumed himself on having stolen a march on
in Paris. Prussia, declaring that he would never have such a
fine opportunity again. The effect that the incident of Ems,
and above all Bismarck's *communiqué*, would produce in such
an atmosphere may well be imagined. On the 14th the Council
received news from Benedetti and held anxious consultations.
One of the Ministers, taking the Emperor aside, brutally informed
him that for the Empire defeat meant revolution. Lebœuf
reported preparations on the part of Prussia—the recall of
members of the *Landwehr* from abroad, and the purchase of
horses, and at last obtained permission to call up the Reservists.
Nevertheless, Gramont, who seemed to be recoiling from the
conflagration which he himself had started and which was
already smouldering, put forward the idea of a European Congress to confirm the principle that no royal representative of a
Great Power should be allowed to accept a foreign throne
without the consent of Europe. Ollivier drew up a message to
the Palais Bourbon to this effect. It was then six o'clock in
the evening. The Emperor returned to St. Cloud, where the
Empress criticised the idea of a Congress and of assuming an
attitude of moderation, declaring that the country was in favour
of war. Whereupon the Emperor summoned another council
to meet that same evening at St. Cloud. Meanwhile Gramont,
at the Quai d'Orsay, was informed by his agent in Switzerland
of the gist of Bismarck's *communiqué*, and he immediately
rushed to Ollivier. "Prussia has just given France a slap in
the face; I shall resign my portfolio rather than submit to such
an outrage!" The "red rag" had produced its effect. At
the council meeting at St. Cloud in the evening, Gramont gave
way to violent abuse of Prussia, and the Empress herself intervened, conjuring the Council to decide in favour of war. The
idea of a Congress was abandoned, and it was decided to
announce the declaration of war in the Palais Bourbon on the
following day.

On the 15th of July Ollivier attended the Legislative Body
and read out the declaration which that very morning had been

c c

approved by the Council at St. Cloud. "Our surprise was intense when yesterday we learnt that the King of Prussia had informed our Ambassador through an aide-de-camp that he would not receive him again, and that, to make his refusal perfectly plain, his Government had officially communicated it to the Cabinets of Europe. . . . (Cries of shame!) To make any further efforts towards conciliation would have amounted to imprudence and a surrender of dignity. We have left no stone unturned to avoid war; and we will prepare to meet the conflict that is thrust upon us, leaving to every man the share of responsibility that comes home to him. (Cries of *Vive l'Empereur!*)"

Thiers then asked to be heard, and in the face of insults from the Right, made a vain appeal to reason and calm judgment.

Thiers' Appeal for Peace. At heart he was in favour of war; but although he was awaiting an opportunity for avenging Sadowa and regarded conflict with Prussia as inevitable, he was of opinion that the moment was inopportune, that it would be better to wait, and not break off relations on a matter of pride, and give Europe time to intervene : "Is it or is not true," he asked, "that since your demand with regard to the Hohenzollern candidature has been fully satisfied, you are breaking off relations on a matter of wounded susceptibilities? Do you wish people to say, do you wish all Europe to say, that though fundamentals were conceded, for a mere question of form you determined to shed torrents of blood?" There were cries of dissent from the Right. "You are the anti-patriotic trumpet of disaster!" In vain, supported by Favre and Buffet, did he demand to see the telegrams which had led to the declaration of war, for his part declining all responsibility for a conflict for which there was so little justification. "From this moment," retorted Ollivier, won over to the idea of war, "we are saddled with a heavy responsibility which we accept with a light heart." As there were cries of protest he added : "I mean with a confident heart which is not weighed down by remorse, for . . . our cause is just and is confided to the care of the French army." A futile explanation. Ollivier remained the "light-hearted" man, and this appellation, even more than the fall of the Empire, was responsible for the irrevocable termination of his political career.

DISASTER

In the meantime Gramont arrived in the Senate and referred to the refusal to receive Benedetti : " It is an insult to the Emperor," he declared, " and an insult to France. And if, by some inconceivable chance, there exists in this country any Chamber ready to defend or support it, I refuse to remain Minister for Foreign Affairs five minutes longer ! " The Chamber refused to insist upon the telegrams being made public, and the Commission which was sitting heard the words " We are ready ! " dinned into their ears in season and out of season by Lebœuf, who also assured them that France was better prepared than Prussia, while Ollivier slipped away.

Gramont had to be fetched and cross-questioned. " Did you always make the same demand—that you wanted to know that **Gramont** the renunciation had been approved and guaranteed **Cross-** by the King ? " Gramont did not deny it : " In **Questioned.** his eyes the two points were identical " (P. de la Gorce). He referred to the incident of Bismarck's *communiqué*, of which, by the way, he had not got the text. And when mention was made to him of alliances he replied pompously : " If I kept you waiting just now it was because I was engaged in conversation with the Austrian Ambassador and the Italian Minister. I hope you will not press me further." The Commission expressed its approval of the Minister, quoting a telegram from Ems which contained inaccuracies and was wrongly dated. Meanwhile the people were singing the *Marseillaise* at the tops of their voices on the brilliantly lighted boulevards and shouting " To Berlin ! Down with Prussia ! " The Chamber held a night sitting and listened to the report of the Commission which was presented by the worthy Talhouët, one of the deputies who that very morning had voted for demanding the publication of **Gambetta's** the telegrams, and had succeeded in inspiring con- **Speech.** fidence. " To-day," declared Gambetta, who made a speech, " we have one and all abandoned the calm composure and measured judgment with which resolutions of such magnitude should be made. . . . You can count upon the sympathy of Europe and the support of France only if the explanations you have to offer prove that you have really been subjected to outrageous insult. . . . But your Ambassador has sent no sign of protest, no indignant telegram ; he has not been

387

of opinion that the situation demanded the return of his papers. . . ." Nevertheless, the Chamber followed the findings of the Commission; it voted the supplies for which it was asked and authorised the calling up of the *Garde Mobile* and the enlistment of volunteers.

Gambetta, in his speech, had given a correct definition of the war, which he declared would " settle the question as to whether the French or the German race was to gain the upper hand." And it was indeed the inevitable conflict foreseen ever since 1866 between an arrogant Government which considered itself the leader of Europe, and a young upstart nation which also had pretensions to hegemony—two village cocks who, after having menaced and provoked each other for a long time, ended up in a good scuffle to settle which was to be master. Nobody could pull them apart. In vain did England offer mediation, calling to mind a wish expressed by the Paris Congress in 1856 to the effect that " States between whom serious differences had arisen should before rushing to arms have recourse to the good offices of a friendly Power." On the 19th France declared war against Prussia.

War declared.

The French army, " the Rhine army," in which the whole country had absolute confidence, consisted, in addition to the Guard commanded by Bourbaki, of seven Army Corps under the command of MacMahon, Frossard, Bazaine, Ladmirault, Failly, Canrobert and Félix Douay. The Emperor himself was to direct operations, with Lebœuf as his Chief of the General Staff. A Bonaparte owed it to the name he bore to take command in person, and in virtue of this tradition the old man, sick and worn out and with but little military science at his command, placed himself at the head of 250,000 men. The eight Army Corps, conveyed chiefly by train, took up their positions in Lorraine and Alsace from Thionville to Belfort. Were they going to attack and penetrate into Southern Germany or menace Mainz? The one thought obsessing the minds of Gramont and Lebœuf was ever to outstrip the enemy. Prussia was apprehensive of the French attack. " The French offensive may be expected at any

The French Army.

388

moment," said King William on the 19th of July. Vain fears! The French army was very far from being ready. It had been concentrated on the frontier before it had really been placed on a war footing; the Reservists, summoned to their depots, where they were equipped in leisurely fashion and often short of arms and accoutrements, were to join their units at the frontier. Thus some of them went from Dunkerque to Strassburg viâ Perpignan, while others from the north reached Alsace viâ Marseilles and Oran. It was estimated that the army of 190,000 on active service would be augmented by 160,000 Reservists. But by the end of July less than 40,000 had joined their units, and barely 50 per cent had joined before the 6th of August. Disorder reigned supreme; Generals were searching for their brigades, and there was a shortage of everything—doctors, nurses, wagons, horses, tents, mess-tins, camp kettles and saucepans. Many of the Reservists did not know how to use the *chassepot*. War material arrived at the station of Metz and was heaped up in inextricable confusion. How could an attack possibly be made before this disorder was cleared away? And would it be sufficient, as had been the case in other wars, to muddle through somehow?

Disorder.

It was only on the 28th of July that the Emperor, in General's uniform, accompanied by the young Prince Imperial in the uniform of a second lieutenant of the Grenadiers, left St. Cloud to join the army. He was sad, dejected and downcast. Two days before, together with his family, he had received the Communion from the hands of Monseigneur Darboy, Archbishop of Paris, like a man who was marching to his death. Alarmed by the disorder among the troops and the isolation of his country, he was at one moment overcome by an access of panic and meditated treating with William at all costs. He got into the carriage at the station reserved for him at the end of the park, and when the Empress had made the sign of the cross on the forehead of the little Prince, the train steamed in the direction of the front, avoiding Paris. Metz was reached that evening, and a council of war was held at the prefecture. The days passed by. Journalists and spies had free entry to headquarters at the Hôtel de l'Europe, they all knew how the troops were being distributed and made

Departure of the Emperor.

public the information.   At last, in order to show some signs
of activity and risk a thrust at the enemy, Frossard made a
sudden attack on the 2nd of August against Sarre-
Sarrebruck. bruck, or rather on the hills which, to the south of
the town, separate the Sarre from the frontier.   The troops
occupied them without suffering much loss, but they did not
even trouble to cut the bridges in the town or to destroy the
station and the telegraph lines.   The *communiqué* extolled the
machine guns and the courage of the Emperor and the Prince
Imperial.   But that same evening the Emperor had a bad
attack of nephritis.   The affair of the 2nd of August was mere
play for princes.   The real war was to begin two days later,
when the sixteen German Army Corps, amounting to 500,000
men, had reached the spot and were ready to attack an enemy
inferior to them in point of numbers by over 50 per cent.

On the 4th of August, at Wissembourg on the Lauter, on the
northern frontier of Alsace, 6,000 men under Abel Douay, one
of MacMahon's divisional commanders, were surprised
Wissem- by 30,000 Prussians.   At one moment the bridges
bourg. across the Lauter were held by Turcos and infantrymen.   But the German artillery silenced the French guns and set
fire to the town.   Douay was killed, and in face of a threat of
being outflanked on the south, the French troops were obliged to
beat a retreat, after having desperately defended the station of
Wissembourg.   The order to fall back reached the defenders of
the town too late and they were captured.   On the hills to the
south, Pellé, who had taken Douay's place, was in the end
outflanked and the Prussians advanced into the hop-fields surrounding the Castle of Geisberg, where Cécile, who was in
command, organised the defence.   But the castle fell under the
fire of the Prussian guns, though, thanks to the resistance it
offered, the rest of the division was able to escape.   The French
had 1,200 killed or wounded and 800 taken prisoner, while the
enemy lost 1,500 men.   It was merely an advanced guard
action, but, as P. de la Gorce points out, it was a picture in
miniature of what the war was going to be.

On the following day MacMahon took up his position with
40,000 men at Froeschwiller, facing east, about nine miles south
east of Wissembourg, behind the Sauer and the village of Wörth,

on flat ground covered with vines, orchards and woods, and intersected by hedges and ravines, the last spurs of the Basses-Vosges abutting on to the Alsatian plain, a district that had long been known as a good defensive position. He succeeded in having Failly put under his command and urged him to join him. But Failly, on the pretext of keeping his front intact, sent only one division. In face of the advancing hosts of Germans, Ducrot, one of MacMahon's divisional commanders, wanted to retreat. But the outposts on the Sauer worried them all through the night of the 5th to the 6th, and on the morning of the 6th a reconnoitring in force on the part of the enemy in the direction of Wörth, launched at the instigation of one of the German Generals, developed into a battle. On the left wing, to the north of Froeschwiller, Ducrot arrested the advance of the Bavarians. In the centre, a Prussian Staff Colonel, who had been sent forward to the outposts, took it upon himself to engage a whole corps : 180 German guns prepared the attack, and the Prussians crossed the Sauer at Wörth, but were unable to debouch, the fire from Raoult's division obliging them to remain at the foot of the slopes. Whereupon a Prussian corps commander, disregarding the order he had just received from the General of the army not to accept battle, summoned two neighbouring corps to his help. One of them attacked the French right to the south of Froeschwiller; their artillery swept the wooded slopes of the Niederwald and the village of Morsbronn, and by the afternoon 75,000 men were engaged against MacMahon's 40,000. On the right Lartigue's division at first held its ground, but was eventually forced to evacuate Morsbronn. Lartigue had at his disposal Michel's brigade of cuirassiers and some lancers. In desperation he hurled them on Morsbronn. And the cuirassiers and lancers, in two successive waves, charged through the vineyards, the orchards and the hop-fields, and riddled by Prussian bullets hurled themselves into the one street of Morsbronn, where they fell before a barricade or were shot from the windows and roofs of the houses. The bullets rattled on the cuirasses like hail on panes of glass. In a few minutes the nine squadrons had lost 800 men, two-thirds of their number. This charge of the cuirassiers

Froeschwiller.

at Morsbronn (incorrectly called the charge of Reichshoffen, a neighbouring village) was a useless sacrifice. The Zouaves, after having defended the Niederwald inch by inch, entered Morsbronn and Froeschwiller, but were obliged to retreat.

In the centre, the Prussians won some ground before Wörth. Three French counter-attacks, at first successful, eventually failed under the fire of the Prussian guns; Generals and Colonels were killed. The little hamlet of Elsasshausen, between Froeschwiller and the Niederwald, where MacMahon had taken up his position and was watching the battle, was bombarded and threatened with capture, and MacMahon had Colson, his Chief of Staff, and Vogué, his aide-de-camp, killed by his side. He was obliged to retreat. The Prussians captured Elsasshausen together with five guns. To cover his retreat, MacMahon ordered General Bonnemains' cuirassiers to charge, but they failed to hold up the enemy. The Turcos, however, who had fought two days before at Wissembourg, made a bayonet charge, led by their Colonel with drawn sword, and recaptured Elsasshausen from the enemy, who fell a prey to panic. In the end the Prussians rallied, regained the positions they had lost, putting between 600 to 800 sharpshooters out of action during the engagement. Froeschwiller was bombarded by 84 pieces of artillery, and Raoult was killed. The village was captured. The rest of the French troops retreated in disorder to Reichshoffen, under the protection of the Zouaves. It was at this moment that the division sent up by Failly arrived—too late to take part in the action. During the day the French had lost half their forces—11,000 men killed and wounded and 9,000 prisoners. The Germans had lost 10,000 men. Alsace was invaded, and three days later the siege of Strassburg began.

On the same day the French suffered another reverse in Lorraine. Frossard had left the immediate neighbourhood of Sarrebruck, where he held a salient, and had taken up a position two or three miles south, facing north, his right resting on the wooded hills round Spicheren, his left in the Stiring ravine, through which the road and the railway from Sarrebruck to Metz passed. It was a position of which Frossard had made a special study and which he regarded as impregnable. He himself was in the ravine slightly to the rear, at Forbach. He had

DISASTER

28,000 men and thought he could count on the corps under Bazaine, who had been put in command of the Lorraine army.

Forbach. On the 6th a Prussian divisional commander of the advanced guard opened battle. After an artillery duel, the enemy attacked and tried to outflank the French, but experienced great difficulty in advancing. Two frontal attacks failed. At this juncture Frossard had the superiority in numbers, but he failed to exploit his advantage in order to attack and overcome the enemy and drive them back on the Sarre. He was a sapper General and did not possess the vision and determination of the tactician. As for Bazaine, owing to his ambiguous orders, he failed to send up in time the reinforcements for which Frossard asked him. Meanwhile German reinforcements had arrived, and in the end 30,000 men were put in the field. These fresh troops advanced in the environment of Stiring and in the woods north of Spicheren. The French counter-attacks were unsuccessful; Generals and Colonels were killed, among them one divisional commander. Laveaucoupet fought sword in hand. A vigorous French counter-attack freed Stiring and recaptured five guns. But the German artillery destroyed the French positions, and the enemy took the Forbacher Berg between Stiring and Spicheren and again menaced Stiring. In vain did Frossard beg for help from Bazaine. In the evening a Prussian division, marching to the sound of the guns, arrived on his left wing and threatened to turn it. A handful of men stopped it and allowed the rest of the troops to retire from the fight without being pursued by the enemy. The French had lost 2,000 killed and wounded and 2,000 prisoners; the enemy had 4,000 killed and wounded. Three of Bazaine's divisions arrived at night, when all was over. And it was necessary to fall back on Metz. Fortunately the enemy, who in spite of their successes still lacked self-confidence, followed up half-heartedly.

What was to be done? At one moment a counter-attack was meditated, and during the night of the 6th–7th a train stood ready waiting in Metz station to convey the Emperor, who actually got into it. Then at four o'clock in the morning this ambitious plan was abandoned, and far from advancing it was suggested that Metz should be abandoned and a retreat made in the direction of Châlons in order to escape from the grip of the enemy. But how could Lorraine be abandoned in this way? There was another change of plan. One day it was decided to remain in Metz; on the next to defend Frouard in front of Nancy, and on the day after to defend the outposts of Metz on the Nied to the east of the town. At all events an attempt was made to persuade the Emperor that it would be better for him to leave the army and return to Paris. He did not dare to do so. But he handed over the whole of the Lorraine army to Bazaine, who was very popular at the time, especially in Paris among the Opposition. And Bazaine ordered the army to retreat to the shelter of the Metz forts. Eventually, in conformity with the express desire of the Empress, telegraphed from Paris, Lebœuf sent in his resignation and Bazaine became Commander-in-Chief (12th of August).

The idea was now revived of a retreat in the direction of Châlons and Paris. The enemy was obviously manœuvring to cut off Metz on the south, to cross the Moselle above the town and take up a position to the west of the fortress in order to bar the way to the French. It was imperative at all costs to save the army from being besieged and put out of action and thus rendered incapable of defending Paris. But Bazaine, wavering and undecided, immersed in detail, and still dreaming of an offensive or a retirement on Frouard, found it difficult to reconcile himself to the idea of this retreat, and lost time. And his ill-temper towards Jarras, whom he had had forced upon him as Chief of Staff, was not calculated to advance matters. He even omitted to have the bridges over the Moselle, south of Metz, blown up.

On the 14th the Emperor left Metz in a carriage, accompanied by his Cent Gardes. In his rear the army was breaking up, and in the midst of incredible confusion he drove through the town, crossed the bridges over the Seille and the Moselle and departed in the direction of Verdun. Late in the afternoon the guns boomed out to the east of the town; and the enemy attacked and took the village of Colombey. Were the French going to fall back without retaliating, and allow the Prussians to reach the forts which bristled on the heights and barred their path? The soldiers, however, tired of retreating, suddenly

394

DISASTER

turned round and faced the enemy before the village of Borny. Bazaine was annoyed, but in the end accepted battle, though he gave orders that matters were not to be carried to extreme lengths—a half-measure which could not fail to hamper the action of the army without allowing of complete victory. There was furious fighting to the north of Borny and in the hamlet of Bellecroix, and Decaen, who had succeeded Bazaine in command of the 3rd corps, was killed. Bazaine himself was slightly wounded. It was traditional for the Commander-in-Chief to be in the thick of the fight. A sunken road in the neighbourhood, to the south of Bellecroix, was destined from that day forward to bear the name of *l'Allée des Morts*. Further north, Grenier's division of Ladmirault's corps held the wood and the village of Mey for a long time, lost it and captured it again. At last night fell. The French had lost 3,600 men, the enemy 5,000. Both sides claimed the victory. The French congratulated each other. "You have broken the spell," the Emperor observed to Bazaine. Meanwhile the Prussian bands were playing behind the camp fires. The French, it is true, had held their positions. But what was the use, since they voluntarily evacuated them shortly afterwards to return to Metz? And precious time had been lost for the retreat.

On the 15th the retreat continued slowly westward of Metz; at certain points inextricable confusion prevailed. Meanwhile the German army hastened to cross the Moselle to the south of the fortress and to continue in a northerly direction in order to cut off the road to Verdun. The Emperor was still with the troops, at Gravelotte, hesitating as to whether he should leave the army. It was the 15th of August, the imperial fête day, and he was presented with flowers. . . . Tragic hours! His one thought now was to avoid a serious defeat which would prevent the alliances with Italy and Austria of which he was still dreaming. At last, on the morning of the 11th, he took his departure in the direction of Conflans and Etain; and from the latter place the Prince Imperial telegraphed to his mother : "Everything is going better and better." It was open to Bazaine to take the initiative in the fight and launch the attack, and possibly surprise the enemy on the march. But he waited; he

(Borny.)

waited until his corps had finished crossing Metz. And it was
the enemy who took the French troops by surprise when they
were resting, the men drinking their soup and the horses being
watered.

The battle of the 16th took place on the high-road running
east and west from Metz to Verdun viâ Gravelotte, Rezonville,
Vionville and Mars-la-Tour. The enemy came from
Rezonville. the south-west and south of the Moselle, which they
had just crossed, and advanced up the ravines which wound
between wooded hills towards the north and ended in the
plateau across which the high-road ran. At first there was a
panic in Vionville. In those days the wagons were driven by
civilians. Under the hail of shells these drivers took fright and
fled for their lives, spreading disorder among the neighbouring
troops under Frossard, who fell back, but afterwards recovered
and reoccupied Vionville. The enemy then made an unsuccessful attack with another corps in the wooded region south of
Rezonville. But Bazaine allowed the opportunity for a counter-
attack to slip. The French fought with spirit but showed a
lack of initiative, making no attempt to impose their will or
any particular plan of battle upon the enemy. German reinforcements came up, the Prussian artillery opened fire, and
then the infantry attacked. To the east, that is to say, due
south of Rezonville, they came up against Jollivet's and Lapasset's brigades, and were unable to advance or debouch from
the woods. To the west they captured Vionville from Bataille's
division, but, under the fire of the French guns and of Canrobert's
corps north of the road, were unable to advance in the direction
of Rezonville. To the south-east, however, the enemy made a
rapid advance as far as the hamlet of Flavigny, occupied it, lost
it, set it on fire with their guns and reoccupied it. Rezonville
was menaced. Lapasset's lancers and the cuirassiers of the
guard under General de Preuil charged in turn, waving their
swords and shouting " *Vive l'Empereur!* " and hurled themselves
on the enemy, who had formed square. But they were obliged
to fall back on their own lines with the German hussars hard
on their heels. The latter reached a French battery whose
position one of the Generals was examining. The latter, drawing
his sword, galloped up to a Prussian officer, some French troops

396

rushed forward and the enemy fled : " Fortune favoured the Prussians up to the end, so that Bazaine was saved for the army and for France " (P. de la Gorce). For this General, who in the thick of the fight was acting the part of an artillery captain, was none other than the Commander-in-Chief. P. de la Gorce is severe, but his dictum is perhaps justified. *Perhaps*— for it is by no means certain that any other man would have done better than Bazaine !

The Prussian Hussars again charged from Flavigny in the direction of Rezonville, but came up against the Guards, who put them to flight. At the same time German cuirassiers and Uhlans debouched from the north of the high-road and cut through the front lines of Canrobert's corps. But they pulled themselves together, and Prince Murat's dragoons, Valabrègue's chasseurs and Gramont's curaissiers charged in their turn against Pierrot Wood north of Rezonville and decimated the cavalry of the enemy, who afterwards called this episode the Ride of Death. But meanwhile Bazaine did not attack ! He kept his troops in reserve in the direction of Gravelotte, obviously afraid of being cut off from Metz, and, ever undecided, still hesitated between a definite movement in the direction of Châlons and a retreat to the shelter of the fortress walls.

It was at this juncture that on the extreme right of the French Ladmirault came up, having advanced under gun-fire with his 4th corps. He overwhelmed the enemy's left, captured Tronville Wood, to the north of the high-road, and entered Mars-la-Tour and Vionville. His cavalry also reached Mars-la-Tour. He did not dare to push further, but waited for one of his divisions under Cissey, which was late. Enemy reinforcements were now arriving and Ladmirault fell back from Tronville Wood and occupied the northern slopes of a ravine known as the Fond de la Cuve, running east and west. Here Cissey at last joined him, surprising and crushing the Westphalians, who were advancing up the ravine, and taking 400 prisoners. But again the French allowed this opportunity of making a counter-attack to slip through their fingers. In vain on their extreme right, to the north of Mars-la-Tour, did General du Barail's African chasseurs charge the German artillery. In vain did Legrand's hussars and dragoons rush upon the enemy's cavalry

with drawn swords. Legrand was killed, and after a terrible
encounter the French cavalry fell back towards their lines,
without, however, being pursued by the enemy. Meanwhile
the sun was setting, and furious fighting was resumed round
Rezonville, which the enemy, in spite of all their efforts and
cavalry charges, were unable to reach. The French lost, retook,
lost again and once more retook the farm known as the Maison
Blanche. Night fell at last and put an end to this battle of
Rezonville, in which 140,000 Frenchman fought 90,000 Germans,
but where their leaders exploited their forces so badly that
they were only just able to hold their own without taking the
initiative which would have given them the victory and opened
the road to Verdun. The French had lost 13,700 men and the
Germans 15,000. Each side claimed the victory. But during
the night Bazaine gave orders for the army to fall back on
Metz owing to shortage of food and munitions. As a matter
of fact the shortage was not sufficiently acute to necessitate
such an order, and at the same time it amounted to confessing
that Rezonville had been a defeat, since the French had been
obliged to give way to the enemy's plan of campaign and had
allowed themselves to be surrounded. Although inferior in
numbers, the Germans had been so eager to take the offensive
and had fought with such zest that in the end they had carried
the day.

On the 17th the various French corps fell back, with the
German army close on their heels. On the morning of the
18th the French found themselves occupying a position facing
west, that is to say, facing France, with their backs to Metz,
on a series of hills and plateaux, which, as a matter of fact,
constituted a very strong situation. Spreading out north and
south was Frossard's 2nd corps, at Rozérieulles, spanning the
Metz–Verdun road, and facing Gravelotte; the 3rd corps under
Lebœuf was resting on large farms scattered over the plateau;
the 4th under Ladmirault took up positions round the village
of Amanvillers and the railway that was being built between
St. Privat. Metz and Verdun; whilst the 6th, under Canrobert, was on the right wing, near the village of
St. Privat-la-Montaigne. Bazaine had kept the guards in
reserve, but on the extreme left, a long way from St. Privat

398

DISASTER

and the vulnerable point where the enemy intended to make an attempt to break through, and where the 6th corps, which had only just arrived from Châlons, was short of artillery and sappers. In the face of this passive motionless army the Germans quietly carried out their manœuvres; 150,000 men marched in a northerly direction in order to wheel round and face east, and the French allowed them to do so. Meanwhile Bazaine was discussing questions of promotion!

The battle did not open till midday. The enemy attacked the 4th corps, and once again it was on the sole initiative of the General of a Prussian corps that fighting started in the centre. But the attack failed owing to the fact that the *chasse-pots* had a longer range than the German rifles and that the Prussian batteries were decimated by the machine guns. The French took two guns by means of a bold sally. But they did not attack, and reinforcements reached the enemy, who advanced close up to the railway. At the same time, on the French left, the enemy, disregarding orders from headquarters, attacked Frossard and Lebœuf. Several of its attacks failed at Moscou Farm. General Molière held out for a long time at St. Hubert Farm, on the Gravelotte road, and fell back only when the farm was set on fire by the shells and the enemy was gaining the upper hand in all directions. But the Germans were unable to push forward any further or debouch from the Mance ravine running north and south, where they were clinging to the eastern slopes. They hurled themselves on the French trenches, and artillery, cavalry and infantry were decimated. The French left held firm.

But on the right the enemy made a vigorous effort with the object of overwhelming the French and outflanking them at this point. Eighty-eight guns bombarded Ste. Marie-aux-Chênes, an outpost to the west of St. Privat. Prussian Guards and Saxon troops attacked, and, overcoming the French by sheer weight of numbers, captured Ste. Marie. Canrobert, who felt he was being overwhelmed—he was fighting two to one against him—asked for reinforcements from Bazaine. In vain! Bazaine, who had eyes only for the left, kept back his reserves, and himself laid some guns on his extreme left. The Prussian Guard attacked from Amanvillers to St. Privat. The French bullets ricochetted on the hard ground and caused many casualties. But the enemy was unable to make any advance on the open glacis formed by the plateau. The officers fell, and whole companies and battalions melted away under the French fire. If only there had been reserves present to counter-attack and scatter the enemy! But Bourbaki, with the Guards, had received no orders, and remained behind Amanvillers and St. Privat.

It was the decisive moment of the battle, and possibly it was during this short space of time that the war was lost. Fresh reinforcements came up for the enemy. Night was falling. Canrobert was still holding out at St. Privat, going into the front line himself to encourage his men. Eventually 84 German guns were laid at about 1,200 yards from the village, which could no longer be held, and the Saxons and the Prussian Guard hurled themselves forward in a desperate effort and reached the houses. There was bayonet fighting round the church and the cemetery, and the French, overwhelmed, fell back inch by inch. The colours—for in those days the colours were carried in the front line and were not relegated to the rear with the wagons, as was the case in the last war—the colours changed hands five times. Canrobert fell back slowly, still hoping that help would arrive, and marched in a south-easterly direction towards Metz. Ladmirault, whose right was thus exposed, had to fall back in his turn, and evacuated Amanvillers. During the night Lebœuf, who was also exposed, and Frossard were obliged to retire beneath the shelter of the Metz **Metz blockaded.** forts. It was all over! The French army was now blockaded. The battle of St. Privat, which cost the French 12,000 men, and the enemy 19,000, put the coping-stone on the defeat.

Meanwhile what was happening in Paris? On the 6th of August a great victory had been announced at the Bourse, a signal revenge for the reverse at Wissembourg. The **Events in Paris.** *Marseillaise* was sung, and the boulevards were decorated with flags. But, as a matter of fact, on that very day the French were defeated at Froeschwiller and Forbach. Late in the evening the Emperor informed the Empress of the fact. " A state of siege must be declared," he

400

added, "and preparations made for defending the capital." Thus, at the very first reverse, the Emperor took the gloomiest possible view. It was decided to summon all available forces to Paris, to call up the 1870 class, to organise the *Garde Mobile* and to convoke the Chambers. On Sunday, the 7th of August, a proclamation announcing the defeats was posted in Paris. The city was thunderstruck; it had complete faith in victory! Whereupon demonstrations were held; there were appeals for arms and a mass levy such as had been made in '93. On the 8th the deputies arrived in Paris and abused the Government and the Lebœufs, Gramonts and Olliviers who had promised success. A delegation went to the Empress and demanded their dismissal, suggesting that Trochu, who was out of office, should be summoned. He was popular because he had the reputation of being a Liberal and because he had criticised the organisation of the army. They also clamoured for Palikao, who was in command at Lyons and was the only well-known General who was not at the front. At the same time the Minister of the Interior, fearing that a popular movement would sweep away the already tottering *régime*, begged the Empress to summon the Emperor to Paris. She refused—a Napoleon owed it to himself to remain with the army on pain of dishonour. She was even told that the presence of the Emperor at Metz was hampering the command, and was almost convinced and was on the point of telegraphing, when the Privy Council in the end persuaded her to do nothing of the sort. On the 9th the mob held demonstrations on the Pont de la Concorde against Ollivier and also against the Emperor. But a command to maintain order prevented the demonstration from degenerating into a riot or possibly revolution. Meanwhile Favre demanded that the Chamber should appoint a Commission of fifteen of its members to repel the invasion, and that the Emperor should no longer be Commander-in-Chief. Cassagnac replied by threatening him with court-martial. But even Jérôme David, who belonged to the Right, came forward with the assertion that Prussia was ready and France was not. And Duvernois proposed a vote of censure against the Government, which was passed.

On the 10th of August, Palikao, who had been made Minister of

THE SECOND EMPIRE

War, formed a new Cabinet, " imperialistic " in sympathy, with Magne as Minister of Finance, La Tour d'Auvergne as Minister for Foreign Affairs, Jérôme David at the Public Works and Duvernois at the Ministry of Commerce. **Palikao.** The new Government stopped the leaks in the vessel of state as best it could.   Preparations were made for a siege; bachelors and childless widowers between the ages of twenty-five and thirty-five were called up, volunteers were encouraged to enlist, and the National Guard was reorganised in the departments, all men under forty being forced to join.   New divisions and provisional regiments were formed.   The ramparts and forts round Paris were armed, and new works were feverishly constructed, the sailors of the Navy being requisitioned to take a hand, and customs officials, park-keepers, gendarmes, municipal guards and police officers were all mobilised.   Duvernois collected corn and fodder in Paris, as well as cattle, which were put out to pasture in the Bois de Boulogne.   A loan of 1,000,000,000 francs (£40,000,000) was floated, and proved a success.   The issue of bank-notes was allowed to exceed the usual limits by making their acceptance obligatory,[1] and a moratorium was granted for the payment of commercial bills.   Germans resident in the capital were forced to leave and told to go south of the Loire. The masterpieces in the Louvre were sent to Brest, together with the Crown diamonds, some of the cash in the Bank of France and the standards in the Invalides.

Furthermore, steps had to be taken to secure order; for the first reverses naturally gave free rein to demonstrations against the Imperial *régime*, the only reason for whose exist- **Disturb-** ence was victory.   At Marseilles, on the 7th and **ances.** 8th of August, the mob broke into the Hôtel de Ville; in other places the gunsmiths' shops, seminaries and convents were pillaged, and at Lyons the Republic was proclaimed to shouts of " Down with the Empire ! ", and policemen were killed and wounded.   In Paris, on the 14th of August, the day on which the battle of Borny was fought, a body of rioters led by Eudes, a future member of the Commune, killed and wounded some firemen and officials at la Villette.   Above all it was imperative to retain the support of the Legislative Body, which was already

[1] See note on p. 6

402

DISASTER

wavering and perturbed and no longer had any confidence in the new Cabinet. Kératry demanded that a Commission of nine deputies should be appointed to assist the Council of Defence. The Government secured the rejection of this motion of lack of confidence, but placed Thiers on the Council.

Meanwhile Paris and the whole of France were living in a state of feverish excitement. Everybody was expecting news of victories, placing their faith in the " great Bazaine " and the popular hero Trochu, and talking of the massacre of the white German cuirassiers round Metz, of the slaughter of Prussian Princes and of their coffins draped in black silver-embroidered cloth. But the termini on the Chemin de Fer de l'Est gradually receded from the frontier, and thus the progress of the invasion became known. Belgian and English newspapers arrived confirming the bad news which the Government dared only to publish piecemeal. And how could this nation, which but a little while back had been so certain of victory, possibly admit the truth? They could only imagine that they had been betrayed. Lebœuf was a traitor; Frossard was a traitor, and Failly. They saw spies everywhere, and tourists, priests and nuns were arrested. . . . They demanded arms at the mairies. Inventors flocked to the Ministry of War or to Trochu offering murderous weapons and bullet-proof breastplates. Profiteering in arms, accoutrements and food was winked at, and, as always happens in similar circumstances, many contractors made their fortunes very quickly by selling the army bad jam and shoes with cardboard soles. Does not war afford an opportunity for every virtue?

At the same time attempts were still being made to secure the most improbable alliances. At the beginning of August, **Attempt to secure Alliances.** Austria, it is true, was meditating intervention with the support of Italy. But she did not wish to act hastily, and before binding herself waited to see the results of the first battles, more particularly as Russia was also menacing intervention—on the side of Prussia. Italy, for her part, insisted upon having Rome. Napoleon III and Gramont waxed indignant at this; for France it would amount to a breach of honour to give way to such a demand. Whereupon the French reverses at Froeschwiller and Forbach occurred,

THE SECOND EMPIRE

which were naturally but ill calculated to encourage whatever desire for intervention Vienna and Florence might have felt. On the 7th of August an appeal for help was sent to Victor Emmanuel from Paris. He replied that he was sincerely sorry for " the poor Emperor," but begged to be excused; with all the good-will in the world it was impossible for him to be of any practical assistance. Worse still, Florence, London and St. Petersburg came to an agreement on the principle of a league of neutrals—the countries not already engaged in the war agreed not to abandon their attitude of neutrality without exchanging views and consulting one another. France was indeed isolated and Europe formed a circle to watch the conflict.

Nevertheless, after St. Privat, the Emperor made one last attempt. On the 19th, at Châlons, he ordered Prince Napoleon to go to Florence and see the King of Italy, his father-in-law, and persuade him to act ! At one moment the Prince thought he had succeeded and asked Trochu whether the Italians were to march on Belfort or on Munich. But suddenly all his hopes vanished in smoke; in Florence everybody avoided him as though he were an importunate creditor. At this juncture, however, Alexander II, who had at first adopted a violently pro-Prussian attitude towards Fleury the French Ambassador, seemed to be perturbed by the first Prussian successes and meditated a *rapprochement* with Austria and France or an offer of mediation. But it all came to nothing.

Meanwhile Trochu was put in command of a corps that was being organised at the Châlons camp, where the remnants of
The Châlons Camp. MacMahon's corps had sought refuge after a difficult retreat from Froeschwiller, together with Failly's corps, which had remained inactive on the 6th of August between Froeschwiller and Forbach, and Félix Douay's corps, which had also been idle in the south of Alsace throughout the two battles. The Seine *Garde Mobile* was also there, raw untrained recruits. Men, horses and baggage were all heaped up in the greatest chaos and confusion. On the evening of the 16th " another remnant turned up " (P. de la Gorce)—the Emperor, retreating from the battle-field of Rezonville viâ Verdun, had found a dilapidated third-class carriage to convey him to Rheims. On the 17th a council of war was held. Prince

404

DISASTER

Napoleon, who was on the point of setting out for Florence, was of opinion that the Emperor should return to Paris under cover of Trochu's popularity : " God in Heaven ! if we must fall, let us fall like men ! " he exclaimed. The Emperor recognised that since he had left the army and was not with the Government it seemed as though he had abdicated. In the end he decided to return to Paris, and sent back Trochu ahead of him as Governor. The Châlons army, under MacMahon's command, also had to fall back on the capital viâ Rheims and Soissons.

But Paris refused to agree to this plan. The Empress, who had no feelings left for the old husband who had done nothing but betray her, had not a single thought beyond saving her son's throne. She wished to be made Regent, and was prepared to do anything to avoid the awkward presence of the Emperor; while Palikao was too jealous of Trochu to welcome his return. He was far too anxious to win the Marshal's baton not to wish to secure elbow-room for himself in Paris, that is to say, to keep the active army at a distance. The Empress and Palikao conspired together to persuade the Emperor to march on Metz and save Bazaine, a strategic plan which fell in with their ambitions. " No, the Emperor shall not return ! " was the reply given by the Empress to Trochu, hateful Liberal that he was ! As for Palikao, he protested and then countersigned the Emperor's decree appointing Trochu Governor, declaring in the Chamber that he himself had recalled him ! But the upshot was that Paris only succeeded in upsetting the decisions reached by MacMahon and the Emperor, and without anything having been settled, the army, in order to escape from the enemy's advance, left Châlons and fell back on Rheims on the 21st of August. In the evening, Rouher, who was President of the Senate, went to Rheims, where he saw the Emperor and MacMahon, but was unable to prevail upon them to march on Metz, where Bazaine was evidently blockaded, since no news had been received from him. On the 22nd, however, a messenger brought a telegram from Bazaine, who talked of making his escape to the north-west, viâ Montmédy, Sedan and Mézières. That clinched the matter, and MacMahon decided to go to meet him. He set out on the 23rd. In a later telegram Bazaine apparently expressed doubts about being able to march north without compromising the safety of the army; but this telegram, which might perhaps have made MacMahon change his plans and fall back on Paris, never reached its destination.

MacMahon had 120,000 men under him and 470 guns and machine guns : the 1st corps under Ducrot, which had been beaten at Froeschwiller and had been more or less reorganised at Châlons; the 5th corps under Failly, which had not been utilised on the 6th of August; the 7th corps under Félix Douay, which had come from Alsace, and a new corps under Lebrun; in addition there was the cavalry under Bonnemains and Margueritte. The plan was to join hands with Bazaine by marching towards Verdun and Montmédy, relying upon escaping the main German armies who were advancing on Paris. But in the dreary waste of Champagne it was discovered that there was a shortage of rations. And how were the soldiers to be fed on that desolate dry chalk plain, intersected by pine woods, which was almost a desert ? MacMahon turned north towards Rethel in order to obtain supplies. The march was continued extremely slowly in a north-easterly direction, hardly more than six miles a day being covered. Meanwhile the German army of 225,000 men and 800 guns, which was marching on Paris, suddenly changed its direction—cavalry reports and news published in the *Temps* and transmitted to London had enlightened Moltke on the 25th of August.

What was MacMahon going to do ? The Emperor was following him like a shadow without being able to give him the slightest assistance; white-headed, his hollow cheeks lined with suffering, he had suddenly become an old man. He said nothing, his eyes were dreamy, and as usual he was resigned to his fate. From time to time he was shaken by a sudden convulsion and tortured with pain. " Oh, if only I could die ! " he said one day to his aide-de-camp.

MacMahon followed Palikao's instructions, lost time, hesitated and allowed the opportunity of attacking the Germans while they were still divided to slip through his fingers. On the 27th, hearing that Bazaine had not left Metz, he decided to change the direction of his march and to retire in the direction of

Mézières, towards the north-east, to avoid being surrounded by the enemy. But Palikao in Paris did not see the matter in this light. An armchair strategist, his one thought was of the march on Metz and the junction with Bazaine. The Empress agreed with him; Bazaine, " the great Bazaine," must not be abandoned ! Above all the Emperor must be prevented from returning in the direction of the capital.

Trochu, Governor of Paris, was the only person who was anxious for the army to fall back on the capital. But he was suspected of being too Liberal and was regarded with mistrust. Had he not declared that he wished to rely only on " moral force " to govern Paris ? " Language that was unusual in the mouth of a soldier," observes P. de la Gorce. His advice was not accepted, and during the night of the 27th–28th Palikao charged MacMahon not to abandon Bazaine, for if he did " there would be revolution in Paris." MacMahon obeyed, and again changing his plans, marched towards the Meuse in spite of the Emperor's expostulations. Orders and counter-orders and everlasting confusion ! The enemy was already holding the road running directly east and west of Montmédy, being in possession of Stenay-sur-Meuse. It was necessary to find a bridge to the north, further down, at Mouzon, in order to get the army across and then march it in a south-easterly direction on the line Montmédy–Metz. Meanwhile a Staff-Captain, named Grouchy—an ill-omened name for the Napoleons—fell into the hands of the enemy, and Moltke, enlightened regarding MacMahon's plans, acted accordingly.

On the 30th of August the Germans, slipping through the woods, reached Beaumont-en-Argonne to the south of Mouzon. **Beaumont.** The 5th corps was encamped there in a hollow surrounded on three sides by hills, and had failed to protect themselves adequately. Suddenly at midday the German artillery opened fire and scattered confusion far and wide. The French pulled themselves together, but gradually retreated. In vain did Colonels and Generals allow themselves to be killed. The enemy took Beaumont and the French camps. To the north of Beaumont, on the heights over which the road to Mouzon ran, another fight took place and lasted throughout the afternoon. But the other corps were occupied in reaching

407

or crossing the Meuse, and nobody came to Failly's help. He fell back step by step on Mouzon, under the protection of a strong rearguard, the enemy pressing harder and harder on his heels. Near Mouzon, Coutenson's cuirassiers charged and hurled themselves on the German infantry. In the evening the remnants of the 5th corps were all huddled together in confusion under the fire of the German guns in the suburb leading to the bridge at Mouzon. A handful of men, under Failly himself, held the enemy at bay, and enabled the river to be crossed somehow or other. In the end they also prevented the Prussians from debouching from the bridge. During the night, 300 infantrymen who had been forgotten on the left bank and had been reformed by Lieutenant-Colonel Demange, reached the bridge and scaled the barricade under fire. Only 100 reached the French lines. The day's fighting at Beaumont had cost the French a total of 1,800 killed and wounded and 3,000 prisoners.

During the night of the 30th–31st of August, MacMahon, too hard pressed by the enemy, gave up the idea of reaching Carignan and Montmédy, stopped Ducrot, who was already escaping towards Mézières, and decided to concentrate his whole army to the north-west of Mouzon, at Sedan. This

Sedan. " stronghold," the work of Vauban, with its ramparts and fortress, gave a false impression, and the French army instinctively turned to it for refuge. But the town was dominated on all sides by hills. It is true that the valley of the Meuse is fairly broad; the river, running from south-east to north-west, shoots out its branches into the fields in front of the villages of Bazeilles and Balan lying below Sedan, as well as into the heart of the town itself. One of these branches forms a long curve below the town, encircling a sort of peninsula running north and south—the peninsula of Iges; indeed it is really an island, since the two ends of the curve are joined by a canal. The river resumes its course only further down in the direction of Donchery. But all the roads are commanded by the hills : the Donchery–Mézières road, on the left bank downstream by the wooded heights of la Marfée; the Mouzon road, on the left bank looking up-stream, was also enclosed between the spurs of the Argonne hills and the river; and conditions on the right bank were similar, where a road down-stream towards

408

DISASTER

Mézières and the Balan–Bazeilles road which rises up-stream in
the direction of Stenay, and the Carignan-Montmédy road, are
both overhung by the wooded crests of the Ardennes, while
about nine miles away runs the Belgian frontier.   In a word,
Sedan is situated in a passage through which a river makes its
devious way and through which the roads run at the foot of
the hills which line the passage.   Anyone in possession of these
hills would be master of the situation.   The enemy was aware
of this and started a movement for enveloping the town.   While
some of the corps crossed to the right bank of the Meuse and
manned the heights to the east of Sedan, others deployed to
the south and slipped in a westerly direction towards Donchery,
also to cross the river lower down, and cut off the French
retreat at the foot of the Ardennes.

On the morning of the 31st, General de Wimpffen arrived at
Sedan, on Palikao's orders, to take over command of the 5th
corps.   MacMahon received this new colleague, sent
Arrival of Wimpffen. to him from Paris without his having been consulted,
with but little enthusiasm.   And it was Wimpffen
himself who, on meeting Failly, informed him that he had
come to take his place.   Meanwhile the German menace
towards the west was becoming better defined and MacMahon
ordered the bridge at Donchery to be blown up.   Nevertheless,
both he and the Emperor still believed that they would have
time to escape towards Mézières by the road down-stream on
the right bank north of the peninsula of Iges.

Moreover, the telegrams from Paris conjured them to retreat
no further.   And the advisability of once more giving battle
was discussed.   MacMahon remained irresolute.   But the enveloping movement was still continuing.   To the south-east
the Bavarians arrived at the railway bridge at Bazeilles in
time to prevent the French sappers from blowing it up, and
even reached the houses of the village, from which they quickly
dislodged the French marine infantry, but eventually returned
to the bridge.   To the west, at the Donchery bridge, MacMahon's
orders could not be carried out;   a train brought up sappers
and material, but as soon as the sappers got out, the officials
on the train, probably beside themselves with terror, immediately
took the train back in the direction of Mézières, carrying the
409

THE SECOND EMPIRE

powder and instruments with it. The enemy lost no time in
occupying the bridge. Everything was now ready for having
the French army completely encircled on the next day; Lebrun
was on the south-east of Sedan between the Meuse and the
Givonne, Ducrot to the north-east of the town, on the Givonne,
and Douay to the north of Sedan in the direction of Floing.

At dawn on the 1st of September, the Bavarians under von
der Tann attacked Lebrun at Bazeilles—a diversion to the
south to allow the circle to be completed on the east and west.
But the enemy's advance was soon arrested; General Vassoigne's
marine infantry, assisted by his brigadiers Martin des Pallières
and Reboul, had barricaded the streets, crenellated the walls,
and above all organised strong resistance at the Villa Beurmann,
which stood at some cross-roads. Desperate street fighting
with firing at short range took place, and the inhabitants of
Bazeilles picked up the rifles of soldiers who had been killed
and joined in the conflict. The Bavarians were held up.

MacMahon rushed from Sedan to meet Lebrun, but at six
o'clock in the morning, to the north of Bazeilles, he was wounded
by a shell splinter and fainted. When he recovered conscious-
ness, he appointed Ducrot his successor, although he did not
stand first in order of seniority. He was a hot-tempered man,
full of fire and passion, but he knew what he wanted. " He
was a man," observes P. de la Gorce, " at a time when men
were scarce." Ducrot had a plan—to escape in a
north-westerly direction towards Mézières, which he
had wished to do two days before, and thus reach
the north of the peninsula of Iges before the enemy. It was
here that the road ran through a defile between the river and
the wooded heights of La Falizette. He gave his orders. His
staff officers remonstrated at such a shameful retreat. He told
them brutally to hold their tongues. Lebrun, proud of holding
his ground at Bazeilles, also refused to acquiesce tamely in this
plan of escape. Nevertheless, there was possibly yet time to
save the army. But just at this moment, Wimpffen, taking
from his pocket the letter of service given him in Paris appointing him Commander-in-Chief if it became necessary to replace
MacMahon, immediately revoked Ducrot's orders and gave
instructions for Lebrun to be supported at Bazeilles. A dis-
410

astrous change of plan in the middle of a battle! Ducrot, retiring into the background, nevertheless begged Wimpffen to continue the retreat through the exits that still remained open. " Listen ! " he implored. " For two months I have been face to face with the Prussians. I know them. Their aim is to surround us." All in vain ! How could this new Commander-in-Chief, who had arrived the night before, in the intoxication of supreme authority, dream of anything but victory? In his mind's eye he already saw the Bavarians repulsed at Bazeilles, the enemy hurled back into the Meuse and the way cleared to Carignan and Montmédy—to Bazaine. Had not Palikao said four days ago in Paris that he must at all costs rejoin the army at Metz? Fond illusion !

At Bazeilles desperate fighting continued. Bavarian reinforcements took the park surrounding the Château de Monvillers, to the north-east of the village. But in the village itself hand-to-hand fighting took place. The enemy, in order to be able to advance, set fire to the houses. Lacretelle's division, which consisted of raw recruits, came to the rescue together with the marine infantry, and at one moment made some progress. But in the end the Saxons and Bavarians captured the heights to the north of Bazeilles, where MacMahon was wounded, and the Bavarians, under cover of the guns, carried Bazeilles and the Villa Beurmann. At the end of the village, in the direction of Sedan, they came up against Bourgerie's house, where a handful of men, under the command of General Lambert, had entrenched themselves and held out under the German fire to " the last cartridge "—the episode remained famous under that name. It was midday, and the Bavarians completed the burning of the village of Bazeilles, which had resisted them for so long, shooting the civilians who had joined in the fight, and three French officers into the bargain. Altogether the Bavarians lost 2,000 men, and the marine infantry 2,600.

Bloody though this conflict had proved, it was not here that the battle was decided. While the slaughter was going on at Bazeilles, the Prussians, who had crossed the Meuse at Donchery, advanced northwards, to the west of the peninsula of Iges, and gained the defile of La Falizette. With its customary daring, the artillery rushed to the front and began to bombard Douay's corps encamped to the east of the peninsula of Iges, north of Sedan, near the village of Floing. Possibly a sudden attack on the part of the French at this juncture would have thrown the Prussian advanced guard into disorder and captured the pass. " The fleeting moment was not seized " (P. de la Gorce).

Gradually fresh German batteries came up and took their positions. They were accompanied by infantry, but it was the artillery that did all the work. At the same time, towards the east, the Saxons and the Prussian Guard advanced, threw Ducrot's troops into confusion and crossed the Givonne to the north above Bazeilles ; their artillery took up a position at Floing to the rear of the French, who were also exposed at this point to the shells from the south of the Meuse. Ducrot was the heart and soul of the resistance. The French artillery came up and took its position under enemy fire, and allowed themselves to be annihilated. Some of the infantry fell back; Douay rallied the fugitives, but in vain. The cavalry remained, and Ducrot asked General Margueritte to charge and open up the way for the infantry. Margueritte advanced to the north of the French positions, near the crucifix of Illy, in order to reconnoitre the ravine descending in a south-easterly direction towards Floing, where he was ordered to make his men charge. A bullet went right through his cheeks, cutting off his tongue. He rode back to face his men, leaning on his aide-de-camp, the blood running down over his tunic. He could not speak, but pointed to the enemy. " Forward ! " roared his men. " Probably we shall never see each other again," said General de Gallifet to his officers. " I bid you farewell ! " And so saying he gave the order to charge. African chasseurs, hussars, Gallifet's chasseurs, lancers, and Bonnemains' cuirassiers spread havoc among some of the enemy's detachments, but broke up under the Prussian fire or at the foot of the banks rising up from the ground, and came back. Ducrot asked Gallifet for yet another effort. " If all is lost, let it be for the honour of our arms ! " he implored. " Anything you wish, General, as long as I have a man left ! " replied Gallifet and went off again. Ducrot tried in vain to get the infantry to follow him. The second charge failed as the first had done. King William was

DISASTER

watching the episode from the slopes of la Marfée, south of
Sedan. " Ah, what gallant fellows ! " he exclaimed. When
Gallifet retired, having lost a third of his men, the enemy
ceased fire. The officers saluted, shouting " *Vive l'Empereur !* "
and the German officers returned the salute. It had required
this mad charge and this fruitless heroism on the part of an
arm which modern guns had rendered antiquated to provide a
spectacle worthy of the days of chivalry, one last memento of
the wars of other days.

This time it was the end; cavalry, infantry and gunners fell
back in disorder south of the crucifix of Illy, into the Garenne
wood. Soon the German artillery was sweeping the
The End. wood itself, and then the Prussian Guard advanced;
and the fugitives descended towards Sedan under the fire of
400 guns. It was three o'clock in the afternoon.

During the morning the Emperor, who was already done for,
had been wandering between Sedan and Bazeilles. Then he
had returned to the sub-prefecture at Sedan. At one o'clock,
in despair, he ordered the white flag to be hoisted on the fortress;
but the battle continued nevertheless, and the flag was lowered.
At this moment, Wimpffen, who could not resign himself to the
inevitable, informed him that he wanted " to force the line "
on the east, and asked him to join his troops. The Emperor
refused this offer, which was doomed to failure, and again had
the white flag hoisted. Nevertheless, Wimpffen, with a handful
of men, attacked the Bavarians in the direction of Balan–
Bazeilles. But he was unable to advance very far. Meanwhile
Sedan, which was being bombarded, filled up with fugitives,
horses, wagons and guns. Douay, Ducrot and Lebrun made
their way with difficulty through the chaos and disorder, and
as they passed by, some of the soldiers shook their fists at them
calling them " Traitors ! " the insult always hurled at superiors
in defeat. The leaders returned to the Emperor. Ducrot was
still dreaming of a sortie during the night. And who was
responsible for the rumour that Bazaine's army had arrived ?
But shells were bursting in the courtyard of the sub-prefecture.
" The firing must be stopped at all costs ! " exclaimed the
Emperor. The old man, sick and ill, was perhaps frightened,
as was only natural; but in addition the humanitarian was

413

That same evening Palikao received distressing news from General Vinoy in Mézières—MacMahon had been wounded and the army was surrounded. On the following day a telegram from London mentioned a success on the part of Bazaine, who was marching on Sedan. But in the evening Jérôme David, one of the Ministers, received from a trustworthy friend in Brussels a telegram in cipher which allowed of no further doubt : " Great disaster, MacMahon killed, the Emperor a prisoner ! " David informed the Empress and Thiers, and begged the latter to take action. " You can still render invaluable services to the country ! " he declared. But Thiers refused. " It is too late ; where shall we be in a week's time ? " On the 3rd of September telegrams and travellers arrived from Brussels and made known the full extent of the disaster. Mérimée, the Empress's old friend, who was already ill—in a month's time he was dead—went to Thiers and begged him to take up the reins of power. Other messages from the Court followed—but in vain ! The aged Thiers held back, doubtless feeling, with the instinct of a statesman, that the country was on the brink of revolution, and that he had not the strength to prevent it.

In the Legislative Body that afternoon, after Palikao had announced the news of the French reverses with the omissions natural to an unfortunate man overcome by events, Jules Favre demanded that the power should be placed in the hands of a soldier ; he had Trochu in mind. In the Tuileries, the Cabinet was deliberating, but decided nothing, except the official proclamation of the disastrous news and the summoning of the Legislative Body to meet the next day at twelve noon. Schneider, the President of the Legislative Body, in vain proposed that the Regency should hand over its powers to the Assembly—possibly the only means of saving the *régime*. In the evening some of the deputies rejoined Schneider at the Palais Bourbon and insisted that the Chamber should meet without delay. Power must be concentrated in the hands of one man, another Cavaignac must be found. " It is imperative that when the people of Paris hear the official news of the disaster they should also hear what measures have been adopted by the Government authorities." An elementary precaution—

416

how came it that the Cabinet had not thought of it? As a matter of fact they were also afraid of the Left, who were whispering that the Empire was falling. And indeed, at the night sitting which opened at one o'clock, Palikao confirmed the news of the disaster and demanded an immediate adjournment. Schneider wanted to end the sitting, but Gambetta prevented him, and Jules Favre read a motion signed by 27 deputies of the Left : " Louis Napoleon Bonaparte and his dynasty are hereby declared to have forfeited the powers conferred upon them by the Constitution." All these powers were to be transferred to a Commission appointed by the Legislative Body, entrusted with the task of resisting invasion to the death and driving the enemy from the country. It was expressly mentioned that Trochu was to remain Governor of Paris. Favre announced that the motion would be supported by his friends at the next sitting that same day at noon. The Bonapartist majority, stunned by the disaster, offered no resistance. Pinard alone protested that the Legislative Body was not competent to declare the fall of the Empire. The *régime* felt that it had been dealt a mortal blow. " There is nothing more to be done ! " declared Rouher, the President of the Senate, that same night. " To-morrow there will be revolution ! "

On Sunday, the 4th of September, at dawn, Paris learnt from the white official placards that the army had been defeated **The News** and captured, and that the Emperor himself was a **of Defeat** prisoner. Under the rays of the morning sun the **reaches** people spread through the streets. Many of them **Paris.** had again put on the uniform of the National Guard, or if they had not got one, at all events the cap. And instinctively they all made their way towards the Place de la Concorde and the Palais Bourbon, where " something " was sure to happen. Soon there appeared among the crowd men in white blouses, who had come in from the suburbs, shouting " Down with the Empire ! " Without taking any concerted action, all the enemies of the Empire, Republicans and members of the International, felt that their day had come.

Schneider grew anxious; who was going to defend the Legislative Body against a possible, nay, probable attack? There was only one of the leaders who enjoyed sufficient popularity

E E

to impress the mob, and that was the Governor of Paris, Trochu. But, ever a victim to petty jealousy, Palikao did not appeal to him, but wrote direct to one of his subordinates to take defensive measures against the demonstrators. Trochu, cut to the quick, held aloof, shutting himself up in the Louvre and allowing matters to take their course. Mounted gendarmes were posted in the Place de la Concorde, Paris guards at the entrance to the bridge, police officers in front of the gates of the Palais Bourbon, and three battalions behind the gates and in the court. But there was no soul to breathe life into the defence, nobody capable of stopping the insurrection. Loafers, demonstrators, and old " Montagnards " contrived, by showing journalists' cards, to make their way into the galleries, where Étienne Arago demanded the downfall of the Empire and the departure of the Empress. " The Emperor is a prisoner," he exclaimed, " and according to the Civil Code, the wife ought to follow her husband." The phrase had a great success among the jeering guttersnipes.

The sitting opened at a quarter past one. Palikao proposed that the Legislative Body should appoint a Council of Five " to carry on the Government and organise the national defence," of which he himself would be the " Lieutenant-General." He did not refer to the Regent and did not dare to mention her, perhaps imagining that he might save the Empress by refraining from saying anything about her and sharing the power with the Assembly. Favre insisted upon the declaration of the downfall. At last Thiers also proposed that " in view of the circumstances,"—at first he had dared to say " in view of the vacancy of the throne,"—a Commission should be appointed to carry on the Government, organise the national defence and convoke a Constituent Assembly as soon as possible. This amounted to declaring the downfall of the Empire without using the word. It was left to the country to pronounce it. The Empress, whom Buffet had urged to give her consent to this solution, in order that the Assembly might be a legal body and that the Bonapartist majority might not be forced to break their oath of allegiance,—the Empress, after protesting in stereotyped phrases that she would never desert her post, in the end gave way and listened to the advice of her Ministers.

418

DISASTER

Thus the Regent herself handed over her powers to the Assembly, who seized the executive. The session was suspended and the deputies met in chambers and were apparently in favour of Thiers' plan. Was the *régime* going to save itself by means of these backstairs intrigues and negotiations on the terms of motions?

But the people upset all these parliamentary calculations. The mob, among whom the majority were animated more by **The Mob invades the Assembly.** curiosity than by revolutionary zeal, gradually gained the upper hand of the forces of law and order. Worse still, the mounted gendarmes on guard at the bridge allowed armed National Guards, who marched up in fours and were taken for reinforcements, to pass. The latter, stopped by the police at the gates, protested, and prevailed upon the General responsible for the maintenance of the peace to order the police to stand aside. Meanwhile, the men in the galleries, profiting by the suspension of the sitting, came out on to the steps in front of the peristyle and waved their handkerchiefs and hats. Some of the National Guards slipped through the gates, and soon the mob was on their heels, and the raw recruits forming the battalions massed in the court were not made of the stuff to stop them. There were shouts of " Down with the Empire ! *Vive la République !* " Deputies of the Left, including Picard, Crémieux and Gambetta, tried in vain to make the demonstrators listen to reason. About half-past two, the mob, tired of waiting for the session to reopen, burst into the galleries and then into the amphitheatre, to the crash of broken glass. " The people will not wait," observed somebody to Thiers in the corridors. " We waited for you until two o'clock; you are not ready, so we must declare the fall of the Empire ourselves ! " Schneider adjourned the house and went out, followed by the majority of the deputies. He tried to reach the President's house, but was recognised in the garden. " Death to the assassin of Creusot, the exploiter of the workingman ! " With these words he was struck and had great difficulty in escaping from the mob.

Meanwhile the crowd was trampling down the benches and throwing papers about with all the delight of rebellious schoolboys. At last Gambetta succeeded in making his stentorian voice heard. Like Favre and Picard, he had done all in his

THE SECOND EMPIRE

power for the change of Government to be carried out " in a regular and orderly fashion." For these Republicans and lawyers were members of the bourgeoisie and were afraid of being swamped by the men of the extreme Left, the members of the International and of the Clubs. They wanted the revolution to be, so to speak, legal, if the two words are not absolutely contradictory. They were terrified of insurrection. And it was
Gambetta proclaims the Fall of the Empire. this concern for legality which animated Gambetta when he proclaimed the fall of the Empire : " Seeing that the country is in danger, that sufficient time had been given to the representatives of the people to declare the fall of the Empire, and seeing that we constitute the regular power founded upon free universal suffrage, we hereby declare that Louis Napoleon Bonaparte and his dynasty have for ever ceased to reign in France." The mob applauded and cheered. It is true that the majority of deputies had left with Schneider. But the Paris deputies were present, and this proclamation in the Palais Bourbon, which, as a matter of fact, was merely a development of the proposition put forward by Thiers, had a semblance of legality. There were shouts of " Republic ! " and Jules Favre came forward. " To the Hôtel de Ville to proclaim the Republic ! " he shouted. " Follow me ! " And thus the tradition of '48 was revived. And everybody made for the Hôtel de Ville.

This meant the end of the Second Empire. Piétri, the Prefect of Police, rushed to the Tuileries, and told the Empress that
Flight of the Empress. she must take flight immediately if she wished to save her life. She made her escape with Metternich, the Austrian Ambassador, Nigra, the Italian Minister, and her lady reader. She reached the Louvre by the galleries on the bank, and left the palace by the Place St. Germain l'Auxerrois, from the very door, observes P. de la Gorce, by which she had gone out seventeen years previously for her marriage in Notre Dame. They hailed a cab, and a street urchin recognised her. Nigra sternly threatened him and the cab drove away. The Empress wandered from house to house; all the loyal supporters with whom she sought refuge were out. In the end she was taken in by her American dentist, Dr. Evans, who helped her to escape into exile.

420

DISASTER

Thus in a few hours, without a drop of blood being spilt, the *régime* for which seven million Frenchmen had voted *Yea* not

Conclusion. four months previously fell to bits. It is true that only a third of Paris had voted for Napoleon III, and that once again it was Paris that had made the revolution. But who could possibly have defended the Empire which had just suffered such a terrible military disaster? The nation had not become Bonapartist, it had merely been following the Emperor " through inertia." " The Government was merely a group of officials imposed upon the nation without forming a corporate whole with it . . . and devoid of all moral authority " (Ch. Seignobos). A band of adventurers had seized the power by means of a surprise attack on a certain December night in 1851, and had kept it by securing material prosperity and a semblance of glory for the country. And when the crisis arrived, instead of gathering in serried ranks about respected and beloved leaders, the people deserted a Government they had accepted only out of weakness, while the imperial edifice, deprived of its natural bulwark, the army, crumbled to bits almost of its own accord, like a castle of cards under the flick of a child's fingers.

INDEX

423

INDEX

INDEX

INDEX

to recognition of the Kingdom of Italy, 233; 239; her sympathy with Poland, 286; demands mobilisation on the Rhine, 298; 299; visits Amiens during cholera plague, 305; 308, 316; acts as regent, 325; 336, 342, 349, 354; no longer attends Cabinet meetings, 360; in favour of war, 385; 389, 400; refuses to summon the Emperor to Paris, 401, 405; 407, 418, 419; her flight, 420

Evans, Dr., receives the Empress, 420

Eylau, 106

FAIDHERBE, in Senegal, 259

Failly, General de, captures the White Works, 114; 189; in the Franco-Prussian War, 403, 404, 406, 408

Falguière, 311

Falloux, 22, 145; elected to the *Académie*, 149, 203, 238, 351

Falloux, the *Loi*, 1, 44, 45, 46, 47, 48, 140; modification of, 144

Farini, 213

Fathma, a prophetess, 257

Faucher, Minister of the Interior, 35

Favre, Jules, confirms election of Louis Napoleon, 20; 37; defends Orsini, 163, 167, 168; attacks Laws of Public Safety, 226; demands abandonment of the Pope, 227; 252, 253; denounces the Mexican expedition, 276, 277; 327, 342, 344, 345; his reply to a deputation of working men, 336; 350, 351, 352, 353, 364, 368; in favour of accepting German unity, 369; 386, 416; demands downfall of the Empire, 418; 419; leads mob to the Hôtel de Ville, 420

Feast of Fraternity, 1, 4, 11

Ferré, 345

Ferry, Jules, 236, 237, 327, 351, 353, 364

Feuillet, Octave, 329

Five, the, 1, 14, 18, 226, 227; reforms demanded by, 235, 236; 337

Flandrin, Hippolyte, 143, 310

Flaubert, 13, 154, 329

Fleury, 53, 88, 89, 92, 115; sent to Verona, 194; meets Bismarck, 288; 289; sent to Florence, 317; 349, 376

Floccon, journalist, 2

Floquet, 236, 237, 327

Flotte, 48

Flourens, 362; proclaims the revolution, 363

Fonvielle, Ulrich de, 361, 362; attacks the Government, 367

Forbach, Battle of, 392, 400, 403, 404

Forcade, 223, 282; Minister of the Interior, 350; 356

Forey, at Solferino, 189; sent to Mexico, 276; 277; recalled, 278

Fortoul, Minister of Public Instruction, his University reforms, 71

Foucault, 328

Fould, 43, 56; resigns, 68, 91, 130; averse to war with Austria, 177; dismissed, 223; made Minister of Finance, 231; 280, 302

Francis Joseph, Emperor, 187, 190; meets Napoleon III at Villafranca, 194, 195; 271, 279; meets Napoleon III at Salzburg, 316; 320, 376

Francis II, King of Naples, insurrection against, 211; 224, 225

Frederick II, 304

Frederick William, King of Prussia, 87, 92

Free Trade, advocated by Napoleon III, 216, 217, 218, 219; 220

Fribourg, 331

Froeschwiller, 390, 391, 392, 400, 403, 404, 406

Froissard, General, 280

Frossard, 113, 388; opens the attack at Sarrebruck, 390; his failure at Forbach, 392, 393; 396, 398, 399, 403

Fuad Pasha, in Damascus, 268

GABORIAU, Émile, 342

Gaillard, Napoléon, 345, 346; prosecuted, 347

Gallifet, 412

Gallipoli, expeditionary force collects at, 98

Gambetta, 236, 253, 327; defends Delescluze, 347, 348; 351, 352, 353, 357, 364, 365, 368; opposed to accepting German unity, 370; his speech on the eve of war, 387; 418, 419; proclaims the fall of the Empire, 419

Garde mobile, the, creation of, 323; rebellions against organisation of, 342; 373, 379, 388, 401; in the Châlons camp, 404

INDEX

Garibaldi, 42, 201; leaves Genoa with his "Thousand," 211; threatens Rome, 213; his attempt against Rome, 234; 235, 245, 291, 317; in Geneva, 318; at the gates of Rome, 319

Garnier-Pagès, member of the Provisional Government, 2; Minister of Finance, 6; 14, 152, 235; his tour of France, 236; 237, 250, 327, 345, 351, 353

George, King of Hanover, 370

George III, 110

Germiny, President of Mexican Finance Committee, 281

Gérôme, 311

Gicquel, the swindler, 229

Girardin, Émile de, arrested, 30; 33; opposed to restoration of Empire, 81; 145, 373, 379

Girardin, St. Marc, 147, 204, 238, 242, 282, 344

Glais-Bizoin, 242, 358

Goltz, von der, his popularity in Paris, 292; 295, 300, 306

Gomez, 157

Goncourts, the, 329

Gortschakoff, 106, 116; evacuates the Malakoff, 118; 301

Goudchaux, Finance Minister, 2, 4; resigns, 6; his financial measures, 30, 31, 150, 152, 153, 163

Govone, General, sent to Berlin, 294

Gramont, Duc de, French Ambassador at the Vatican, 213; 220; French Ambassador in Vienna, 374; and the Hohenzollern candidature, 378, 379, 381; interviews the Emperor, 382; 383, 385, 387, 401, 403

Gramont, 51

Grand Luxemburg Railway, 372

Granier de Cassagnac, 337

Grassot, actor, arrested, 115

Grenier, 395

Greville, Sir Charles, his opinion of Napoleon III, 220

Grevy, 31, 353, 365

Grouchy, 407

Guéroult, journalist, 132, 237, 249, 351, 353

Gueydon, 318

Guillaume, 311

Guilloutet, 337

Guizot, 34, 79, 130, 139, 147, 204; his condemnation of the decree of November 24th, 1860, 222; 238, 248; preaches the union of all Christian sects, 343; 360

Guys, Constantin, 128

Gyulai, Austrian Commander-in-Chief, 181, 182, 183, 184, 185

Halévy, 313

Hanoverian Legion, the, disbanded, 371

Hausen, his mission to Berlin, 303

Haussmann, Prefect of Bordeaux, 82; rebuilds Paris, 135–138; 161, 226, 231, 349, 351; resignation of, 360

Havin, 237, 327, 331

Hébert, 345, 347

Heliagabolus, 345

Hénon, Dr., 75, 76, 153, 161, 163, 242

Henry V, 50, 146

Herbillon, General, 56

Hérisson, 237

Hérold, 236, 237

Herwegh, poet, 15

Hohenzollern - Sigmaringen, Prince Charles of, given Crown of Roumania, 294. See also Charles, Prince of Roumania.

Holle, 259

Holy Places, the, dispute over, 94, 95

Hortense, Queen, 18, 68, 127, 155, 341

Howard, Miss, 43; official favourite of Napoleon III, 88

Huber, dissolves the Assembly, 17

Hübner, Austrian Ambassador, 84, 92, 120; his opinion of Napoleon III, 124; and of the Empress, 125; 126, 175

Hugo, Victor, 17, 24, 28; lashes the clerical party, 47; his violent opposition to Louis Napoleon, 52; 97, 149, 150, 151, 235, 347, 356, 357

Hume, the medium, 127

Ingres, 67

Inkerman, 105, 106, 116

International, the, 329, 330, 331, 332; its growth, 343, 344; supports the French strikers, 335; meets at Lausanne, 336; extends its activities, 362

International Exhibition, of 1855, 138, 139; workmen's visit to, in London, 249, 250; of 1867, 309, 310, 311, 331; of 1862, 329

Isabella, Queen of Spain, 377

428

INDEX

Isocrates, 352
Issoudun, disturbances at, 13

Janin, Jules, 147
Jarras, 376, 394
Jecker, his Mexican Loan, 273
Jena, Battle of, 284
Jerome, King, 158, 235
Jerome, Prince, 125
Jesuits, hate the Government of their own country, 47
Josephine, Empress, 90
Jouvenel, 266
Juarez, leader of the Liberals in Mexico, 270, 271, 273, 274, 275; flight of, 278, 280
Julian the Apostate, 203
Jurien de la Gravière, Vice-Admiral, 272, 274
Juvenal, 235

Keller, his speech in the legislative Body, 225, 226; 238
Kératry, 357, 402
Kerdrel, 78
Korniloff, Admiral, 102, 103; death of, 104
Kourchid, ex-Pasha of Buirut, 268

Laboulaye, 147, 153, 237, 238, 344
Lacordaire, 145; elected to the *Académie*, 204
Lacretelle, 410
Ladmirault, at Solferino, 189; 388, 395, 397, 398, 400
Lamartine, appoints Provisional Government, 2; his speech to the mob, 4; disavows Ledru-Rollin, 7; 8, 10; makes his will, 11; 13, 14, 15; arrests Barbès, 17; 23, 31
Lambert, 411
Lamennais, 30; funeral of, 151
Lamoricière, 25, 26, 27, 28, 30; arrested, 55, 115, 147; made leader of the Papal forces, 212; 213, 214; capitulates at Ancona, 215; 225
La Motterouge, 184, 185
Lanfrey, 342
Lapasset, 396
Laprade, Victor de, 228
La Ricamerie, massacre of, 354
Lartigue, 391
La Tour d'Auvergne, Minister of Foreign Affairs, 402

La Valette, hostile to Austria, 298; 299, 325, 336, 349
Laveaucoupet, 393
Lavergne, 146
Le Bas, teacher of Louis Napoleon, 18
Leboeuf, hands over Venetia to Italy, 305; Minister of War, 357, 373, 376; prepares for war, 384, 385; declares that France is ready, 387; 388, 398, 399, 400, 401, 403
Lebreton, 27, 28
Lebrun, General, sent to Vienna, 376; 406, 410, 413
Leconte de Lisle, 329
Ledru-Rollin, wants to hold elections, 1; member of Provisional Government, 2; dismisses the Prefects, 7, 8, 9; 10, 11, 12, 14, 15; arrests Barbès, 17; 26, 30; his financial measures, 31; 33, 35, 40, 41; flees to England, 42; 49; in London, 150; 235; a "fashionplate Danton," 327; 358, 363
Leflô, 54; arrested, 55
Lefrançais Millière, 367
Legrand, killed in action, 397
Leipzig, Battle of, 284
Lemoinne, John, 147
Leopold of Hohenzollern, offered the throne of Spain, 377; 381, 382, 384
Leroux, Pierre, 9
Lesseps, his mission to Rome, 1, 38; suddenly recalled, 41
Leverrier, 328
Light Brigade, the, charge of, 104
Ligue Internationale de la Paix, 373
Limoges, disturbances at, 13
Lissagarey, attacks the Government, 367
Loges, Monseigneur des, 343
London, Conference of, 309
London, Convention of, 271
Lorencez, in Mexico, 274, 275, 276
Louis XIV, 370
Louis XV, 92
Louis, King of Holland, 18
Louis Philippe, 50; driven from the Tuileries, 2; the workshop system under, 21; 65; provides for his family, 67; 68; official candidature under, 73; 124, 127, 131, 132, 133, 136, 144; a protectionist, 216; 257
Louis XVI, 45
Lourmel, General, 106
Luxemburg, squabble over, 306, 307; neutralisation of, 309

429

INDEX

Luxemburg Commission, 1, 10
Luzy, 189
Lyons, communism in, 9

MACÉ, Jean, founds the *Ligue de l'enseignement*, 329; 343
Machiavelli, 166
Machinery, imported from England, 3
MacMahon, 1, 18; opposes the Law of Public Safety, 162; 180, 183, 184; made a Marshal, 185; at Solferino, 189, 190; 198, 388, 390, 391; at Froeschwiller, 392; retreats on Paris, 405; 406, 407; wounded, 410, 411, 415, 416
Mage, naval lieutenant, 260
Magenta, Battle of, 183, 193, 197, 199, 209, 298, 320
Magnan, 421; in command of the Paris army, 53; 54; occupies Paris, 55, 56; made Marshal, 86; 92; made chief of the Freemasons, 230
Magne, 56; resigns, 68; 91, 130, 218, 223; opposed to recognition of the Kingdom of Italy, 234; 365; Finance Minister, 336, 356, 402
Malakoff, the, 127
Malon, Benoît, 343
Mamelon, Fort, 112; attack on, 114
Mangin, 28
Manteuffel, 121, 289
Marat, Prince, 397
Marche, 3
Marengo, Battle of, 32, 84
Margueritte, in Mexico, 277; 406; mortally wounded, 412; his death, 414
Marie, member of the Provisional Government, 2; 14; Minister of Public Works, 21; 22, 235; forms a committee, 237; 242, 327
Marie Antoinette, 125
Marrast, journalist, 2; his opinion of Morny, 130; funeral of, 151
Martin, Henri, 237, 331
Marx, Karl, 251; in London, 329; 331
Massol, baritone, 155
Masson, solicitor, 25
Matilde, Princess, 125, 155, 198
Maupas, Prefect of Police, 53, 55, 57, 66, 82, 91, 349
Maximilian, Emperor of Mexico, 271; offered the Crown of Mexico, 278, 279; his difficulties in Mexico, 280; 282, 283; murder of, 313, 314, 335

430

Mayors, system of nomination, 71
Mazzini, 154, 235, 245
Meetings, Law on, of 1868, 338, 339
Meilhac, 313
Meissonier, his picture of Solferino, 192; 311
Méline, 253
Menschikoff, presents ultimatum to Turkey, 95, 96; at the Alma, 100, 101; sinks a Russian ship at Sebastopol, 102; 104
Mentana, Garibaldians defeated at, 319
Merimée, his opinion of Persigny, 241; his opinion of American Puritans, 271; his admiration for Bismarck, 293; 357
Mérode, Monseigneur de, reorganises the pontifical forces, 212, 213; 214, 225
Metternich, 202
Metternich, Prince, Austrian Ambassador, 200, 295; his flight from Paris, 420
Metz, retreat on, 393, 398; blockaded, 400
Meurice, 356
Michel de Bourges, 54
Michelet, 151, 385
Milan, revolution in, 15
Millet, 310
Miramar, Convention of, 279
Miramon, General, head of the Conservatives in Mexico, 270
Mocquard, 53, 82
Moleschott, 328
Molière, General, 399
Moltke, his desire for war, 309; 384, 406, 407; his interview with Wimpffen, 415
Montalembert, Catholic leader, 44; 45, 49; urges people to vote for Louis Napoleon, 49; 61, 64; withdraws his support from Louis Napoleon, 68; his criticism of the Constitution, 77, 78, 79, 141, 145, 238, 242
Montauban, Cousin, in China, 262, 263, 264, 265; 266
Montebello, Battle of, 182
Montijo, Count of, 90
Morny, 36, 43; his master mind behind the *coup d'état*, 53; his ancestry, 53; 55, 56, 57, 59, 61; forbids meetings, 67; resigns, 68; 72, 73, 75; promoted Grand Cross of the Legion of Honour, 86; 88, 89, 91, 128, 147,

INDEX

INDEX

Pellé, 390

Pellerin, artist, 13

Pelletan, 237, 327; founds the *Tribune*, 340; 344, 353

Pereire, brothers, 132

Pereire, Isaac, 133

Périer, Casimir, 242

Persigny, 53; organises propaganda on behalf of Louis Napoleon, 19; 45; advises confiscation of Orleans property, 67; 68, 70; on official candidature, 74; 81, 82; increases the Emperor's Civil List, 86; sent to Prussia, 87; 91, 110, 143, 146, 155, 165; averse to war with Austria, 177; 224, 227; orders the Prefects to forbid meetings, 230; in favour of recognition of Kingdom of Italy, 234; 238; his ill-temper, 239; 241, 242; fall of, 243; his advice to Bismarck, 292; hostile to Austria, 298; sent to Rome, 317, 349, 354

Peyrat, journalist, 253, 347

Peyrouton, 345, 346; prosecuted, 347

Philip II, 370

Pianori, attempts to shoot Napoleon III, 111, 154, 165

Picard, Ernest, 152, 163; criticises Haussmann, 226; 237, 327; founds the *Électeur Libre*, 340; 345, 351, 353, 365, 367, 418, 419

Pie, Monseigneur, 201; virtually ostracised, 228; deceived by Gicquel, 229; 230

Piedmont, King of, 15, 82; one of the first to recognise Napoleon III, 87; 97

Pieri, 156, 157

Piétri, Prefect of Police, 124, 143, 156, 358; helps Empress to escape, 420

Pimodan, General de, 215

Pinard, Minister of the Interior, 336, 347, 349, 350, 365, 366

Plombières, the meeting at, 172, 173, 174, 175, 205

Plutarch, Louis Napoleon a student of, 18

Poland, 1, 4, 15; revolt in, 16; 17; insurrections in, 284, 285, 286, 287

Ponsard, his denunciation of gambling, 130; 313

Posen, revolt of Poles in, 16

Pouyer-Quertier, 220, 252

Prague, Peace of, 302; Treaty of, 315

Prefects, organisation of, 72

Press Law, of July 16th, 1; of 1850, 49; of 1867, 336, 337

Prévost-Paradol, 148, 226, 238, 239, 242, 321, 351, 363; foretells war with Prussia, 370

Prim, General, commander of the Spanish forces in Mexico, 272, 274; rules Spain, 377; and the Hohenzollern candidature, 378

Prince Imperial, the, 142, 153, 198, 292, 312, 342, 365; accompanies his father to the front, 398; 390, 395

Protot, 328

Proudhon, 9; his socialistic scheme, 31; 151, 251, 328, 331

Prussia, admitted to Paris Congress, 121

Public Safety, Law of, 160

Puebla, French defeat at, 275; 277; fall of, 278

Pujol, leads the mob, 22; 23, 24

Pyal, 9, 35, 40; goes into exile, 42; appeals for the murder of the Emperor, 363

Quentin, 346; prosecuted, 347

Quentin-Bauchet, 58

Quinet, Edgar, 150, 235

Raglan, Lord, 98, 103; and the charge of the Light Brigade, 104; 105; dies of cholera, 116

Railways, development of the, 72, 133, 134

Randon, Marshal, subdues Kabylie, 153; made Minister of War, 181; 187, 194; opposed to recognition of the Kingdom of Italy, 233; in Great Kabylie, 257; his disapproval of the Mexican expedition, 278; demands mobilisation on the Rhine, 298; 299, 302; resignation of, 309, 322; 321

Ranvier, 345

Raoult, 391; killed in action, 392

Raspail, 8; arrested, 17; 33, 34, 351, 353

Raspail, Madame, funeral of, 151

Regnault, treacherously killed, 28

Regnault de St. Jean d'Angily, 198

Reichstadt, Duc de, 85

Rémusat, 147, 238, 242, 351

Renan, Ernest, forbidden to lecture, 228; resigns his Chair, 245; 248; 328, 335, 351

INDEX

434

INDEX

INDEX